Burt sc.

A Alexander

THE LIFE

OF

ARCHIBALD ALEXANDER, D. D., LL

FIRST PROFESSOR IN THE THEOLOGICAL SEMINARY,
AT PRINCETON, NEW JERSEY.

BY

JAMES W. ALEXANDER, D. D

PHILADELPHIA:
PRESBYTERIAN BOARD OF PUBLICATION.
821 CHESTNUT STREET.
1870.

PREFACE.

THE reasons for this condensed edition are sufficiently obvious. Many persons who would gladly have perused the larger memoir, found it beyond their reach. It will be seen, on collation, that the abridgment has been slight, and that the narrative is scarcely touched. Especially is the autobiographical part given entire.

In this place I may be allowed to repeat, that the work was one from which I would gladly have shrunk; but it was laid upon me by the highest human authority I ever knew; as he who is the subject of the narrative expressed on his death-bed the desire, that whatsoever should appear in the way of public memorial might proceed from two of his sons whom he named for this purpose. For reasons not interesting to the general reader, the task has devolved solely on me. I girded myself for it under all the disadvantages of a conviction long since formed, that in many respects a son is not the proper biographer of a father. Though his knowledge of facts and character may be supposed to be intimate, he is in danger either of writing a panegyric, or of falling below the truth in attempting to avoid it. In almost every page I confess myself to have been haunted by the apprehension of overstating, overcolouring, and giving undue importance to domestic traits. If this evil has been incurred, it has not been from wilful suppression of truth, but from the warping influence of a loving veneration. It would have been as natural as it was consonant to my feelings, to speak of my dear and honoured father under that tender appellation; but the wish to avoid obtruding my own person every where as thus connected, has led me to name him as he was known by others.

One of the difficulties of the performance ought to be clearly stated. The two ordinary and most copious sources of a religious biography, are a private diary and epistolary correspondence. As it regards the former, my father, after his years of boyhood, kept no personal journal. His letters, it is true, were numerous; but they were to a remarkable extent bare letters of business. Of hundreds now in my hands, the greater part contain no passage which admits of being extracted. and most of the remainder furnish only scattered sentences. My hearty thanks are due to those pupils and other friends of my father, who have sent me letters received from him; the number of such favours has prevented distinct and private acknowledgment. Some of these arrived too late to be inserted in the text. In the absence of the materials just named, I have had to rely upon two classes of authorities. In the first place, my father, after the middle of his life, threw upon paper large reminiscences of his own career, and the history of his early friends and acquaintances. Greater use would have been made of these manuscripts, if he had not expressly forbidden them to be made public in their original form. I have gone to the utmost limit of his supposed permission, in these autobiographical extracts. Unfortunately, they do not extend at all into the second and more conspicuous half of his life. The other source has therefore been the chief reliance, as to this period; namely, my own personal recollections, aided and corrected by those of his family and friends.

In those parts which are made up from his manuscript records, I have once or twice allowed myself, rather than mutilate his account, to repeat the same events and opinions, as expressed by him in different connections. In some few instances, I have been constrained to return to topics already treated and apparently dismissed, thus disturbing the arrangement; because new matter on these points came in while the book was going through the press. The excellent steel engraving which accompanies these pages is from the best representations which art has been able to produce. But it ought to be added, that no likeness has been other than a failure, in respect to the animation of his features and the liquid brilliancy of his eye.

It is my humble prayer, that this memorial of one who devoted his best powers, for a long period, to the service of truth, of the Church, and of the Lord Jesus, may be made conducive to the interests of religion.

New York, *October*, 1855.

TABLE OF CONTENTS.

CHAPTER FIFTH.

1790, 1791.

CHAPTER SIXTH.

1791.

CHAPTER SEVENTH.

1792.

CHAPTER EIGHTH.

1792—1797.

CHAPTER NINTH.

1801.

CHAPTER FIFTEENTH.

1819—1829.

CHAPTER SIXTEENTH.

1830—1839.

CHAPTER SEVENTEENTH.

1840—1851.

CHAPTER EIGHTEENTH.

1851.

CHAPTER NINETEENTH.

1851.

CHAPTER TWENTIETH.

THE LIFE

OF

ARCHIBALD ALEXANDER, D.D.

CHAPTER FIRST.

1772—1788.

DESCENT—THE GREAT VALLEY—OLD ARCHIBALD ALEXANDER—PARENTAGE—NATIVE PLACE—EARLY SCHOOLS—THE WAR—WILLIAM GRAHAM—PRIESTLY—CLASSICAL TRAINING.

ABOUT the year 1736, as nearly as can now be discovered, three brothers named Alexander emigrated to America. Though they came from Ireland, they were of the Scottish race, and their father, Thomas Alexander, had removed from Scotland to the neighbourhood of Londonderry. One of these brothers, Archibald Alexander, settled first in Pennsylvania, where his son William was born upon the river Schuylkill. The three brothers were well educated, and one of them, Robert, was a teacher of mathematics. After a residence of more than two years in Pennsylvania, Archibald Alexander removed to New Virginia, as the country was then called; his son William, being at the time about nine years of age. He was among the earliest settlers of that particular region.

"While he resided in Pennsylvania," says the personal narrative to which we are to be indebted for most of our facts, "the Great Revival which spread its benign influence over so large a portion of America, extended to the congregation in which he lived, and he became a subject of the good work, under the preaching of Mr. Rowland. This fact I learned from old Dr. Robert Smith of Pequea, who knew him well, and told me in 1791, when I was at his house, that he had often met with my grandfather during that period, following Mr. Rowland far and near."

No better notion of the locality here principally concerned can be obtained, than from some paragraphs left by the subject of this narrative. "The Great Valley of Virginia, or as it is commonly called in the State, *the Valley*, is situated between the Blue Ridge and the North Mountain; and its general direction is the same, from northeast to southwest. It is a continuation of the same valley which, commencing on the Delaware at Easton, passes entirely through the State of Pennsylvania, including Bethlehem, Reading, Harrisburg, Carlisle, Shippensburg, Chambersburg, and many other flourishing towns and villages, and extends through Maryland to the Potomac. On the south side of this river the Valley of Virginia commences, and runs nearly through the State, embracing in its whole extent, from the Delaware to the New or Kanhawa River, as rich, as variegated, and as well watered a region, as can be found in the United States. The width of this valley, from mountain to mountain, varies from ten to thirty miles ; fifteen miles may be considered the mean breadth. There is also a great difference in the surface ; in some parts the land is flat, but rises in others into high hills, which every where in their uncultivated state are covered with forests of timber, which is often very large. It is, throughout, a limestone country ; and in some places the rocks almost cover the surface of the ground. Within these rocks are many caverns, in some of which the waters collect in such quantities, that in many places, springs burst forth with a stream sufficient to turn a large waterwheel. The ledges of limestone running above the surface, and generally inclined at a considerable angle to the horizon, cause the roads to be rough and very unpleasant for wheels. Through the whole extent of this valley, wheat and other kinds of corn are cultivated with great success. Perhaps for the extent of it, it is the best wheat land in America. It is an excellent farming country, with a deep stiff clay soil, susceptible when exhausted of great improvement from the gypsum and the lime obtained from the rocks.

"Although the region under consideration is now the central part of Virginia, it generally received its inhabitants from a source very different from that of the remaining portions ; for while the latter are from a pure English stock, the former are Scotch-Irish and German in their origin. The people called the Scotch-Irish are all Presbyterians, and descending from the Scotch, have nevertheless for several generations resided in the north of Ireland. They are a people of marked traits, differing entirely from the native Irish, and from the descendants of the English in Ireland. They have also acquired characteristics which distinguish them from the Scotch. These people settled in Ireland at different periods; but most of them went over in the times of persecution under the Stuarts. When Pennsylvania was laid open for settlement, and freedom of religion was promised to all denominations by William Penn, many emigrated to that colony, and settled in the southern and eastern counties, and in the three counties which have since composed the State of Delaware. As the settlements extended, they spread themselves westward, and were generally among the foremost to occupy new lands. Many of them therefore entered the Great Valley before described, about Harrisburg and Carlisle, also towards the Potomac, and beyond it into Virginia. The time of the earliest emigration from Ireland was probably from 1720 to 1740. About the last mentioned date, some persons had penetrated so far along the valley as to reach the waters of the great Powhatán, commonly called the James River. This part of the valley, though uneven and in many places rocky, was found to be exceedingly fertile, and the 'coves' and gaps in the mountains furnished good grazing for cattle. So favourable a report was brought back by the explorers, that many families in eastern Pennsylvania determined to remove to New Virginia, as that region was then called.

"Between 1740 and 1750 a great emigration took place; and as an unhappy schism then existed in the Presbyterian Church, dividing it into the Old Side and New Side, as the parts were called, the people of these parties settled, not promiscuously, but in separate groups, which became the germs of new congregations; for when a settlement was once made, it was rapidly increased every year by emigrants, not only from Pennsylvania but directly from Ireland. The emigrants from congregations of the Old Side planted themselves in compact bodies in that part of the Valley east and south of Staunton, and even extended themselves over the Blue Ridge at Rockfish Gap, immediately below which they found some rich and beautiful land on Rockfish River. In a very few years there were three ministers of the gospel stationed among them. The Rev. Mr. Craig took charge of the Augusta Church, and that of Tinkling Spring; the Rev. Mr. Miller, of Mossy Creek and Harrisonburg; and the Rev. Mr. Black, of Rockfish, on the eastern side of the Blue Ridge. That part of the valley which lies southwest of Staunton, as far as the Forks of James River, was settled principally by adherents of the New Side. The congregations of Hebron, Bethel, New Providence, Timber Ridge, and the Forks, with some mixture of the others, were chiefly of the New Side. The first minister who settled in this part of the Valley, was the Rev. John Brown, who was born in Ireland, but received his education, at least the finishing part of it, in this country; for he was a graduate of the College of New Jersey. When licensed he visited New Virginia, and received a call from New Providence and Timber Ridge, which then formed but one congregation. The next preacher of this party was, I think, Mr. Cummins, who preached at the North Mountain (Hebron) and Bethel. In the Forks, that is the region about Lexington and further on towards the James River, there was no settled pastor before Mr. Graham."* And here we resume the personal narrative: "The congregation to which my grandfather belonged must have been Norriton, in the vicinity of Norristown, which did not then exist. It was divided into two, and the friends of the revival built a new house of worship, which they called Providence. From this many families emigrated to New Virginia, settled together, and built a meeting-house, which they called New Providence. As the congregation was extensive, they built another on Timber Ridge, ten or twelve miles further along the valley. My grandfather's residence was within the bounds of the latter; my father's farm was adjoining.

"I have often wondered why he chose a residence in a part of the valley so hilly and precipitous, when the whole country was before him, and when land could be had for a mere trifle. But I have understood that the selection was judiciously made, on account of the fine pasturage in the mountains, made accessible to cattle by the gap of Irish Creek."

Archibald Alexander was a man of some remarkable points. At the solicitation of others, and for the sake of his children, he gave lessons to such of the neighbouring youth as would resort to him at night. "The appearance of my grandfather," the narrative continues, "I remember very well. He was rather below the common height, but was thick-set, broad-breasted and strongly built. His face was broad, and his eyes large, black, and prominent. The expression of his countenance was calm and benignant, and his

* MS. Life of the Rev. William Graham.

manner of speaking was very kind and affectionate. He raised a company of men, called Rangers ; and as their captain performed a tour of duty on the Great Kanhawa and the Ohio. For this service he received, in connection with other officers, a right to locate several thousand acres of land in Kentucky. Perhaps no man ever left behind him a higher character for uprightness and benignity, than old Ersbell Alexander, as he was called by the Scotch people. I have heard him spoken of by men of all classes, without any variation in their testimony to his worth. A large part of Rockbridge County was included in a grant made by the King to a certain Mr. Burden, and was called, within my memory, Burden's Tract. When Burden died, he left my grandfather sole executor of his will, with authority to sign numerous deeds for land already sold. This high trust he executed with fidelity ; and although he had such opportunities of appropriating to his own use any quantity of good land, he never seemed to have the least desire to become wealthy. When he first came to the country, he only took up as much land as would make moderate farms for himself and his two sons ; and to each of these, when grown, he gave portions. They, however, surveyed tracts on Irish Creek, which at this day are among the most valuable lands in the neighbourhood."

William Alexander, son of the preceding, enjoyed fewer opportunities of education ; yet, being of an active mind, and having more access to books than his companions, he acquired a considerable fund of knowledge. It is indicative of the domestic habits of the day, that he knew the whole

Larger Catechism, and remembered almost all Watts's Psalms and Hymns. He united the pursuit of merchandise to that of agriculture, but suffered greatly by the depreciation of the continental currency. He was an elder in the Presbyterian church, but did not attain to the Christian eminence of his father. William Alexander married Ann Reid, the daughter of a wealthy landholder, of the same Presbyterian colony. She was a retiring and humble, but affectionately pious woman. The latter years of her life were made sad by a total loss of sight.

Archibald Alexander, the subject of this narrative, and the son of William and Ann above mentioned, was born on the seventeenth day of April, 1772.

"The house in which I was born," says his own account, "was built of square logs, as were most of the houses at that time. The place is rough, and is near a little mountain stream, called the South River, which, after joining the North River, falls into the James River, just above its entrance into the mountains. Nearly opposite to the place, Irish Creek, a bold stream from a gorge of the mountain, falls into the South River. This my birthplace was at that time in Augusta County, which was unlimited to the west; it is now in Rockbridge County, and is about seven miles from Lexington, in an eastern direction.

"I was the third of nine children, seven of whom are still living (July 26, 1839). My brother Andrew was the oldest. The next in order was my sister, Margaret Graham. The others, in the order of nativity, are Sarah, John, Nancy (who died in childhood), Phebe, Elizabeth, Nancy, and Martha.

"My father, having in the year 1775 removed from his place on the South River to the Forks, that is, to the south of the North River, just this side of the site of Lexington, began to carry on his mercantile business there. Indeed, to get into a more public and convenient situation, was, I suppose, his only motive for this change. He purchased the house now owned by my oldest brother. As the buildings were poor, and on the wrong side of the farm for his purpose, he erected a house and a store near to the present site of Jordan's Mills. By this removal he went out of Augusta into Bottetourt County; for the North River was the dividing line. But soon after this a new county was taken from the two, and called Rockbridge, from the Natural Bridge, which was within its limits. Lexington was fixed on for the seat of justice; and a town was laid off, which took its name from the place of the first battle and first bloodshed of the Revolution. But the war came on, and all mercantile business was necessarily suspended; and my father now acted as deputy-sheriff to his father, in the new county."

A lively affection appears to have subsisted between the brothers and sisters of the family. Of his brother, the late Andrew Alexander, a Christian of high respectability and strong points of character, he thus writes: "My brother was four years older than myself, and perhaps two brothers were never more unlike. From his early childhood he was sober and careful, fond of work, and always contriving something. I have heard my mother say, that while the family sojourned at Irish Creek, when he was only five or six years of age, he made for himself a booth in the garden, where ne would sit and work with awl and needle, making himself a shot pouch ; for at that period every thing had a military complexion, the alarm of war having sounded through our peaceful country. But my brother was at the furthest remove from a warlike spirit. All his life he was so devoted to peace, that he would at any time rather suffer loss than enter into contention. His youth, manhood, and old age corresponded with his childhood. He was of uninterrupted veracity, and so honest that no temptation could ever seduce him to take an advantage."

The country was new, and the times were difficult, in consequence of which the youth of that day grew up with hardier habits than ours. Dr. Alexander used repeatedly to tell his children that his father gave him a rifle the day he was eleven years old ; and how he would spend days in the mountains in search of cattle which were lost, able to catch and discriminate the bells of his father's herd at a distance which seems almost incredible. He was an expert swimmer, and grew up with that perfect knowledge of horsemanship which is still common to all young Virginians. Trifles serve to colour the picture of the times. The dress of the children was grotesque. "Long hair," says he, "tied down the back, was all the mode ; and every little fellow was cherishing his hair. I, among the rest, had a little dangling queue, which from the thinness of the hair was very small. On this account, some of the boys called me 'My Lord Pigtail.' A great laugh was raised against me, by my having complained to the master of this, as a breach of the third commandment.

"Some judgment may be formed of the privations of the people, consequent on the long continuance of the war, from the fact, that it was very difficult for our teacher to obtain a penknife, to make and mend the pens of the scholars. Hearing that my father had been on to the North for goods, I was mounted on a horse and sent home to get a knife. There had been a great rain and the streams were swollen. Arriving at the North River, on the opposite bank of which my father's house stood, I found that the river was too high to be forded by so young and weak a horse as the one I rode. I knew not what to do. The only house near was a cabin of one John Montgomery, an old cedar-cooper. To cross the river, which is always deep at that spot, John had made a bark canoe, such as is used by the Indians. I sat nearly all day, but knew not how I should pass the night. But towards sunset the old man said he would go up with me to the ford, and would try to make the family hear our call, that a servant with a strong horse accustomed to the ford might be sent over. In this we succeeded. Davy, a black boy, crossed, and taking me behind him on a tall horse, led the one I had ridden, but it was not without danger."

These details, as belonging to the history of Virginia, could not well be omitted. We shall gather from the narrative some account of his early lessons and teachers, which will not be without their interest.

Schools were very scarce. I recollect that after our settlement in the Forks, as the whole country was then called between the James River and its North Branch, on which last we resided, my eldest brother and sister went to a school kept in the woods, half a mile north from where my brother Major Alexander now lives. The master was one Carrigan. They were every day carried across the river on horseback. About this time, that is, the next year after our removal, my father went on a trading expedition to Baltimore, and there purchased several convict servants, who had been transported for crime. Among these was a youth about eighteen or twenty named John Reardon, born, as he said, in Ireland, but reared from a child in London. He had been for some time at a classical school, and had read Latin books as far as Virgil, as well as a little in the Greek Testament. He wrote a fair hand and had some knowledge of book-keeping, but had never been accustomed to labour. This young fellow, it was thought, might teach school, in default of a better, and accordingly a hut of logs was erected at the foot of Paxton's Meadow, where there was a spring. When last in that country, I visited the spot and recognised the little knoll on which the house stood, but no vestige of it remained, and nothing around except the meadow furnished me with any associations of my earliest school. For though this place was a mile from our house by the direct path along the creek, which was narrow and disagreeable, and a mile and a half by old Letty Campbell's place, thither I trudged along every day, with my short legs and little feet, when not more than five years old. The master, as being my father's servant, lodged at our house, and often carried me in his arms part of the way. I had no fear of him, as at home I was accustomed to call him Jack, and often conveyed my father's commands to him. By some means, I know not how, I had learned to read in the

New Testament, before I went to this school. I remember a *horn-book*, and a folded pasteboard, with letters and pictures, but this is all. The school was large, and some of the scholars were nearly grown. It consisted of both boys and girls. Our little Englishman made himself very familiar with the larger boys, and did not pretend to exercise any authority over them. But he would lay about him stoutly with his long switch upon the smaller urchins, when they were guilty of looking off their books. The custom was, to read with as loud a voice as we could while getting our lessons, as it was called. When within a quarter of a mile of a country school, one might hear like a distant chime the united voices of the scholars. Upon reflection, I cannot think that I derived the smallest benefit from the year or part of a year spent in this school, unless my lungs may have been strengthened by perpetual exercise. Before the year was out, the war had commenced, and the drum and fife of the recruiting sergeant were heard in all public places. Many companies of regulars were enlisted in that region. There were but two tories in the whole country, and these were obliged to fly. Most of the English convicts, whether they had served out their time or not, enlisted. All who were in my father's service, namely, James Malone an Irish papist, Joe Lyon a thievish Jew, and John Reardon, went off; for these men generally cherished a deadly hatred to England."

"Malone and the Jew enlisted before Reardon. The former, as we heard, was killed in Carolina. Lyon, who was a very bad man, deserted to the British. Soon after Wallace's company reached the scene of warfare, Colonel Beaufort was attacked by Tarleton's corps in North Carolina. The Colonel, seeing his men in confusion, fled at the beginning of the battle, and almost the whole of his command was cut to pieces by the dragoons. Wallace disdained to fly, and being surrounded by the British horse, sold his life dearly, having first killed three or four men with his spontoon. Reardon, being a small man, was soon cut down. He had three deep wounds in the arms, one bayonet wound through the side, which only penetrated the flesh, and a severe cut on the head. After the battle he lay bleeding almost to death, among the slain and wounded, totally unable to move himself, but perfectly in his senses. When night came on, the moon shone, and he perceived a man passing near him, and wherever he observed signs of life despatching the sufferer with his bayonet. He presently approached Reardon, his musket was raised and his bayonet directed, when by the moonlight Reardon perceived that this murderer was his old fellow-servant, Joe Lyon. He immediately said, 'What, Joe—you will not kill me!' Lyon dropped his weapon and appeared amazed; but he sat down beside him, bound up his bleeding wounds as well as he could, brought some spirits and water, and remained by him a good part of the night; and before day dragged him to a small hut near the battle-field. Reardon, from whose lips I often heard the story, believed that the kind care of Lyon saved his life. Soon afterwards the battle of Guilford took place, in which it was said that Lyon was mortally wounded. Reardon returned to school-keeping on Timber Ridge."

At the age of seven, he was sent away to board at the

house of a relation, and attend a school on Timber Ridge. He represents himself as very small for his age, and both timid and peevish. Having previously learned the Shorter Catechism, he was now put to learn the Larger. "When I returned, the war was raging, and I frequently saw companies of backwoodsmen, with their rifles, brown hunting-shirts, and deer's-tail cockades, passing on to the theatre of conflict." The young subject of our memoir after going for some time to the school of one Stevenson, was again placed under the care of Reardon, who had been released from the wars and healed of his wounds. While here he had the early grief occasioned by hearing that his father had been draughted as a soldier; his place was however taken by his half-brother, John Alexander. He next went to school to John Rhodes, an Englishman, and also a "redemptioner," as such bondmen were called. "I remember this year," says he, "with much satisfaction. We had many pleasant schoolmates, and were pleased with our learning. I spent much of my time at the writing-desk, but made poor progress. In arithmetic and English grammar I did better; but at that time we had no grammar but the one appended to the spelling-book, which was founded on the Latin. This I laboriously committed to memory, but it was not of the least use to me. I was now ten years old; and my father having determined to give a liberal education to one of his sons, selected me, saying to me that learning was to be my estate. The Reverend William Graham, a graduate of the College of New Jersey, had set up an academy at Timber Ridge Meeting-House, and had obtained an ample charter from the Legislature. He travelled through the New England States, soliciting benefactions for his seminary. Several small neat buildings were erected for the use of the students, and a good house on the New England model was reared for the rector. Students came in a goodly number, mostly grown young men. Every thing promised success ; but war came on and obstructed the progress of the institution, which was named Liberty Hall. The school indeed existed before Mr. Graham came into the State, but had its seat at Mount Pleasant, near to the site of the village of Fairfield, six or seven miles to the east of Timber Ridge. Here Mr. Graham taught for a year or more, but being a man of much enterprise, he wished to rear a seminary after the model of Princeton College. Having received a call to take charge of the congregations of Timber Ridge and Hall's Meeting-House, he removed the school to the former place, where he conducted it for several years. But finding an opportunity to purchase a farm which pleased him on the North River, not much more than a mile from the present site of Lexington, he transferred it to that place, and had influence with a majority of the trustees to give their assent. The spot was on the extreme part of my father's property. My father was pleased to have the school brought so near him, and made a donation of as much land as was needed for the buildings. In the mean time, studies were pursued in an upper room of Mr. Graham's. Here I first entered on classical learning."

This is the proper place for giving some account of the Reverend William Graham, whose name must occur so frequently in these pages. To no man did Dr. Alexander own himself more indebted, in regard to the direction of his studies and the moulding of his character. Such was his uniform testimony through life; and we cannot do better than to subjoin his own estimate of this truly great thinker, gathering it from a discourse delivered in 1843, among the very scenes of his early studies.

"Mr. Graham possessed a mind formed for profound and accurate investigation. He had studied the Greek and Latin classics with great care, and relished the beauties of these exquisite compositions. With the authors taught in the schools he was familiar by long practice in teaching, and always insisted on the importance of classical literature, as the proper basis of a liberal education. He had a strong leaning to the study of Natural Philosophy, and took great pleasure in making experiments with such apparatus as he possessed. As he was an ardent patriot and thorough republican, the times in which he lived led him to bestow much attention to the science of government; and one of the few pieces which he wrote for the press was on this subject. By some he was censured for meddling with politics; but it should be remembered that at this period, the country having cast off its allegiance to Great Britain and declared itself independent, had to lay the foundation of governments, both for the States and the Nation; and the welfare of posterity as well as of the existing inhabitants of the land was involved in the wisdom with which this work was done. The talents of any man, capable of thinking, seemed to be fairly put into requisition. It is a sound maxim, that men living at one time must not be judged by the opinions of an age in which all the circumstances are greatly changed. At the adoption of the Federal Constitution, which according to its original draught he did not approve, he relinquished all attention to politics for the remainder of his life.

"The science, however, which engaged his thoughts more than all others except Theology, was the Philosophy of the Mind. Though acquainted with the best treatises which had then been published, he carried on his investigations not so much by books, as by a patient and repeated analysis of the various processes of thought as these arose in his own mind, and by reducing the phenomena thus observed to a regular system. The speaker is of the opinion, that the system of mental philosophy which he thus formed, was in clearness and fulness superior to any which has been given to the public, in the numerous works recently published on this subject. It is greatly to be regretted that his lectures were never committed to writing, for the benefit of the world. It was, however, a fault of this profound thinker, that he made little use of the pen; and it was also a defect, that in the latter years of his life he addicted himself little to reading the productions of other men, and perhaps entertained too low an opinion of the value of books.

"Mr. Graham, in his theological creed, was strictly orthodox, according to the standard of his own church, which he greatly venerated; but in his method of explaining some of the knotty points in theology, he departed considerably from the common track, judging that many things which have been involved in perplexity and obscurity by the manner in which they have been treated, are capable of easy and satisfactory explanation, by the use of sound principles of philosophy. As a preacher, he was always instructive and evangelical; though in common his delivery was feeble and embarrassed, rather than forcible; but when his feelings were excited, his voice became penetrating and his whole manner awakening and impressive. His profound study of the human heart enabled him to describe the various exercises of the Christian, with a clearness and truth which often greatly surprised his pious hearers, to whom it seemed as if he could read the inmost sentiments of their minds. When his object was to elucidate some difficult point, it was his custom to open his trenches, so to speak, at a great distance; removing out of the way every obstacle, until he was prepared to make his assault on the main fortress. Thus insensibly he led his hearers along step by step, gaining their assent first to one proposition and then to another, until at last they could not easily avoid acquiescence in the conclusion to which he wished to bring them. As a clear and cogent reasoner, he had no superior among his contemporaries; and his pre-eminence was acknowledged by all unprejudiced persons.

"The great error of his life was his relinquishing the important station in which Providence had placed him, and for which he was so eminently qualified, and this at a time of life when he possessed the ability of being more useful than in any former period. Having removed to the banks of the Ohio, he fell into great embarrassments, in the midst of which he died, in consequence of a violent fever contracted by exposure to drenching rains, while on a journey to Richmond. In that city he breathed his last, in the house of his friend, the late Colonel Robert Gamble; and his remains were deposited very near the south door of the Episcopal church on the hill, over which is placed a plain marble slab, with a short inscription." *

Concerning the school which Mr. Graham taught in his own house, we have some remarks of Dr. Alexander, penned, as we believe, in the last months of his life. "Here," says he, "the writer commenced his literary career, when a small boy. With the romantic scenery around, he has many interesting associations; but these are feelings which cannot be communicated. Of the whole number of youth whom he found in this school, he supposes that not one remains in the land of the living. And when he recollects the sportive and joyous hours, and the little foresight which any of the number had of their future course of life, he experiences an indescribable emotion, especially when he follows them, as he can in most cases, in their various fortunes. All the pupils were older than himself, and most were full-grown men; and while some rose to eminence in different professions, others pursued a devious and downward course, and scarce lived out half their days." †

The private narrative goes on with further particulars concerning this infant college: "Mr. Graham was so completely occupied with his new farm, that he paid little personal attention to the school. But his usher, James Priestly, was fully competent. Mr. Graham had perceived his extra-

* "Address before the Alumni of Washington College," Lexington, 1843.

† MS. Life of the Rev. William Graham.

ordinary memory, while yet a small boy, at a catechizing in the congregation ; and little Priestly was domiciliated with the minister. Here his progress in learning Latin and Greek exceeded any thing that had been known in that country. His memory, indeed, was so retentive, that he seemed to forget nothing that he read or heard. It was the custom for all the boys who boarded with the rector, to give an account of the sermons on Sabbath evening. Priestly, who seemed asleep all the time of preaching, would, nevertheless, repeat the sermon almost verbatim. The classics commonly read at school, he had so completely by heart, that I hardly ever saw a book in his hand, when hearing classes in Ovid, Virgil, Horace or Homer. He would sometimes take his pupils to a large spring, which bursts from the side of a steep hill, and rushes with noise into the river just below. The place is very romantic, and worth a visit from any one who is in Lexington. Hither Priestly would resort with his larger scholars, to spout the orations of Demosthenes in the original, with all the fire of the Grecian orator himself. He had about him an enthusiasm which transported him beyond himself, when the sentiments which he uttered were sublime. Twenty years later, I have seen him in a school of two hundred boys ; and when one of them did not declaim to his mind, he would jump out into the floor, and deliver the speech as he conceived it ought to be spoken.

"Mr. Priestly did not continue to be a teacher in the school more than a year after my entrance. He directed his course towards Maryland, and soon received employment as a classical instructor, first in Annapolis, and then in Georgetown."

After removing to Kentucky as a lawyer, he resumed the business of teaching, and returned to Georgetown. After some time, he transferred his abode to the city of Baltimore, where I visited him in 1801. A few years after this he received an invitation to take charge of the Cumberland College, as it was then called, at Nashville. Here he spent the last years of his life; and though all were impressed with his extraordinary learning, and his high qualifications as a classical teacher, he did not succeed well in organizing and arranging an infant college. He was, indeed, a very eccentric, though a very amiable man, and married a woman as eccentric as himself." "Dr. Priestly," says the Lexington Address, above cited, "possessed an enthusiastic ardour in behalf of education, which I have never seen surpassed, and succeeded in inspiring his pupils with somewhat of the same. From him the speaker derived the first impulse in his literary course, and he, therefore, feels a pleasure in having this opportunity of paying a deserved tribute to the memory of a teacher who was an ornament to this institution in its earliest days."

Even under such teachers, the attainments of our young scholar, as he represents them, were humble. Under Priestly he became thoroughly versed in Ruddiman's Latin Grammar, which stuck to him through life. He was encouraged by learning that the usher had spoken of him to his father as a boy of great promise, because, says he, "from my earliest years a sense of deficiency has preponderated over all vain conceit of my own abilities." Under Mr. Graham, he proceeded in his study of languages. He speaks of being surrounded by evil companions. The school became exceedingly corrupt. A bashful and timid disposition kept him from many excesses ; but he records and laments his initiation into various dangerous games and foolish practices. About the time that he began to read Horace, he enjoyed the able instructions of a new usher, Archibald Roane, afterwards Governor of Tennessee.

In the life of one who afterwards attracted notice as a public speaker, the following incidents ought to have their place. " The students were permitted, in order to improve themselves in speaking, to have public exhibitions, in which plays were acted. Much of our time was taken up in rehearsal. I always had the part of a female, as being of the proper size. This I disliked very much, but it was pressed upon me. As to other speaking, I made a poor hand of it, and was seldom able to get through my speech. In writing and composition, nothing could be more miserable. My handwriting was as bad as it well could be, and I felt unable to compose any thing. Once I attempted to take part in a debate, but it was an utter failure. After the departure of Mr. Roane, we fell again under the tuition of Mr. Graham, and as he was fond of Natural Philosophy, he devoted himself most cheerfully to the improvement of the pupils. The course which we followed was that which prevailed at Princeton under Dr. Witherspoon. We had the same textbooks, and even transcribed his lectures on Moral Philosophy and Criticism. Much attention was then paid to practical mathematics, surveying, mensuration and navigation."

During the whole time of his connection with the

Academy he was, according to subsequent and sober views, making very little advancement in mind or morals. Environed by many idle and some profligate boys, he joined them in many of their ways ; though not without pungent checks of conscience. But the regular course of study had been passed through, and it was the desire of the Principal that he should take a regular degree, conformably to powers which had been granted by the Legislature. For the necessary examinations he now began to prepare with great diligence. "I was, however, conscious," says he, "that I had passed over most of the studies superficially, although at every public examination I had been placed in the first grade, more on account of my youth and small size and the promptitude of my answers, than any solid desert. But I had not proceeded far in my review, when my father returned from a journey to Fredericksburg, and informed me that he had made an engagement for me to be a tutor in the family of General Posey, of the Wilderness, twelve miles west of Fredericksburg. It is a little remarkable that on that journey he staid all night at the house of Dr. Waddel (afterwards my father-in-law), and had nearly made an arrangement for me to be his assistant in the school which he kept. I was only a little turned of seventeen. My father was very peremptory in his orders, and I could do nothing but obey."

Before we leave this beautiful and picturesque scenery of Rockbridge, we think it suitable to give some view of the impression which it made on the subject of this narrative.

It was a topic on which he loved to dwell in animated conversation, even to his latest days. His own words are these :

"Whether the scenery with which our senses are conversant in early life, has any considerable effect on the character of the mind, is a question not easily determined. It would be easy to theorize on the subject ; and formerly I indulged in many lucubrations, which at the time seemed plausible, all tending to the conclusion that minds developed under the constant view and impression of grand or picturesque scenery must in vigour and fertility of imagination be greatly superior to those who spend their youth in dark alleys, or in the crowded streets of a large city, where the only objects which constantly meet the senses are stone and brick walls, and dirty and offensive gutters. The child of the mountains, who cannot open his eyes without seeing sublime peaks, penetrating beyond the clouds, stupendous rocks, and deep and dark caverns, enclosed by frightful precipices, thought I, must possess a vivid impression of the scenes of nature, by which he will be distinguished from those born and brought up in the city, or in the dull, monotonous plain, where there is neither grandeur nor variety. Perhaps there might be a little vanity mingled with these speculations, as it was my lot to draw the first breath of life at the foot of a lofty mountain, and on the bank of a roaring mountain torrent ; where the startling reveillé was often the hideous howling of hungry wolves. But when I attempted to recollect whether I had, in the days of childhood, ever experienced any sensible impression from the grandeur of surrounding objects, or had ever been led to contemplate these objects of nature with any strong emotion, I could not satisfy myself that any thing of this sort had ever occurred. The only reminiscence was of impressions made by the novelty of some object, not before seen ; or some fancied resemblance to something with which I was familiar. Two mountains, somewhat remarkable, were frequently surveyed by me with delight ; the House Mountain, and the Jump Mountain ; both appertaining to a ridge, called in the valley the North Mountain. The first of these is a beautiful mountain which stands out at some distance from the main ridge, and from the middle of the valley exhibits something of the shape and appearance of a house. From Lexington and its vicinity, the view of this mountain is pleasant and imposing. The idea of its resemblance to a house took strong hold of my imagination ; and especially because at the western end there was the resemblance of a shed, which corresponded with such an appendage to the house in which my childhood was spent. And now, when I revisit the place of my nativity, whilst almost every thing else is changed, the House Mountain remains the same, and I gaze upon it with that peculiar emotion which attends the calling up in a lively manner the thoughts and impressions of infancy. The idea of a perfect resemblance to a house was so deeply imprinted on my mind, in relation to this mountain, that I was greatly discomposed and disturbed in my thoughts, when a boy, by having occasion to travel a few miles towards the east end of the mountain, and finding that every resemblance of a house was gone ; and when instead of one beautiful, uniform mountain, as smooth and steep as the roof of a house, I now beheld two rough-looking spurs, separated at a considerable distance from each other. This obliteration of a pleasing idea from the mind was painful; and whenever I was in a situation to see the mountain under this aspect, the unpleasant impression was renewed. Every traveller among mountains must have noticed how remarkably they vary their appearances, as he changes his position; and not only so, but from the same site a prominent mountain exhibits a wonderful variety of aspects, according to the state of the atmosphere. This I believe is what is called *looming*, and was much noticed by Mr. Jefferson from Monticello, particularly in relation to that remarkable isolated mountain, called Willis's, which elevates its head to a considerable height, at a great distance from any other mountain or hill.

"But to return to my favourite, the House Mountain. In the days of my childhood—and perhaps it is still the case—this mountain was commonly burnt over every year; that is, the dry leaves on the ground were burnt. When the fire extended in a long crooked string along the side of the mountain, and especially when near the top, the appearance was grand and beautiful in a very dark night. It had all the appearance of a zig-zag fire in the sky; and whenever it occurred, greatly attracted and delighted the boys. It was in those days held as a maxim among boys, that no one ever had ascended, or could ascend to the ridge or summit of the House Mountain; but since that time I understand that not only men, but women, have been successful in reaching the top; and have thence surveyed the varied and delightful landscape of the valley, with its villages, and its farms, its rivers and smaller streams. I can scarcely conceive of a pleasanter prospect than that which might be enjoyed from the summit of the House Mountain.

"As to the Jump Mountain, it was only occasionally that I got a view of it ; and although the descent is very abrupt on the north side, so that the top of the mountain actually seems to project, my mind would have received a slighter impression from it, had not the first view of it been associated with a story told me by an older boy, that the reason why it was called the Jump Mountain, was because, at a certain time, a man had actually jumped off the top of the mountain, and fallen dead at its foot. This made a deep impression on my mind, and although I have seen the mountain hundreds of times since, I believe I never saw it without thinking of the man who took such an awful leap. When that species of taste is developed which delights in landscapes, I have not been able, with any precision, to ascertain. As far as my own experience goes, or rather as far as memory furnishes me with facts, I think that while a boy at school, I had no consciousness of the exercise of any such faculty. The love of novelty is almost coeval with our existence ; but the love of the beauties of nature is slow in its development, and when there is no culture, it is often scarcely observable in mature age. Some men cast their eye over a lovely landscape with as little emotion as is experienced by the horses on which they ride. The only thought perhaps is, how rich the land ? how many barrels of corn, or hogsheads of tobacco, or bushels of wheat, might be raised here, to the acre ? And even the horse will experience an emotion as elevated as his rider's, if there should happen to be a good clover-field in sight. As it relates to objects of sublimity, I have found it, except in a few cases, difficult to distinguish this emotion from mere wonder, or admiration. But in this same valley, and not very remote from the objects of which I have spoken, there is one which, I think, produces the feeling which is denominated the sublime, more definitely and sensibly than any that I have ever seen. I refer to the Natural Bridge, from which the county takes its name. It is not my object to describe this extraordinary *lusus naturae*, as it may be called. In fact, no representation which can be given by the pen or pencil can convey any adequate idea of the object, or one that will have the least tendency to produce the emotion excited by a view of the object itself. There are some things, then, which the traveller, however eloquent, cannot communicate to his readers. All I intend is, to mention the effect produced by a sight of the Natural Bridge on my own mind. When a boy of fourteen or fifteen, I first visited this curiosity. Having stood on the top, and looked down into the deep chasm above and below the bridge, without any new or very strong emotions, as the scene bore a resemblance to many which are common to that country, I descended by the usual circuitous path to the bottom, and came upon the stream or brook some distance below the bridge. The first view which I obtained of the beautiful and elevated blue limestone arch, springing up to the clouds, produced an emotion entirely new ; the feeling was as though something within sprung up to a great height by a kind of sudden impulse. That was the animal sensation which accompanied the genuine emotion of the sublime. Many years afterwards, I again visited the bridge. I entertained the belief, that I had preserved in my mind, all along, the idea of the object; and that now I should see it without emotion. But the fact was not so. The view, at this time, produced a revival of the original emotion, with the conscious feeling that the idea of the object had faded away, and become both obscure and diminutive, but was now restored, in an instant, to its original vividness, and magnitude. The emotion produced by an object of true sublimity, as it is very vivid, so it is very short in its continuance. It seems, then, that novelty must be added to other qualities in the object, to produce this emotion distinctly. A person living near the bridge, who should see it every day, might be pleased with the object, but would experience, after a while, nothing of the vivid emotion of the sublime. Thus, I think, it must be accounted for, that the starry heavens, or the sun shining in his strength, are viewed with little emotion of this kind, although much the sublimest objects in our view; we have been accustomed to view them daily, from our infancy. But a bright-coloured rainbow, spanning a large arch in the heavens, strikes all classes of persons with a mingled emotion of the sublime and beautiful; to which a sufficient degree of novelty is added, to render the impression vivid, as often as it occurs. I have reflected on the reason why the Natural Bridge produces the emotion of the sublime, so well defined and so vivid; but I have arrived at nothing satisfactory. It must be resolved into an ultimate law of our nature, that a novel object of that elevation and form will produce such an effect. Any attempt at analyzing objects of beauty and sublimity only tends to produce confusion in our ideas. To artists, such analysis may be useful ; not to increase the emotion, but to enable them to imitate more effectually the objects of nature by which it is produced. Although I have conversed with many thousands who had seen the Natural Bridge ; and although the liveliness of the emotion is very different in different persons ; yet I never saw one, of any class, who did not view the object with considerable emotion. And none have ever expressed disappointment from having had their expectations raised too high, by the description previously received. Indeed, no previous description communicates any just conception of the object as it appears ; and the attempts to represent it by the pencil, as far as I have seen them, are pitiful. Painters would show their wisdom by omitting to represent some of the objects of nature, such as a volcano in actual ebullition, the sea in a storm, the conflagration of a great city, or the scene of a battle-field. The imitation must be so faint and feeble, that the attempt, however skilfully executed, is apt to produce disgust, instead of admiration."

CHAPTER SECOND.

1789.

TUTORSHIP—RELIGIOUS VIEWS—GENERAL POSEY—MRS. TYLER—AWAKENING—FLAVEL—WORK OF GRACE.

BEFORE we accompany the youthful teacher on his travels, it is proper that we should gather some notices of his moral and religious experience, during the period of childhood and youth. This we shall do chiefly from certain volumes of manuscript Reminiscences, in the hands of his children.

Having been religiously and even strictly educated, after the manner of the old Presbyterians, he was not without solemn awakenings from time to time. At an early age, he received deep impressions from the sermon of a travelling minister; but, as a caution to parents, he records that these instantly vanished upon his hearing the discourse disparaged by his father and mother. At the particular period last mentioned by us, his religious views were crude and insufficient. "My only notion of religion was that it consisted in becoming better. I had never heard of any conversion among the Presbyterians.——The state of morals and religion in that country, after the Revolutionary War, was very bad. The old continental soldiers, many of whom in that quarter were convicts, now returned, and having received certificates for their wages, were able to live for a while in idleness and dissipation. Robert * * *, a shrewd, intelligent man, who was one of this number, had acquired a house in Lexington, the old farm-house of Isaac Campbell, who owned the land. Here he collected all the vagrants in the country, and a drunken bout would be kept up for weeks. They called themselves the Congress, and made Bob their president. Hard battles were fought here. The better class of people were as much injured by the profane and licentious manners of the officers of the disbanded army, as the lower classes by the soldiery.

"There were a few pious people in the land, who kept up the power of religion, and were as salt to preserve the mass from universal putrefaction. Among these, the elder John Lyle, and his wife Flora, my aunt, were conspicuous; to whom may be added an old Mr. M'Nutt, Alexander Walker, John Wilson and Hugh Weir; the two last being ruling elders in Monmouth. These persons spake often one with another about the affairs of the Kingdom. They were exceedingly dreaded by the wildest of the people, being both reverenced and hated. I remember having been at a dance in Lexington, when John Lyle, the elder, called to see a man with whom he had business; and it is inconceivable what a consternation was spread through the company, when his grave and stately form was seen to approach the house.

"Much of our time, which should have been spent in study, was consumed in playing cards, at which I became a great adept ; so managing, however, as to avoid detection, except in one instance. The vacation had taken place, and a number of us agreed to meet in the Academy, and there pursue our usual amusement. But while we surrounded the table, and after the cards had been dealt, Mr. Roane entered the room. Seeing what we were about, he seemed confounded and passed along. We were in great alarm, and fell into a hot dispute as to whether he had made any discovery ; when after a few minutes he returned and spoke to us in a very serious and admonitory manner. But he said that if we would pledge ourselves never to be guilty of such an offence again while we were students, he would not inform against us. To this we readily agreed, and I kept my promise, for I have never thrown a card from that day to this."

From what has been said, it is sufficiently obvious, that he left his father's house with no tokens as to the manner of life which he was destined to lead. His journey was a solitary one, across the Blue Ridge, a distance of one hundred and forty miles. And this brought him to a new and important period of his history.

At the early age of seventeen Archibald Alexander left his father's house, to become a private tutor in the family of General John Posey, of the Wilderness, in the county of Spotsylvania The family residence was in a very retired situation, where a few persons of wealth had valuable estates. Among these, visits were frequent, but few other persons came into the neighbourhood. General Posey had done service in the Revolution as a commander of riflemen in Morgan's famous corps, in which he finally rose to be Colonel. He was a man of noble appearance and courtly manners. Mrs. Posey, who had been a beauty in her youth, was now at the age of forty a fine and stately person. She was addicted to the pleasures of society, but generally took the side of religion, in a day when it was frequently impugned, and seemed to be vacillating between duty and the world. Though somewhat decayed in wealth, the Poseys maintained much of the style which belonged to old Virginia families. The pupils were John Posey and George and Reuben Thornton, sons of a former marriage; a daughter, Lucy, came in for occasional lessons.

The young preceptor felt the embarrassment of his new situation, and was burdened with a sense of his incompetency. One of the scholars was larger than himself, and they had all been taught with some accuracy. Their youthful tutor, though he had read largely, was well grounded in nothing but the grammar. Cornelius Nepos, which he read with them, was new to him and offered many difficulties, and his nights were often spent in preparing for the next day's lesson, amidst regrets that he had not made more faithful preparation. But he ascribed to this pressure all the accuracy which he afterwards attained in the Latin language. In the latter part of his life he has been heard to say, that during the half-century then past, he had read more Latin than English. He carried some of his scholars into Cæsar and Virgil. The house contained a small country library, and he devoted his spare hours to the reading of history, of which his knowledge was scanty. In this way he perused with much avidity Rollin's Ancient History, his History of Rome, in sixteen octavo volumes, Rapin's England, besides books of travels. He attempted Locke's Essay, but with little comprehension of the argument. In after life he was accustomed to dissuade instructors from entering their pupils prematurely into philosophical works, and said in reference to this ineffectual attempt, "This fact shows that a capacity and relish for any particular study may be late in developing itself. Mental Science became afterwards my favourite study." He speaks about this period of one Mr. Jones, a neighbour, who had Cartesian books, to whom he lent Martin's Grammar of Philosophy, as this friend was unacquainted with the Newtonian system. In the seclusion of the Wilderness, far from all congenial company, he was seldom without a book in his hand, except when he was giving up his mind to solitary meditation.

As to his religious views at this time, the records which he has left are happily full and explicit. He had learnt the Shorter Catechism and a good portion of the Larger, but without reflection, so that he describes his ignorance as profound. With an utter aversion to what was spiritual, he cherished a strong predilection in favour of religion in general, and particularly in favour of that in which he had been brought up. Of the two classes of professors in his native county, his father belonged to the more liberal and accommodating; and the son had been wont to laugh at any who gave signs of extraordinary devotion. Up to this time he had never felt any thing like a serious influence, except of the most transient kind. From Mr. Graham, the Rev. John B. Smith, and other preachers of the time, who visited Rockbridge, he sometimes heard startling truth, with a momentary effect. He remembered all his life a sermon of Adam Rankin, who vehemently cried in one of his addresses, "O ye people of Timber Ridge, if you are determined not to go to heaven, I will go without you!" "It is remarkable," said he, "that I never paid any attention to what our own preacher said in the pulpit. His voice was very low, and much interrupted by continual hemming, or clearing the throat. I thought him the worst preacher of all that I ever heard, but was astonished to hear a sensible man, who had no love to him, say that he had more sense than all the rest put together. While I was under his tuition, he resigned the charge of both his congregations, and then preached in the Academy to the students; but the house was crowded with the people of his late charge. The students were warned, that these sermons they must remember, for they would be required to give the substance in writing. This caused us to hear with attention. He began with the proofs of the being of a God, and went on systematically. I remembered a good deal, but understood nothing. One day however he took a practical subject, and discoursed about the new views given by the illumination of the Holy Spirit. My attention was gained at the commencement and fixed throughout the sermon. It seemed as if a new world had suddenly risen to my view; but as soon as the discourse ended the scene vanished, and for years afterwards I never once recollected that I had such new views." Such was the state of mind, when he was brought by Divine Providence into a situation which was to prove so important to his higher interests.

In the house of General Posey, an aged Christian lady, Mrs. Tyler, had found a refuge. She was a Baptist, and was well bred and well informed, having seen better days. In the embarrassing circumstances of the young family tutor, Providence raised him up an invaluable friend in this excellent woman. She corrected his opinions and guided him in the choice of useful books. Sometimes she related her own religious experience. In early life she had been gay and fond of admiration. The only form of Christianity with which she was then acquainted was that of the English Establishment. When the Baptists first began to preach in the country she held them in contempt, and used to go to their meetings purposely to ridicule the blunders of their ministers. But under a discourse from an aged stranger, she found her peace of mind effectually destroyed. In her deep and continued distress she was without any adviser, and knew not whither to look for direction and relief. At length she came deliberately to the conclusion that she should certainly be lost. Her efforts were vain, and she sank into a calm despair. But she remembered to have heard that the souls in perdition blaspheme God in their anguish. This she felt that she could never do. She should for ever bless God for his goodness. Thinking thus, she found the plan of salvation by Christ opened to her view, and, filled with admiration, she owned herself willing to take up the cross and follow Christ. Nor was the self-denial small to which she was called. The Baptists, under whose ministry she was awakened, were a despised people in Virginia. Yet she joined them, in the face of remonstrance and contempt from all her connections. Such was the narrative which she gave, adding as she turned to the inexperienced young man, "Now I know all this must appear utter nonsense to you, who have felt nothing of the kind." He was silent, but was deeply convinced, from the solemnity of her manner, that there must be a reality in these things.

Mrs. Tyler did not address to him many observations as to his own particular case, but she often spoke of religious matters. In her view, the Presbyterians, as she had seen them, were sound in doctrine, but deficient in inward experience. She was anxious that he should listen to the best preachers of her own persuasion. This was not easy, as those who appeared in Spotsylvania were of an inferior sort. The Baptists were divided into two classes, known respectively as the Regular and the Separate; and the former regarded the latter as wild and fanatical. The Church of the Wilderness was served by the Separate Baptists. "Their stated preacher was Aaron Bledsoe, a stout, corpulent man, who, when he preached in warm weather, took off his coat and neckcloth, threw open his collar, and generally became so earnest that before he was done he was black in the face. In every sermon he gave an account of his own experience." The people of wealth seldom attended, but when any such happened to be present, Bledsoe treated them without leniency, and sometimes inveighed against learning, it was supposed for the benefit of the young teacher. These meetings exhibited those strange bodily agitations which afterwards became so frequent in the Southern revivals. Not only were there enthusiastic responses and outcries, but leaping, contortions, swooning, and convulsions.

Mrs. Tyler was mortified at these exhibitions, and often expressed the wish that her young friend might hear her own minister, whose name was Frisbie. For this purpose they once set out on a short journey beyond the Rappahannock. The river was high, and they crossed it on horseback at some peril. At the house of a worthy Scotch Presbyterian named Morrison, they enjoyed a hospitable reception. It was the time of a great meeting, or sacramental season, among the Regular Baptists. The assembly was too large to be contained by the small meeting-house. Mr. Frisbie preached out of doors. His text was, "We preach not ourselves, but Jesus Christ, and ourselves your servants for Jesus' sake." Mr. Alexander records that he was too much occupied with the strange and promiscuous assembly to pay much attention to the discourse. It contained, however, a fling at learning, and yet was highly pleasing to Mrs. Tyler, who was disappointed that it had made so little impression. But the words of the private record will best continue this part of the narrative.

"About this time General Posey had a mill built on his plantation, and the millwright was a Baptist by the name of Waller, a brother, I think, of a famous Baptist preacher called Jack Waller. I often talked with this man about his business and other matters; but one day he unexpectedly turned to me and asked me whether I believed that before a man could enter the kingdom of heaven he must be born again. I knew not what to say, for I had for some time been puzzled about the new birth. However, I answered in the affirmative. He then asked whether I had experienced the new birth. I hesitated, and said, 'Not that I knew of.' 'Ah,' said he, 'if you had ever experienced this change you would know something about it!' Here the conversation ended; but it led me to think more seriously whether there were any such change. It seemed to be in the Bible; but I thought there must be some method of explaining it away; for among the Presbyterians I had never heard of any one who had experienced the new birth, nor could I recollect ever to have heard it mentioned. This became about the same time a subject of discussion at the table, after old Mrs. Tyler had withdrawn, especially on Sunday. In these conversations Mrs. Posey, who professed to be a 'seeker,' defended the Baptist opinions, and so did old Mrs. William Jones, who I believe was a truly pious woman. General Posey declared that he did not believe in any such miraculous change, but added that he would credit it, if Mrs. Posey should ever profess that she had experienced it. Mr. William Jones was a good-natured, luxurious, skeptical man, who avoided giving offence by any avowal of his opinions, but plainly insinuated that religion was a disease of weak and superstitious minds, and that all that was necessary for a cure was an acquaintance with philosophy. Major Jones cared for none of these things. His opinion was that preaching was as much a trade as any thing else." These details give glimpses of a state of society which many a reader will recognise as familiar.

Mrs. Tyler pursued her calm religious course amidst all

these misapprehensions. She loved the writings of John Flavel, and could not but desire to make them known to the youthful Presbyterian inquirer. As her eyes were weak she often sent for him to read to her, a request with which he complied at first out of courtesy, and afterwards from some increase of interest in the author. Learning that Flavel was a Presbyterian, he took pains to discover what were his views of regeneration. He had never read any thing upon the evidences of Christianity. Though he knew of infidel books in the hands of other young men, he had never read them, feeling no interest in the argument. But now, when his mind began to be enlarged by the reading of history, and he found that there were other religions, the professors of which were fully confident of their systems, he was staggered, and asked himself what basis he had for his own belief. This doubt was increased by the knowledge that many intelligent men in the country rejected revelation, and under the influence of French philosophy that these opinions were rapidly on the increase. Still he felt a strong reluctance to give up the truth of Christianity, and the prejudices of education were salutary.

"So ignorant was I (thus he writes) that I did not know that any book had ever been written in defence of Christianity; of course, I knew not whither to go to have my doubts removed and my faith strengthened. My mind became anxious on the subject, which frequently dwelt on my thoughts. It happened, providentially, that into a trunk of classical and scientific books, sent to me from home at my request, some lady had thrown a coarse pamphlet, which I had often seen tossing about at home ; and when I now saw it, I felt displeased that this old pamphlet should have been sent. But on looking at the title-page, I observed the word 'Evidences,' and it struck me immediately that it was possibly something in favour of Christianity. On further inspection, I saw that I was not mistaken, for the whole title was 'Internal Evidences of the Christian Religion, by Soame Jenyns, Esq.' I was rejoiced ; and as all the family had gone to church, I sat down and began to read. At every step conviction flashed across my mind, with such bright and overwhelming evidence, that when I ceased to read, the room had the appearance of being illuminated. I never had such a feeling from the simple discovery of truth. And it is my opinion, that no argument of the external or historical kind would have produced such a conviction." This incident sufficiently accounts for the warm terms in which, even to the close of life, Dr. Alexander was accustomed to recommend this treatise of Jenyns, though with an earnest protest against the whimsies of the brilliant but sometimes chimerical author.

What has been related shows a mind under divine leadings. In addition, he says of himself, that he had often prayed mentally when he was in danger, or when his friends were ill, but was wholly a stranger to secret prayer, as a habitual practice. Now he began to have a concern about his salvation, which led him to retirement. Every morning, when the weather would permit, he took a long, solitary walk through the fields, terminating it at the Wilderness Creek, which ran along the border of the plantation. Here he found some plots of green grass, surrounded by thickets, and overhung by great birch trees; and here, with his knife, he made a booth or arbour. To this sequestered spot he used to retire for prayer, taking some volume with him, on the Lord's day. He records that on a certain Sunday evening, his meditations of God and divine things became solemn and delightful, so that he was unwilling to withdraw his thoughts from these objects, when it became necessary to return home. But all this was without a radical reformation of character.

"My services as a reader (such is his own account) were frequently in requisition, not only to save the eyes of old Mrs. Tyler, but on Sundays for the benefit of the whole family. On one of these Sabbath evenings, I was requested to read out of Flavel. The part on which I had been regularly engaged was the 'Method of Grace;' but now, by some means, I was led to select one of the sermons on Revelation iii. 20, "Behold I stand at the door and knock," &c. The discourse was upon the patience, forbearance and kindness of the Lord Jesus Christ to impenitent and obstinate sinners. As I proceeded to read aloud, the truth took effect on my feelings, and every word I read seemed applicable to my own case. Before I finished the discourse, these emotions became too strong for restraint, and my voice began to falter. I laid down the book, rose hastily, and went out with a full heart, and hastened to my place of retirement. No sooner had I reached the spot than I dropped upon my knees, and attempted to pour out my feelings in prayer; but I had not continued many minutes in this exercise before I was overwhelmed with a flood of joy. It was transport such as I had never known before, and seldom since. I have no recollection of any distinct views of Christ ; but I was filled with a sense of the goodness and mercy of God ; and this joy was accompanied with a full assurance that my state was happy, and that if I was then to die, I should go to heaven. This ecstacy was too high to be lasting, but as it subsided, my feelings were calm and happy. It soon occurred to me that possibly I had experienced the change called the new birth. But as I was walking homeward, the thought presented itself, that if this was indeed conversion, the effect would be that I should leave off all my sins ; and I was willing to make this the criterion of my state. For a few days I guarded against every thing which I knew to be wrong ; but in a week my former feelings returned, and when exposed to temptation I transgressed as before. The next day the recollection filled me with unutterable anguish ; for, agreeably to my own judgment, my hopes of heaven, which had been so strong, were all blasted. I make no remarks on this joyful frame. Such experiences are not uncommon, and are often taken for conversion."

By reading so much in Flavel, and hearing the remarks of his aged friend, he began to emerge somewhat from his former ignorance, and to comprehend the cardinal doctrines of Christianity. About this time, a little book, "Jenks on Justification by Faith," fell into his hands. This treatise he read with an effect not unlike what had proceeded from and perplexity as to the way of acceptance with God, or, as he expressed it, he was leaning on the old covenant. "Now every thing appeared as clear as if written with a sunbeam. The effect on Mrs. Posey was similar; for she spoke of the book in the most exalted terms. I recollect that the author, who was a clergyman of the Church of England, confesses he had preached for a long time without knowing the true method of salvation. And when his eyes were opened, he published this little volume, to open the eyes of other legalists. It is somewhat remarkable, that from that day to this, a period of half a century, chiefly spent among books, I have never seen another copy of this work, and have never conversed with any one who knew it; so that at length I began to think that I had forgotten the true title; but about a year ago, I happened to see a favourable mention of it, under the very name which I had preserved in my memory.

"I now began to read Flavel for my own instruction, and also Burkitt, which was the only commentary in the house. The two great doctrines of Justification and Regeneration I began to understand, at least in theory. A good sermon was now a feast to me. At the Wilderness meeting-house, one Sunday, we found in the pulpit a grave, well-looking man, named Saunders, who had for his text, 1 John ii. 2, 3. His explanation of Christ's propitiatory work for the whole world, in which he opposed the Arminians and Universalists, gave me great satisfaction. He was one of the Regular Baptists.

"This year, 1788–89, was in many respects the most important of my life. If I had not the beginnings of a work of grace, my mind was enlightened in the knowledge of truths, of which I had lived in total ignorance. I began to love the truth, and to seek after it, as for hid treasure. To John Flavel I certainly owe more than to any uninspired author. During the year I paid one visit to my friends in Lexington, and heard Mr. Graham preach a sermon on the text, 'For our righteousnesses are as filthy rags.' The utter insignificancy of our own works, and the need of a better righteousness than our own, were of course the subjects. It was the first intelligent discourse to which I had listened since my new understanding of the doctrines in question, and it gave me great satisfaction; but when I looked around upon the people, I had the impression that they were generally in the same state of darkness and legality in which I had lived so long. As good Mrs. Tyler, who I doubt not had a tender concern for my salvation and prayed often for me, was a Baptist, she naturally wished me to know what she believed to be the truth on that subject; and she put into my hands Gill's work on Baptism. This perplexed me not a little, for I had strong predilection for the way in which I had been educated, especially as I found that Flavel was a Presbyterian. And in turning over the large volume containing his works (the two being bound in one) I met with a controversial piece on this very subject, written against Cary. This I read with avidity and with full conviction that his arguments were valid, though I now doubt as to the conclusiveness of some texts on which he mainly rests the cause."

At the close of the year he returned to his native scenes, in the beautiful and romantic county of Rockbridge.

CHAPTER THIRD.

1789—1790.

RETURN HOME—GREAT REVIVAL—VISIT BEYOND THE MOUNTAINS—REVIVAL SCENES—STRUGGLES OF SOUL—SAMUEL MORRIS—JOHN BLAIR SMITH—WILLIAM GRAHAM—PROGRESS OF INWARD WORK.

THE period to which our narrative now brings us was remarkable, in the history of the Southern churches, for that wide-spread religious movement known as the Great Revival. As few were more familiar with this awakening than Dr. Alexander, and few have left more copious notes in regard to it, we feel justified in giving particulars which may sometimes lead us to deviate from the strict line of biography. Many of the sketches of eminent men are too interesting to be omitted, and belong to the characteristic history of the times.

It must have been in the year 1789 that the young preceptor returned to his father's house, with a determination to supply the defects of his intellectual training. We find him therefore retiring for days to the woods, and devoting himself to Euclid and Horace. But the year was to be signalized by higher progress. He found his eldest sister much changed, and earnestly engaged in seeking acquaintance with God. A startling death among the connection brought him into new terrors. At the same time he was thrown into confusion by Dr. Chauncy's defence of universal salvation, which was officiously put into his hands by a latitudinarian doctor. There was at this time no church in Lexington; but he speaks of a funeral discourse which so affected his mind that he retired into a grove with a volume of Whitefield's sermons, and spent the afternoon in reading and prayer; and with his characteristic attachment to localities, he adds that this grove is now cut down. On a vacant Sunday he heard one of Willison's Sermons on the Lord's Supper read to the congregation, and was convinced of his duty in regard to this ordinance, while he knew that he was destitute of preparation.

A rumour had come into the quiet settlement, of an extraordinary religious awakening, on the other side of the Mountain, as the great dividing Blue Ridge is familiarly called. The Rev. Mr. Graham prepared to visit the scene of these wonders, and proposed to take young Alexander among other companions. All such journeys were of course made on horseback, and amidst mountain scenes and in a hospitable country were sufficiently exciting. "On our journey," says he, "Mr. Graham was very open and communicative; at first on philosophical subjects, in which he took great delight, and then upon religious matters, when he found me interested in these. We discoursed particularly on the subject of Justification by Faith and Regeneration. My companion, Samuel Wilson, was astonished to hear me converse on topics, concerning which when together at the Academy neither of us had formed any opinions. Mr. Graham also

4

was surprised at the extent and accuracy of the knowledge which I appeared to have on subjects to which very few young men in our part of the country had turned their thoughts. The fact was, I purposely turned the conversation to those interesting truths on which my mind had been so much exercised, merely with a view to ascertain whether the conclusions to which I had come after much thought and inquiry were in unison with his views, and whether he agreed with Flavel and the other authors I had been reading. I had no thought of making any display of knowledge ; for it never entered my mind that I had acquired any stock of theological doctrine. These conversations, however, had a depressing influence on my companion, who was several years older than myself, and who was conscious that he knew little about matters on which I talked so freely."

The party was hastening to arrive at a celebration of the Lord's Supper, at a place called Briery, near the borders of Charlotte and Prince Edward Counties. On their way they were entertained at Liberty, in the house of Michael Graham, father of the late Professor Samuel L. Graham, of the Union Theological Seminary. The whole time was spent in hearing from him and especially from his pious and more eloquent wife, accounts of the revival, with narratives of particular cases. Here they heard of the conversion of James Turner, afterwards known as one of the most remarkable masters of natural but irresistible oratory. Turner had been a profligate and a ringleader in all the profane and violent amusements of the time. But now he was holding meetings and exhorting. Pursuing their expedition they came to the house of Major Trigg, whose aged mother was one of the Rev. Samuel Davies's communicants, a woman of great piety and goodness. She spoke of Mr. Davies with much reverence and affection. She said to Mr. Graham, "I have never attained to the faith of assurance, but only to the faith of reliance." He answered promptly, "If you know you have the faith of reliance, you have the faith of assurance also." The month was August, and our travellers were exposed to the rays of a Virginian sun, without the shelter of an umbrella, a convenience (our journalist notes) which had not then come into use. But they were joyfully welcomed to the house of Samuel Morris, a name sacred in the annals of American Presbyterianism, which may justly detain us for a little.

Mr. Morris had removed from Hanover, and was now residing in the lower end of Campbell County. It was he who was instrumental in the revival of gospel truth, by the reading of evangelical books in the Reading-House of Hanover County, long before the arrival of any Presbyterian missionary. "As we approached through the fields, we saw the old gentleman walking homeward, as if like Isaac he had been meditating." "Samuel Morris was at this time between seventy and eighty years of age, but had the appearance of firm health. But for his being bowed with age, his stature must have been six feet. His frame was large, his shoulders were broad, and though he was somewhat bald, the thick hair about the sides of the head was not gray. He had one son, and a number of daughters. Mr. Morris gave Mr. Graham a detailed account of the origin and progress of Presbyterianism in Hanover, before Mr. Davies came to settle there; the same, I presume, which he put into writing for Mr. Davies, who included it in a letter to Dr. Bellamy. The old gentleman had heard of the revival in Prince Edward, and seemed to be much interested in it. He said he understood that one of the preachers, Mr. Lacy, resembled Whitefield."

There had never been any revival in the Valley, and few of the Scottish Presbyterians there resident had much faith in these sudden awakenings. They had heard of a work of this kind in Western Pennsylvania, under the labours of the Rev. Joseph Smith, the Rev. John M'Millan, and others; but the general impression was that these religious commotions would pass away like the morning cloud. John Lyle, an eminently vain, ostentatious, and dissipated young man, who had avowed infidel opinions, returned from Franklin, now East Tennessee, with a mind and character signally renewed, and this served to awaken new expectations of the scenes which they were about to visit.

As the travellers approached the place of their destination, there was an interesting meeting between the two great preachers of Virginia. Mr. Graham had enjoyed very little friendly intercourse with Mr. Smith for a number of years; indeed a certain coolness existed between them in consequence of some difference in Presbytery, which was not however of a personal nature. But now Mr. Smith had specially invited Mr. Graham to come over and see the great works of the Lord. The Rockbridge party turned aside from the road to await the arrival of the people returning from the Saturday's service, which usually preceded the communion. "While we were here," says the narrative, "a novel and solemn scene presented itself. A large company of young people on horseback, as they slowly passed along, were engaged in singing hymns. Most of this company, I afterwards learned, were young converts, who had come over from Caswell County, North Carolina, with the Rev. Nash LeGrand. They had travelled fifty or sixty miles to attend the sacrament, and were full of zeal and affection. The music resounded through the woods in an agreeable and impressive manner. Mr. LeGrand, who had been remarkably converted during the revival, having just finished his college course, was, with very little preparation, except an ardent zeal, brought into the ministry by Dr. Smith, and sent into North Carolina, where a powerful influence seemed to accompany his preaching. After nearly all the people who were returning had passed, came Dr. John Blair Smith, accompanied by several of the elders of his church, and other friends. As soon as he espied Mr. Graham, he stopped and received him with a hearty greeting."

They were now in the very midst of revival scenes. Among the persons, then in youth, whom they here met, was William Hill, now the venerable Dr. Hill of Winchester.

But the prominent figure in every group was undoubtedly Dr. John B. Smith. It is unnecessary to adduce many facts concerning a man so well known in our history. He was a son of the Rev. Dr. Robert Smith, of Pequea, Pennsylvania, and of course a brother of the Rev. Samuel Stanhope Smith, D. D., of Princeton. Smith, as well as Graham, was educated at the college of New Jersey, and wher his brother Samuel founded Hampden Sidney College, John became a tutor or professor in the same, and was licensed by the Presbytery of Hanover. When his brother was called to Princeton, John Blair Smith was made President of Hampden Sidney.

"His natural disposition was full of vivacity, his temper quick, and his action rapid. At the beginning of his ministry he did not manifest great zeal, and his preaching was less impressive than his brother's; but at the commencement of the great revival in 1786 or 1787, he underwent a remarkable change in his own feelings and in the fervency of his preaching, so that he became one of the most powerful preachers I ever heard. In person he was about the middle size. His hair was uncommonly black, and was divided on the top, and fell down on each side of the face. A large blue eye of open expression was so piercing that it was common to say Dr. Smith looked you through. His voice had an unusual solemnity, and always affected me, whatever was said. Dr. Smith was as fearless a man as ever lived, and his quickness of temper sometimes led him to act rashly, and incur enmity which might have been avoided. As a companion, he was most agreeable. His treatment of young ministers was soothing to the diffident, and his manner of introducing them to strangers was peculiarly agreeable to their feelings. His preaching was far from being uniform, for sometimes he fell short of his usual force from the state of his feelings. His sermons were always well prepared, but nothing was written out, except the introduction, which he commonly prepared with great care ; and its only fault was that it was grandiloquent. Within the leaves of a small Bible which he held in his hand he had a small paper containing the introduction, all the divisions and subdivisions, leading thoughts, and cited texts, which last he always read out of the Bible. His speaking was impetuous ; after going on deliberately for a while, he would suddenly grow warm and be carried away with a violence of feeling, which was commonly communicated to his hearers. If opposed to him in sentiment they were often aroused to great wrath. The most powerful sermon I ever heard from him was in defence of the revival as a work of God. It was directed more especially against the Seceders, who, to a man, set themselves in opposition to it. It was delivered in the grove near New Monmouth, immediately after the communion, to the largest congregation which had ever been collected in that county. Many of the leading Seceders were present. He told them of the opposition of their sect to Whitefield, and to the revival at Cambuslang. Next day I heard one of them say that if ever any man was possessed of a devil in modern times, it was John Blair Smith when he delivered that sermon. He was eminently discriminating and perspicacious ; but if he failed to see through a difficulty at the first glance, he commonly failed to do so by any further attempt. He was perhaps censorious in his judgment of professors who discovered any lukewarmness, and would often declare to his friends of such and such persons, that they did not possess a spark of religion. No man in Virginia was so much admired as a preacher ; but after his removal to Philadelphia, where he bestowed more care on accuracy, he lost much of that impressive manner, which carried away and captivated his hearers during the revival."

On arriving at the neighbourhood of Little Roanoke Bridge, the company addressed themselves to preparation for the approaching solemnities. There were strangers from every quarter, including fifty from Carolina. Some of them were newly converted young men, who spoke with warmth and freedom of their late worldliness or even infidelity, and their present faith and joy. "The meeting was very much crowded. Here (says the record) I first got a fair sight of Dr. John Blair Smith. His appearance was more solemn than that of any one I had ever seen, and caused a feeling of awe to come over me. As Mr. Graham was exhausted by riding in the heat, Dr. Smith called on a very young man, Mr. C., to pray. Next he called on William Hill to exhort. This astonished me. How a person so young should have the courage and ability to speak in public and before such an audience, I could not conceive; but he delivered a warm and pungent address, on the Barren Fig Tree, which affected my feelings very much. Then, after prayer, Dr. Smith himself addressed a powerful and solemn discourse to the company.

"My mind was considerably excited by what I saw and heard on the Saturday evening. The question of professing my faith returned upon me with force. Having never spoken freely to any one of my own religious exercises, I felt great backwardness to open the subject, and indeed I had had no opportunity of conversing with my pastor. On the morning of the Sabbath the roads were covered with multitudes flocking to the place of worship, at Briery. The house was not sufficient to hold half the people ; an arbour had been prepared, with a stand for the preachers, and the intention was to have the sacrament as well as the sermon out of doors. Dr. Smith preached the Action Sermon, as it was called in Scottish phrase. The text was Psalm li. 17, 'The sacrifices of God are a broken spirit : a broken and a contrite heart, O God, thou wilt not despise.' It was especially intended to comfort diffident and discouraged believers. The evidences of piety which he laid down were such as I could for the most part find in myself; so that I felt much regret that I had not taken measures to partake of the ordinance. Though the morning was clear, the appearances of rain were threatening ; after consultation it was therefore determined to administer the sacrament within the house. Notice was given that while arrangements were making, Mr. LeGrand would preach in the grove behind the church. I resorted to the place, where I first had a sight of this successful young minister. At this time there was much that was striking in his aspect. He was tall, but rather bending in his attitude, and his countenance was solemn and benignant, with a shade of melancholy. He stood upon a horse-block, and preached a discourse which, though inaccurate and incoherent, was delivered with peculiarities of voice that made their way to the feelings. After the communicants had retired, the Rev. Samuel Houston preached to the non-communicants under the arbour. After hearing Mr. Houston, whose sermon was interrupted by the rain, I pressed with much difficulty into the house, where Mr. Graham was preaching. Little did I think, that I should ever preach in that pulpit, and become the pastor of that people! There was on the face of the assembly an appearance of tender and earnest solemnity. Never had I heard my pastor speak with such warmth and pathos as on this occasion. His text was Isaiah xl. 1, 'Comfort ye, comfort ye my people,' etc. The part which I heard was the address to the impenitent, in which under a series of particulars he showed them their comfortless state. The good people of Briery were entranced. They had expected a very cold and dry discourse. Dr. Smith afterwards said to me of this sermon, that it was the best he had ever heard, except one; and the one excepted was preached during the revival by the Rev. James Mitchell, who was never reckoned a great preacher. Every mouth was filled with expressions of admiration, and from this time, Mr. Graham was considered one of the ablest preachers in the land."

"On Monday after the Communion, we went to Hampden Sidney, in the county of Prince Edward, where Mr. Lyle, already named, showed us much attention and introduced us to the Rev. Drury Lacy, who then as Vice-President had charge of the institution, in consequence of Dr. Smith's having resigned the presidentship. I was much pleased with the free and candid manners and conversation of Mr. Lacy. By the early loss of his left hand, from the bursting of a gun when a boy, Mr. Lacy had been led to fit himself for teaching an English school. In this calling he early acquired a high reputation, especially as he wrote an incomparably beautiful hand. As he taught for some time in Cumberland, where Dr. Smith preached on the alternate Sabbaths, he received an invitation to come and learn at the College. Having about that time experienced a change of heart, he joyfully accepted the offer, immediately began the study of Latin, rapidly passed through the curriculum and was licensed to preach as a probationer. Having a voice which was loud and clear, and a very distinct articulation, with a warm heart, he was from the first very popular and effective as a preacher. And as the great revival in the vicinity soon commenced, Mr. Lacy was much employed in various places, but being fond of teaching continued his residence at the College. By many, his preaching during the revival was preferred even to that of Dr. Smith; it was plain and experimental, and there were manifest seals to his ministry. Though deficient in accuracy he was unusually acceptable abroad, and at presbyteries and synods, when the assemblies were large and the services in the open air, he was commonly chosen for the work, as his penetrating tones could reach the outskirts of any congregation. He was a man of great humility, remarkably exempt from envy, of a sociable and friendly temper, and greatly esteemed and beloved by his brethren. Having suffered long with a calculous affection, he resorted to the surgical aid of the celebrated Dr. Physick of Philadelphia; but a fever ensued, and in a few days he expired. I had at his request taken my passage in the stage-coach for Philadelphia to see him; but before the hour of departure I received a note from his kind host Mr. Robert Ralston, advising me not to come, lest it should agitate him too much, especially as I had received from Dr. Hoge the sad intelligence that Mrs. Lacy, whom he left in health, had died of the putrid fever. He left the world in ignorance of this bereavement, to enjoy the surprise of meeting his beloved wife in the invisible state. His remains lie in the cemetery of the Arch Street Church. Two of his sons, and three of his grandsons are in the ministry."

During this excursion, Mr. Alexander was taken by Mr. Graham to visit the celebrated orator, Patrick Henry ; to whose eloquence he had several opportunities of listening, at a later period. Mr. Graham remained more than a week in Prince Edward, and preached several times at private houses. His sermons were intended to discriminate between what was essential and what was incidental in religious experience. He was careful to show that true religion consisted more in the strength of the habitual purpose of soul, than in high affections. "I understood his discourses," it is here added, "and thought I could find the evidences of vital piety, as proposed by him, in myself. But hearing much of sudden conversions, and of persons being convulsed with severe conviction, I concluded that the hopes which I entertained must be fallacious, and that they prevented my being truly convinced of sin. This occasioned great perplexity, and I felt a strong desire to make my case known to Dr. Smith. As we were to journey together to Bedford, I hoped for an opportunity to have his judgment. Mr. Graham had hitherto said nothing to me about my personal feelings ; but when we returned to Charlotte, at our lodging at old Mrs. Morton's at Little Roanoke Bridge, he took me out and conversed with me. I freely related my difficulties, but he made little or no reply. Dr. Smith was to preach the funeral sermon of an unfortunate young woman, who had been killed by falling from a horse as she was returning from an entertainment. To this solemnity I looked forward, as one well suited to produce conviction. On the way I fell into company with Susan Watkins," afterwards by a second marriage the wife of the Rev. Dr. Hoge, "and found her remarkably communicative, so that I could open my mind to her with less restraint than to any one I had met. She told me her own experience and encouraged and exhorted me to go forward in seeking religion. My expectations of being deeply affected by Dr. Smith's sermon on this sorrowful occasion were utterly disappointed. I was not only conscious of no suitable emotion, but my thoughts were to an uncommon degree wandering. I however had the opportunity of conversing with Dr. Smith. I related to him my various exercises, but added that I had still fallen into sin after these exercises ; upon which he said, in his decided, peremptory way, that then they were certainly not of the nature of true religion, which always destroys the power and dominion of sin ; and he proceeded to account for the joy I had experienced, on other principles. From this time I abandoned all persuasion that I had experienced regenerating grace. My desire now was to be brought under such alarming convictions of sin, as I had heard of in the case of others. But that evening, which I spent in the forest, I was greatly distressed on account of my exceeding hardness of heart. I rolled on the ground in anguish of spirit, bewailing my insensibility. We lodged at the house of a pious man, a nephew of Samuel Morris, and the next day went on to Bedford.

"When we arrived at Liberty, we met nearly thirty of our friends from Rockbridge who had come over to the sacrament, among whom was my eldest sister. They seemed already under a solemn impression, even before attending any services. The preaching was continued several days at the Peaks Meeting-House, and the communion was on the Sabbath. It was a time of great emotion, and none seemed more affected than the Rockbridge company.

"While I was at Liberty I experienced exercises of mind which were remarkable. The place was a little out of the town in a thicket, at the edge of a wood. I had in the morning walked out into this grove, and while thus engaged in meditation and prayer, I was suddenly visited with such a melting of heart as I never had before or since. Under a lively sense of Divine goodness my eyes became a fountain of tears. The most prominent feelings were a sense of ingratitude for the innumerable mercies which had been richly and constantly showered upon me. When I now reflect upon it, it seems like a sudden change in the animal system, and a relief arising from a vent found for tears. The immediate result was a sweet composure of spirit. I cannot remember that I had any thought of Christ, or much contrition for my sins; and this melting frame, the counterpart of which I never experienced, led to no permanent change in my condition; in a few hours I felt much as before it occurred."

The progress of this mental conflict may be noted in the following record, concerning a later day, in the same journey. "The former part of the day I spent in the woods, ruminating on my sad condition and future prospects. The train of my thought was, that I had enjoyed the very best means and opportunities of salvation, but these had produced no good effect; that I was now going where all were careless of these things, and where the means would be far less favourable. The conclusion forced itself upon me that I should certainly be lost for ever. My mind was calm and my thoughts deliberate, and when I came to this result I was nowise agitated, but began to contemplate the justice of God in my condemnation. It was evident to me that as a righteous Governor he could not do otherwise than condemn me to hell; and I could not but approve the sentence of my own condemnation. Yet I felt that I could never entertain any hard thoughts of God, even when suffering under his heavy displeasure. These views were so far from increasing my distress, that I experienced a degree of composure which I had not had for a long time. The awful question in regard to my destiny appeared now to be settled, and I felt no need of prayer or further waiting on God. I returned to the house, and there found the Rev. James Mitchell, pastor of the Presbyterian church in that county. He had never been introduced to me, but invited me into an adjoining room. He then began to enumerate the high privileges which I had enjoyed in my visit to Prince Edward, and said he hoped I had received abiding impressions from the many powerful sermons which I had heard, and from seeing so many young people engaged in religion and forsaking all for Christ. I answered deliberately, that what he had remarked about my privileges was very true; but that however great the means, they had proved of no avail to me; I had not yet in any degree experienced those convictions without which I could not expect to be saved, and that being now about to leave all these means, I had that day come to the conclusion that I should certainly be lost ; that I knew it would be just, and that I had no one to blame but myself. To which he answered, that no certain degree of conviction was prescribed ; that the only purpose which conviction could answer was to show us our need of Christ, 'and this,' added he, 'you have.' He then represented Christ as an Advocate before the throne of God, ready to undertake my cause, and able to save to the uttermost all that come unto God by him. A new view opened before me at this moment. I did feel that I needed a Saviour, and I knew that Christ as an Advocate was able to save me. This mere probability of salvation, after having given up all hope, was like the dawn of morning upon a dark night ; it was like life from the dead. From that instant I entertained a joyful hope that I should yet be saved. These new views affected me exceedingly. I was like a man condemned to die, who is unexpectedly informed that there is a friend who can obtain a reprieve. I was unable to say any thing. My tears prevented utterance."

In continuing the journey, "I rode along alone," says he, "and my mind was in a state of delightful repose ; cheering promises came into my mind, as though they dropped from heaven. When Mr. Mitchell commenced the prayer-meeting, at a town on the way, he called upon my companion, Samuel Wilson, to pray. After a word or two of exhortation, and a hymn, I was in like manner called upon, and did not hesitate to make the attempt, although in any other state of mind in which I had ever been, I should as soon have agreed to rise and preach extempore. I was astonished at myself, and though altogether unaccustomed to pray, I was delivered from the fear of man, and was enabled to get through without serious obstruction. This manner of treating young persons under religious impressions, I have always disapproved. It was intended to bring us to take a decided part, before we returned home; and it no doubt had the effect of causing us to feel that we were now committed. The next morning we set out for Lexington, about thirty in number, and sang revival hymns as we rode along. On the top of the Blue Ridge we halted at a spring to partake of a viaticum, which some of the company had been provident enough to bring along. Mr. LeGrand appeared to be very happy, and talked freely with us all, exhorting us to persevere boldly in the cause of Christ when we reached home."

CHAPTER FOURTH.

1789—1790

REVIVAL IN ROCKBRIDGE—EXTRAORDINARY EXPERIENCE IN THE FOREST—CHARACTER OF THE WORK OF GRACE—PRINCETON COLLEGE—ILLNESS—JOURNEYING—RECOVERY—PROGRESS.

THERE is something of amiable youthful simplicity in the confidence with which the returning company expected an immediate manifestation of awakening grace on their arrival at Lexington. Notice was duly given of a meeting for prayer, to be held on the evening after their return. The service was under the direction of Mr. LeGrand. We resume the narrative: "I had the trial of being called upon to pray, in the presence of all my young acquaintances. My timidity, however, was in a manner gone. I now calculated fully on a revival in Lexington. Before the meeting I conversed privately with some of my associates, and found them favourably disposed. The news of our arrival, and of the spirit in which we had returned, spread rapidly through the country around. The next day the public service was at New Monmouth church. Mr. LeGrand preached in the morning on Isaiah xlv. 22, 'Look unto me and be ye saved, all ye ends of the earth.' After which Mr. Graham gave a narrative of all that he had seen and heard in Prince Edward and Bedford, and then addressed the great congregation in the most penetrating and pathetic manner, the tears meanwhile streaming from his eyes. The assembly was deeply and solemnly moved. Multitudes went weeping from the house. Another meeting was appointed for the evening, in the town, in a large room which had been used for dancing. Here the solemnity was greater, if possible, than at the church. Many remained to converse with the ministers, and a person of the most sedate habits and moral life cried out in an agony, 'What must I do to be saved!' Every thing went on prosperously, and I was in expectation that all, or nearly all, the people would be awakened. Several of my companions, educated young men, came forward and professed their determination to be on the Lord's side. I had not heard a whisper of opposition, but next morning my uncle, Andrew Reid, who had not been at any of the meetings, brought to our house a volume of Locke's Essay, with the page turned down at the chapter on Enthusiasm. My sister, to whom he spoke with some severity, was surprised and confounded, and grew faint with agitation, so that she was constrained to go to her couch. It struck me as amazing that any man of sense could think us in danger of enthusiasm. We soon found that there were many enemies of our proceedings, and that some of the young men ridiculed the whole affair. But the work went on, and we were gratified to find that cases of awakening occurred at almost every meeting, and the religious concern continued to diffuse itself through the country. These were halcyon days for the church ; and as for myself, though I did not regard myself as converted, I was so occupied with the cases of others, and with the opposition, that for a while I almost forgot my own case.

"Mr. LeGrand remained with us a week or two. His natural disposition was very uneven. He was either exceedingly lively, or in an awful gloom, in which he continually expressed a desire to die. At the time of his awakening, in Cumberland, he lay, I have been told, for hours in convulsions, produced by convictions, which were followed, it is thought, by believing views of the Saviour. Great success attended his earliest labours. His countenance, though youthful, was marked with sadness, and his voice had a mellowness and tenderness which I have never heard surpassed.

"Being much dissatisfied with my state of mind, and now sensible of the corruption of my heart, I resolved to enter on a new course, and determined to give up all reading except the Bible, and to devote myself entirely to prayer, fasting, and the Scriptures, until I should arrive at greater hope. My life was spent almost entirely in religious company, but our conversation often degenerated into levity, which was succeeded by compunction. Telling over our private exercises was carried to an undue length, and instead of tending to edification, was often injurious. But reserve on this subject was considered a bad sign ; and on meeting, the first inquiry after salutation was concerning the state of each other's souls.

"A young woman of my acquaintance, who, with others, had gone over to Bedford, appeared more solemnly impressed than most of the company. All believed that if any one had experienced divine renewal, it was Mary Hanna. One afternoon, while reading a sermon of Tennent's, on the need of a legal work preparatory to conversion, she was seized with such apprehensions of her danger, that she began to tremble, and in attempting to reach the house, which was distant only a few steps, fell prostrate, and was taken up in a state of terrible convulsion. The news quickly spread, and in a short time most of the serious young people in the town were present. I mention this for the purpose of adding that I was at once struck with the conviction that I had received an irreparable injury from the clergyman who had persuaded me that no such conviction as this was necessary. I determined, therefore, to admit no hope until I should have the like experience. I read all the religious narratives I could procure, and laboured much to put myself into the state in which they described themselves to have been, before enjoying hope. But all these efforts and desires proved abortive, and I began to see much more of the wickedness of my own heart than ever before. I was distressed and discouraged, and convinced that I had placed too much dependence on mere means, and on my own efforts. I therefore determined to give myself incessantly to prayer until I found mercy, or perished in the pursuit.

"This resolution was formed on a Sunday evening. The next morning I took my Bible and walked several miles into the dense wood of the Bushy Hills, which were then wholly uncultivated. Finding a place that pleased me, at the foot of a projecting rock, in a dark valley, I began with great earnestness the course which I had prescribed to myself. I prayed, and then read in the Bible, prayed and read, prayed and read, until my strength was exhausted; for I had taken no nourishment that day. But the more I strove the harder my heart became, and the more barren was my mind of every serious or tender feeling. I tasted then some of the bitterness of despair. It seemed to be my last resource, and now this had utterly failed. I was about to desist from the endeavour, when the thought occurred to me, that though I was helpless, and my case was nearly desperate, yet it would be well to cry to God to help me in this extremity. I knelt upon the ground, and had poured out perhaps a single petition, or rather broken cry for help, when, in a moment, I had such a view of a crucified Saviour, as is without a parallel in my experience. The whole plan of grace appeared as clear as day. I was persuaded that God was willing to accept me, just as I was, and convinced that I had never before understood the freeness of salvation, but had always been striving to bring some price in my hand, or to prepare myself for receiving Christ. Now I discovered that I could receive him in all his offices at that very moment, which I was sure at the time I did. I felt truly a joy which was unspeakable and full of glory. How long this delightful frame continued I cannot tell. But when my affections had a little subsided I opened my Bible, and alighted on the eighteenth and nineteenth chapters of John. The sacred page appeared to be illuminated; the truths were new, as if I had never read them before ; and I thought it would be always thus. Having often thought of engaging in a written covenant with God, but having never before found a freedom to do so, I now felt no hesitation, and having writing materials in my pocket, I sat down and penned it exactly from my feelings, and solemnly signed it as in the presence of God.*

"I expected now to feel uniformly different from what had preceded, and to be always in lively emotion, thinking my troubles all at an end. As I had been much distressed by discovering the sins of my heart, and as I read in Scripture that faith works purification, I resolved to make this the test. At the time, indeed, I had no doubt as to the sincerity of my faith ; and in the paper of self-dedication above-mentioned I expressed the assurance that if I had never before received Christ I did then and there receive him. For several days my mind was serene. But before a week had elapsed, darkness began to gather over me again. Inbred corruption began to stir. In a word, I fell back into the same state of darkness and conflict as before."

Shortly after this, in the autumn of 1789, he made a profession of his faith. But he describes his first approach to the Lord's Table as destitute of high comforts. His thoughts were much distracted, and his soul was harassed with awful fear lest he should eat and drink damnation to himself. And after receiving, this dreadful suspicion haunted him, until he felt convinced that this enormous sin had been

* This document is in our possession.

committed. But at his second communion, which was at New Monmouth, he enjoyed a delightful day of clear assurance. "The sermon by Mr. Graham," says he in a very late record, "was on the text, 'The Sun of Righteousness shall arise,' etc. The preacher compared the beginnings of true religion in the soul to the rising of the sun; sometimes with a sudden and immediate clearness, sometimes under clouds, which are afterwards dispersed. As he went on, it occurred to me with great distinctness, that the Sun of Righteousness began to rise on me, though under a cloud. When conversing with Mr. Mitchell in Bedford, I was relieved from despair by the persuasion that Christ was able to save even me. This shows how seldom believers can designate with exactness the time of their renewal. Now, at the age of seventy-seven, I am of opinion, that my regeneration took place while I resided at General Posey's, in the year 1788."

It seemed proper to dwell at some length on the traits of this remarkable and extensive religious awakening, because it shows how familiar the subject of this memoir was with the good and the evil of such excitements; especially as in a later period of his life, when he felt constrained to unite with other wise men in protesting against enthusiastic excesses and false doctrine, he was frequently treated by opponents as a rigid book-divine, who had grown up in cold forms, without acquaintance with great outpourings of the Holy Spirit. How far this was from the true state of the facts, will have been sufficiently apparent in the preceding extracts.

It was a remarkable peculiarity of this great popular reformation, that amidst all its outbreaking enthusiasm and strange animal agitation, it was not carried forward by means of corrupt doctrine. Aberrations from the truth there doubtless were in the case of individuals, and even bodies of errorists broke away on one side and the other, especially in the West ; but all the preachers whom we have had occasion to name, were zealously attached to the sound Nonconformist theology of the seventeenth century. Minor points were indeed brought into question among the active minds of inquirers, stimulated by greatly exalted feeling ; but the fundamentals of reformation truth were left undisturbed. Most of those in the Valley who professed their faith maintained their constancy, but some who persevered most faithfully were not the most prominent at the beginning. "Much conversation took place concerning the nature of faith, the necessity of legal conviction, and the question whether there was an operation on the soul itself prior to all spiritual views, or whether regeneration was effected by the introduction of truth to the mind. When we brought our various opinions to Mr. Graham for his decision, we found that his judgment was peculiar. He maintained that as conversion is the change of a rational agent, it must be a matter of conviction and choice ; and that it was absurd to suppose any physical operation on the soul itself to be necessary or even conceivable. This opinion therefore became prevalent. The opposite, supposed to be that of many called Hopkinsians, was that no change takes place in the views of the understanding, but such as arises from a change in the feelings of the heart. But some of us were not satisfied with either of these explanations. We supposed that a soul dead in sin was incapable of spiritual views and feelings, until made partaker of spiritual life ; that this principle of life was imparted in regeneration ; so that the natural order of exercises was, that the quickened soul entertained new views, which were accompanied by new feelings in accordance with the truths presented to the mind. This opinion I then adopted and have always held. The Spirit operates on the dead soul, communicating the principle of life. The Word holds up to the view of the regenerated soul the evil of sin which leads to repentance, and shows the excellency and suitableness of Christ as a Saviour in all his offices, and reveals the beauty of holiness.

" Among other practical books, Marshall on Sanctification came into use, strongly recommended by some, as exhibiting the only true view of saving faith, and as fitted at once to give peace to the troubled conscience. Some who had received little comfort in religion, seized on this notion of faith, persuaded themselves that their sins were pardoned and that Christ and all his benefits were theirs, and exulted for a time in the pleasing delusion. But they generally fell back into doubt and distress. The instances of persons professing a full assurance were few. Great caution was exercised, to guard against deception ; which perhaps led to undue nicety in the attempt to discriminate between the exercises of the believer and the hypocrite, and to a multiplication of marks and evidences, some of which were not deduced from the Holy Scriptures. This caused perplexity in the minds of many sincere persons, and detracted from the peace which they might have enjoyed. Nevertheless just views were generally entertained on this subject, and our pastor was lucid and discriminating as to the nature of true religion."

"With many the impressions suddenly made vanished away by degrees, so that they became as careless as ever; and some no doubt entered the communion of the Church who had not the root of the matter in them. But a large number continued to give evidence of the depth and reality of the work of grace in their hearts. Some of the most lively Christians were of the female sex."

Of the period concerning which we have been writing there remain several little books, chiefly in cipher, containing a brief journal of the writer's private exercises. They begin when he was eighteen years of age, and extend with interruptions for about six years. For several reasons we make no use of them; partly because of their scantiness, partly because his mature judgment seems to have been adverse to such diaries, but chiefly because he has given elsewhere as much of these transactions between God and his soul, as he desired to be remembered.

The records from which we make these extracts contain narratives of fearful apostasy, in a few remarkable instances; full of interest and warning, but too extensive in their details to find a place in our pages. Some of these fatal results are attributed by the writer himself to the practice common in most revivals of dragging young and obscure persons into public view, and to the ill-judged stress laid on apparent gifts of fluent and acceptable prayer in seeming converts On this subject his views corresponded with those of Robert Hall, who in reviewing his own juvenile experience in respect to this matter, writes as follows : " I never call the circumstance to mind but with grief at the vanity it inspired ; nor, when I think of such mistakes of good men, am I inclined to question the correctness of Baxter's language, strong as it is, where he says, 'Nor should men turn preachers as the river Nilus breeds frogs (saith Herodotus), where one half *moveth* before the other is *made*, and while it is yet *but plain mud !*' "*

Sixty years ago, when Archibald Alexander was struggling to acquire an education, there was no such provision of literary apparatus as in our day. Single volumes passed from house to house, as great treasures, and the youth was happy who could own any one of those works which now greet us with profusion. Our young student speaks of several authors who influenced his mind in this its forming state. First among these were such as met the demands of his troubled mind during early awakenings ; Owen, Baxter, Alleine, the Erskines, Willison, Doddridge, Whitefield, Jenyns and Dickinson's Letters.

At the instance of General Andrew Moore, young Alexander was induced to think of going to Princeton College, then under the presidentship of Dr. Witherspoon. To this plan his father was very favourable ; his clothes were packed up and actually forwarded a certain part of the way. A

* Memoir of Robert Hall, Vol. III., p. 5.

day or two before setting out, however, he waited on Mr. Graham, from whom he desired to take letters. To his surprise Mr. Graham disapproved the whole scheme, and gave such a description of the inconveniences to which he would be subjected as an undergraduate, and the advantages of deferring this step until he should take degrees at Lexington, that he was persuaded to remain at home. Gen. Moore was chagrined, and the family of Mr. Reid were much displeased. It must be admitted that the difficulties suggested by Mr. Graham were imaginary. But Providence directs in all such conjunctures, and the very next day Mr. Alexander was seized with a fever, which held him many weeks in great suffering and danger. The physician who was called in, came to the bedside drunk. For a large part of the time the patient was in a raging delirium. At one stage of the disease he lay speechless, and the family was called to see him die. One morning, about daybreak, he heard the voice of a neighbour at the door, inquiring, "Is he still alive?" It was the preposterous custom of the country for every one to have access to the sick room, and one day when a sermon was preached in the house, half the congregation came in to see him, and some good but unwise men undertook to talk with him on religious subjects, while his mind was alienated. But it was God's purpose to spare him for usefulness. For several weeks he was lifted out of bed, as an infant. His constitution, which was vigorous before, received a shock, from which, as he supposed, it never fully recovered. He was seized with an excruciating sciatica, and suffered for months with a distressing cough; so that during the whole winter and spring of 1790, he was in feeble and as it seemed declining health.

The Sweet Springs had already become a place of frequent resort, and thither he was accompanied by his father in the ensuing summer. The scenes were new to him, and we would fain believe are such as no longer present themselves in that beautiful locality. "A company of gamblers never intermitted their games day or night, Sunday or workingday, during the whole time I was there. They relieved one another, and would sometimes come out to the fountain, adding not a little to the horrid symphony of oaths and imprecations which filled the air at these gatherings. They strove to outdo one another in the rapidity and novelty of their profane expressions. Some of these persons came every year, and had their log cabins to dwell in. Besides other invalids there were old broken-down debauchees, who were endeavouring to prop up a shattered and polluted constitution. There was an old Baptist by the name of Cox, from North Carolina, who had been here every season for a number of years. He was treated with a sort of respect by the profane, although they would throw out a jest at his sobriety; to which he would reply, 'Gentlemen, if there is no future state, your course may do, but if it should turn out that there is, I should fear to be in your place.'" He adds a painful account of a dying man, who though belonging to the convivial circle was abandoned by his comrades. "They would only come within twenty or thirty yards of the cabin, and ask how he did; but I could hear their oaths as I sat beside him. I found on his table, Law's Serious Call, which I had never ceen, and which I read through that night. Nothing ever more goaded my conscience ; yet I believe it did me little good, for I was in a despondent state."

During most of his sojourn he was in the family of Mr. Lewis, the proprietor of the Sweet Springs. Here he met with the Rev. Mr. McRoberts, of Prince Edward, whose name will appear again in our narrative. Mr. LeGrand also came to the Springs, and preached to the visitors. The sketches which follow are too characteristic to be omitted, especially as the memorials of this period are scanty.

"My health was improving, and several weeks remained of the time allotted to my stay, but finding a man from Augusta returning with a led horse, I prevailed on him to convey me to Rockbridge, which would be only a few miles out of his way. We set out rather late and were unable to reach our lodging place before night ; and being near the banks of Jackson's River we lost our way, and took a path which led us off from the main road directly across the hills towards the river. For a time our situation was not only painful but perilous, as the ravines which we descended were very deep. After wandering some time we saw a distant light, and with some difficulty reached a cabin in the low grounds. We found two women in the house, one aged, and the other young, but the mother of several children, who were sleeping in the room which we entered, of course the only one in the house. There was an evident reluctance in these persons to comply with our request for lodging, the reason of which transpired in due time. The matron set to work, however and provided a supper, which to our appetites appeared very good. Scarcely had we ended our repast, when the man of the house came home in a state of intoxication. He was very noisy before he came in, but when he found two strangers, he became outrageous and ordered us to depart. We expostulated, reminding him that the night was dark and that we could not possibly regain the high-road. The wife and mother joined their entreaties to ours, and he at length consented to furnish provender for our horses, and soon fell into a sound sleep. His wife spread a bed on the floor.

"We rose early, on a lovely Sabbath morning; my plan in setting out having been to reach the forks of Jackson's River and the Cow Pasture, where I knew Mr. LeGrand was to be. The man of the house arose early also, and with a marked change in his demeanour. He was deeply mortified at the inhospitality of the previous night, and sought in every way to make amends for it. Our way lay all the morning along the bank of the river, and in some places there was scarcely room for a bridle-path between the mountain and the channel. The ride was delightful and refreshing, and before reaching the junction of the Cow Pasture, we passed what I have always admired as a most picturesque spot; I mean that where Jackson's River makes its way through the high and steep mountain. The fissure is very narrow, and the sides abrupt, with piles of rock at the bottom. The two sides of the breach seem to correspond with each other, showing that there had once been a continuous ridge.

"We arrived at Mr. Davidson's long before the hour of public worship. The people seldom heard a sermon; being so strung along the narrow valleys, that they can never form self-supporting congregations, but must always depend on itinerants, or the transient visits of ministers from a distance. In such regions it is pleasing to see the ardour with which the mountain people flock to the place of meeting; issuing from every hollow of the neighbouring hills, on horseback and on foot. When the young preacher arose, with his singular advantages of mien and voice, an unwonted air of solemnity and interest pervaded the assembly. Mr. LeGrand again preached much to my heart; seldom have I spent a happier day. We had two sermons, with a short interval. When he met me at the edge of the dense forest whither he had retired for devotion, his face seemed like that of Moses to shine, and as we were on terms of great intimacy he said to me, 'If I ever enjoyed sensible communion with God, it was within the last half hour.' And his sermon bore witness that he had been with Jesus. These discourses were not in vain. The seeds of piety were sown in many young hearts that day. Several members of Mr. Davidson's family dated their serious impressions from that day. I reluctantly parted with Mr. LeGrand in the morning, as my travelling companion was becoming impatient to be on his way. My leaving the Springs at this time was imprudent; as I now believe that if I had remained, my health would have been entirely restored. As it was, though much recruited by the use of the waters, I soon fell back into a state of debility."

CHAPTER FIFTH.

1790—1791.

PREPARATIONS FOR THE MINISTRY—THEOLOGICAL CLASS—FIRST ATTEMPT AT EXHORTATION—VISIT TO PHILADELPHIA—GENERAL ASSEMBLY—GREAT MEN OF THE DAY—RETURN.

THE time had arrived when it was natural and almost necessary for Mr. Alexander to choose a profession for life. The subject had been forced upon his mind during all the months of his religious inquiry. At the Sweet Springs he conversed freely on this point with Mr. LeGrand. The ministry of the gospel was clearly his choice, but he conceived himself altogether unfit for a work of such importance. Mr. Legrand however urged him to engage at once in the study of divinity. After the disappointment experienced in regard to Princeton, he privately read from time to time such books as he could procure, and so far as his health permitted. "I doubted my call," says he, "to this high and holy office. The only other pursuit which entered my thoughts was that of agriculture; and I pleased myself with the thought of retirement and escape from the awful responsibilities of the ministry. I still however went on with my studies. While before I had been reading at random every good book I could lay hold of, I now thought it necessary to commence the study of theology with more method. I expected to be put to reading many ponderous volumes in Latin, and endeavoured to brace my nerves for the effort. Accordingly I went to Mr. Graham with a request that he would direct my studies. He smiled, and said, 'If you mean ever to be a theologian, you must come at it not by reading but by thinking.' He then ridiculed the way of taking our opinions upon the authority of men, and of deciding questions by merely citing the judgments of this or that great theologian; repeating what he had just said, that I must learn to think for myself, and form my own opinions from the Bible. This conversation discouraged me more than if he had told me to read half a dozen folios. For as to learning any thing by my own thoughts, I had no idea of its practicability. But it did me more good than any directions or counsels I ever received. It threw me on my own resources, and led me to feel the necessity of disciplining my own thoughts and searching into the principles of things.

"My thoughts were entirely absorbed in theological questions, and as there were several young men of education in Lexington, we carried on daily discussions. Taking nothing for granted without proof, we debated especially all the points in controversy between Calvinists and Arminians. The Methodists who professed Arminian doctrine were spreading their opinions on all sides. When I first began the study of theology I had no companion but John Lyle, who had been for some time a pupil of Mr. Graham; but after a while we had half a dozen. Every Saturday we met at our preceptor's study, for recitation and debate. Even at this time Mr. Graham was much engaged in the study of Mental Philosophy. He had a natural turn for such investigations, and had observed for himself with great acuteness. He had recently obtained the works of Reid and Beattie, with others of the Scottish school; but he thought he could construct a better system than any proposed by these writers. Accordingly he digested a series of lectures, which he frequently delivered to his students and to a class of young ladies. They were perspicuous and methodical and rested on observations made by himself. I believe they were never written out, for he had a strong aversion to the pen, and in speaking he had such a command of his knowledge as to require no assistance from notes. During the time of my theological studies I perused no great number of volumes, but some I read with much care. Among these were Edwards on the Will, on Original Sin, and on the Affections; Bates's Harmony of the Divine Attributes, and some treatises of Owen and Boston."

In the autumn of the same year, 1790, the Presbytery of Lexington was to meet at the North Mountain Meeting-House, in the county of Augusta. This church is now called Hebron. Mr. Alexander was prevailed upon by his friends and teachers to present himself to that body in order to trials for the ministry. He describes his feelings on this occasion as very uncomfortable, from remaining doubts as to his being called to the work; but he was averse to disregard the advice of his honoured preceptor, who had acquired an influence over him which he could hardly resist. The Presbytery perceived his gifts, and encouraged him to proceed. It appears from their records that this event took place on the 20th day of October, 1790. Mr. Graham had resolved to get the permission of the Presbytery that the candidates under their care should have the privilege of exhorting in social meetings for religious worship ; for in that day the function of public teaching had not been distributed so lavishly among the lay brethren, as in our own time. And to quiet the scruples of Mr. Alexander, he was informed that his actual entrance on the ministry might be postponed as long as he chose. On returning home from the Presbytery, he soon received notice that authority had been given to him and his fellow-student, Mr. John Lyle, to exercise their gifts in exhortation. Mr. Graham was accustomed to hold a meeting at Kerr's Creek, at the house of old John McKee. This place was therefore selected for the debut of the young candidates. But the event is too interesting not to be related in his own words. It is seldom that we have such descriptions of a first effort from one who was destined to become eminent in this very field of labour.

"The thing was new in that part of the country, and many came together. I was exceedingly apprehensive that I should utterly fail, and not be able to say any thing, for I had never spoken in public except what I had committed to memory. I had once attempted to speak in a juvenile debate, without the least success. We arrived at the place early in the evening, and retired to the grove. When we returned to the house Mr. Lyle appeared to be much animated and elevated. He told me that he had a remarkable flow of thought, and seemed confident of a prosperous issue; which only discouraged me the more, as I was weighed down with a heavy burden. After singing and prayer, Mr. Graham called first upon Lyle, who arose with an awful cloud upon his brow, seized fast hold of the chair upon which he had been sitting, and with many contortions of countenance forced out a few words; but his flow of thought had deserted him. He hemmed and groaned, rolled up his pocket-handkerchief into a ball, made a few convulsive gestures, and sat down. After another prayer and hymn, I was called upon. Although I did not know a single word which I was to utter, I began with a rapidity and fluency equal to any I have enjoyed to this day. I was astonished at myself, and as I was young and small, the old people were not less astonished. From this time I exhorted at one place and another, several times every week. It was still a cross for me to hold forth at Lexington; and after efforts unsatisfactory to myself, I often suffered keen anguish of spirit, from various causes. At other times my heart was enlarged, my feelings were lively, so that I found delight in the utterance of truth. At that time I seldom followed any premeditated train of thought; the words which I first spoke generally opened a track for me, which I pursued."

It is a proper addition to this statement to say that, throughout his life, the extemporaneous discourses of Dr. Alexander, which indeed were the highest effusions of his mind, partook of the character of these early efforts; and he has been heard to say again and again, that if he were to stake his life on a single effort, he would, if familiar with the general subject, abandon himself entirely to the impulse of the moment.

During the continuance of the revival, Mr. Graham was much engaged in preaching, not only at home, but in many other congregations, for there was an awakened attention to religion almost throughout the Valley ; and in the remote and destitute places there was an uncommon desire to hear the Gospel. He therefore made some preaching tours among the mountains, and along the streams, where the population is too much extended through narrow vales to admit of compact societies. On one of these excursions he was accompanied by his young pupil. They crossed the North Mountain at what is called the New Gap, where the ascent is exceedingly steep. After leaving the mountain they fell down upon the James River near the place where it takes that name, that is, just below the junction of the Jackson and Cow pasture Rivers. Mr. Graham preached to these scattered people with a clearness which made all understand, and with an earnestness and affection which caused deep feeling. One of their meetings was at the house of a rich old German. "In the morning," says a narrative from which we derive these facts, "Mr. John Lyle, my fellow-student and travelling companion, informed me that before sunrise he had seen a labourer take the German Bible from the house into a neighbouring thicket, where he kept it about half an hour and then went to his work. We agreed to have some conversation with the man, and learned from him that he lived at a distance, but that he was now engaged for a time in attending to some hemp, in a piece of land allowed him by the farmer. We found that he had not been present at the sermon the day before. He gave us the following narrative. 'I have lived, ever since I was married, on the Cow pasture River, where the Gospel is seldom preached. For a few months we engaged a man to preach, and poor and careless as we were, I subscribed a dollar, and then thought I would go and get the worth of my money. I frequently felt my conscience moved, but the impression soon went off. Soon after the preacher left us, I was one day riding by myself, when all at once I had such a view of my lost condition and sinfulness, that I felt as if the earth would open and swallow me up. Though the awful feeling of that moment subsided, I fell into a state of settled distress. I knew that I was a sinner, but knew not how my sins could be pardoned. I was advised to read the Bible, which I did ; but the more I read, the more was I condemned, and my distress was thereby increased, so that for a while I shut up the book and put it away. Yet I could not find rest, and so returned to reading. My neighbours were of various opinions respecting my case. Some were of opinion that my reason was touched, others said it was low spirits.

"'My distress of mind began to wear me away, until at last I was unable to work in the field, and my wife and children were likely to come to want. At length I scarcely had strength to walk the floor. One Sunday evening a little before sunset I was sitting on the side of my bed, where I had been reading my Bible, when all of a sudden my mind seemed to be full of light and my heart of love and joy. I thought that Christ had died for my sins, and that God had forgiven me for his sake. It was so plain, I wondered that I had never seen it before. The joy was so great that I sank down on the bed, and almost swooned. My wife shrieked, thinking I was about to die. But I was soon able to tell her that I was happy—as happy as I could be—that I had seen Christ to have died for me on the cross, and that God had pardoned all my sins. In this happy state I remained for some time ; but by degrees I began to believe that it was a delusion. Darkness came over me and my distress returned ; but not as at first, for I now knew that whether I had received it or not there was pardon for miserable sinners. But for several years I have had no comfort. I read and pray, and sometimes have a faint hope, but for the most part am in darkness. It is now nine years since I had this wonderful discovery, and during all that time I have never heard a sermon, nor ever before met with a single person who understood my case.'

"When the poor German had proceeded thus far, we had reached the place of meeting, and found the house full. We were very solicitous that Mr. Graham might be led to choose a subject suited to the case of our German brother, for such we esteemed him. And it was so ordered that the text led him to open the way of salvation, and to describe the exercises of a soul when closing with Christ on the terms of the Gospel. That day we heard more for the afflicted man than for ourselves. He never took his eyes off the preacher, and during the hour of the sermon they were full of tears. His emotions were evidently various. We were incapable of entering into the feelings of a man who had been converted for nine years, and yet had never heard a sermon, and who for seven years had been walking in darkness and doubt, without once meeting with man or woman who knew any thing of experimental religion. As he had to return immediately, we followed him to his horse as he came weeping from the house. His heart was too full for utterance. At length he lifted up his hands, and thanked God for the mercy bestowed on him, in giving him opportunity to hear the precious Gospel that day. He said that his distress had forsaken him, and something of his first joy filled his heart, but that he had much sorrow for sin mingled with his comfort. He took leave of us with tears, tenderly thanking us for having procured him this inestimable privilege.

"Mr. Graham's preaching for fifteen years had been attended with so little apparent effect, that it is not easy to conceive of the joy with which he witnessed so great a change in the religious aspect of the community. For some time he devoted himself entirely to the work of the ministry. His preaching at this time was evangelical and powerful. The writer is now of opinion, that he never heard from any man a clearer and stronger exhibition of the Gospel than in the sermons of Mr. Graham during this period."*

An event of more than ordinary moment in the quiet career of a student in the mountains, was his making a visit in the spring of 1791 to Philadelphia. In his mature years

* MS. Life of William Graham.

he was accustomed to speak with regret and reprehension of one part of the counsel of his invaluable friend and preceptor. The General Assembly was about to convene, and Mr. Graham, desiring his young and promising pupil to attend on that judicatory, conceived the strange design that he should go in the capacity of a ruling elder. He was little satisfied with the arrangement, but acquiesced.

These were days of equestrian travel, and they set out as for a long journey. An agreement had been made to meet Dr. John B. Smith at Winchester, and to attend the communion at Shepherdstown, where Mr., afterwards the Rev. Dr. Moses Hoge was pastor. Mr. Alexander rode a young horse, unaccustomed to travelling, which was foundered about the third day. They stopped with Mr. Solomon Hoge, brother of the clergyman, with whom resided his venerable father. Mr. Graham, after as much delay as he could afford, resumed his journey. The horse did not amend, and this caused a halt of some days.

"Old Mr. Hoge," so he writes, "though eighty-four years of age, was in the fullest vigour of intellect, and delighted in theological discussion. He gave me a narrative of the state of the Presbyterian Church in Pennsylvania during his youth. At the age of one and twenty he carefully read over every article of the Westminster Confession of Faith, to see whether he could adopt the whole; which he was able freely and deliberately to do. At the time when I met him he was in connection with the Seceder Church. He did not inform me how this came about, but some years afterwards Dr. Hoge told me that his father left our church on account of the 'Adopting Act,' which permitted candidates to make some exceptions when they received the Confession. I know not that I ever received so much instruction in the same time from any one as from this old gentleman. Certain difficulties, which I had on some points, he entirely removed to my satisfaction. What he told me of the mother Presbytery, of Philadelphia, would have been of value if I had written it down from his mouth, but before I recognised its importance, the facts had become dim in my memory."

Mounting his crippled horse, he attempted to press forward, but before reaching Winchester he found him unable to proceed. Here occurred an incident of travel, which belongs to the picture of life. "After struggling along a few miles, I came to Opekan Creek, where the low grounds were covered to the depth of two or three feet by reason of back-water from a mill below. When I had reached about midway, the horse determinately refused to proceed, and there I was, seated on his back in the midst of the water. There was no way left but to dismount into the water, but this I was afraid to do on account of my feeble health. Observing a house at some distance I called as loudly as I could, and at length made myself heard. A large, lazy looking German came down and asked why I was sitting there. I told him, and entreated him to get a horse and bring me out, but he said there were no horses near. The want of sympathy in this man aggravated my distress. At length a man came along on horseback who immediately led my horse out; and not only so, but continued with me until nine o'clock at night, when I arrived at the place to which I had been directed.

"I found old Mrs. Riley alone; all her sons had gone to the sacrament at Shepherdstown, where Dr. Smith and Mr. Graham were assisting Mr. Hoge. The next morning which was the Sabbath, I went into the neighbourhood to hear a Methodist preacher. At the close of his sermon he gave notice that a Presbyterian minister would preach at Mrs. Riley's that evening. At first I wondered who it could be that had come into the place, but it soon occurred to me, that it arose from a misapprehension of something I had said to Mrs. Riley. The mistake disturbed me not a little. I went to the stand on which he had preached—for the sermon was in the open air—and begged him to correct the mistake, but he made light of the difference between a preacher and an exhorter. In the evening a multitude collected, so that the house could not contain them. When I arose to speak I explained the matter, and then delivered an exhortation of some length, as the people seemed greedy to hear. Indeed there was a considerable excitement among them, which had been produced by the preaching of Mr. Hill and also of the clergymen with whom I was travelling."

Provided here with a fresh horse, he set out and pressed on with all his force to overtake these companions. The next day he arrived at a neighbourhood where Dr. Smith had just been preaching, and the evening after arrived at the house where he was lodging. Dr. Smith's cordiality and courtesy here appeared to great advantage, and he had it in his power to communicate great relief to the young and embarrassed stranger. The company went onward by the way of York, and at length reached the little town of Pequea, a spot somewhat remarkable in the history of our church. Here the venerable Doctor Robert Smith, the father of the President, was still pastor. Here likewise the sacrament was to be celebrated on the approaching Sabbath. The congregation was large, but without those signs of popular feeling to which our Virginians had been accustomed at home. On Monday, in conformity to the old Scottish practice, Mr. Graham discoursed; his sermon was powerful and pungent, and a certain young man was struck to the heart, and came to the house inquiring what he should do to be saved. On Tuesday the four travellers set their faces towards Philadelphia, and their number was increased by old Dr. Smith and his wife. We shall here annex copious extracts from the personal narrative, both as giving a simple description of the impressions made by novel scenes on an unsophisticated mind, and as affording more particulars than are elsewhere extant concerning a very important General Assembly.

"I felt a great awe on my spirits at the thought of entering the great city. My impression was that all eyes would be directed towards me. As we approached, our company separated, as they expected to lodge in different places. Mr. Graham and I stopped at a farm-house near Gray's Ferry, where we made an agreement with the host, a quaker, for the keeping of our horses. As we rode along the streets and beheld the people pressing forward with rapid steps, I was surprised and relieved to find that they took no notice of us. The tavern where we dismounted was, I think, in Chestnut Street. Here we found a hale corpulent man of forty, bouncing about and attending to his guests with little aid. The floors were not carpeted, but were scoured very clean, and thickly sprinkled with very white sand.

"After adjusting our dress, we repaired to the church at the corner of Third and Arch Streets, where the Assembly was to be opened by a sermon from the Reverend Robert Smith, D.D., the late moderator. I went under a painful apprehension that the appearance of such a youth, under the denomination of a ruling elder, must excite the contempt or pity of every member. Indeed it was an ill-judged thing. What struck me with astonishment was that although thousands of people were passing the doors, there were not a hundred in the church. Dr. Smith preached a sermon of which I heard very little, as his enunciation was impaired by the loss of his teeth. He wore a very large white wig, coming down far over his shoulders, and being short in stature presented an appearance somewhat grotesque. Most of the clergy wore wigs; all from the cities and great towns wore powder, as did many gentlemen whom we met in the streets. The discourse was delivered with great earnestness, and the opinion which I formed of the preacher was that he possessed uncommon ardour of piety. He said much of the great revival in which he had been a labourer, but seemed much afraid of the wildfire and disorder, which so much injured the cause in those days. In private he expressed apprehensions lest his son John Blair Smith and Mr. Graham were engaged in sending raw and unfurnished ministers into the work. He treated me with great tenderness, but was surprised to hear that I was to be a member, and asked whether I came as priest or Levite. The excellent old man lived but a year or two after this time.

"Some interest seemed to be felt as to the choice of Moderator. The Rev. Dr. John Woodhull, of Freehold, N. J., was nominated, but Mr. John B. Smith came round to us, and solicited our votes for Mr. McCreary, an old minister from Maryland or Delaware, who was said to be a godly and evangelical man ; but Mr. Woodhull had a large majority. The body was small, consisting of not more than thirty or forty members. The leading ministers were Dr. Alison of Baltimore, Dr. McWhorter of Newark, Dr. Ewing of Philadelphia, Nathaniel Irwin of Neshaminy, James F. Armstrong of Trenton, Joseph Clark of New Brunswick, Dr. Cooper, Dr. Latta, and Nathan and Jacob Ker. Dr. Nisbet was in constant attendance, but I have forgotten whether he was a commissioner. But all Presbyterian ministers were invited to sit as correspondent members. President Witherspoon came about the middle of the session, and after a day or two gave place to Dr. Samuel Stanhope Smith. There were few from the south, besides our little company. I remember one by the name of Templeton. Colonel John Bayard, father of John, Samuel, and James A. Bayard, was there as an elder, and took an active part in all business, receiving much deference, as he had occupied high civil offices. Dr. Green was not a member, but came every day and sometimes engaged in discussion. At that time he must have been above thirty years of age ; his appearance was dignified and lofty, and except that he was pale he was at a distance a very handsome man. His peruke was the finest I ever saw, falling over his shoulders in great curls, which were white with powder. I was filled with admiration to hear so fine a man talk seriously about religion ; for I had imbibed the prejudice widely prevalent among the Methodists, that men or women who dressed fashionably and wore powder and the like ornaments, must be destitute of religion.

"Dr. Woodhull the Moderator was a man of good appearance, about forty-five years of age. If I remember aright, William M. Tennent, afterwards Dr. Tennent of Abingdon, was the recording clerk, and Mr. Armstrong the reading clerk. The member who took most upon him, explaining every thing minutely and tediously, was Dr. McWhorter of Newark. But though unnecessarily prolix his remarks were always earnest and judicious. Dr. Nisbet seemed desirous to learn all that was said ; being somewhat deaf he would go up close to the speaker and turn to him the hearing ear. His appearance was singular. He was short in stature, but broad in the face and shoulders and whole frame, and wore a gray wig which reached far down his back. He took much snuff and seemed to have the habit of talking to himself, for his lips were in frequent motion, and as he sometimes trotted from one speaker to another he would utter something audibly. On one of these occasions as Dr. Hall of North Carolina was making an earnest speech, with great solemnity of manner, Dr. Nisbet as he returned to his seat near the Moderator was heard to ejaculate, 'Poor human nature, poor human nature!' Some one was officious enough to tell this to Dr. Hall, who was grievously mortified and offended. Nathaniel Irwin of Neshaminy was an influential member of this Assembly. He was very tall, and had a voice the sound of which produced alarm, on a first hearing. He always took his stand at a place the most remote from the chair, and seemed to utter every thing with the greatest sound he could command. It was easy to discern that as his head was literally long, so it was intellectually. The very first draft of a plan for raising a permanent * * * proceeded from him during this Assembly. Joseph Clark of New Brunswick, afterwards Dr. Clark, was a speaker who occupied much time, from the extreme slowness of his observations.

"About the middle of the Assembly Dr. Witherspoon came from Princeton, and took his seat. He immediately participated in the business, and evinced such an intuitive clearness of apprehension and correctness of judgment, that his pointed remarks commonly put an end to the discussion. In most cases I thought I perceived how things should be decided, and was gratified to find my opinions frequently confirmed by those of Dr. Witherspoon. But in one instance, in which John D. Blair of Richmond took an active part, I was entirely misled. The question was whether an offending member's profession of repentance was a sufficient ground for immediate restoration. Mr. Blair read the passage in which our Lord says, 'If thy brother offend against thee seven times in a day,' etc. This seemed to me as clear as the light; but Dr. Witherspoon arose and dispelled the delusion, by distinguishing between a private offence, concerning an individual, and a public offence which affected the church, as also between the offence of a private member and the offence of a minister.

"Dr. Witherspoon remained only two or three days, after which Dr. Samuel Stanhope Smith took his place. When he entered the house I did not observe him, but happening to turn my head I saw a person whom I must still consider the most elegant I ever saw. The beauty of his countenance, the clear and vivid complexion, the symmetry of his form and the exquisite finish of his dress, were such as to strike the beholder at first sight. The thought never occurred to me that he was a clergyman, and I supposed him to be some gentleman of Philadelphia, who had dropped in to hear the debate. I ought to have mentioned that Dr. Witherspoon was as plain an old man as ever I saw, and as free from any assumption of dignity. All he said, and every thing about him bore the marks of importance and authority. Dr. Green had just returned from the General Association of Connecticut, which he had attended as a delegate. He gave an account of his reception, and brought forward a resolution to agree with them in a concert of prayer for the revival of religion. This was opposed by Dr. Alison, in a speech of great power and eloquence. I never heard a man who could pour out such a torrent of strong thoughts and expressions, without the least appearance of effort ; for he made no attempt to play the orator, but commonly leaned over the side of the pew and seldom raised either his head or his hands. Dr. Green made an able and pious speech in reply, in the course of which he mentioned that the only three men who opposed it in the General Association were a Mr. Church, a Mr. Lord, and a Mr. Devotion. Dr. Smith was also opposed to it, and had caused it to be cast out in the Synod of New-York and New Jersey. But our Southern ministers, fresh from a great revival, were zealously in favour of it, as were the members from the west of Pennsylvania. So that the resolution was carried by a large majority.

"The only difficult and unpleasant cases, which came before the Assembly of 1791, were the following. A certain minister had been guilty of a great crime, which was not mentioned; after a season of the deepest sorrow and full confession and profession of repentance, he was restored by the Presbytery of Newcastle by which he had been deposed. He soon afterwards removed up the North River, carrying with him clear credentials. But after a while the report of the crime followed him; the Presbytery within whose bounds he now was found the charge to be true, and brought a complaint against the Presbytery of Newcastle, for dismissing the member as in good standing, who had been thus guilty. There was much warmth among some of the old men about this matter. Dr. Cooper was not, I think, a regular member of the Assembly, but spoke as a correspondent. A severer countenance I never looked upon, and in debate his words were sharp as a two-edged sword. He made a reply to a speech of Dr. Samuel S. Smith, which was very tart and cutting. The other case was a complaint of Newcastle Presbytery against that of Lewes, because the latter had taken under their care and licensed a candidate while he was under censure of the former.

"Our ministers were warm from a great revival, and for a year or two had been engaged in organizing a plan for sending out missionaries. Indeed the Synod of Virginia had at this time four or five young men in the field. These were Nash LeGrand, William Hill, Cary Allen, Robert Marshall, and John Lyle.

"While in Philadelphia I was frequently at the house of old Mrs. Hodge, the grandmother of Professor Hodge. Here John B. Smith and his family were entertained, and here I saw also the widow of President Finley of Princeton, who was at this time entirely blind. Dr. J. B. Smith remained in Philadelphia, as the Third Presbyterian Church (of which the writer was afterwards pastor) had given him a call, after the death of Dr. Duffield."

It was now the month of June, and as the weather was extremely hot and the roads were dusty, the little party determined to lie by during the day and travel by night. They crossed the Blue Ridge at Black's Gap, by the light of the moon, which was then near the full. But after midnight they began to feel sleepy, and having cleared the mountain sought for some lodging-place. Part of the company found a house on the right; Mr. Graham and his young companion went further, and turned into a farm-clearing on the left. It was a log house, and the family were asleep in bed. But in conformity with the hospitable customs of the land, the mountaineer arose and admitted them, and took charge of their horses. The guests were shown up stairs, or rather up a ladder, to a loft under the roof. Here they were made acquainted with the German fashion of sleeping under a bed, in lieu of other covering The next day Dr. Hall proposed to introduce them to a case of somnambulism or irregular mental action, which carried some appearance of the supernatural. The person was a young woman of the neighbourhood, who every day at a certain hour seemed to fall into a trance, and uttered wonderful things.

"We pushed hard," says the narrative, "to get to the house by the hour of her paroxysm, which was one o'clock. Her name was Susannah Orendorf, and she was the daughter of a farmer near Sharpsburg. The young woman was reclining on a bed, very pale, and clad in white. She was attended by an elder sister, who with the parents agreed in asserting that she had eaten nothing for five or six months, and that the only thing which entered her lips was a sip of sweetened water, of which a tumbler stood near her on the table. This was considered miraculous by many, and the Methodists preached about Susannah, and related her sayings in their sermons. Multitudes came to see her; some above a hundred miles; so that there would sometimes be two hundred people there at one time. After coming out of one of her epileptic fits, she would tell those around her what she had seen in heaven; and so credulous were some that they came to ask whether she had seen certain friends of theirs who had lately died. On this point, however, she could give no satisfactory information. Some wished to know which religious denomination was most approved in heaven.

The girl answered more discreetly than could have been expected from her education—for she was very ignorant—saying, 'In the other world people are not judged of by their professions, but the sincerity of their hearts, and the goodness of their conduct.' Some very noisy persons came from Newtown to see her; and as a great company was collected they engaged in devotional exercises. One of their number, John Hill, a man of great muscular power and a stentorian voice, exerted himself to the utmost in prayer, keeping time with one of his feet and both his hands. When he was done, Susannah asked him, 'Why do you speak so loud? Do you think the Almighty is hard of hearing?'

"At nearly the same hour every day, after a little convulsive agitation she seemed to fall into a swoon, ceased to breathe, and lay calm and motionless as a corpse. As she recovered herself a sound was heard, as if issuing from her breast, and she commonly awoke singing. We asked her for some account of what she had seen in her last visit. Without hesitation she began a narrative of her journey to heaven, which greatly resembled some of Mohammed's descriptions. She went over a very high and beautiful bridge, which appeared to be made of ivory. She entered paradise, where she beheld the angels flying about in all directions, and heard companies of them singing. On her arrival she was presented with bread as white as snow and exceedingly delicious, which she ate every day, and by which she was nourished, so as to have no need nor appetite for earthly food. The most remarkable occurrence was that a beautiful and majestic person, whom she took to be our Saviour, came to her, and gave her a white flower, which she took to be a token of his love. On being requested to sing one of the tunes which she had learnt in heaven, she complied without reluctance ; uttering in a soft and somewhat melodious voice a strain, which however consisted of only a few notes continually repeated. Being then accustomed to learn tunes by ear, I caught up this strain, and could repeat it, but have long since forgotten it. This was no doubt a case of epilepsy, which continued more than a year, and then gradually left her ; but she did not live long after her recovery."

In looking back on this visit to the great city of America, Mr. Alexander was accustomed to say, that he found less of that warm and impulsive religion which the revivals of Virginia had made dear to him, than he expected. But he often recurred with pleasure to the animated piety of Joseph Eastburn, and of Mrs. Hodge, a venerable Christian lady of Philadelphia.

CHAPTER SIXTH.

1791.

THEOLOGICAL STUDIES—LICENSURE—EARLY SERMONS—CHARACTER OF PREACHING—MR. HOGE—LABOURS IN BERKELEY—ENGAGEMENT AS MISSIONARY.

AT the period to which our narrative relates, the means of education for the ministry were few and irregular. Mr. Alexander enjoyed, however, the guidance of Mr. Graham, whom through life he continued to regard as the chief instrument employed by Providence in educing and disciplining his faculties. "For a number of years," he records, "candidates for the gospel ministry had been very few, so that there seemed no prospect of a supply to the churches, when the acting ministry should pass away. But now the scene was changed. A number of young men who had finished their academical course, were arrested in their career and brought under the influence of the truth. These were now disposed to devote themselves to the important business of preaching the gospel. This not only furnished to Mr. Graham a pleasing prospect as it relates to the Church, but opened a field of useful employment in preparing these candidates for the ministry. It was a work for which in many respects he was well fitted, and in which he evidently took much delight, especially when he had pupils who received instruction with docility and entered fully into his views and explanation of doctrines. For although he constantly inculcated the right and duty of searching for the truth, free from the trammels of authority, he was never well pleased if any of them thought differently on any subject from himself. A theological class was formed, whose reading he directed, and who attended at his study on one day of the week, where they read their compositions on prescribed subjects, and discussed subjects previously given out; while he presided, and in the conclusion gave his own views of the matter. By this kind of training a number of young men, who afterwards were well known and esteemed in the church, were prepared. Though Mr. Graham had a scientific turn, and delighted much in experimental philosophy, it was the philosophy of the mind which was his favourite study; and this he had long pursued, not by reading books on the subject, but by paying close attention to the exercises of his own mind. He had reduced his thoughts to a system, which he was fond of unfolding to his pupils; so that he contracted a liking for this department of philosophy. His thorough knowledge of the laws of thinking evidently gave him a great advantage in explaining many difficulties which are frequently met with in religious experience. He was not much read in books, and for many years perused few, and commonly expressed a low esteem for what he read. There were few authors of whom he spoke with entire approbation. He continually recommended to his pupils to think for themselves, and to depend on their own resources rather than on authors. On some this had a good effect; but it was a saying which all could not receive. In almost every case his students adopted his views of theology, and held them at least for a while with much confidence. On all points he was strictly Calvinistic; but he had his own method of explaining things. One of his radical principles was that the rational soul of man can undergo no moral change, except through the influence of motives, or the presentation through the understanding of such objects as excite the affections. He therefore scouted the opinion that in regeneration there is any physical operation on the soul itself, and held that by the influence of the Holy Spirit truth is presented in its true nature to the rational mind, and when thus perceived cannot but produce an effect correspondent with its nature. He therefore fully held what has been called in some places the 'Light-scheme'; believing that all moral changes must be produced by new views, and can be produced in no other way. But how the dead soul could have truth thus presented to it, without being first vivified, he did not explain. In effect, however, he held with those who believe that all moral acts and exercises are produced by the operation of the truth, justly apprehended, but that in order to this a regenerating influence must be sent forth to render the soul capable of such views of truth as will produce these effects.

"His views of justification by the imputed righteousness of Christ were very clear and sound; but he considered faith to be simply a *belief of the truth*, under a spiritual apprehension of its nature. Nor would he agree that any affection or emotion which flowed from such belief properly belonged to its nature, as distinguished from other graces. His idea of the primitive state of man was, that though an accountable moral agent without any supernatural influence, he could be preserved from falling, when exposed to temptation, only by the indwelling of the Holy Spirit. He therefore thought it the easiest thing in the world to show how a human being, though perfectly holy, might be seduced into sin when left to himself. The divine influence, which was absolutely gratuitous, being withdrawn, man, though still possessing ability to perform his duty, is exceedingly liable to be led away, on account of natural imbecility, a complicated constitution,* and strong natural propensities. Respecting the whole mediatorial work, Mr. Graham was entirely sound ; and in his preaching the doctrines of grace were always prominent."†

Books were scarce, and he mentions the inconvenience which it cost him to carry a quarto copy of Blair's Lectures, which his preceptor had bought in Philadelphia. This work he read with avidity, but he found that the rules were chiefly such as had already occurred to his own mind. He had perused Witherspoon's Lectures on Moral Philosophy, which he had transcribed from a manuscript, as the book was not yet published. He confesses that this subject, which afterwards occupied so much of his attention, did not

* The manuscript is here doubtful.

† MS. Life of the Rev. William Graham.

then awaken any interest in him. The remainder of the summer was spent in vigorous study. There were now more than half a dozen divinity students, whose intercourse was fraternal and advantageous. He also exercised his gifts in religious meetings, generally with much ease and fluency ; but he records that when on some occasions he failed, his feelings of mortification were excruciating. It was however in such exercises as these that he laid the foundation for that habit of extraordinary extemporaneous discourse which was his grand peculiarity as a preacher and teacher, and which was in no degree abated after threescore years of ministry.

Though his health was still unsettled, he found it necessary to devote himself with spirit to his theological preparations. Besides a compendium of Turrettine in Latin, he resorted to the Writings of Owen and Edwards ; and perused Bates's Harmony of the Divine Attributes, which was one of his favourite works as long as he lived. He conversed almost daily with his preceptor, though the regular meeting of the young men in Mr. Graham's study was only once a week. As there was now a class in theology, and as other young men who had not completed their academical course, were pious and interested in such subjects, much time was spent in free conversation and animated discussion. "Among those of the latter class," says he, "who were still engaged in classical learning, was George Baxter, afterwards so highly distinguished as a preacher and a theologian. He had a mind formed for accurate distinctions and logical discussion." During the year, besides other compositions, he wrote seven sermons, which were read before the class, and criticised by Mr. Graham. The first of these he preserved as a curiosity; it was on Acts xvi. 31, "Believe on the Lord Jesus Christ," etc. At the meeting in the spring of 1791, held at New Monmouth, he exhibited several of his pieces of trial, and was examined on the sciences and languages. With the measure of Latin which he then had attained, his *Exegesis*, as it is oddly named, gave him no small trouble. His Critical Exercise was on Heb. vi. 1–7; and this also vexed him considerably, as he spent much time on the subject without arriving at satisfaction. His Popular Lecture, or *Homily* as it was then called, was on the difference between a living and a dead faith. "The essay," says he, "is I believe still among my old papers, and the view taken of the subject is not materially different from that which I should now take."

These preparations gave him more than the usual amount of trouble, from the low condition of body in which he still found himself. In September the Presbytery met at the Stone Meeting-House in Augusta. He had at this time gone through all his trials, except the examination in theology and the "popular sermon." He was however very reluctant to be licensed, on account of an abiding sense of unfitness. On this subject he had many conversations with Mr. Graham, in which he strongly and repeatedly stated his objections. But his pastor and teacher disregarded the scruples, and urged him to enter on the work of preaching, for this among other reasons that his health might be confirmed by travelling; adding that he might continue his studies as usual and make excursions among the destitute, as he felt inclined. At this time his stature was small and his whole appearance was strikingly boyish. "The Presbytery," we use his own words, "had given me a text for a popular sermon which I disliked exceedingly, as it brought to my mind the circumstance which distressed me in the view of entering the ministry, namely my youth and boyish appearance. The text was Jeremiah i. 7, 'But the Lord said unto me, Say not, I am a child, for thou shalt go to all that I shall send thee, and whatsoever I command thee thou shalt speak.' I read the sermon from the pulpit, but with very little satisfaction to myself. As the ministers were on their way to the Synod, they had not time to examine me on theology, and so adjourned to meet at Winchester. When we arrived there a meeting was held in the house of James Holliday, where I was examined, principally by the Rev. John Blair Smith; but as he was taken suddenly ill before it was concluded, the examination was continued by Mr. Hoge. It was then determined that I should be licensed in the public congregation, on Saturday morning, October the first, 1791. This was indeed a solemn day. During the service I was almost overwhelmed with an awful feeling of responsibility and unfitness for the sacred office. That afternoon I spent in the fields, in very solemn reflection and earnest prayer. My feelings were awful, and far from being comfortable. I seemed to think, however, that the solemn impressions of that day would never leave me. O deceitful heart!"

In regard to the text abovementioned, it is said in another manuscript; "It was assigned to me by the Rev.

Samuel Houston, not only because of my youth, but because I had strongly remonstrated against having my trials hurried to a conclusion, as I did not wish to be licensed for several years. The house was full of people, and the whole Synod was present. When I stood up to answer the questions," which were proposed by Dr. Smith, though only a corresponding member, "I felt as if I could have sunk into the earth." The sermon mentioned above was most happily recovered by us, among the papers of the late Mrs. LeGrand. It bears marks of careful preparation, though written in a hand as yet quite unformed. Notwithstanding the suggestion of the text, there is a characteristic absence of all allusion to his own youth or any thing personal. It is a plain, but clear and sensible discussion of that great topic, a Call to the Ministry. Equally beyond our expectation was it to recover the first sermon which he ever wrote, while yet a student, and of which mention has been made. It is upon Acts xvi. 31, and bears the date, 1790.

Having now been licensed as a probationer, it was his intention to return home and devote himself to study; but the purpose was overruled by a clear providence. Tidings came that the Rev. William Hill (a servant of Christ who has gone to his rest since we last mentioned his name) was prevented by a fever from continuing his labours in Berkeley, now Jefferson County. Some religious awakening had taken place in that region, and the neighbouring ministers urged Mr. Alexander to come to their aid. Mr. LeGrand also was desirous of making an excursion, and offered an inviting field of labour in his congregations of Opekan and Cedar Creek, including Winchester. A revival had been in progress among his people for some months. The following is an abridged record of some of these earliest labours.

"After the Synod adjourned, I went with Mr. LeGrand to an appointment which he had at old Mr. Feely's, some fifteen miles from Winchester. He told me that I must preach, but I positively refused. He said nothing at the time, but when the congregation was assembled, he arose and said, 'Mr. Alexander, please to come forward to the table, and take the books and preach.' I knew not what to do, but rather than make a disturbance I went forward and preached my first sermon after licensure, from Galatians iii. 24, 'Wherefore the law was our schoolmaster to bring us unto Christ.' Among the hearers was old General Morgan, whose residence was in the vicinity.

"My next sermon was preached at Charlestown, from the text, Acts xvi. 31, 'Believe in the Lord Jesus Christ, and thou shalt be saved.' I had prepared a skeleton of the sermon and placed it before me; but the house being open a puff of wind carried it away into the midst of the congregation. *I then determined to take no more paper into the pulpit;* and this resolution I kept as long as I was a pastor, except in a very few instances.* I had, it is true, written seven sermons, but had committed none of them to memory, and to this day though I have made several efforts I have never succeeded in getting a discourse by heart. Having of

* "From that time for twenty years, I never took a note of any kind into the pulpit; except that I read my trial sermon at ordination."----*MS. Reminiscences.*

late been much accustomed to exhort in public, I felt little embarrassment and went on fluently enough."

If we were more fully provided with reports other than his own of these early efforts, we should doubtless find that in the estimation of all who heard them they were of a high order. So far as he could be drawn out to speak of his own performances—a subject which he always avoided—these were equal to any public endeavours of his life. Great interest was added to his other qualities by the juvenile appearance of the preacher; indeed he seemed but a little boy. His complexion was fair, his eye was dark and penetrating, and his voice according to every witness of that period was incomparably clear and flute-like. It always was both resonant and penetrating, but at this time was of a silvery tone both in speaking and singing. His fluency and command of words were extraordinary ; and in these youthful discourses he gave full swing to an imagination which he learned more and more to chasten in later years. The Rev. Dr. Speece, once speaking to us concerning his early exuberance, said, "You think him animated now, but if you had heard him in his youth, you would compare him to nothing so readily as to a young horse of high blood, let out into a spacious pasture, exercising every muscle, and careering in every direction with extravagant delight."

There are no circumstances which bring out the gift of pulpit eloquence more fully or speedily than those in which he was now placed. Going rapidly from assembly to assembly, followed by awakened and admiring crowds, in times of great revival, and during all the intervals plying the same work among warm and affectionate brethren, by conversation, prayer and praise, he was kept in that state of healthful and pleasurable excitement which animates and exalts the powers, and forms habits of ready and powerful expression.

So accustomed was he to associate pleasurable sensations with pulpit-work, that even in later years he used to laugh at the notion of any one's being injured by preaching. And it was commonly observed, through most of his life, that however depressed in spirits he might be before the service, he always came from it in the highest state of exhilaration. Never was he more free or full in conversation. These were the times at which to draw from him his most elevated religious discourse, as well as his liveliest narratives; and his own household, or those in which he was a guest, remember such hours with a pensive delight. Like good Rowland Hill, he was cured of many an ailment by the delivery of a long and animated sermon.

After visiting Shepherdstown and preaching for Dr. Hoge, he returned to Frederick, to supply Mr. LeGrand's place according to appointment. Gladly would we multiply such recitals as that which follows: "The weeks which I spent at Opekan passed pleasantly. Besides the services of the Sabbath we had a weekly meeting at Major Gilkin's. These were delightful gatherings, for the presence of God seemed to be with us. I remember one meeting in particular in which all present seemed to be melted down in a remarkable manner. On one of the days on which I attended there, an old man, after sermon, told me that he wished to speak with me. He led me as far from the house as he could do without crossing a high fence, and then burst into tears, saying, 'I am a poor old sinner!' His weeping was so profuse that he could say no more, except to request me to visit him at his own house. This I promised, and next day I found my way through a desolate pine wood and an intricate path, to the dwelling, where the poor old man was trying to spell out some sentences in the New Testament. He said that he was unable to read, but could spell a little, and thus could make out some things which gave him much satisfaction. But he informed me that his boys, who were now absent, could read pretty well, and that they had spent nearly all the preceding night over the New Testament; for his sons were as anxious to learn as himself. The old woman was busy spinning on a flax wheel, and continued to work while I conversed with her husband. At length I turned to her with the words, 'And what does your wife think of these things?' She immediately ceased from her work, and burst into tears, but answered not a word. Here was a family, of which the heads had grown gray without having ever attended public worship; and who until now knew no more of a Saviour than the heathen. But they were now like persons come into a new world. Indeed all their views and feelings were entirely new. Salvation had come to their house. I learned that a multitude of poor people lived in these pines, who seldom heard a sermon except when some itinerant Methodist passed through the settlement. I was desirous to preach to them; and the opportunity was afforded by an invitation to the house of a Mrs Carlisle, the wife of a Quaker miller, who had been read out of meeting for marrying a person not of the Society. But he retained all his attachments to Quakerism, and was rather crusty towards his wife when she wished to have Presbyterian ministers at the house, and commonly went out of the way. Mrs. Carlisle's mother, Mrs. Douglass, lived with her, a convert of Whitefield, and a woman of uncommon piety. From her I heard much about the preaching of that great man. She had resided at White Clay Creek, where Charles Tennent was minister, and where Mr. Whitefield preached several days in succession to thousands of people. The old lady was now and had long been a Seceder. Knowing the opposition of that people to Whitefield, I thought it surprising that one of his admirers should have joined herself to them. But she thus explained it. The opposers of the revival, in the Presbyterian Church, were called the Old Side, and where she lived they had manifested a malignant opposition to the work of grace, insomuch that the new converts considered the Old Side as the declared enemies of the revival. But after some time a union was effected, which so offended some of the zealous disciples of Whitefield, that when about the same time the Seceders made their appearance, they were joined by the disaffected persons, Mrs. Douglass being included. She was the mother of James and Daniel Douglass, of Alexandria, Va., and the grandmother of the Rev. James W. Douglass, who died at Fayetteville some years since."

After supplying Mr. LeGrand's pulpit until his return, Mr. Alexander proceeded to aid his friend Mr. Hill, preaching often in private houses, and sometimes in the small

Presbyterian church at Charlestown. "Here," says he, "I first saw old John White, the father of Judge White of Winchester, and grandfather of the minister at Romney, in Hampshire. The whole White family were remarkable for strength of mind and acquaintance with the Scriptures. The old gentleman had Erskine's Gospel Sonnets by heart, and was eminent for simple piety. I think he dated his religious impressions from hearing Mr. Robinson, the first regular Presbyterian minister who entered Virginia. I was now in the region where I was to labour, and made my home at Alexander White's, the son of the fore-mentioned. The winter was hard, and the farm-houses in which I preached during the week were very uncomfortable places for speaking. The attention of the common people was awake for a considerable distance around, but they were generally very ignorant of the doctrines of religion, and my preaching was more of the didactic than the hortatory kind. I had no books with me but my small pocket Bible, and found very little to read in the houses where I stopped. I was therefore thrown back entirely on my own thoughts. I studied every sermon on horseback, and in bed before I went to sleep, and some of the best sermons that I ever prepared were digested in this way and at this time."

In reading records like these we are led to see the force of such remarks as those of the Rev. Dr. Hall, who says "It deserves to be noted by all ministers and candidates, that one of the chief external means by which Dr. Alexander attained what are often called his inimitable excellencies as a preacher, was his spending several years after licensure and ordination, in itinerant missionary service, preaching in the humblest and most destitute places, often in the open air, and adapting his language and manner to minds that needed the plainest kind of instruction. It will be a good day for the ministry and the church, when the performance of a term of such itinerant service shall be exacted as part of the trials of every probationer before ordination."*

In a record contained in another manuscript, the same subject is touched. "Some of the sermons which I most frequently preached during my ministry I studied out this winter, without putting pen to paper. Indeed I had no opportunity to write sermons. The houses in which I lodged had but one [sitting room], and I remained but a short time at any one place. When Mr. Hill returned from Charlotte, I was at liberty to give up the field which I had occupied; but the winter was severe and travelling unpleasant, and Mr. Hoge urged me to continue in the neighbourhood until spring. For all the labours of the winter I received not one cent, and indeed expected nothing. But as I came from home without expecting to be long absent, I found that if I remained I must provide myself with some articles of clothing. Upon my mentioning this as a reason for returning home, Mr. Hoge took me to a store and became responsible for what I needed; and as soon as I returned home I sent him the money which was due.

"While I remained I continued to preach frequently, for Mr. Hoge, for Mr. Hill, and for old Mr. Vance of Tuscarora,

* Sermon on the death of Dr. Alexander, in 'Home, the School, and the Church,' Vol. iii. p. 98.

who then lay upon his death-bed. In his congregation I met with one Robert Campbell, whose memory was prodigious. The Rev. Dr. McKnight had formerly been his pastor, and was held by him in great admiration. Campbell could repeat many of the Doctor's sermons verbatim. After removing to New-York Dr. McKnight resolved to publish several sermons on Faith, but he had lost the manuscript of one among them. He had recourse to Mr. Campbell, who supplied what was missing, and, as I was informed, with great exactness."

There were few of Dr. Alexander's early friends and counsellors of whom he spoke oftener or more affectionately than Mr. Hoge, the father of the President. "As Mr. Hoge lived only eleven miles from Charlestown, the centre of my operations,—here we resume his own narrative,—"whenever I could get a day or two I would spend it at his house, and though he was very poor and lived on a mere pittance, he always received me kindly and gave me free use of his books. But my highest privilege was his conversation; in which he assumed no magisterial air, but treated me as if I had been his equal. His disposition was in contrast with that of Mr. Graham, who was very dogmatical, treated with contempt all opinions which he rejected, and was impatient of contradiction. But Mr. Hoge patiently and candidly listened to every argument and objection brought against his opinions, and proposed his own views with so much modesty that I felt altogether at my ease in conversing with him. He caused me still more to hesitate about certain opinions which I had heard proposed by my teacher; and this not by making any direct attack on them, but by gently insinuating doubts and considerations which led me to a more thorough inquiry. One of these opinions was that regeneration is produced by light. Mr. Graham always ridiculed the idea of a moral change being produced in any other way than by motives or a view of the truth. This seemed to some as evident as an axiom ; but Mr. Hoge stated difficulties about this light. How can light shine into a blind mind, without some previous operation on that mind ? The natural man cannot know the things of the Spirit of God, because they are spiritually discerned ; and before they can be spiritually discerned the eyes of the mind must be opened. It is true that all pious exercises are produced by a view of the truth, but this view of the truth is the effect of regeneration, not the cause ; unless we confound regeneration and conversion. The Spirit of God, by an instantaneous touch, prepares the soul to apprehend the truth. By an act of omnipotence he communicates spiritual life, and the soul thus quickened, begins to see with new eyes, and experience new emotions and affections. These views I have entertained since my youth ; being intermediate between two extremes ; first, that we are regenerated by light let into the mind, or by a presentation of the truth objectively to the soul ; and secondly, as the Hopkinsians maintain, that the understanding needs no change, but to have the truth doctrinally apprehended ; that all depravity is in the heart, and therefore that regeneration is merely a change of the heart or feelings, while the views of the understanding remain as they were before regeneration.

"As I had an ardent thirst for knowledge, the time which

I spent under this quiet roof was diligently employed in reading and conversation ; except when we attended religious meetings, in which Mr. Hoge took great delight, being gratified when there was the least appearance of lively feeling. He seemed never to be discouraged, and surely did not despise the day of small things. At this day, when books are so abundant, it may surprise some to learn that until now I had never seen a copy of the Septuagint ; and that which Mr. Hoge had was not complete. I seized it with great avidity, and read as much as I could during the time I spent there. Here I also read Chrysostom on the Priesthood, in an English translation ; so that Mason errs in saying that his is the first translation ever made into English. This work produced a very solemn impression on my mind, but it seemed to relate [to matters] of which before I had no conception. I also read Riccaltoun's Exposition of the Epistle to the Galatians, and with considerable profit."

From a private record of texts and places, we find that in the first fifteen months of his ministry he preached one hundred and thirty-two sermons.

In the month of March, 1791, he turned his face homeward, having preached all winter without stipend. "Indeed," says he, "I never thought of compensation for what I did, not considering my labours as of any real value." At Millerstown, or Woodstock, as it is now called, he was detained some days by a flood. He lodged with a Mr. Morris, from Newcastle in the Northern Neck, the only Presbyterian in those parts, except the German Reformed. He preached in a house belonging to the Germans. The village was at that day noted for irreligion and wantonness. On his way to Lexington he stopped at Staunton. The town contained no place of worship but an Episcopal church, which was without a minister. "It was proposed," he continues, "that I should preach in the little Episcopal church; to which I consented with some trepidation; but when I entered the house in the evening it was crowded, and all the gentry of the town were out, including Judge Archibald Stuart, who had known me from a child. I took for my text, 'What is a man profited,' &c. My first head was to show the worth of the soul, the second how it might be lost, and the third the unprofitableness of all other acquisitions, if the soul should be lost. As I was very young, not yet twenty years of age, and my friends were well known here, I was heard with great attention. In speaking of the worth of the soul, I undertook to give a brief analysis of its powers. Judge Stuart expressed surprise that I should know any thing of the philosophy of the mind, a science then little cultivated. But it had been the favourite study of Mr. Graham, my preceptor; who, while he read little on other subjects, had sent for the writings of Reid and Beattie which had just come out. After reading these, however, he planned a system of his own, remarkable for its simplicity and perspicuity, which he communicated to all his students; and this gave my mind a turn to this study which may account for any proficiency I may have since made in it."

It would be unpardonable to omit the account of his return home, given by the subject of the narrative himself. "When I reached home," so he wrote almost half a century after the event, "there was a great curiosity in men, women, and children, to hear me preach. They had often heard me speak in public, but preaching was another thing. Accordingly, on the next Lord's Day a great congregation filled the Court House, which was then used for public worship, for at that time there was no church in the place. My text was John ix. 25, 'One thing I know, that whereas I was blind, now I see.' My delivery in those days was fluent and rapid. I never appeared to hesitate or be at a loss for words; my thoughts flowed too fast for me. I laboured under two great faults as a public speaker; the first was extreme rapidity of utterance, not so much from indistinct articulation as neglect of pauses. I ran on till I was perfectly out of breath, so that before I was done my inhalations became audible; the other fault was looking steadily down upon the floor. This arose from a fear of losing the train of my thought; for my sermons were closely studied, though not written. My voice, though not sonorous, was uncommonly distinct and clear, so that without painful exertion I could be heard in the largest churches, or by a great assembly out of doors. I preached but one other Sabbath in my native county, and that was not in the town, but at Oxford meeting-house. I had very little knowledge of the estimation in which my preaching was held, and was always surprised to hear of a favourable opinion expressed by any one; for I was so conscious of my own defects, that often after preaching I was ashamed to come down from the pulpit, and wondered that any could speak kindly to me."

"As my health was now good, and I had no thought of

taking a pastoral charge, I embraced an offer to travel as an itinerant missionary in Eastern Virginia. This mission was in pursuance of a plan adopted by the Synod of Virginia, at their second meeting, in 1789. "There was a Commission to superintend this important matter, by whom were appointed, successively, Mr. LeGrand, Mr. Hill, Mr. Cary Allen, Mr. Marshall, Mr. John Lyle, and Mr. Alexander. Respecting the last named, the minutes contain this statement, under date April 9, 1792: 'Upon motion, the Commission elected Mr. Archibald Alexander, a probationer under care of Lexington Presbytery, to the office of missionary; upon condition that the Presbytery recommend him. Mr. Graham and Mr. John Lyle are directed to apply to the Presbytery for such recommendation.'*

"The common sentiment was against my remaining at home in study, and Mr. Graham urged me to accept the appointment. Another young preacher, Benjamin Grigsby, a friend and acquaintance of mine from my youth, had received license in the spring, and he and I were sent together to preach to a people of whom we knew nothing. Grigsby was a young man of talents and scholarship, and was also a fine speaker, and possessed of easy and popular manners. In the theological class which studied under Mr. Graham he was undoubtedly the favourite of his teacher. But though respected, he was never much a favourite with his associates. He was two years my senior, but I was licensed six months before him. Our directions were to proceed to Petersburg, and there separate. While he went eastward from that place,

* See Foote's Sketches of Virginia, p. 529.

I was to turn westward, along the North Carolina line Being both furnished with good horses and other appointments, we took our departure from old Mr. Grigsby's on Hart's Bottom. Our first effort was to cross the Blue Ridge at Prior's Gap, over the steepest part of the mountain, by a bridle-path. We found no difficulty, as we both had been accustomed to mountain climbing. For hours however we talked but little, as it was necessary to ride singly in the path. We had been advised to lodge the first night on the Amherst side of the Ridge at the house of Captain David Crawford, several of whose sons had been at the Academy, and of whom one was now an Episcopal minister. We were kindly received by the family, especially by the young parson of the parish, who laid himself out to make us comfortable. Appointments for us to preach in his church had been sent on, for we were so ignorant, that it never occurred to us that any objection could arise. Let it be noted, that there was not then any Episcopal minister in Rockbridge or Augusta. Mr. Charles Crawford had received the notice and published it to his small congregation, near the Tobacco Row Mountain. He also accompanied us to the church, where we found about twenty respectable planters, to whom Mr. Grigsby preached. After service, Mr. Crawford, having first conversed with the few people who were out, came and presented in a very formal manner the thanks of the congregation to Mr. Grigsby for his excellent sermon. The next day young Mr. Crawford gave us letters to an acquaintance at whose house we might lodge, and then took his horse and accompanied us part of the way."

The next day our young travellers reached the mansion of Colonel William Cabell, of whom the manuscript notes that he was the grandfather of Doctors John, Robert and William Breckinridge, and the brother of Mrs. Paulina Read, afterwards Mrs. LeGrand; names which cannot be omitted in any contribution to Presbyterian annals. Crossing the James River at Warminster they reached the house of Colonel Joseph Cabell, and thence proceeded to their lodgings at the New Store. The manners and customs of that region have changed since the statements which follow were penned. "We were not aware that this neighbourhood was famous for the abuse of travellers. At an 'ordinary' not more than a mile from the place, on the great Buckingham road, a set of fellows used to meet for carousal, who never failed to maltreat any traveller who came to the house. One night they caught an old man named Ross, from Richmond, and held him in the well for some time with his head downward. Another stranger they threatened to throw into the well, unless he would consent to dance for them; and at this exercise they kept him until a late hour of the night; when some intermission being allowed, he slipped out to the stable, saddled his horse and fled, being forced to swim over the Appomatox River."

The next morning brought them to the hospitable mansion of old Mrs. Venable, on the edge of Prince Edward County. She was of the Michaux family and a descendant of Huguenots who had settled on the James River; a matron of great shrewdness, information and piety. Her husband had long been dead, and her children were grown up

There was an important vacancy, caused by the resignation of Dr. John B. Smith, who had served the united congregations of Cumberland and Briery. Mr. Grigsby was sent to the former and Mr. Alexander to the latter; little supposing, as he records, that he should ever become their pastor, as he was not seeking for a settlement. On Sunday evening he went to Little Roanoke Bridge, and became first acquainted with Mrs. Paulina Read, whose name must often be mentioned in these pages. He preached at the house of old Mrs. Morton, where he had attended a meeting in 1789. On Wednesday he preached to a small congregation at Hampden Sidney College. But the instructions of the young missionaries did not permit them to spend more than one Sabbath among these "affectionate and delightful people," and they directed their course towards Petersburg.

During this brief visit Mr. Alexander became acquainted with Col. Samuel Venable, a man of great distinction, whom he used to name in connection with Graham, Hoge and Smith, the counsellors of his youth. His notes concerning this invaluable friend have great interest, and cannot be inserted in a more suitable place. "Three brothers were among the first settlers in Prince Edward. Nathaniel owned the place on which the Court House was built, and was for a long time an elder in the church, and represented the county in the Legislature. He was also an active trustee of Hampden Sidney College. . . . . . Samuel was his oldest son, who, though grown up when Samuel Stanhope Smith opened the Academy of Hampden Sidney, betook himself to learning, and followed Smith on his removal to

Princeton, where he was graduated [in 1780], as were also three of his brothers, Abram, Richard and Nathaniel. William and Thomas were alumni of Hampden Sidney.

"Samuel Venable intended to study law, but was led by some circumstances to engage in merchandise. This business he carried on in a very judicious manner, so as to accumulate a large estate. He was a man of clear head and sound judgment, and had made observations on the characters of men as they passed before him; and these observations he had reduced to maxims. He was confident in the opinions which he had formed, but not inclined to dispute with those who did not agree with him. He used to say that when a young man he was fond of disputation, and thought he could bring others to see as he did, but that after some experience he found it to be vain, and therefore suffered others undisturbedly to enjoy their own opinions. His wife was the daughter of the elder judge Paul Carrington, and sister of the younger; a woman of uncommon vivacity, wit, and power of sarcasm. They had twelve children.

"When Col. Venable was about fifty years of age, he thought of giving up active business, and retiring to pursue a course of reading and study, which a busy mercantile life had prevented. He therefore placed a younger brother in the firm, and built for himself an office or study separate from his dwelling, where he anticipated much repose and gratification. But the event was different. After quitting business he fell into a hypochondriac state, in which he fancied that his lungs were ulcerated, and that he could designate the precise spot where the disease was seated. He was a man of robust frame, and had a broad projecting chest, and no symptoms of any real pulmonary disease. The opinions of friends and even of physicians had no effect to convince him of his error; he persisted in maintaining his opinion. At this time his nerves became so affected, that he could scarcely sit still for a few minutes. He kept a horse saddled at the door, and whatever company he had he would abruptly leave them when the fit seized him, and would ride for miles. Nothing seemed to relieve him except smoking the pipe, a thing which before this he abhorred. . . . . . The disease received no effectual check until he was induced to engage again in active business, which occupied his attention; and a portion of his former cheerfulness returned. But he never afterwards possessed the firmness and confidence which had characterized him before. He died suddenly at the Virginia Springs, leaving a large family well provided for."

During the whole of his life Dr. Alexander was accustomed to speak of Col. Venable as the most remarkable instance of wisdom matured by experience and observation, that he had ever known; in which respect he was fond of comparing him with Franklin. The descendants of the three brothers above mentioned now amount to some hundreds in Virginia and the new States; and of these a remarkable number are zealous and efficient members of the Presbyterian Church.

CHAPTER SEVENTH.

1792.

MISSIONARY TOUR—LUNENBURG—THE MILLWRIGHT—CAPT. CRAIGHEAD—MR. HUNT—WILLIAM COWAN—NOTTOWAY—AMELIA—PETERSBURG—MR. JARRATT—MECKLENBURG—MR. PATILLO.

FROM Prince Edward the young preachers went towards Lunenburg. Before sunset they arrived at the house of a Mr. Yarborough, a Baptist of some wealth, who received them with Christian and Virginian hospitality. Here they gained acquaintance with a man whose case is too remarkable and characteristic of the times to be omitted. And as the memorandums of Dr. Alexander respecting his contemporaries furnish facts which would otherwise be entirely lost, we feel justified in frequently turning aside to diversify our story by such episodes.

"Mr. Yarborough took occasion to inform us that there was a Baptist preacher in his employment as a millwright, who would be at the house as soon as his work was finished. Accordingly about the dusk of the evening, an old man in coarse garb, with leathern apron, and laden with tools, entered the house and took his seat on the stairs. Neither Mr.

Grigsby nor I had ever been acquainted with uneducated preachers, and we were struck with astonishment that this carpenter should pretend to preach. When we retired, Mr. Shelburne, such was his name, was put into the same room with us. I felt an avidity to question him respecting his call to the ministry, taking it for granted that the old man was ignorant. I therefore began by asking him what he considered a call to the ministry. Mr. Shelburne perceived the drift of my question, and instead of giving a general answer proceeded to a narrative of his own experience, and to state the circumstances which led him to suppose that God had called him to be a preacher. The substance of his story was as follows:

"'I was born in one of the lower counties of Virginia, and when young was put to learn the carpenter's trade. Until I was a man grown and had a family, I never heard any preaching but from ministers of the Established Church, and did not even know that there were any others. About this time came into the neighbourhood a Presbyterian minister, by the name of Martin, whom I went to hear; and before he was done I was convinced that I was in a lost and undone condition. He made no stay, and I heard no more of him. But a wound had been left in my conscience which I knew not how to get healed, and no one about me could give any valuable advice as to a cure. I went from day to day under a heavy burden, bewailing my miserable state, till at length my distress became so great that I could neither eat nor sleep with any peace or comfort. My neighbours said that I was falling into melancholy or going mad, but not one of them had any knowledge from experience of the nature of my distress. Thus I continued mourning over my miserable case for weeks and months. I was led, however, to read constantly in the Bible ; but this rather increased than lessened my distress ; until one Sunday evening I saw as clearly as I ever saw any thing how I could be saved, through the death of Christ. I was filled with comfort, and yet sorrow for my sins flowed more copiously than ever. I praised God aloud, and immediately told my wife that I had found salvation ; and when any of my neighbours came to see me, I told them of the goodness of God, and what he had done for my soul, and how he had pardoned all my sins. As I spoke freely of the wonderful change I had experienced, it was soon noised abroad, and many came to see me, and to hear an account of the matter from my own mouth.

"'On Sabbath evenings my house would be crowded, and when I had finished my narrative I was accustomed to give them a word of exhortation. And as I could be better heard when standing, I stood and addressed my neighbours, without any thought of preaching. After proceeding for some time in this way, I found that several others began to be awakened by what they heard from me, and appeared to be brought through the new birth much as I had been. This greatly encouraged me to proceed in my work, and God was pleased to bless my humble labours to the conversion of many. All this time I did no more than relate my own experience and then exhort my neighbours to seek unto the Lord for mercy. Thus was I led on from step to step, until at length I actually became a preacher, without intending it. Exercised persons would frequently come to me for counsel, as I had been the first among them to experience the grace of God; and that I might be able to answer their questions I was induced to study the Bible continually; and often while at work, particular passages would be opened to my mind; which encouraged me to hope that the Lord had called me to instruct those who were more ignorant than myself; and when the people would collect at my house, I explained to them those passages which had been opened to my mind. All this time I had no instruction in spiritual matters from any man, except the sermons which I heard from Mr. Martin. But after a few years there came a Baptist preacher into our neighbourhood, and I found that his doctrine agreed substantially with my experience, and with what I had learned out of the Bible. I travelled about with him, and was encouraged by him to go on in the exercise of my gift of public speaking, but was told by him that there was one duty which I was required to perform, which was that I should be baptized according to the command of Christ. And as we rode along we came to a certain water, and I said, See, here is water, what doth hinder me to be baptized? Upon which we both went down into the water, and he baptized me by immersion in the name of the Father, the Son, and the Holy Ghost. From that time I have continued until this day, testifying to small and great, to white and black, repentance towards God and faith in our Lord Jesus Christ; and not without the pleasure of seeing many sinners forsaking their sins and turning unto God.

" 'Now,' said he, 'you have heard the reasons which

induce me to believe that God has called me to preach the Gospel to the poor and ignorant. I never considered myself qualified to instruct men of education and learning. I have always felt badly when such have come to hear me. But as for people of my own class, I believed that I could teach them many things which they need to know ; and in regard to such as had become pious, I was able, by study of the Bible and meditation, to go before them, so that to them also I could be in some measure a guide. I lament my want of learning, and am deeply convinced that it is useful to the ministry of the Gospel ; but it seems to me that there are different gifts now as of old, and one man may be suited to one part of the Lord's work, and another to another part. And I do not know but that poor and ignorant people can understand my coarse and familiar language better than the discourses of the most learned and eloquent men. I know their method of thinking and reasoning, and how to make things plain by illustrations and comparisons adapted to their capacities and their habits.'

"When the old millwright had finished his narrative, I felt much more inclined to doubt my own call to the ministry, than that of James Shelburne. Much of the night was spent in this conversation, while my companion was enjoying his usual repose. We talked freely about the doctrines of religion, and were mutually gratified at finding how exactly our views tallied. From this night James Shelburne became an object of my high regard, and he gave abundant testimony of his esteem for me. Whenever I visited that part of the country, he was wont to ride many miles to hear me preach, and was pleased to declare that he had never heard any of the ministers of his own denomination with whose opinions he could so fully agree as with mine. I had the opportunity of hearing him preach several times, and was pleased not only with the soundness of his doctrine, but the unaffected simplicity of his manner. His discourses consisted of a series of judicious remarks expressed in the plainest language, and in a conversational tone, until he became by degrees warmed with his subject, when he fell into a singing tone, but nothing like what was common with almost all Baptist preachers of the country at that time. As he followed his trade from day to day, I once asked him how he found time to study his sermons; to which he replied, that he could study better at his work, with his hammer in his hand, than if shut up and surrounded with books. When he had passed the seventieth year of his age he gave up work, and devoted himself entirely to preaching. Being a man of firm health, he travelled to a considerable distance and preached nearly every day. On one of these tours, after I was settled in Charlotte County, I saw him for the last time. The old man appeared to be full of zeal and love, and brought the spirit of the Gospel into every family which he visited. He was evidently ripening for heaven, and accordingly, not long after, he finished his course with joy. Thus I have anticipated much that relates to my old friend, although his end did not occur until many years after this time." *

* See also an account of the same man, in the 'New Orleans Protestant' for 1846 or 1847.

At Reedy Creek the travellers met with some persons from whom they acquired many important facts as to the early plantation of our church in Virginia. Distinguished among these was Captain William Craighead, an intimate friend of the Rev. Samuel Davies of Hanover, with whom he served as an elder. He cordially welcomed the missionaries, as his family and that of William Cowan, Esq., were the only Presbyterians of the neighbourhood. He produced a file of letters received from President Davies after his removal to Princeton, and said it was his custom to read them over on a certain day in every year. From his ardour of disposition, activity, fluency of speech and religious zeal, the Captain was well fitted to be a useful officer in the church. In all the negotiations touching Mr. Davies's removal he bore a prominent part, and afterwards was several times a commissioner to convey a call to other northern ministers; among the rest to Mr. Kirkpatrick of New Jersey. After many disappointments the Hanover people were at length visited by the Rev. David Rice, who became their pastor. After Mr. Rice's departure, the congregation remained many years vacant, and the church declined more and more.

The notices respecting another old Christian of that country aid our conceptions of the type of religion which prevailed. This was Mr. Hunt, the father of Craighead's second wife. He was a subject of the work of grace in Hanover, before they had any preaching. He was old enough to have a family around him, when the awakening began, in consequence of finding and reading certain old books. He remembered Mr. Robinson's visit, and gave a particular account of the circumstances attending his arrival. He had a notion that when a young man God had called him by name, it is believed in Williamsburg. Sitting up till midnight he heard a voice from above distinctly calling him, James Hunt, James Hunt! Contrary to what is usual in such visitations, the voice was distinctly heard by two women who were ironing in a room near at hand. From that time he had very serious thoughts about religion, but was ignorant of its nature, until the famous "reading" commenced at Mr. Morris's house, in the neighbourhood of which he lived. The genuineness and sincerity of Mr. Hunt's religion were rendered evident by a life of even, humble piety, during seventy years. "In his ninety-second year," says Dr. Alexander, "he read Paine's Age of Reason, not long after which I visited him, at the house of his son Gilbert, on Staunton River; and was struck with the remarks which he made on that infidel performance. At that time he related to me an experience which he had had many years before. One morning as he arose from his bed, he had so ravishing a view of the glory of God, that for some time he stood in mute astonishment. And when this passed away he enjoyed for a fortnight such a peace, that he could conceive of no greater happiness."

Another person whom the missionaries found in Lunenburg was William Cowan, a Scotchman by birth, a lawyer of some eminence, and a man of eminent piety. Having come to this country when a lad, with an elder brother, he fell in with the Methodists, exhorted in public, and was elated with his supposed success in public speaking. He used to relate that he felt sure he could produce a sermon off-hand on any text in the Bible ; and that to make a trial, he opened the book at random, and alighted on these words, Obadiah 3, "The pride of thy heart hath deceived thee," &c. This came home to his conscience and feelings with a power so convincing that he fell prostrate on the ground, and from that hour a great change was wrought in his character, and he became an humble man for the rest of life. When a suitable occasion offered itself he returned to the bosom of the Presbyterian Church, in which he had been baptized. "Mr. Cowan," says our manuscript, "was certainly one of the most uniformly serious men I was ever acquainted with. In his arguments at the bar, his solemn voice and formal manner of dividing his subject much resembled preaching. Though always grave he was not austere, and the impression which he made on men of the world, and especially on his associates, was exceedingly favourable, while his profound skill in jurisprudence was universally acknowledged. He was no orator, but in causes requiring legal acumen and judgment, he was by many preferred to Patrick Henry, with whom he practised in the same courts for many years, living in habits of intimacy with that great man. When the war was ended he was almost entirely occupied in collecting moneys due to the Scotch merchants, who had generally gone off at the commencement of the Revolution; a business which was attended with little difficulty after the confirmation of Jay's Treaty. But immediately after the Revolution the payment of these debts was resisted, and Patrick Henry, as I have been informed, never made a greater display of his extraordinary abilities, than in a speech before the Supreme Court against the equity of these claims; so that the British agents who were in court said to one another, 'We had better go home, for this man, before he is done, will make us the debtors instead of the creditors.'

"When Mr. Cowan retired from the bar, and confined himself to collecting the aforesaid debts, he came often into the part of the country where I resided, and I had the opportunity of being much with him. And having observed his solemn manner at the bar and his uniform seriousness and devotion, I, as well as others, concluded that he ought to become a preacher of the gospel. One day, therefore, when riding with him from the place of worship, I ventured to broach the subject. He said it had often been suggested to his mind, but that after the most mature deliberation he had come to the conclusion that it would be unwise for him to enter the ministry. That the habits of one profession long fixed could not be easily laid aside to assume those of another; that he had had much to do in worldly business, and had been obliged in the course of his profession to offend many persons; that many were prejudiced against him on account of his being the attorney for British merchants, to whom almost all were indebted; and especially that he still was concerned in cases which could not be terminated for many years. I was much impressed with the solid weight of these reasons.

"He was deeply sensible of the evils of slavery, and one day said to me that there was a secret policy in the minds of some leading men in the state, to tax slaves very heavily, so as by degrees to render them unprofitable ; as they were convinced that the mass of slaveholders would never consent to emancipate them while they were profitable."

After Mr. Grigsby had preached at Reedy Creek, to a small congregation, he and his companion were met by Capt. Craighead, who took them to his house and entertained them with much kindness. On the next Sabbath they went to Lunenburg Court House, two or three miles distant, where Bishop Madison was to preach. They heard him discourse on standing in the old paths. The object of this visitation—and he made but few—was to win back the people into the old church. The state of episcopacy in Virginia at this period may be learnt from the history of Dr. Hawks. Captain Craighead and Mr. Cowan expressed the opinion that there was no vitality in the body, except in the parish of old Mr. Jarratt, of whom more will be said hereafter. In the afternoon both the young Presbyterians preached in the Court House, to a large and attentive audience, of whom most had never heard a minister of this persuasion. The youthful appearance of the speakers attracted much attention. In the county of Amelia they found no Presbyterians, but were warmly entertained by an old Col. Brooking, who, with his wife, had been accustomed in their youth to hear Mr. Davies. "They informed us that John Rodgers Davies resided near them, and was frequently their guest. Old Mrs. Brooking added, that she had once asked him to do her a special favour, and on his consenting, informed him that she desired him to take home and read the little poem which his father had written on the occasion of his birth. He answered that he could not do it, and that he had never perused any of his father's writings.

"Six or seven years after this, I made a tour through the counties south of James River, and found that he had removed to Sussex. The man with whom I staid, a Mr. Chapel, a Methodist, told me that there was a Presbyterian gentleman near him, who never attended any of their meetings, and that he was glad I had come. Mr. Chapel urged me to preach in the evening; and went himself to inform Mr. Davies of the service. But he could not by all his arguments prevail on him to come. And finally, to get clear of his importunity, he said, 'If the Apostle Paul was to preach at your house to-night, I would not go; nay, if my own father was to preach there I would not go.'"

It deserves to be mentioned that great assemblies were gathered to the preaching of Mr. Alexander during this visit to Amelia. A report had been circulated that he was only fifteen or sixteen years of age, which indeed his appearance seemed to justify, though at this time he was nearly twenty. From all the accounts which we have been able to obtain during a residence in the same region nearly thirty years ago, when many were surviving who remembered these juvenile efforts, we are induced to believe that at no period of his ministry was the preaching of Mr. Alexander more attractive and powerful than at that very time. With little of that culture which he afterwards received in large measure, he had the glow and exuberance of youth, a fund of brilliant imagery and copious words, a magical fascination of voice, and above all a spirituality of mind, which was the chief endowment in the apprehension of those aged persons who gave the report. His labours were abundant, sometimes involving successive days of preaching, at places far apart; and they were doubtless instrumental in promoting the growth of that Church to the service of which his whole energy both in youth and age was consecrated.

Continuing their journey in the direction of the rivers towards tidewater, our missionaries went next to Petersburg. They were consigned by letter to Mr. Thomas Shore, of Pocahontas, on the side of the Appomatox opposite to the town. This gentleman's father, Dr. Shore of Hanover, had been one of Mr. Davies's elders. They took up their abode, however, with a Mr. Dodson, who proved to be an obliging and serious man, but unconnected with any religious body The good man informed the young preachers that there would be no difficulty in procuring them a place in which to hold meetings, assuring them that they might have either the Episcopal church, or the Methodist church in Blandford. He accordingly agreed to go and see the principal local preacher of the Methodists, a considerable merchant, of whose liberality he spoke in high terms. "It was also agreed," says Mr. Alexander, "that Mr. Grigsby should go to Blandford and secure the Episcopal church there, so that each might have a place of preaching. We thought every thing was to go on swimmingly. After dinner we stepped into a store in the old town, as Mr. Grigsby wanted a pair of black silk gloves for the pulpit. While he was chaffering at the counter, the owner of the store said to me, 'When

I saw you ride into town, I thought you were Methodist preachers, but now I find I was mistaken; pray, to what denomination do you belong?' On our replying, he said, 'Ah! Presbyterian!' with a peculiar tone and expression of countenance; 'We have a man in town who was once a Presbyterian preacher, but is now a merchant; for he says he can't sell goods and preach too.' I replied, that I thought the man was perfectly right, as no man could fulfil the duties of the sacred office and be a merchant at the same time. His colour rose at this, and he said, with a smarter tone, 'Then you do not agree with the Apostle Paul, for he preached and wrought at the trade of tent making.' I answered that I did agree with Paul, who had given solemn directions to Timothy that ministers should give themselves wholly to their work; and that Paul's labouring was from necessity, and to take away all occasion of prejudice from his enemies. Here we left the store, and on relating what had passed to Mr. Dodson, were informed that this man was a preacher and a leading person among the Methodists."

There is much naïveté in the description of these first attempts to exercise their gifts in a large town. "On Saturday, Mr. Grigsby proceeded to Blandford and Mr. Dodson applied to the local preacher, requesting their house at hours which would not interfere with their worship, and was confounded to find that it could not be had. Mr. Dodson was greatly mortified, as he said he and many others who were not of their society had helped to build the house. When Mr. Grigsby returned from Blandford, he told us he had visited Mr. Cameron, the rector, from whom he had received an unceremonious refusal. He had, however, met with a Dr. Hull, born in Augusta and bred a Presbyterian, who insisted that we should dine with him the next day. I hesitated, but thinking a private house would be more agreeable than Mr. Dodson's boarding house, I consented. The question as to a place of preaching was not yet satisfactorily answered. We made many inquiries, but nothing presented itself. At length I asked Mr. D., if they never had field-preaching about the town. He said there was a spring about a mile off called John Baptist's Spring, because an old Baptist, a black man named John, sometimes held forth there. I replied that this should be our preaching place ; but how to give notice was the difficulty. At length Mr. Dodson suggested that he had a smart negro boy, who could go through the town with a bell, carrying the notice in his hand to be read by all who might meet him. I was much pleased with this scheme, and we prepared in a large legible hand a notice that two young Presbyterian ministers would preach at the 'stand' of John the Baptist, at four o'clock in the afternoon. Our little black was already summoned, when information came that Mr. Prentiss, the printer, had offered for our use a large unfurnished house in Bolingbroke Street.

"In the morning I went with Mr. Dodson to the Methodist church, and Mr. Grigsby went to Blandford to hear Mr. Cameron. The circuit rider who attended in Petersburg on that occasion was no indifferent speaker. He was either an Englishman, or had caught the swell and rotundity of English elocution from preachers who had come over from

10

that country. But after he had proceeded some length in his discourse, he went out of his way to warn the people against a set of preachers who taught that the righteousness of Christ was imputed to the believer. He said this was a dangerous doctrine, and before he was done called it imputed nonsense and blasphemy. I was astonished, not being then aware of the Methodist hostility to this doctrine. After sermon I went over to Blandford to meet Mr. G. at Dr. Hull's. Here I learned that Mr. Cameron also had uttered a violent tirade against Calvinists, and warned the people against hearing them, as he understood some preachers of that description had come to the place. Thus were we met with opposition on all sides.

"Soon after our arrival the company began to come in, carriage after carriage. We found to our chagrin that a large party had been invited, and as Archibald Gracie of New-York and some other guests were late, the hour for preaching had nearly come before we sat down. We expressed our uneasiness to the host, who said we should be there in full time. But before we had made our way half through the elegant dinner, which did me no good, the hour arrived. We unceremoniously rose from table, in the midst of a smart thunder shower. The rain prevented many who would have come, for the refusal to let us preach had excited much feeling. The house, however, which was in a very rough state, was well filled, and Mr. Grigsby preached a plain, solemn and impressive sermon, on John iii. 3. The people were very attentive, and an old Mr. Angus took us cordially by the hand, and in a strong Scotch accent asked us to go home with him, to which we agreed. He informed us that the majority of Parson Cameron's hearers were Scotch people, who had been brought up Presbyterians; 'Yes,' he added, 'and he also was brought up a Presbyterian.' Before the people were dismissed, we learned that application had been made for the use of the Masonic Hall, a spacious building in Blandford, but that an old lady, whc taught a dancing school there, strongly objected, fearing lest we should injure her craft. But when the Master Mason heard this, he brought the key of the Hall and delivered it to one of our friends. The next day, therefore, I preached tc a very large congregation in this fine room; and Mr. Grigsby preached on the day following. During these days an earnest application was made, for one of us to remain and preach there statedly. And if we could have staid, a Presbyterian congregation might have been gathered fifteen years before such an organization actually took place. But each of us had a tour of six months before him.

"We now took our leave of Petersburg and of one another. This last we were very reluctant to do; for we had found that 'two are better than one,' and that the plan adopted by our Saviour was better than any other. No sooner had I turned my face westward, than I began to feel solitary and dejected. Grigsby's exuberance of spirits had previously kept me up, but now I was left to my own gloomy forebodings of innumerable difficulties."

The name of the Reverend Devereux Jarratt is well known by all the friends of evangelical religion in Virginia, where he shone as a light in a dark place, during a season when the Episcopal Church had few to declare the gospel in its simplicity. Having heard much of his piety and eloquence, Mr. Alexander determined to spend the next Sabbath with him. The good old man had lately attended the diocesan convention at Richmond, and had preached a pungent and faithful discourse, which was then fresh from the press. He was found in his spacious old-fashioned house, in the midst of a large plantation, without children, but surrounded by sleek, happy-looking servants. "But I confess," says the narrative, "I was much better pleased with Mrs. Jarratt. There was so much of sweetness and kindness in this old lady, that I have seldom seen the like. Mrs. Grammar, of Petersburg, known to me long afterwards, was in affability, goodness, and Christian courtesy the exact resemblance of Mrs. Jarratt. Indeed, she was brought up under her tuition, and her son now occupies Mr. Jarratt's place in the parish of Bath. The old gentleman seemed at first reserved and austere. I was a perfect stranger to him, very young, and younger in appearance than in reality, and as far as I remember, brought no introductory letters; they were less common in those days than now. He did not leave his study to keep me company, but left the good lady to attend on me, which she did in a manner that could not but be most soothing to the heart of a stranger, much disposed to melancholy thoughts. After a little, however, Mr. Jarratt began to unbend; and the first thing he did was to examine me on the Evidences of Christianity, and to get something of my history, and of my purpose in visiting that part of the country. Finding me not altogether ignorant, he proceeded to converse with me freely. He related a controversy which he had had the week before with the Methodist Presiding Elder of the district; in the course of which the latter asked in regard to something which he had asserted, 'How should you know any better than I?' 'Because,' answered Mr. Jarratt, 'I had read more books before you were born, than you have done in your whole life.'

"He said his parish was much reduced, and that the state of religion was very low; but he described scenes of a truly animating kind which had been witnessed there. When he first preached there, as the people were gay and careless, he prepared a few flowery discourses, *ad captandum*, and brought out but little of the gospel plainly. This he justified by the case of Paul, who became all things to all men. But it was a doubtful expedient, and an experiment replete with danger. As to his own church, he knew but one man in the ministry whom he regarded as an experimental Christian; this was a Mr. Ball. But as he has published an account of his own life, which is a curious picture of manners in Virginia at that period, I will not attempt to sketch his character. His zeal, together with a voice of great power and melody, carried him forward and raised him high as a preacher; and as he and Mr. McRoberts were the only two who zealously preached the gospel in the church as by law established, their prominence was marked. Some years afterwards I heard him preach at Hampden Sidney College; the sermon was evangelical and fervent, without signs of care in the preparation, and his voice was then broken. A good idea of his labours may be obtained from his printed sermons. His theological opinions, as he informed me, were in conformity with those of Richard Baxter, except that he held, and in several publications endeavoured to maintain, the possibility of attaining sinless perfection in this life."

The path marked out for Mr. Alexander lay in the direction of the North Carolina border. From Petersburg, therefore, he retraced his steps through the counties of Amelia, Nottoway, and Lunenburg, where he fulfilled engagements made in the former visit. He then entered Mecklenburg, where the Rev. Mr. Patillo was accustomed to preach once in the month. Here the Methodists had enjoyed much success for a time. A lady is remembered, who a few years before had made much noise. Such was her zeal and enthusiasm, that she spoke and exhorted in public assemblies, even when a number of preachers were present. Her figure was commanding, and her address won public admiration. The young missionary here records a misadventure not uncommon in such itinerations; his horse escaped, and was missing for some days. In this great embarrassment, his gloomy thoughts were dispelled by a discourse which he casually opened upon in a friend's house, on the words, "Shall we receive good at the hands of the Lord, and shall we not receive evil?" It was in Bennet's Oratory, a work on Prayer, for which he always retained a strong attachment.

At the Blue Stone Meeting-House, he first fell in with the Rev. Henry Patillo, who had come over from Granville County in Carolina, to administer the Lord's Supper; and of whom he gives the following notices. Mr. Patillo was born in Scotland, and was brought to this country by an elder brother, when only nine years old. While yet a young man, he became acquainted with Mr. Davies, and having experienced the power of grace he entered on studies preparatory to the ministry, receiving aid from some persons of benevolence. But his chief resource was in his own labours as a teacher, by which he was enabled to sustain himself. In due time he was licensed by the Presbytery of Hanover, at that time the only one in Virginia. This was probably about the year 1760. For some years he preached in Cumberland, Prince Edward, and Charlotte ; but on receiving an invitation to North Carolina, he removed to Granville County, and had for his charge the congregations of Grassy Creek and Nutbush, with which he remained till the close of his life.

Mr. Patillo was above the middle size, of robust constitution and uninterrupted health. His aspect was benevolent, and his manners were simple and affectionate. He was free from envy and jealousy, and even in old age had no austerity or moroseness. He was especially affable with young ministers, delighting in their gifts, for which he gave thanks to God. The most untutored and the youngest were perfectly at ease in his company ; as he seemed to esteem himself the least of all God's servants. Yet he was an incessant reader, and remembered almost all that he read. In the pulpit, he was plain and practical ; but it was evident that much pains had been bestowed on his discourses. His voice was commanding, and he was generally heard with attention. His disposition was so contented, that nothing seemed to disturb the serenity of his mind. As far as was possible for the head of a family, he divested himself of all worldly cares. He was always poor, and used to express his thankfulness to God for having kept him entirely exempt from the snares of wealth. The only kind of property on which he set much value, was books. He had a great avidity for learning, rather than for accumulating a fine library; but was generous in parting with his treasures to those who needed them more than he. "Until this period of my life," says Mr. Alexander, "I had never seen a Hebrew Bible, or any other Hebrew book; and some time after this, having found a mutilated copy among the relics of old Robert Henry's books in Charlotte, I begged it of the family, and then travelled into North Carolina, to procure a Bythner's Lyra Prophetica, from old Mr. Patillo." On a certain occasion, while Mr. Patillo was absent, his house was consumed by fire. On his return, he exclaimed to his wife, "O my dear, are my books safe?" And on being assured that they were, he devoutly praised God.

Late in life, Mr. Patillo became an author. His principal work was an abridgment of Leland's Deistical Writers; a very seasonable production, at a time when French infidelity was rife. The other was a series of plain sermons. A note appended to one of these, broached the same doctrine concerning Christ's human nature, which has since been so offensively taught by the famous Edward Irving. It will cast light on the ministerial life of those days, here to insert a statement of Dr. Alexander's, though out of its chronological place. "While I was minister in Charlotte, the old gentleman came once to pay his last visit to his friends in Virginia. I made a string of appointments for him, reaching from Cub Creek to Cumberland, and accompanied him the whole round. It was previously suggested to a few as we passed from place to place, that it would be well to make a contribution, to aid the aged servant of God. When we had finished our tour, I had in my saddle-bags about thirty dollars, which the people had freely given. As I handed him the silver coin (for we had then never seen a bank-note), the good old man appeared to be penetrated with gratitude." Mr. Patillo is supposed to have been more than seventy years of age at the time of his death.

Among the early settlements of Presbyterianism in this region, Mr. Alexander occasionally found persons of character so marked, as to deserve a passing notice. He names a Mr. John Young, a warm friend of Mr. Patillo, and a person of plain unassuming manners, who was remarkable, in years of scarcity, for selling corn at a uniform price, even when it would bring twice as much in the market. Col. Smith was another leading Presbyterian of the same neighbourhood, who had a daughter of extraordinary knowledge and piety. The personal narrative says of her: "She understood the Calvinistic doctrines better than any woman I ever saw. I have spent days in conversation on theological points with Polly Smith. Her religion was not merely theoretical, but deeply practical. She was a truly devout and humble person. She became the wife of the Rev. William Williamson, of Ohio." Chesley Daniel and an old Mr. Lewis, are also mentioned as pious friends of this period. The only contemporary journal of this tour which remains to us, is a fragment of just six pages; which nevertheless contains two somewhat interesting entries. "Tuesday, August 7, 1792. I preached at Sandy River. The house was very full of people, who seemed desirous to hear. I don't remember that any to whom I have preached since I was on my tour, were apparently more affected than these." "Thursday, Aug. 30. I preached at Chestnut Meeting-House, to a small congregation. In the time of sermon, the people appeared to be impressed, and to drink in the Word with greediness. I therefore continued my discourse for nearly two hours, and then dismissed the congregation. I sat in the pulpit about fifteen minutes, but no person in the house offered to go away. After some time I arose and told the people, that as they were not disposed to leave the house of God, their meditations might be assisted by singing a hymn; after which I again spoke about three quarters of an hour. There were few individuals in the house who did not appear deeply affected."

From the borders of North Carolina, Mr. Alexander returned by the way of Charlotte, in Virginia. In fulfilling his appointments, it is believed in Mecklenburg, he met with the following interesting occurrence; "A young man named William Boyd was afraid to come into the house of worship, lest he should be seized with religious impressions; but feeling a strong curiosity to hear the young preacher, he at length returned and took a seat near the door, that he might go out immediately if any thing touched him. Though the bow was drawn at venture, the arrow took effect; he went home under strong convictions and was soon hopefully converted, and at an early age became an elder in the church. This account I received from his own mouth. He was a man of a tender and gentle spirit." In Charlotte, he fell in with Moses Waddel, afterwards the Rev. Dr. Waddel of Georgia, but then a tutor at Hampden Sidney College.

CHAPTER EIGHTH.

1792—1797.

PRINCE EDWARD AND CHARLOTTE—EARLY PREACHERS—MR. ROBINSON—MR. HENRY—PROGRESS IN LEARNING—SMITH'S RIVER—PASTORAL SETTLEMENT—MODE OF PREACHING—PATRICK HENRY AND JOHN RANDOLPH—HAMPDEN SIDNEY COLLEGE—JOHN H. RICE—CONRAD SPEECE—PRESIDENTSHIP OF THE COLLEGE.

THE part of Virginia with which our narrative must now for some time be concerned, is highly interesting to those who wish to study Southern institutions in their connection with Christianity. There is no portion of the State or country where the bright side of the planter's life is more agreeably exhibited. The district has always been remarkable for its adaptation to the culture of a particular variety of tobacco which usually commands high prices, and it has therefore abounded in slaves. Although the estates are less extensive than in the cotton districts of the remoter South, the proprietors enjoy the comforts and luxuries of life in a high degree, and almost every family has some man of liberal education within its bosom. Hospitality and genial warmth may be said to be universal. Nowhere in the South has the Presbyterian Church had greater strength among the wealthy and cultivated classes. It was to be for a long time the theatre of Mr. Alexander's labours; and throughout life he looked back on these as halcyon days. Some of the reminiscences gathered by him in his excursions from persons long since dead must find a place in these pages.

The Rev. Mr. Robinson, one of the pioneers of Virginia, preached in the Caldwell settlement on Cub Creek, in the county of Charlotte. It was a small colony of Scotch-Irish Presbyterians. Among the first ministers settled in Virginia, after Mr. Davies, was the Rev. Robert Henry, who was pastor of this church on Cub Creek. He was a pious but blunt man, whose natural passions were strong and not altogether disciplined. His preaching was unpolished but warm and evangelical. It should never be forgotten that like Davies he laboured faithfully for the salvation of the negroes, many of whom were converted under his preaching. The number of black communicants in this church was greater than in any within our bounds; and in general these converts maintained a consistent Christian character. Even at this moment the fruits of these labours are apparent. From the time of Mr. Henry the names of black communicants exceeded those of the whites, and were probably more than a hundred.

Some characteristic anecdotes of Mr. Henry are recorded in the manuscripts before us. On his way to Briery Meeting-House, where he regularly preached once a fortnight, he was accustomed to lodge at Mr. Morton's, near the Little Roanoke bridge. It was his manner, on turning into the forest through which the road lay, to throw the reins upon the neck of his horse, and to engage in prayer aloud. On one occasion he was so absorbed in this exercise, that the horse reached the door before Mr. Henry had ended his devotions. Such was his absence of mind that he sometimes mistook his own horse on coming from the place of worship.

Mr. Henry was a native of Scotland, but his name appears among the early graduates of Princeton, in 1751. At that time all who had not taken regular degrees elsewhere were required by their Presbyteries to pass through the College of New Jersey.

"The Hebrew Bible," says the narrative, "which I found among the old books in the house of Mr. Henry's widow, I brought with me to Philadelphia. Having there obtained one more complete, I transferred this to Mr. Belleville, then a student, who with a pen very neatly supplied the chapters which were wanting. Since the establishment of the Seminary, this very volume has come in as a present, and may be seen in the library. I found here also several books of Latin theology, but all much injured. Among them was Chemnitius's *Examen Concilii Tridentini*, from which I derived my first accurate knowledge of the Romish tenets.

The Rev. William Robinson, already mentioned as the first preacher in the Caldwell Settlement, came from the Presbytery of New Brunswick. He formed the purpose of visiting all the scattered Presbyterians in Virginia and North Carolina, and as many others as might be willing to hear. When he first arrived in these parts great joy was felt by the pious settlers. A stand, or tent (for both names were used), was made ready, and notice was sent round in all directions that a preacher had come from the North. "Among others one Austin, a half-breed Indian, was called upon. This man was notorious for violence of temper, a quarrelsome disposition, and shocking profaneness. His wife expressed some desire to go to the meeting, which he swore she should not do. But he nevertheless went himself, and not intending to hear any thing lay down on some leaves, near the outskirts of the large congregation. Here he was apparently slumbering, when the preacher announced his text, 'Awake thou that sleepest!' The words conveyed a barbed arrow to Austin's conscience. In a moment he started to his feet, and fixed his eyes on the speaker, gradually advancing towards the stand, until towards the close of the discourse he was standing near Mr. Robinson's feet, gazing into his face, while streams of tears ran down his tawny cheeks. After sermon he returned home in silence. He appeared to be in great agony of mind, so that his wife was in excessive terror. At night, instead of going early to bed, as was his custom, he walked to and fro before his house until midnight; when unable any longer to conceal his distress, he came into the house, and declared that he was an undone sinner, and that he had heard that day things which had never come to his ears before. For a day or two this distress continued, and then he obtained relief by as clear views of the Gospel as he had previously had of the Law. This profane and violent man was become as meek as a lamb. To this account I received some additions from old Mrs. Morton, of Little Roanoke Bridge, who said she had often conversed with Mr. Davies, Dr. Waddel, Dr. Smith, and many other eminent ministers, but with none from whom she received so much edification as from Austin. When persons were in distress about their salvation, it was common to send for him ; and in one case he had been summoned to go thirty miles into Lunenburg."

These journeys of Gospel service were not without their crosses. Mr. Alexander speaks of preaching at Tomahawk in Pittsylvania, while racked with toothache, and then riding seventeen miles in the rain, without an umbrella. At this time he had apppointments to preach almost every day for many weeks. In some places the avidity of the people to hear the Word was such, that he speaks of having preached "night and day for a good part of a week." He penetrated into Henry County, preaching on his way at Leatherwood, in the house where Patrick Henry lived several years after leaving Prince Edward. In his later years Dr. Alexander used to relate with much animation his meeting, in this county, with several pious but illiterate Baptist preachers, by whom he was very cordially received. They marvelled at the pocket Greek Testament in which he read, and invited him to a council of ministers. "The affair, however, was not ready for the trial, and Father Anthony, the pastor, went round to the clergy present, offering each one his small Bible, to go up into the pulpit and preach ; but all refused. Upon which the old gentleman said, 'Brethren, if none of you will consent, I will preach myself, and my text shall be concerning that wicked and slothful servant who would not do his

Lord's work. I know why you are all unwilling; it is because so few are out. But I tell you there are more here than you will be able to convert. The best sermon I ever preached was to two persons; and by the blessing of God they were both converted.' After this pithy little *concio ad clerum*, he approached one of them, saying, 'Brother Hall, preach;' and the other without a word of excuse ascended the pulpit, and gave us a very passable sermon."

The country into which his mission now took him is eminently picturesque. "Smith's River," to use his own words, "rises in the Blue Ridge, and its head spring is very near the head spring of New River, which falls into the Ohio, as Smith's does into the Roanoke. The mountain range at this place sinks low, and is cultivated on both sides nearly to the top. On the eastern side there is a beautiful cove of table-land, where a number of mountain streams come together and form Smith's River. The soil along these waters is exceedingly fertile, and the land lying low and sheltered on all sides by mountains, enjoys a very temperate climate in winter. Except over the Blue Ridge, there is but one way into the settlement which is practicable for wheels, and this winds so much that for twelve or thirteen miles there were no habitations on the road. Along this way I entered from old Mrs. Houston's, where I had lodged. The leading man in this settlement was one Squire Pilson. He had been a Presbyterian elder for eighteen years, without knowing any thing experimentally of religion, until Mr. Mitchell and Mr. Turner, from Bedford, made a preaching visit to this sequestered spot. He was then remarkably converted. He took every opportunity of making religious addresses to his neighbours, and was always greatly rejoiced to see any minister arrive, hoping that a blessing would attend his labours. Books were rare in this nook of the mountains. He had fallen upon Gregory's Legacy to his Daughter, and invited some of his neighbours to come to his house and hear it read. This meeting took place the day after my arrival. He read the book through, and in so doing shed many tears."

Dr. Alexander was often heard to describe the odd appearance of the women in this out-of-the-way place. Having little intercourse with the rest of the world, they cut their dresses after the exact pattern which their grandmothers brought with them. Mr. Pilson had been with his wagon to Petersburg, and had brought his daughter a beautiful piece of changeable silk. This she made up after the fashion aforesaid, with cuffs upon cuffs, reaching almost to the ground, a stomacher broad at the top and tapering downward to a point, with ribbons crossing each other very elaborately.

Among these secluded people he preached a number of times. But even here there were religious animosities, which operated as hinderances to the truth. One of the principal men was a bigoted opponent of Watts's Psalms. He had gone to hear the Reverend William Calhoon, and had contended with him on this subject; so that when the next itinerant missionary came, he would not go to hear him. From Smith's River Mr. Alexander went into Franklin County, where there was a small place of worship, called, it is believed, Wood's Meeting-House. But as he had now traversed all the counties included in his commission, and as the Virginia Synod was soon to meet, he prepared to go homeward. Mr. Calhoon, afterwards a connection by marriage, here became his companion. They crossed the Blue Ridge at one of its lowest passes. The record of these events takes notice of a mountain spring of uncommon beauty. "It boiled up in the midst of clear white sand, which it threw up in a jet, and covered a considerable circular space. The outlet was like a mill-tail, and within less than two hundred yards of the fountain, two mills were turned by the water." The travellers were very desirous to overtake Mr. Matthew Lyle, who, as they learned, was before them; they therefore pushed on to Fincastle. Here they met with an experience which is not without its instruction.

"We put up at the principal inn, and the people appeared civil enough, and the house was quiet; but we were scarcely seated before a great company of gentlefolks arrived from the Sweet Springs. The house was soon full of noise and confusion; for these persons affirmed that they had that day crossed no less than seven mountains; they were accordingly fatigued, hungry, and out of humour. In those days it was customary for the preachers in Virginia to have worship wherever they stopped for the night. On this occasion I was in favour of dispensing with the service, as we could hear the noise and profaneness of the new-comers. But Mr. Calhoon, always one of the most conscientious men, insisted that we should do our duty, and inquired of the host whether he would have any objection to our holding family worship with him and his guests. But no sooner was it mentioned to the visitors than the whole house was in uproar ; some calling for candles, and some for slippers, till the whole of a large company of gentlemen scampered off to bed, to escape the infliction of a prayer. The tavern-keeper, however, brought in his wife, and Mr. Calhoon, who officiated, vociferated so loudly, that no one in any part of the building, or of the neighbouring houses, could fail to hear him. I felt uncomfortable, and was led to think that this method of forcing prayers on irreligious people could do no good."

The analogy of the subject leads us here to introduce a couple of anecdotes, which he used to tell with much enjoyment ; we are able to give almost his very words, but the charm of his narrative must be supplied by those who remember the humorous vivacity of his manner. "In travelling to the north," said he, "I lodged in a large and pleasant public-house at Elkton. There was no company, and the host appeared serious and intelligent. We conversed all the evening on the subject of religion. I did not tell him that I was a clergyman, but supposed that he would infer it. When it drew near bed-time, I said to him, in as gentle a manner as possible, 'Have you any objection to having prayers in your house?' He was much confused, and after stammering a little, replied, 'You must excuse me—you must excuse me ; I live here in a public way—but I hope I do not forget the proper reflections when I lie down at night.' I was astonished, both at his refusal and his reasons ; and it was not until I was in bed that the true state of the case flashed upon my mind. Recalling the form of my request, I perceived that he thought I was asking him to officiate in family worship. When I went to the bar to pay my reckoning, he was reserved and distant; no doubt thinking me an impudent fellow, who wanted to set him a-praying in his own tavern."

The other story is a kindred one. "Once when I was going," said he, "from the Northern Neck to Richmond, the sun went down as I approached a tavern well known as the Piping Tree. Finding no company, and seeing many servants about the house, I felt it to be a duty to ask the privilege of praying in the family. The innkeeper was quite an old man, of hoary head, and yet as thoughtless of religion as a child. He said he belonged to the old English church; but that it had now gone down. He spoke of abundance of Baptists and Methodists in the neighbourhood; and against the latter his feelings were much aroused. I requested him to call in his family, saying I should like to pray with them. 'Bless you,' said he, 'I have no family; I have had the misfortune to have two wives, and have lost them both.' I replied that there were numerous servants, and that their souls were precious. 'To be sure—to be sure!' said he, and began to call in one and another, so that the room was soon pretty well filled. I said something to them, and offered a prayer. A large, fine-looking black man remained to take my boots and show me to bed. But before we left the room my host approached the negro with a threatening countenance, and began to berate him for being a Methodist. 'There,' said he, 'there now's a prayer for you! Did you ever hear a Methodist make a prayer like that? No, you black fool, you never did—you never did.' I was really afraid he would make an assault on my poor attendant, who however got off with me to my chamber, where I talked with him, and found him to all appearance an humble, pious man."

Returning to our narrative we have to record, that the next day they joined Mr. Lyle, and went to the house of the Rev. Edward Crawford, the only Presbyterian minister in Botetourt County. He was a native of the Valley, and a graduate of Princeton, in the year 1775. Thence they went to the Pastures, to the celebration of the Lord's Supper, in the church of the Rev. John Montgomery. This good man had a gift of pleasing eloquence, and was settled in a field of much extent, where, however, he seems to have had small success. This was the last stage of our young missionary before reaching his native place, where he arrived with greatly improved health, after a tour of six months, in which he had visited the counties of Amherst, Rockingham, Prince Edward, Charlotte, Lunenburg, Nottoway, Amelia, Dinwiddie, Prince George, Mecklenburg, Halifax, Pittsylvania, Patrick, Henry, Franklin, and Botetourt, in Virginia, and of Granville, Wake, and some others in North Carolina. After making his report to the Commission of Synod, he was directed to return at once to Lunenburg and Nottoway, with permission to spend a few weeks in Prince Edward. On arriving in Nottoway he found the appearances less favourable than on the previous visit. After passing a few weeks there, he therefore proceeded again along his former track, with events very similar to those which have been recited.

It has been already stated that the Rev. John Blair Smith had accepted a call to Philadelphia. Upon this the congregations of Briery and Cumberland, together with the Trustees of Hampden Sidney College, invited Mr. Graham to take charge of both the college and churches. The call was unsuccessful, and the attention of the people was at once turned to Mr. Alexander. All the Presbyterian congregations in that part of the county were vacant, namely, Cumberland, including the College, Briery, Buffalo, and Cub Creek, including Charlotte Court House. Mr. Lacy was a regular supply for the two first named. After consultation it was determined that all these churches should unite in calling two ministers, who should serve them in rotation. The number of preaching places was six, and the persons designated were Mr. Lacy and Mr. Alexander, who both signified their acceptance. They immediately entered on their laborious circuit, the field being not less than sixty miles in length and thirty in breadth, distances which they were to traverse on horseback.

Although Mr. Alexander was induced to take a pastoral charge so early, from a desire to pursue theological study, he now found that he must spend most of his days in the saddle. The plan was moreover found to be unsatisfactory to the people, who were too far removed from their pastors. It was therefore agreed that a division of the parochial diocese should take place; in pursuance of which, Mr. Alexander received for his share the churches of Briery and Cub Creek.

His residence was in the county of Charlotte, at the house of Major Edmund Read. And by a remarkable coincidence, one of his sons, when first settled in the ministry, dwelt in the same house thirty years afterwards, and enjoyed the hospitality of the same Christian lady, Paulina LeGrand, formerly Mrs. Read. Here, at the mansion still known as Retirement, about two miles from the Court House, Mr. Alexander resided three or four years. The lofty oaks under which he walked and sat still remain, among the noblest of their kind, and when we last saw the place, a small separate house used by him as a study, was yet standing.

Mrs. Read, afterwards Mrs. LeGrand, was widely known and honoured among Christians of every name in Virginia. It is probable that no house in the land ever opened its doors to more ministers of the Gospel. A whole Presbytery was sometimes sheltered under her roof. Her wealth was largely dispensed in acts of charity. Though of a desponding turn as to her own spiritual state, she was perpetually occupied with religious thoughts and employments, and was a devoted hearer of the word. Having been recently brought to the knowledge of evangelical truth, she was at this time full of zeal, and unwearied in her endeavours to second all Gospel labours. Her recollections of Mr. Alexander and his youthful ministry were lively and affectionate. She loved to expatiate on his ardent piety and acceptable preaching. From her representations, it would appear that at this period of his life, he was burning with desire to save the souls of men, and frequent in his personal addresses to all who were accessible on this all-important subject. While in her house, he redeemed much time for study, and though his discourses were extemporaneous, he sometimes wrote them out with much care after delivery. We have seen in the hands of Mrs. LeGrand, a manuscript volume containing nine sermons, thus written in a fair and beautiful hand. They were remarkable for the same simple perspicuity which characterized whatever proceeded from his pen. This volume, after some effort, we have not been able to recover, though we have a few scattered discourses of the same period. The date of his ordination and installation was May 5, 1795.

Some of the anxieties of a young pastor, overburdened by the greatness of an unaccustomed charge, may be discovered in the following narrative. "As the chief reason for the division just mentioned was the desire expressed by many, that they might have pastoral visits, and an opportunity of knowing their minister, I determined to begin a regular course of this kind. I accordingly went to Col. Charles Allen, the elder who lived furthest east, and gained his consent to go with me through that section of the congregation, beginning with old Mr. Redd's, on Bush River, as the remotest house. We arrived pretty early in the day. The old gentleman was out in a distant part of his estate, where the hands were clearing ground, but was sent for by his wife. Although we told her that we came not to dine, she gave no heed, but set all around her in motion to prepare viands. The chickens were chased in all directions, fires were kindled, closets were searched, and I soon found that we should scarcely be able to get away. After some time, the old gentleman came in ; but before he could be seen he must shave his beard and put on some clean clothes. We now repeated our wish to see the family collected, but the mistress and her maids were now in the act of preparing a fat turkey for the spit. For hours we had none to converse with but the master of the house, and conversation with this old tobacco planter was not easy. He seemed like one sitting on nettles. I informed him of the object of our visit.—'Very good.—Very glad to see the parson.—Live so far from church that I can seldom get there.' At length he thought he would use his privilege of asking a question. And that which he propounded was about the meaning of that passage, where it is said that seven women should take hold of one man. I was obliged to tell him that I did not know, intimating that the knowledge of this was not essential to salvation. 'Very true,' said he; 'but I have thought it might refer to our times, when so many men have been killed in the French Revolution, and in the consequent wars.' Late in the day the table was spread with an enormous dinner. By the time this was concluded, a thunder-storm burst over us, and detained us until near sunset. Thus a whole day was wasted in visiting one family, and that without the least benefit. I found that among a people so widely scattered, and unaccustomed to such a thing, no progress could be made in this way. I adopted the method of preaching in different parts of the bounds, in private houses. But here a mischievous custom existed. After worship was over, as many as thirty persons would sometimes stay to dine. This was by invitation of the family, and to some must have been a heavy tax. But the old

Virginians never count the cost of dinners, even when they give very little for the support of the Gospel."

The habits of preaching which marked the whole ministerial life of Dr. Alexander were formed during this period; and he may be considered the best witness as to his own methods. "While itinerating," says he, "I studied my sermons in my mind; and seldom preached without intense application of my thoughts to the subject beforehand. Texts of Scripture would often open to my view, and these I would seize upon for discourses. The necessity of thus composing in the evening and morning where I lodged, or as I rode along the way, proved a good discipline, as it accustomed me to close thinking and to going over and over the same train of thought. I was, however, often greatly disappointed and mortified; for when I had great freedom in premeditation I naturally expected the same in preaching. But this was sometimes far from being the case. On some occasions a text would strike my mind shortly before speaking, accompanied with a strong aversion to the subject proposed. I commonly ventured on the new topic, and in such cases almost always had better success than usual. Not unfrequently, while I was preaching, my subject would present itself in new lights, much more favourable than preceding ones, so that I have often changed my whole plan of treatment. Though the thought was often suggested to me, 'that is very good,' yet when I was done I was greatly humbled, and sometimes so discouraged as to feel as if I could never venture into the pulpit again. I have commonly felt that the people who admired my preaching were deceived."

From following a premeditated train of thought, he fell into a habit of fixing his eyes on the floor, which was a great hinderance. In later years no man could be more free from any such fault; as all his hearers will remember the piercing look with which he was accustomed to single out individuals in the congregation. In reference to this early period, he describes his own preaching as occupied much with Christian experience. When his text was figurative, he usually carried the imagery through the whole discourse. He allowed himself a license of accommodation which his later judgment disapproved. The parables were favourite themes. The excessive rapidity of his utterance sometimes exhausted his natural fervour before he had arrived at the application. But while he speaks thus humbly of his own performances, it is certain from the testimony of others, that his popularity was unbounded, and that he already ranked in public estimation among the first preachers in the country.

In his manuscript record he turns aside from time to time to speak of his private friends, some of whom were eminent in the church. Among these a place is justly given to the Rev. Samuel Brown, who was now one of his fellow-labourers. Mr. Brown was a native of Bedford, and a subject of the revival already mentioned. "He began his classical course after he was grown, and was hurried in his studies. But his original mind was constantly employed in thinking out difficult points in theology; so that by the time he was through his course he was in many respects a profound theologian. His religion was of the best kind; deep, lively, and Scriptural. He became early attached to the writings of President Edwards ; and this both encouraged and directed him in his investigations. Indeed he always appeared to me to have a mind much like that of Edwards ; not remarkable for quickness, but profound and sure, and free from the aberrations to which men of greater vivacity are subject. Whatever he read seemed to be merely the occasion of opening new trains of thought to his own mind. He possessed great ardour and generosity, and was susceptible of the strongest attachments of friendship ; indeed all his affections were of uncommon vigour. If he had possessed advantages of person and voice, he would have exceeded as a preacher all that I ever heard. Though he had a fine eye, deeply sunk in its orbit, and much benignity of countenance, his face was plain, with a slight distortion of the mouth, and a certain efflorescence over the cheek bones which was unsightly. Nevertheless he was a clear, original, powerful and often eloquent preacher. Even his voice became forcible and penetrating, when toned by strong feeling ; and he succeeded in communicating to his hearers the elevation of his sentiments and the benevolence of his feelings. Sometimes, indeed, when his mind was not roused, his preaching was indifferent ; but on occasions which called forth his powers, or when his pious feelings were in lively exercise, his performances were certainly among the best I ever heard. He excelled in apt illustration, and was thus able to render abstract truth plain to men of common minds.

"Mr. Brown accepted a call to the church of New Providence, west of the Blue Ridge. He had a turn for business, both mechanical and agricultural, and finding his family increasing around him he devoted himself with much ardour to secular pursuits; so that for some years his improvement was not equal to what might have been expected from his talents. As far as is known to me he never published any thing. His most elaborate trains of thought were studied without a word being committed to paper. Mr. Brown felt a deep interest in all that related to the welfare of his country, and therefore, without being a politician, entered warmly into those views which he believed to be dictated by sound policy. He patronized with zeal the College of Washington, of which he was a trustee at the time of his death.

"The close of this good man's life was somewhat remarkable. He had sold the farm on which he first settled, and bought another, larger and better situated, on which he was engaged in erecting a commodious dwelling-house. As he was dextrous in the use of tools, he often put to his hand to help forward the work. One day, some exertion being required to remove some timbers, he turned in, and while thus engaged suddenly complained of being sick, sunk down, and expired in a few minutes, in the very prime of life. His successor, the Rev. Mr. Morrison, married his only daughter. Five of his sons are now ministers of the Gospel, and the sixth has received a liberal education, and is I believe a communicant in the church."

The connection of Mr. Alexander with a number of congregations, sometimes as a temporary supply and sometimes as pastor, leads to so much confusion, that we prefer to throw together the several dates, as collected by the Rev

Dr. Foote. It appears, then, that he presented his testimonials to the Presbytery of Hanover, November 8, 1793, at which time he received calls to become collegiate pastor with Mr. Lacy of Cumberland, Briery, Buffalo and Cub Creek; which calls he did not accept. On October 22, 1794, he received calls from Cub Creek and Briery. He was ordained at Briery, June 7, 1794, and was dismissed from Cub Creek, April 11, 1797, and from Briery, November 16, 1798. He took his seat as President, May 31, 1797.

Being now established in a charge, it was natural for him to desire that some of his early associates should be near him. After a disappointment in regard to Mr. Brown's settling in Mecklenburg, he turned his attention to Mr. Matthew Houston, as a friend remarkable for his free and pleasant temper. Houston had been a student at the Liberty Hall Academy. He was frequently under religious concern, and amidst impressions received during the revival made a profession of his faith, though without pungent convictions or any strongly marked exercises. He had a vein of wit, and fell into levities which attracted attention. With moderate talents, but warm feelings, he spoke with fluency and acceptance. Houston received an appointment to be a missionary for six months in Mecklenburg. But his frivolity alienated the more serious of his people, and his animated and shallow preaching had little effect. He removed to Kentucky, where he became popular. About the year 1800, a great awakening spread like wildfire through Kentucky, and Houston being a combustible material was soon ignited. His mind became bewildered and deeply infected with the prevalent enthusiasm ; until, in 1801, he and his wife and a number of his people were so infatuated as to join the people called Shakers. Both church and congregation were hereby broken up. At first a society of these fanatics was formed in the immediate neighbourhood ; but they all soon removed to Ohio, where for many years he was the presiding elder at Lebanon. When he was just seventy years of age, he sent to Dr. Alexander, then of Princeton, a copy of the Shaker Testimony, accompanied with a short note, in which he declared that since uniting with this people, he had enjoyed uninterrupted happiness. Of his subsequent history nothing is known.

In the occasional retirement of his rural study, the young pastor endeavoured to make up for lost hours. Most of the books which he had read up to this time, were either borrowed or picked up at the places where he lodged ; but their rarity led him to devour rather than to peruse them. Sometimes he found in unexpected places scarce volumes, which he continued to read while he was in those neighbourhoods. This pursuit of knowledge under difficulties left its mark on his mind. We remember to have heard him recite events from the History of the Arabians, which he had not opened for sixty years. At the house of an old German on James River, he first met with Stillingfleet's Irenicum, which he read with great avidity, and with a valuable accession to his knowledge on controverted points in church polity. The main principles of that work he retained through life as his own ; though the distinguished author is said to have abandoned them. Though he preached in three large counties, he continued to redeem some time for study, and laid out a small sum for books. Among these early purchases, he mentions the works of Reid and Stewart, so far as then published.

He was further stimulated to laborious investigation by the alarming prevalence of infidelity in his native State. Paine's Age of Reason was widely circulated and much read by the young men of the country. "Indeed," says he, "most of our educated and professional young men became Deists, or worse. Young lawyers openly reviled religion, and boldly attacked its serious professors. Many of those who entertained such opinions occasionally attended public worship; and in these circumstances it was needful to study the evidences of Christianity with care. My mind was so occupied with the subject, that I often preached on it. My trial-sermon for ordination was entirely on this topic; the text being John xvii. 17, 'Thy Word is Truth.' I also undertook an answer to Paine; but his Second Part was soon published, and then Watson's Apology, which I considered far better than any thing I could produce. Murray's Evidences appeared to me popular and convincing; but I have since never seen a copy."

"It was perhaps an advantage to me that my collection of books was small, and that my attention was devoted to few subjects. On a copy of the British Encyclopedia I seized with much avidity, and thus learned something about the progress of the Sciences. My thirst for knowledge was always great, and its pursuit was never a weariness to me." It is not improper to add, that throughout his whole life he retained a lively interest in mathematical and physical investigation; delighting in the severe methods of the old geometry, and keeping himself acquainted with the course of discovery to an extent which was surprising to all around him.

As these pages, if read at all, will be read by persons living in the very region where the scenes here described are laid, we have thought it expedient to introduce notices of families and individuals who were active in the promotion of religion, and who "addicted themselves unto the ministry of the saints." Among other good results it will serve to show how extensively the blessings of grace continued to descend in the lineage of the righteous. The large and Christian connection of the Venables has been already mentioned. To these we must now add the Allens. They lived chiefly in Cumberland, but also in Prince Edward, and many of them were parishioners of Mr. Alexander. The root from which they all proceeded was (like various eminent persons named in our memoir) a member of Mr. Davies's church in Hanover, and was converted, it is thought, under the missionary labours of Whitefield. Mr. Alexander heard from an eye-witness that while Whitefield was preaching, Mr. Allen fell at full length, as suddenly as if shot through the heart, and lay for the remainder of the evening as one dead. He had four sons. "James, the eldest," says the manuscript, "was one of the most venerable men I ever saw. When I came to the country he was above seventy years of age, and lived alone. He was more than six feet in height, slender and pale, but of benignant countenance, and with hair white as snow. The most of his time he spent over a large family Bible, which lay open before him on a small table, and which he often moistened with his tears. His son, also named James, was, before his conversion, irascible in the extreme, and often engaged in broils, being of great muscular power. On one occasion he came home in a rage, threatening to flog a man who had said that his father was an old hypocrite. But the father said meekly, 'Jemmy, my son, be not angry about it ; for I assure you it is the very thing I have been suspecting of myself for twenty years.' Besides James, he had two sons, Benjamin and Charles, who were elders in the Cumberland church, while I was minister there, as was also their uncle Benjamin Allen. His brother Daniel was the father of the Rev. Cary Allen. James Allen, the younger, died by the slow torture of a cancer, which began in the middle of the lower lip. But though naturally a man of strong passions and unquiet temper, he was now as patient as a lamb, and edified all who came to see him by his heavenly conversation."

The particulars which he gives of the Morton family afford glimpses of a state of society now existing only on the frontiers. The founder of this family, called Little Joe, to distinguish him from another of the same name, was a bold and enterprising pioneer, a staunch hunter, and employed by the Randolphs and others in exploring the country not yet inhabited, in order that they might lay their warrants on the good lands and have them surveyed. "I believe that all the fine lands on Staunton River were first discovered by him." He was skilful in catching wild horses, which abounded in the unsettled parts of the country. They were commonly taken in pens, into which they were decoyed; and several streams in that region have hence derived the name of *Horsepen*.

Joseph Morton, with a young wife, built a log cabin near Little Roanoke Bridge. Mrs. Morton, when an aged widow, informed Mr. Alexander that for several years she had not a neighbour nearer than thirty miles, and that during the greater part of the time her husband was absent, and she and her young children were alone in the forest. Such was Morton's knowledge of woodcraft, that he could pursue a horse for any distance by means of his tracks, and this even if the road was crossed by thousands of other tracks. On one occasion he was sent for to follow a horse-thief, which he did for more than a hundred miles, and with success, although the fugitive had taken all imaginable means of concealing his course. This account was given by his son, Col. William Morton, a man of undoubted veracity. Joseph Morton left his sons possessed of good estates.

"His character was remarkable in several respects. He possessed a most unshaken firmness, and rigidly adhered to what appeared to him to be duty. He was brought up an Episcopalian; but the Rev. Mr. Davies, in one of his preaching tours, was taken to his house by John Morton, a young cousin. Being a rigid Churchman he was reluctant to consent, but after some consultation with his wife, he agreed that the newlight preacher should come. Mr. Davies, by the dignity and suavity of his manners, made such an impression on both, that when he departed they accompanied him to Cumberland, to the administration of the sacrament. His wife had become deeply concerned from the first evening, and was anxious about partaking of the Lord's Supper. But she was afraid her husband would not agree to it. She however broke the matter to him on Sunday morning. Though surprised, he told her to do as she thought proper. In the intermission after the 'action sermon,' he called out Mr. Davies, and told him he wished to join in communion with the church. Mr. Davies, after a little conversation, gave him a token of admission, and the husband and wife went together to the Lord's Table. From this pair sprang a large Presbyterian population, spread far and wide through Prince Edward and Charlotte counties. Not long after, he and a number of others united in building a house of worship at Briery; and in a short time they obtained one half the labours of the Rev. Robert Henry. When there was no sermon, Mr. Morton regularly attended, read a discourse, and catechised the children. So consistent was his character, and so beneficial his influence, that he was a blessing to the whole community in which he lived. As a justice of the peace, he exerted a salutary influence in suppressing profaneness and other immorality. Being visited by one of his wealthy correspondents from below, who was exceedingly profane, Morton gave him warning, that as a magistrate he was bound to put into execution the law against swearing. The other disregarded his threats, and was fined accordingly. I never saw him, but I have been in no neighbourhood where any man had left on the minds of all a stronger impression of his integrity and piety. Mrs. Morton lived to the age of ninety-two, and died some time after I was settled in Charlotte. She was a very pious woman, whose house was always open for ministers and religious people, and for the preaching of the Gospel."*

From John Morton, named above as the guide of Mr. Davies, also a numerous progeny descended. Of his sons, one of the same name spent his life chiefly in France. The eldest, Maj. James Morton, was a revolutionary officer, and long an active elder in the church at Prince Edward. The Rev. Dr. John H. Rice married his daughter, a lady of known Christian excellence, who still survives.

The County of Charlotte, where Mr. Alexander now laboured, is remarkable for having been the residence of two very celebrated orators, belonging to two successive periods in our national history; we mean Patrick Henry and John Randolph of Roanoke. During Mr. Alexander's earliest visit, he was invited to accompany his preceptor, Mr. Graham, in a visit to Mr. Henry, who then lived in Prince Edward, seven or eight miles from the college; but the plan was disappointed by the straying of the horses. Mr. Graham went alone, and spent a day with the old patriot, to his own great satisfaction; for they were of one mind in politics, both being exceedingly opposed to the Constitution which had that year been adopted. At a later

* Josiah, the oldest son, was the father of Col. William Lewis Morton. William, the second son, was for many years presiding judge of the county court of Charlotte. The third was oddly enough named Little Joe. The fourth was Col. Jacob Morton. Three of these were ruling elders in the Briery church.

period, however, he was brought into nearer acquaintance with Henry's powers. The account of this in his own words, as published in 1850, we can by no means omit.

"From my earliest childhood I had been accustomed to hear of the eloquence of Patrick Henry. On this subject there existed but one opinion in the country. The power of his eloquence was felt equally by the learned and the unlearned. No man who ever heard him speak, on any important occasion, could fail to admit his uncommon power over the minds of his hearers. The occasions on which he made his greatest efforts have been recorded by Mr. Wirt, in his Life of Henry. What I propose in this brief article is to mention only what I observed myself more than half a century ago.

"Being then a young man, just entering on a profession in which good speaking was very important, it was natural for me to observe the oratory of celebrated men. I was anxious to ascertain the true secret of their power; or what it was which enabled them to sway the minds of hearers, almost at their will.

"In executing a mission from the Synod of Virginia, in the year 1794, I had to pass through the county of Prince Edward, where Mr. Henry then resided. Understanding that he was to appear before the Circuit Court, which met in that county, in defence of three men charged with murder, I determined to seize the opportunity of observing for myself the eloquence of this extraordinary orator.

"It was with some difficulty I obtained a seat in front of the bar, where I could have a full view of the speaker, as well as hear him distinctly. But I had to submit to a severe penance in gratifying my curiosity; for the whole day was occupied with the examination of witnesses, in which Mr. Henry was aided by two other lawyers.

"In person, Mr. Henry was lean rather than fleshy. He was rather above than below the common height, but had a stoop in the shoulders which prevented him from appearing as tall as he really was. In his moments of animation, he had the habit of straightening his frame, and adding to his apparent stature. He wore a brown wig, which exhibited no indication of any great care in the dressing. Over his shoulders he wore a brown camlet cloak. Under this his clothing was black, something the worse for wear. The expression of his countenance was that of solemnity and deep earnestness. His mind appeared to be always absorbed in what, for the time, occupied his attention. His forehead was high and spacious, and the skin of his face more than usually wrinkled for a man of fifty. His eyes were small and deeply set in his head, but were of a bright blue colour, and twinkled much in their sockets. In short, Mr. Henry's appearance had nothing very remarkable, as he sat at rest. You might readily have taken him for a common planter, who cared very little about his personal appearance. In his manners he was uniformly respectful and courteous. Candles were brought into the court house, when the examination of the witnesses closed; and the judges put it to the option of the bar whether they would go on with the argument that night or adjourn until the next day. Paul Carrington, jun., the attorney for the state, a man of large size and uncommon dignity of person and manner, and also an accomplished lawyer, professed his willingness to proceed immediately, while the testimony was fresh in the minds of all. Now for the first time I heard Mr. Henry make any thing of a speech; and though it was short, it satisfied me of one thing, which I had particularly desired to have decided; namely, whether like a player he merely assumed the appearance of feeling. His manner of addressing the court was profoundly respectful. He would be willing to proceed with the trial, but, said he, 'My heart is so oppressed with the weight of responsibility which rests upon me, having the lives of three fellow citizens depending, probably, on the exertions which I may be able to make in their behalf, (here he turned to the prisoners behind him,) that I do not feel able to proceed to-night. I hope the court will indulge me, and postpone the trial till the morning.' The impression made by these few words was such as I assure myself no one can ever conceive by seeing them in print. In the countenance, action and intonation of the speaker, there was expressed such an intensity of feeling that all my doubts were dispelled; never again did I question whether Henry felt, or only acted a feeling. Indeed, I experienced an instantaneous sympathy with him in the emotions which he expressed; and I have no doubt the same sympathy was felt by every hearer.

"As a matter of course the proceedings were deferred till the next morning. I was early at my post; the judges were soon on the bench, and the prisoners at the bar. Mr. Carrington, afterwards Judge Carrington, opened with a clear and dignified speech, and presented the evidence to the jury. Every thing seemed perfectly plain. Two brothers and a brother-in-law met two other persons in pursuit of a slave, supposed to be harboured by the brothers. After some altercation and mutual abuse, one of the brothers, whose name was John Ford, raised a loaded gun which he was carrying, and presenting it to the breast of one of the other pair, shot him dead, in open day. There was no doubt about the fact. Indeed, it was not denied. There had been no other provocation than opprobrious words. It is presumed that the opinion of every juror was made up from merely hearing the testimony; as Tom Harvey, the principal witness, who was acting as constable on the occasion, appeared to be a respectable man. For the clearer understanding of what follows, it must be observed that said constable, in order to distinguish him from another of the name, was commonly called 'Butterwood Harvey;' as he lived on Butterwood Creek.

"Mr. Henry, it is believed, understanding that the people were on their guard against his faculty of moving the passions and through them influencing the judgment, did not resort to the pathetic, as much as was his usual practice in criminal cases. His main object appeared to be, throughout, to cast discredit on the testimony of Tom Harvey. This he attempted by causing the law respecting riots to be read by one of his assistants. It appeared in evidence, that Tom Harvey had taken upon him to act as constable, without being in commission; and that with a posse of men he had entered the house of one of the Fords in search of the negro, and had put Mrs. Ford, in her husband's absence, into a great terror, while she was in a very delicate condition, near the time of her confinement.

"As he descanted on the evidence, he would often turn to Tom Harvey—a large bold-looking man—and with the most sarcastic look would call him by some name of contempt; 'this Butterwood Tom Harvey,' 'this *would-be-constable*,' &c. By such expressions, his contempt for the man was communicated to the hearers. I own I felt it gaining on me, in spite of my better judgment; so that before he was done, the impression was strong on my mind that Butterwood Harvey was undeserving of the smallest credit. This impression, however, I found I could counteract the moment I had time for reflection. The only part of the speech in which he manifested his power of touching the feelings strongly, was where he dwelt on the irruption of the company into Ford's house, in circumstances so perilous to the solitary wife. This appeal to the sensibility of husbands—and he knew that all the jury stood in this relation—was overwhelming. If the verdict could have been rendered immediately after this burst of the pathetic, every man, at least every husband in the house, would have been for rejecting Harvey's testimony; if not for hanging him forthwith. It was fortunate that the illusion of such eloquence is transient, and is soon dissipated by the exercise of sober reason. I confess, however, that nothing which I then heard so convinced me of the advocate's power, as the speech of five minutes, which he made when he requested that the trial might be adjourned till the next day.

"In addition to this, it so happened that I heard the last public speech which Mr. Henry ever made. It was delivered at Charlotte, from the portico of the court-house, to an assembly in the open air. In the American edition of the New Edinburgh Encyclopedia an account of this speech and its effects is given, so charged with exaggeration as to be grossly incorrect. There is more truth in the statements contained in Mr. Wirt's memoir. In point of fact, the performance had little impression beyond the transient pleasure afforded to the friends of the administration, and the pain inflicted on the Anti-federalists, his former political friends. Mr. Henry came to the place with difficulty, and was plainly destitute of his wonted vigour and commanding power. The speech was nevertheless a noble effort, such as could have proceeded from none but a patriotic heart. In the course of his remarks, Mr. Henry (as is correctly stated by Mr. Wirt) after speaking of Washington at the head of a numerous and well appointed army, exclaimed, 'And where is the citizen of America who will dare to lift his hand against the father of his country, to point a weapon at the breast of the man who had so often led them to battle and victory?' An intoxicated man cried, 'I could.' 'No,' answered Mr. Henry, rising aloft in all his majesty, and in a voice most solemn and penetrating, 'No; you durst not do it; in such a parricidal attempt, the steel would drop from your nerveless arm!'

"Mr. Henry was followed by a speaker afterwards noted in our national history; I mean John Randolph of Roanoke; but the aged orator did not remain to witness the debut of his young opponent. Randolph began by saying that he had admired that man more than any on whom the sun had shone, but that now he was constrained to differ from him *toto coelo.* But Randolph was suffering with the hoarseness of a cold, and could scarcely utter an audible sentence. All that is alleged in the Encyclopedia, about Henry's returning to the platform and replying with extraordinary effect, is pure fabrication. The fact is as above stated. Henry retired to the house, as if unwilling to listen, and requested a friend to report to him any thing which might require an answer. But he made no reply, nor did he again present himself to the people. I was amidst the crowd, standing near to Creed Taylor, then an eminent lawyer, and afterwards a judge; who made remarks to those around him, during the speech, declaring among other things that the old man was in his dotage. It is much to be regretted that a statement so untrue should be perpetuated in a work of such value and celebrity.

"Patrick Henry had several sisters, with one of whom, the wife of Colonel Meredith of New Glasgow, I was acquainted. Mrs. Meredith was not only a woman of unfeigned piety, but was in my judgment as eloquent as her brother; nor have I ever met with a lady who equalled her in powers of conversation.

"At an early period of my ministry, it became my duty to preach the funeral sermon of Mr. James Hunt, the father of the late Rev. James Hunt, of Montgomery County, Maryland. The death occurred at the house of a son who lived on Staunton River: Mr. Henry's residence, Red Hill, was a few miles distant, on the same river. Having been long a friend of the deceased, Mr. Henry attended the funeral, and remained to dine with the company; on which occasion I was introduced to him by Captain William Craighead, who had been an elder in President Davies's church. These gentlemen had been friends in Hanover, but had not met for many years. The two old gentlemen met with great cordiality, and seemed to have high enjoyment in talking of old times.

"On the retrospect of so many years I may be permitted to express my views of the extraordinary effects of Henry's eloquence. The remark is obvious, in application not only to him but to all great orators, that we cannot ascribe these effects merely to their intellectual conceptions, or their cogent reasonings, however great: these conceptions and reasons, when put on paper, often fall dead. They are often inferior to the arguments of men whose utterances have little impression. It has indeed been often said, both of Whitefield and of Henry, that their discourses, when reduced to writing, show poorly by the side of the productions of men who are no orators. Let me illustrate this, by the testimony of one whom I remember as a friend of my youth. General Posey was a revolutionary officer, who was second in command, under Wayne, in the expedition against the Indians; a man of observation and cool judgment. He was in attendance on the debates of that famous convention in which there were so many displays of deliberative eloquence. He assured me, that after the hearing of Patrick Henry's most celebrated speech in that body, he felt himself as fully persuaded that the Constitution if adopted would be our ruin, as of his own existence Yet subsequent reflection restored his former judgment, and his well considered opinion resumed its place.

"The power of Henry's eloquence was due, first, to the greatness of his emotion and passion, accompanied with a versatility which enabled him to assume at once any emotion or passion which was suited to his ends. Not less indispensable, secondly, was a matchless perfection of the organs of expression, including the entire apparatus of voice, intonation, pause, gesture, attitude, and indescribable play of countenance. In no instance did he ever indulge in an expression that was not instantly recognised as nature itself; yet some of his penetrating and subduing tones were absolutely peculiar, and as inimitable as they were indescribable. These were felt by every hearer, in all their force. His mightiest feelings were sometimes indicated and communicated by a long pause, aided by an eloquent aspect, and some significant use of his finger. The sympathy between mind and mind is inexplicable. Where the channels of communication are open, the faculty of revealing inward passion great, and the expression of it sudden and visible, the effects are extraordinary. Let these shocks of influence be repeated again and again, and all other opinions and ideas are for the moment absorbed or excluded; the whole mind is brought into unison with that of the speaker; and the spell-bound listener, till the cause ceases, is under an entire fascination. Then perhaps the charm ceases, upon reflection, and the infatuated hearer resumes his ordinary state.

"Patrick Henry of course owed much to his singular insight into the feelings of the common mind. In great cases, he scanned his jury, and formed his mental estimate ; on this basis he founded his appeals to their predilections and character. It is what other advocates do, in a lesser degree. When he knew that there were conscientious or religious men among the jury, he would most solemnly address himself to their sense of right, and would adroitly bring in Scriptural citations. If this handle was not offered, he would lay bare the sensibility of patriotism. Thus it was, when he succeeded in rescuing the man who had deliberately shot down a neighbour; who moreover lay under the odious suspicion of being a tory, and who was proved to have refused supplies to a brigade of the American army.

"A learned and intelligent gentleman stated to me that he once heard Mr. Henry's defence of a man arraigned for a capital crime. So clear and abundant was the evidence, that my informant was unable to conceive any grounds of defence, especially after the law had been ably placed before the jury by the attorney for the commonwealth. For a long time after Henry began, he never once adverted to the merits of the case or the arguments of the prosecution, but went off into a most captivating and discursive oration on general topics, expressing opinions in perfect accordance with those of his hearers ; until having fully succeeded in obliterating every impression of his opponent's speech, he obliquely approached the subject, and as occasion was offered dealt forth strokes which seemed to tell upon the minds of the jury. In this case, it should be added, the force of truth prevailed over the art of the consummate orator."*

* Princeton Magazine, 1850.

From manuscript authorities we add a few traits. At first sight Mr. Henry's appearance struck him as being not unlike that of an old clergyman. There was a peculiar earnestness in all that he said, and his small gray eyes seemed to be in perpetual motion. "The only time," says he, "that I ever was in Mr. Henry's company, was a few months before his decease, when I was sent for to preach at the funeral of old Mr. James Hunt, the father of the Rev. James Hunt. This man had been brought up in the same neighbourhood with Mr. Henry, and resided near him during his last years. Old Captain Craighead had late in life married a daughter of Mr. Hunt, and it was he who introduced me. I had, however, little conversation with him. After the sermon he asked Capt. Craighead what we meant by talking so much about grace, and added that he did not understand it. He was, however, a firm believer in Divine Revelation, and spent much of his time during his retirement in reading the works of such authors as Sherlock and Tillotson ; and he warmly recommended religion to those young friends who came to see him." Some years ago we obtained from the Clerk's Office of Charlotte County a certified copy of an extract from his last will and testament, which is in these remarkable words : "This is all the inheritance I can give to my dear family. The Religion of Christ can give them one which will make them rich indeed."

The College of Hampden Sidney derived its name from two great English patriots. It was founded for the purpose of raising up an evangelical ministry. As early as 1771, in consequence of representations made by Mr. Samuel Stanhope Smith, afterwards President Smith, of New Jersey, the Presbytery of Hanover began to consider the subject of education. The first attempts were humble, and did not contemplate any thing so elevated as a college. One or two schools, under presbyterial direction, were during the following years taught in different places, till at length in 1773 it was determined to open a seminary in the county of Prince Edward. Mr. Samuel Stanhope Smith was appointed the rector, and became at the same time pastor of the congregations of Prince Edward and Cumberland. Land was given and moneys were raised for books and apparatus. The revolutionary troubles greatly impeded, but did not utterly hinder the progress of the institution. In 1776, Mr. John Blair Smith, so often mentioned in this narrative, became the assistant of his brother, and there were other instructors. After some time Mr. John B. Smith became principal of the seminary, as well as pastor of the churches of Cumberland and Briery. Mr. Smith was chosen captain of a company of the students, about sixty-five in number, and Mr. David Witherspoon, his assistant, was first lieutenant. The charter of Hampden Sidney as a College was obtained in 1783, and its first literary degrees were conferred in 1786. In 1788, on the retirement of President Smith from the active duties of the college, the Rev. Drury Lacy was made Vice President. In September, 1789, Mr. Smith resigned his presidentship, and for several years efforts were made, without success, to obtain the services of the Rev. William Graham. "The attention of the Board"—we here quote from Dr. Foote—"was then turned to the Rev. Archibald Alexander, a member of Lexington Presbytery, recently licensed to preach the gospel, a pupil of Mr. Graham. He was invited to unite with Mr. Lacy in the government and instruction of the College, with equal authority and emolument."

We are happily able to give Mr. Alexander's own statement with regard to this important step in his life. "In this retirement," says he, "I spent a few years, when the Trustees of Hampden Sidney elected me to the office of President. The condition of the college was as low as it could be to have an existence. Mr. Lacy set up a school in the vicinity, which was attended by most of the youth who had been at the college. But the Trustees were determined to resuscitate it if possible. At first I was very averse to an undertaking of so little promise. But at length I was persuaded to make the trial; and the consideration had much weight with me, that if I did not succeed, I should leave matters no worse than they were, but that if I had success, I might be doing some public good. I accordingly consented in the autumn to go to the college in the following spring; and immediately applied myself to the studies connected with my office.

"John H. Rice, then about the age of twenty, had been engaged in teaching below Richmond, and not being satisfied to remain there, was employed by the Trustees of the College to take charge of the few students who were preparing for entrance. During the winter I visited him frequently, and conversed with him respecting the enterprise. I soon found that he was no common man. His appetite for books was rabid. Having access now to the college library, which, though small, contained some well selected works, he was like a hungry ox when let into a rich pasture. Before he had half finished one volume, he would be forcibly drawn to another, and thus he roamed from book to book, and from shelf to shelf. I found him also to be fond of composition. He read to me many of his pieces, most of which were seasoned with no little sarcasm. He had a peculiar disposition to satirize the fashions of the times, without any thought of publication; but it was customary with him to give his essays to the students to be pronounced as orations."

It is scarcely needful to add, that the person here named is the same who in later years, as the Rev. Dr. Rice, filled so large a space in public observation, as a preacher, an author, a controvertist, and a theological professor. During all his life he was one of the most intimate and cherished friends of Dr. Alexander.

The name of Rice suggests that of Speece, another ornament of the Virginian church, and likewise closely allied to the subject of these memoirs. Conrad Speece was the son of a German who lived in Campbell County, some miles east of New London. The grandmother of Conrad, living at this town, used to receive frequent visits from the boy, whose education had been neglected, but who had a turn for music, so as to play on several instruments. On one occasion the boy composed a humorous description of some Christmas sports which had taken place at the village tavern. The verses were shown to a number of persons and were thought extraordinary for a boy of thirteen. At that time Mr. Edward Graham, afterwards the brother-in-law of Dr. Alexander, taught a school in New London. By his encouragement young Speece turned his attention to regular study. He was large for his age, and had a rough and uncultivated appearance. But he learned readily whatever was assigned to him. He did not, however, commit the Latin Grammar to memory as speedily as another boy in the school; but as soon as he began to read, and to apply the rules to the structure of language, he seemed to have awaked to a new sense, and began to study with extraordinary delight. He soon finished the first book, leaving all his classmates far behind. Rising to a higher class he distanced them in like manner, until at the year's close he stood at the head of the school, and was able to translate Cicero and Horace with more than common accuracy and even elegance. Nothing could now cool his ardour of desire for a liberal education. After struggling through many difficulties he at length realized his hopes and entered Washington College in Lexington, where he took his degrees with high distinction, and became one of its tutors.

"I first knew him," says Dr. Alexander, "when on a visit to my friends. On leaving college he returned home and began to read law, but his health seemed so much impaired that for a while he gave up study and travelled on foot to the Sweet Springs, where he spent the usual season of attendance, bathing and drinking the waters. Another teacher being needed at Hampden Sidney, I turned my attention to Speece, who had now returned home, whither I went to seek him out. I found the dwelling of his father in a rough country, at a romantic and sequestered spot. Conrad was at home, in coarse farmer's dress, and seemed pleased with the idea of spending his life in husbandry. But after deliberating upon my proposals, he agreed to come to us at the commencement of the next session. He came accordingly, and he, John H. Rice, and I, performed the duty of professors without the title."

The intimacy of these three young men was so close and affectionate, that we seize with avidity on any estimate which any one of them formed of the others; and we therefore introduce here, by a little anticipation, some remarks of Dr. Rice, in which he sketches his two associates. "The eldest of them" (whom he calls Paulinus, but who is evidently Mr. Alexander,) "had been a preacher ten or fifteen years, is endowed with faculties of the highest kind, and has cultivated them with great assiduity. No man of his age has greater extent or variety of information. His powers are peculiarly fitted for the investigation of truth. With a sound judgment, a vigorous understanding, a quick perception, a great compass of thought, he has the capacity of holding his mind in suspense, until a subject be viewed in all its bearings and relations, and until the rays of evidence, however widely they are dissipated, are all brought to a focus on the point under investigation. Possessing such intellectual powers as these, he is animated with a love of truth, and thirst after knowledge, which prompt to unwearied diligence in research, and unremitting application to study. His knowledge, then, must be considerable. His taste is refined, his imagination rich in imagery, his elocution copious, and his trains of reasoning are close and logical; his eye sparkles with intelligence, and his voice is as melodious as the notes of the nightingale. But in addition to all these excellencies, he is remarkably modest; it is impossible for you to be in his company without seeing his superiority, and yet such is his modesty, that it gives you no pain to acknowledge it."

"The second" (Philander, or Mr. Speece,) "is a younger man and a younger minister. He also possesses real genius. The most remarkable quality of his mind is vigour; in argumentation he resembles one of the Ajaxes of Homer, with his mace of iron, at every vibration overthrowing whole troops of Trojans. His conception is very clear; and of course he is perspicuous, precise and fluent in elocution. From the comparison just used, however, it is not to be supposed that there is any thing of coarseness in his mind. Far from it. His imagination is delicate, and his taste refined." He adds, "The piety of both these gentlemen is warm and unaffected. They have hearts formed for friendship. Possessing the highest talents, and the best means of information that Virginia could afford, they would have been capable of filling any office, and might have risen to the first eminence in the State. But such was their devotion to the cause of Christ, that they left all and followed him." *

To return to our narrative; when Mr. Alexander went to the college he resigned his more distant charge, and divided his preaching between the congregations of Briery and Prince

* Virginia Religious Magazine, Vol. iii. pp. 170, 171. Maxwell's Life of Rice, pp. 39, 40.

Edward. His friends in Charlotte, and especially Mrs. Read, were much opposed to his removal. On going to Hampden Sidney he had possession of the president's house, but usually took his meals at the common table. At no time of his life did he feel more keenly the stimulus to application, and he declared in later years that whatever accuracy he possessed in classical and scientific knowledge was acquired during such periods, under the spur of necessity. He began by insisting on the utmost exactness, and took pleasure in drilling the young men in those rudiments which they had neglected. The number increased rapidly, but there were as yet no regular classes, and very few took a complete course. Yet all the branches then common in colleges were taught, and some of them thoroughly; the studies being arranged in some degree after the method then prevalent at Princeton.

It is to be regretted that of that very interesting period of his life, we have but slender memorials from his own pen. He was earnestly engaged, even beyond his strength, in accumulating and systematizing stores of knowledge; and in conscientiously endeavouring to lift up an institution which had sunk almost to the lowest point. At the same time he was laborious in preaching the Gospel, not only to his two congregations, but, according to the custom of the country, in many places on every side. To this part of his duties he always recurred with most pleasure in the memory of later years. Though he had under his care many promising and interesting pupils, some of whom live to remember his kind instructions, he never felt himself completely at home at the head of a college. There was, however, much solace in the cordial intimacies of a cultivated and Christian people, who have been and still are noted, even among Virginians, for the warmth of their attachments and the largeness of their hospitality. These years, spent amidst many anxieties, were, nevertheless, profitable in no common degree, in the corroboration of principles, and the moulding of character.

The history of any human mind is incomplete unless it affords us some knowledge of inward struggles in regard to the acquisition of truth and the performance of duty. One of these crises occurred in the life of Mr. Alexander, while he was president of the college; and we must interrupt the regular narrative, to give some account of his difficulties respecting Baptism. His own record of this is so extensive that it might even form a separate publication. For our present purposes we must endeavour to afford an honest representation of the whole, in the way partly of abridgment and partly of extract.

"About this time," says he, probably indicating some part of the years 1797, 1798, or 1799, "I fell into doubt respecting the authority of infant baptism. The origin of these doubts was in too rigid notions as to the purity of the church, with a belief that receiving infants had a corrupting tendency. I communicated my doubts very freely to my friend Mr. Lyle, and to Mr. Speece, and found that they had both been troubled by the same. We talked much privately on the subject, and often conversed with others in hope of getting some new light. At length Mr. Lyle and I determined to give up the practice of baptizing infants, until we should receive more light. This determination we publicly communicated to our people, and left them to take such measures as they deemed expedient; but they seemed willing to await the issue. We also communicated to the Presbytery the state of our minds, and left them to do what seemed good in the case; but as they believed that we were sincerely desirous of arriving at the truth, they took no steps, and I believe made no record.

"Things remained in this posture for more than a year. During this time I read much on both sides, and carried on a lengthened correspondence, particularly with Dr. Hoge. Two considerations kept me back from joining the Baptists. The first was that the universal prevalence of infant baptism, as early as the fourth and fifth centuries, was unaccountable on the supposition that no such practice existed in the times of the apostles. The other was, that if the Baptists are right, they are the only Christian church on earth, and all other denominations are out of the visible church. Besides, I could not see how they could ever obtain a valid baptism."

Mr. Speece was, however, more precipitate, and having concluded that the Antipedobaptists were right, strongly urged his friends to join him in going over. They endeavoured to retard his progress, but his mind was naturally inclined to peremptory conclusions, and impatient of dubiety. One Sunday morning, therefore, he went to a Baptist meeting, held within two miles of the college, and without having given notice of his intention, was there re-baptized by immersion. On his return he seemed much satisfied with what he had done. The church soon licensed him to preach, and he began to go about the country with his Baptist brethren. "He attended an Association in Cumberland, where he preached; some of the ministers informed him that he aimed well, but that if he would do execution he 'must put to more powder.' They gloried much in their acquisition, and the day was often fixed by public rumour for my baptism and that of Mr. Lyle. It was evident, however, that Mr. Speece was not perfectly happy in his new connection; yet he said nothing."

To those who know the character of Dr. Alexander's mind, his reverence for Scripture as the sole authority, and his extraordinary acquaintance with the various literature of this controversy, it is scarcely necessary to say, that his ultimate determination was founded exclusively on the word of God. Historical and patristical arguments cleared away prejudices, and brought him with an unbiassed judgment to the record. None know better than those Baptists, who were once his pupils, how largely and thoroughly he investigated the purely biblical sources of opinion on this topic, and how entirely he repudiated all other grounds for pedobaptism. The contrary has been disingenuously insinuated by some whose personal knowledge might have prevented the convenient error. In the very manuscript from which a portion has been selected for the Memoir, as having some novelty, there is a sketch of the scriptural argument. It is omitted by us, from our persuasion that none even among opponents will allow themselves to quote such silence as proof that Dr. Alexander remained a pedobaptist without biblical warrant. In that sketch, which is too long for our narrative, he passes under review the arguments for infant baptism which controlled his life-long judgment; the apostolic baptism of households, as explained by proselyte baptisms; the inclusion of infants in churches; the federal consecration of infants; the analogy of circumcision; the identity of the Jewish and Christian church; our Lord's treatment of little children. The expansion of these and like arguments, in his elaborate lectures, is remembered by hundreds, who learned from him to go to the Scriptures for the settlement of their doubts.

By this process of diligent inquiry his mind was at length brought to peace upon a subject which had given him great distress for as much, it is believed, as two years. He quietly resumed the practice of the church, in which he was joined by his friend and relative Mr. Lyle. And after a short time Mr. Speece returned to the bosom of the church, of which he remained for many years an ornament.

It is not without entertainment that we read the account of these events in the "History of the Rise and Progress of the Baptists in Virginia," by the Rev. Robert B. Semple. He is speaking of the Middle District Association.

"The sessions were as usual, until October, 1800, when they met at Tarwallet Meeting-house, in Cumberland County. This is said to have been one of the most unpleasant, and, indeed, confused meetings, that the Association had ever witnessed. The consequences did not subside for several years, as we shall presently show. It was at this session that Mr. Conrad Speece (now a Presbyterian preacher), who had been baptized in the course of the year, by elder James Saunders, was introduced as a Baptist preacher, and was found, both in the pulpit and private conference, agreeable and clever. He was a man of considerable learning, having been educated for a Presbyterian preacher. By reading some treatise on believers' baptism, as 'tis said, he became convinced of the impropriety of infant baptism. After some time devoted to the study of the subject, he offered himself as a candidate for baptism, and was accordingly baptized by Mr. Saunders. Soon after this Association, he professed to be again convinced of the validity of infant sprinkling, and wrote a letter to Mr. Saunders, to that effect. He rejoined the Presbyterians, and has since continued with them. Of his motives it is difficult to judge. By some it was said that he was disgusted with the turbulent proceedings of the Association at this session; by others, that Mr. Speece was much disappointed on finding that Baptist preachers received little or no compensation for their ministerial services. It is, perhaps, more probable, that he found the general tenor of the manners and customs of the Baptists quite different from his own and those of his former associates. Finding his temper soured at the loss of society to which his habits were assimilated, and not able at once to accommodate himself to that into which he had now fallen, he was the more easily persuaded of the truth of principles, which but a few months previously he had renounced as erroneous and false. It has sometimes been made a question in private companies, whether it would not have been more wise, on this occasion, to have separated baptism and church membership. *There were at this time several other eminent Presbyterian preachers, halting between two opinions.* It was thought they were perfectly persuaded of the impropriety of infant baptism, and therefore did not for many years baptize a single child, but were averse to joining the Baptists, or, however, from some cause, did not do it. Now, say some, had one or more of these been baptized, without requiring them to become members of the Baptist Church, he could have baptized the rest, and they might have formed a society to themselves, in which the ordinances would have been preserved pure, although their church government and general manners would have been different from the other Baptists. These suggestions were wholly speculative ; one thing, however, is certain, that when Mr. Speece deserted the Baptists, the scruples of all the others were quickly removed, and they resumed the absurd practice of sprinkling children. Of Speece we must say, we wish that he had either never submitted to baptism, or that, being baptized, he had not again turned away." pp. 197, 198.

The family of Dr. Alexander have repeatedly heard him speak of a long journey of exploration which he made during these years into what is now the State of Ohio. He travelled on horseback, with a mounted and armed servant. But we can turn to no living person who can give us the date. We remember his evening stories about his meeting a bear at night, and his coming suddenly on a camp of hunters who were rejoicing over great spoil. And he has often been heard to say, that in Chilicothe, which is now a city, the best room in the best house, at the time of his visit, had the stump of a tree remaining in its earthen floor.

Aged persons remember the days in which he was a daring horseman, an accomplishment certainly not rare among gentlemen bred in the South. This must seem strange to those whose memory recalls only the contrast of his later years, when he never mounted a horse, and seldom entered a vehicle. The sister is still living in a serene and lovely old age, who in childhood accompanied the young missionary on a journey of more than sixty miles, clinging behind his saddle. It was a preaching tour; and with that spirit of adventure which belonged to his nature, and that contempt for mere conventionalities which never forsook him, he took the child of ten years as his companion. The expedition is fresh in her memory after sixty years. She speaks of crossing the mountain range of the Blue Ridge, where there was no road but a bridle-path, and of the high excitement awakened by the fresh forest and the unwonted scenes of sublime nature. And she tells how her brother, wearied with her unceasing prattle, vexed withal with toothache, and perhaps, as his manner was, studying as he rode, offered her a silver dollar if she would hold her peace. Our informant is Mrs. Elizabeth McClung, of Staunton, now the sole survivor of all those sons and daughters; and the living resemblance in face and manner of her departed brother.

Since the more extended memoir was written, a number

of little pocket memorandum books have come to light, which contain accurate lists of all the discourses preached during this period. In later years, this method was dropped, as, indeed, was every thing which looked like an enumeration of duties and performances, or connected the personality of the preacher with the great and paramount work of God by him. In all his life, he knew nothing of gratulatory assemblages, ministerial anniversaries, or jubilees; while his peculiar tolerance and candour kept him from censuring those who accepted such offerings of partiality.

CHAPTER NINTH.

1801.

RESIGNATION OF PRESIDENTSHIP—JOURNEY NORTHWARD—DR. WADDEL—AMOS THOMPSON—FREEMAN THE FANATIC—PHILADELPHIA—THE GENERAL ASSEMBLY—PRINCETON—NEW-YORK—GENERAL ASSOCIATION OF CONNECTICUT—HARTFORD—DR. STRONG—NEWPORT—DR. HOPKINS AND DR. PATTON—DR. EMMONS.

AFTER remaining at Hampden Sidney until the spring of the year 1801, Mr. Alexander resigned his office as president, and resigned his pastoral charge. His motive was twofold; first, the restoration of his health, which had been impaired by several severe attacks of illness, and a desire to visit New England, which he had long cherished. An expectation prevailed among most of the people that he would return after a few months to resume the duties of his post, and hence no efforts were made to fill the vacancy. Indeed, he was assured by the Trustees of the college, and the elders of the churches, that they would gladly receive him after the temporary absence. He resolved, however, to fetter himself by no engagements, so that he might be free to accept any situation of greater usefulness which might be presented. He was chosen by the Hanover Presbytery as a commissioner to the approaching General Assembly.

Travelling on horseback, and at a time when bank-notes were little in use, he carried his money in his saddle-bags. The first night after leaving home, in the county of Cumberland, he was robbed, by some one who cut the leather containing his little store. On the day after leaving this place, he was seized with so violent a chill, that he was obliged to turn into a house not far from the road, and seek permission to lie down. Pursuing his journey, he is led to observe, that the whole course of a man's life may depend on a determination which he makes from motives of very little weight. For he hesitated for some time whether he should go the upper road, by the Rev. Dr. Waddel's, or the lower road, by the Rev. John Todd's, who had requested him to attend the communion of their church. His preference of the former led to one of the most important events of his life.

The Rev. Dr. James Waddel, celebrated as the Blind Preacher of Wirt's British Spy, was now in old age residing on his estate, at the junction of the three counties of Louisa, Orange and Albemarle; his dwelling being in the first named of these. He was born in Ireland, in 1739, and was educated in Pennsylvania, under the care of the Rev. Dr. Finley, afterwards president of New Jersey College. He was licensed as a probationer by the Presbytery of Hanover, in 1761, and in the same year received calls from five congregations at once ; none of which he accepted. In 1762, he became pastor of the churches of Lancaster and Northumberland, lying between the great rivers Potomac and Rappahannock. Here he would cheerfully have spent his life, amidst extraordinary usefulness, and in the bosom of a loving people, but for the ill effects of the climate. About the year 1777, with a constitution almost ruined, he accepted a second call to the church of Tinkling Spring, in Augusta. The last earthly removal of Dr. Waddel was to an estate called Hopewell, on the other side of the mountain. It was here that Mr. Alexander was about to visit him.

Dr. Waddel was one of the most distinguished clergymen of his time. To great learning, he added an eloquence so remarkable, that the traditionary accounts of it seem almost fabulous. It was of that sort which electrifies whole assemblies, transferring to them the speaker's passion, at his will ; a species, we must own, which has prevailed very much at the South. Under his preaching, audiences were moved simultaneously and irresistibly, as the trees of the wood are shaken by a tempest. Especially was his power great, in so painting his sacred scenes as to bring the hearer into the very presence of the object. When he rose in scornful argument, it was like a sweeping torrent, which carries every thing before it. He died on the 17th of September, 1805. During some years of his life, he was afflicted with blindness. A cataract seized first one eye, and then the other, leaving him in total darkness. By means of the operation of couching, he recovered the sight of one eye.

During this great privation, he still retained his ardent thirst for knowledge, and caused many volumes, some of which were in the Latin tongue, to be read to him by his daughter Janetta, whose name now becomes connected with our narrative.

Mr. Alexander had seen this young lady before, in visits which he had made at Hopewell, the residence of Dr. Waddel. Her beauty had struck him, but the impression was transient. When he now saw her again, waiting with filial piety on her venerable father, and during a sojourn of several days learned more fully the excellencies of her character, he determined to seek her hand, and being accepted, proceeded on his journey with a pleasing obligation to return; though, as he says, his resolution had been to go to the North untrammelled.

"While I remained here," so says the narrative, "a clergyman came to the house, of whom I had often heard, though I had never seen him. The Rev. Amos Thompson, who had long resided in Loudon County, Virginia, was a man of gigantic frame, but not in the least inclined to corpulency. His bodily strength was prodigious, several proofs of which I had from himself. He came to the northern part of Virginia, before the Revolutionary War; and before his arrival, the Baptists were the only dissenters in that part of the country. Old Father Thomas, one of their leading preachers, and a man of many oddities, had been threatened with personal violence by a set of profane and lawless men, if he should ever show his face in a certain pulpit, where he had preached for some time. The old man took a journey of twenty or thirty miles, to obtain the presence of Amos Thompson at the aforesaid place. Thompson, being fearless and fond of adventure, at once agreed to go and preach for him. When they arrived, a great multitude had assembled, some to hear the preacher, and some to see the sport, for the ruffians had sworn that they would beat old Thomas. While Mr. Thompson was at prayer, a company armed with bludgeons entered the house, and took their position just before the pulpit ; but when they saw the brawny arm and undaunted appearance of the preacher, they became alarmed, and permitted the service to go on to its conclusion. I ought to have stated, that at the close of his discourse, Mr. Thompson addressed himself directly to these men, and expostulated with them on the unlawfulness of their proceedings ; assuring them, that Mr. Thomas, though a dissenter, was under the protection of the law, and that if a finger should be raised against him, the law should be put in force, for that he would spend all the little property he possessed in seeing that justice was done. He concluded by saying, that although he was a preacher, and a man of peace, he held it to be right, when attacked, to defend himself, which he was ready and able to do. When the meeting was ended, he went out of the house and inquired for the captain of the band. Being led to the spot where they were collected, he approached this man, and asked him to go aside with him. A stout, bold-looking man walked off with him towards the wood, on entering which he appeared to be panic-struck, stopped, and raised his club. Thompson said, 'Fie, man, what can you do with that ?' and in a moment wrested it out of his hand, adding that he intended no violence, but that if so disposed, he could hurl him to the earth in a moment. The ruffian was completely overawed, and was glad to escape from so powerful an antagonist. Father Thomas received no further molestation.

"Thompson was a graduate of Princeton College (in 1760), while Mr. Davies was President. He was, I think, a native of Connecticut. Soon after being licensed, having heard that the Rev. Samuel Hopkins had adopted some novel opinions in theology, he took horse and travelled to Newport, to converse with this celebrated man, and if possible to convince him of his errors. The result was, that after discussing the disputed points for several days, he came away a thorough convert to Dr. Hopkins's system, to which he tenaciously adhered until his dying day, and which he preached on all occasions, filling the minds of the untheological Virginians with astonishment, and often with displeasure.

"When I met Mr. Thompson at Hopewell, he was about seventy years of age, and had been journeying to Henry Court House, more than three hundred miles from his residence, to attend on a lawsuit, for a piece of land to which he thought that he had a title; I travelled for several days with him. As he often alighted to get fire for his pipe, which he kept almost continually in his mouth, we made slow progress. Soon after this, the old gentleman died suddenly, I believe."

Pursuing his journey northward, Mr. Alexander passed through Alexandria, Georgetown and Washington. At the last-named place, he met with Adam Freeman, lately a minister of the Gospel, but now a wild enthusiast. The case of this unfortunate man is too full of warning, to be passed over without particular notice.

Adam Freeman was a schoolmaster at Lexington, during the revival times. He was remarkable for a long visage, large mouth, very black hair, and lips which scarcely concealed his teeth; he was tall, raw-boned, and of knotty joints. He attended a dancing-school, but with no very notable amendment in his carriage. In 1789, having been lately admitted to the bar, Freeman became interested in the great revival, of which much has already been said. From the first, he seemed to possess a full assurance of the favour of God. He was licensed to preach the Gospel, and inveighed earnestly against intemperance in eating, and the excesses of female dress. After obtaining a settlement, he became much distressed at the wicked and corrupt state of the church, and after revolving the matter for some time, resolved to demand of every communicant in his charge a full account of his inward state, and to warn such as seemed unfit, against approaching the Lord's Table. He was next led to attribute the corruption of the church, to the membership of infants, and published a pamphlet, entitled "The Death and Burial of Infant Baptism." The principle which he now adopted, was, that nothing in religion was to be practised, for which we can find no example or explicit command in Scripture. Hence, he would neither pray nor sing before preaching, and likewise disused family worship. But he had not been many weeks among the Baptists, before he found that they needed further reformation.

Being unsuccessful in his endeavours, he published a philippic against the Baptists, and gave notice that he had set up a church of his own ; into which, however, he could gather but nine persons.

Giving a literal interpretation to the last chapter of Mark, he next attempted to perform a miracle, by healing a woman who was ill. The failure on this occasion only convinced him that his faith was not genuine, and he went home in the greatest distress. He gave himself up to fasting and prayer, and after much study came to the conclusion, that no part of the Bible is inspired except the books of Ezekiel and Revelation. In process of time, he declared himself to be the Shiloh of the prophecy. While in this frenzy, he went to a neighbouring town, directed as he said to observe a fast of three weeks, and to warn the people of impending destruction. For months he had allowed his beard to grow, and now wore a long white garment, so that his appearance was terrific. He passed through the streets in this guise, crying, "Wo, wo, wo!" He was apprehended, and on being brought before the magistrates, made a defence of great ability and severity. He left the place denouncing anathemas, and shaking off the dust of his feet against it. Soon after this, he appeared at the house of a gentleman of Alexandria, clothed, and in his right mind, but declaring, that as to religion, he would have nothing more to do with it. He went to the remote south, and resumed the practice of the law ; but was seized with a fever, which soon put an end to his life.

But we must accompany Mr Alexander on his journey

northward. He arrived at Philadelphia, and attended the General Assembly, which met on the twenty-first of May, 1801. He was the only commissioner from his Presbytery, and there were only three from the Southern States. It may remind us of the growth of our church, that seventeen Presbyteries were represented. Here, however, he was brought into a nearer acquaintance with several eminent men, among whom were the Rev. Dr. Jonathan Edwards, Dr. McMillan, the patriarch of western Pennsylvania, Dr. Green, Dr. Woodhull, and Dr. McKnight. Here also he first met with the Rev. Samuel Miller, with whom he was to spend more than thirty-five years of harmonious labour, but who was now in the early bloom of manly vigour. Reports were brought to this Assembly, of the remarkable revivals in the West, by which our churches were largely extended in that growing region ; and the Synod of Virginia made it known, that they had employed six missionaries to labour west of the Allegheny. This Assembly was further remarkable for the adoption of regulations for the government of churches in the new settlements, where Presbyterians and Congregationalists are intermingled. The whole acts of this Assembly bear marks of a zeal for the extension of the church, and of a missionary spirit in regard to the heathen. Mr. Alexander was appointed a delegate to the General Association of Connecticut, together with Dr. McKnight, of New-York, and young Dr. Linn, of Philadelphia.

Here he had another attack of remittent fever, the last which ever visited him. We were informed by the late Rev. Dr. Hillyer, of New Jersey, that he fell in with Mr. Alexander during this sojourn; that the latter considered his state of health as threatening, and was much impressed with a belief that his labours were soon to end.

On leaving the great city, he proceeded, still on horseback, through New Jersey to New-York. His companion was Mr. Charles Coffin, a young minister of New England, who had been sent out to East Tennessee, where he united with the Rev. Hezekiah Balch, in gaining many adherents to the new views of Hopkins. He was an alumnus of Harvard, and a man of respectable talents, but strongly attached to the scheme of Emmons. On the first day they reached Trenton, where they lodged with the Rev. James F. Armstrong.

"The next stage," says he about 1849, "we travelled no further than Princeton; the first time I ever saw the place where I have already spent above thirty years of my life, and where I shall in all probability lay my bones. Such a view of futurity as should have presented to me the events of my life, would then have appeared very strange." He renewed his acquaintance with President Smith, who had known his father and grandfather, and had been seen by him at meetings of the General Assembly in Winchester and Philadelphia. In those days the talk in Princeton was about Godwin's Political Justice, a book which has lost its interest, and about a young man, lately a tutor in the college, whose eloquence was awakening attention. This was the celebrated Henry Kollock.

"The next day we went on to New Brunswick, where we intended to pass the Sabbath. Colonel John Bayard, the father of Andrew, Samuel, James, and John, had met me in Philadelphia and kindly invited me to stop at his house. In the afternoon I preached for the Rev. Dr. Clark, in my usual Virginia style, without notes, on the conversion of Paul. Here I became acquainted with Judge Paterson, with whom I was greatly pleased. With great talents, extensive knowledge, and profound legal attainments, he was as gentle and unassuming as any man I ever met with. Dr. Clark was an excellent man and greatly esteemed by his people. Col. Bayard was a gentleman of generous feelings, who had been much in public life, both civil and ecclesiastical; for he had been President of Congress, and often in the General Assembly.

A single stage brought them to New-York, where Mr. Alexander was courteously entertained by the Rev. Dr. McKnight. There he was brought into more close acquaintance with the Rev. Samuel Miller, as yet unmarried, and resident with his distinguished brother, Edward Miller, M. D. Dr. Rodgers was now advanced in years, but still occupied the pulpit of the First Church in his turn.

At Horse Neck, in Connecticut, now Greenwich, they enjoyed the hospitality of Dr. Isaac Lewis, at the finely situated dwelling which is still occupied by his descendants. Dr. Lewis was a man of science, and had been thought of as qualified for the presidentship of Yale College, when his neighbour, Dr. Dwight, was chosen. This excellent clergyman was the father of Mr. Zechariah Lewis, of New-York. Their next stage was Norwalk, on the Sound, where they were kindly received by Dr. Burnett, who had received his education at Princeton. At Danbury they fell in with Doctors McKnight and Linn, on their way to the General Association, and the whole company was entertained by a wealthy deacon. Here they saw a few Sandemanians collecting for their worship. Here, also, they saw still in use the pillions on which women rode to church behind their husbands and fathers. At every step they had cause to admire the unaffected hospitality of New England. Some sketches in the words of the manuscript journal will be acceptable to the reader.

"From Danbury we proceeded to Litchfield, and arrived early in the day on which the General Association was to meet. The appearance of the old country clergymen was to me novel and grotesque. They came into town on horseback or in chaises, wearing cocked hats, and sometimes queues dangling down the back. The opening sermon was preached by Dr. Perkins, of Hartford. The ministers all met at the house of the pastor, Mr. Huntington; and the first thing was a distribution of long pipes and papers of tobacco, so that the room was soon filled with smoke.

"According to usage the delegates were lodged at the house of the pastor, a very polite and hospitable man, who soon afterwards became a Unitarian. Dr. Linn requested me to go into the pulpit with him. About the time of assembling, a black cloud arose, causing such darkness that long before he had got through his sermon he was unable to decipher his manuscript. Mr. Huntington sent the sexton for candles, and these were placed in candlesticks on the pulpit. The windows however were open, and the wind being high, the lights flared so much that Dr. Linn could not make out to read what lay before him, and taking the paper in his hand, held it first to one candle and then to the other, until at length he impatiently threw down his manuscript, and attempted to conclude his sermon extempore. But he succeeded poorly in a kind of preaching to which he was little accustomed. He was, nevertheless, a man of genius and a splendid orator. He died by the rupture of a bloodvessel, at the early age of twenty-six. His ability as a writer may be learnt from from his controversy with Dr. Priestley respecting the divinity of Christ. He was the colleague of Dr. Ewing, whom he succeeded in the First Church in Philadelphia.

"The General Association seemed to have little business, and there were no set speeches. The famous 'Plan of Union,' which made so much noise in after years, had been adopted by the Presbyterian Church this year, under the influence of Dr. Jonathan Edwards, president of Union College, and was ratified by the Association without discussion. Dr. Nathan Strong was evidently the leading spirit.

"After the General Association was over, Coffin and I mounted our horses and took the direction of Hartford. About the middle of the day we arrived at the house of the Rev. Mr. Cowles, whom Coffin said we must not pass, as he was a clergyman of some distinction and a writer on Infant Baptism. At Hartford I went to the Rev. Dr. Strong's, who had reached home before us, and now received me cordially. Dr. Strong was somewhat humorous in his conversation. The next day was the Sabbath, and I preached for him. I found throughout New England that expressions of approbation and even admiration in regard to sermons, were much more unreserved than in Virginia; and it affected me strangely to have my preaching praised. My sentiments suited Dr. Strong, on this account, that he had drawn back from the ultraism of Hopkins, Emmons and others, and that Coffin, as it appeared, had delivered a discourse in which he recognised the doctrine, that God is the efficient cause of sin. With this Dr. Strong was dissatisfied, and in the morning spoke to us both, as though we entertained that opinion; but I immediately disclaimed it, and left Coffin tc defend his own tenets.

"The year before there had been a glorious revival in Dr. Strong's congregation, more considerable than any which had occurred since the great awakening in the time of President Edwards. The enthusiasm and divisions which brought disgrace on that work, had left in the sober-minded a dread of all religious excitements. When the revival began in Hartford, as Dr. Strong told me, he was alarmed and thrown into great perplexity, as to whether he should encourage or suppress it. Labouring under this anxiety he went for advice to Chief Justice Ellsworth, on whose judgment he placed great reliance. The Judge counselled him to go forward, encouraging the seriousness, but to guard against extravagances. A similar awakening was experienced in most of the congregations in the State; of which a full account may be seen in the Connecticut Evangelical Magazine. Dr. Strong took me in his chaise to visit Judge Ellsworth in North Hartford I had a particular desire to see this distinguished man ; but we were not so fortunate as to find him at home. In returning we called and took tea with Mr. Rowland, the minister of North Hartford. We found here the Rev. Dr. Lyman, of Hatfield, on his way to New Haven, to plead for a church there against their minister. He was famous, as I learned, on such occasions, and was sent for from far and near. Dr. Lyman, though dry and metaphysical, and apparently not susceptible of tender feeling, was a sound theologian, and a clear-headed and truly benevolent man. The zeal and constancy with which he sustained the cause of Foreign Missions, furnish good evidence of his enlarged and Christian views. I was told that there was not a family in Hatfield which did not belong to his charge ; and that the manners of the people retained all the puritanic simplicity of the preceding century.

"Much attention was paid to church music at this time in New England ; but the taste was not the most pure and refined. Choirs were found every where, and the singing was very much confined to them. This struck me unfavourably. There was little appearance of devotion in the choir, and less in the congregation. In Dr. Flint's church, I was informed before I went, that the chorister would send into the pulpit the psalms which were to be given out.

"In the evening of the Sabbath we had a delightful meeting in Dr. Strong's lecture-room, where I was again called upon to speak. A large portion of the assembly was made up of new converts, fruits of the late revival, with whose appearance I was greatly pleased. The Rev. Mr Cooley has informed me, that he came there that evening in great distress of mind, under which he had laboured for months, and that he found peace and comfort to his soul. There still remained some cases of obstinate dejection. Among these was a young son of Dr. Strong, about sixteen or seventeen years of age. I conversed with him, at the request of the father, but could not succeed in dispelling the darkness which hung over his mind.

"Dr. Strong was a graduate of Princeton College, and in principle a Presbyterian as to church government. He was much celebrated for his powers of wit and satire. He published two volumes of sermons, such as he preached to his people. They are more practical and experimental than any discourses issued in New England about this time. But they are deeply imbued with the new theological opinions now generally embraced in that country. He published also a volume on Universal Salvation, in answer to a posthumous work of his intimate friend, Dr. Joseph Huntington, entitled 'Calvinism Improved.' The argument is founded on the optimistic principle, that the introduction of sin and its eternal punishment tend to the highest possible degree of happiness in the universe. On this principle, the reasoning is ingeniously and forcibly conducted. The work gave great satisfaction to all Hopkinsians in New England, but has been little read elsewhere. Nevertheless, Dr. Strong, like Dr. Dwight, drew back from the opinion that God is the author of sin, and also from making a willingness to be damned a sign of grace, and from denouncing the use of means in the case of the unregenerate. These three things they were accustomed to name as the characteristics of Hopkinsianism; so that when Dr. James P. Wilson visited President Dwight, he was assured by him that there were no Hopkinsians among them, and was referred to these tenets as the criterion.

"Leaving Hartford, we directed our course towards New London. About the middle of a very hot day we arrived at Lebanon Crank, where we observed that the church was full of people. We put up our horses at the tavern, went into the assembly covered with dust, and took our seats near the door. The clergyman, a middle-aged man of low stature, had just finished the introductory services, and seeing us enter, suspected us to be travelling ministers, came down to inquire, and finding his surmises correct, entreated and insisted that one of us should preach for him. He informed us that an extensive revival was in progress among his people. Mr. Coffin put the service off upon me, and up I went with all my dust unbrushed, and gave an extempore lecture on the Parable of the Sower. The pastor thanked me over and over for the discourse, which he said was exactly adapted to his people's present condition; but expressed some astonishment that I could go regularly through such an exercise without any sign of a note. He said that the aid was most opportune. He had been so occupied with counselling inquirers and preaching lectures, that he had never before had so little preparation. He took me home with him, and gave me a particular account of the origin and progress of the awakening, which may be found described in the magazine above named." Twenty or thirty years afterward, the Rev Mr. Wright, a missionary to the Choctaw Indians, called on Dr. Alexander, and informed him that he was then present, under his first religious impressions.

The following day they were at Norwich, with the Rev. Joseph Strong, a brother of Dr. Nathan Strong of Hartford. "In the morning we arrived at New London, and having been previously invited, lodged with the Rev. Mr. Channing, an uncle of the great Channing of Boston, a sensible man, but evidently no friend to evangelical religion or to revivals. Crossing the Thames next day we came into the wildest part of the State of Connecticut, which borders on Rhode Island. The change became more manifest every mile we travelled, and we were soon in the midst of the Narraganset country, famous for its milk and cheese. About noon we met crowds of people in the road, returning from a Baptist meeting, where nearly thirty ministers had convened to ordain a brother over a vacant church ; but we were informed that the ordination did not take place, because the church refused to promise any salary to the candidate. The evident rudeness and want of courtesy in the people whom we met, differed widely from any thing which we had before observed in New England. When we came to the church, we found a concourse of hearers still there, and could hear the voice of a preacher, with the intonation with which I had been well acquainted at home. But going a quarter of a mile further, I saw what I had never known to take place at an ordination, namely, a horse-race, in a field adjoining the highway, and hundreds of people collected for the sport.

"In passing over to the island, I began for the first time to breathe the bracing and exhilarating air of the ocean.

Its effect on me was suddenly and sensibly beneficial. The first day I spent on the island restored me to vigorous health; at least I grew better from that time. Mr. Coffin, to whom I resigned myself, took me to the house of the Rev. Mr. Patton, afterward Dr. Patton, one of the meekest and gentlest men I ever saw. It was every where a matter of curiosity to hear an orthodox man from Virginia, which was supposed to be given up to Deism. Here for the first time I entered the pulpit in a gown; and it sat awkwardly upon me, for Mr. Patton was a much taller man, the pulpit was high, and the stairs steep, so that in mounting I became entangled in my own train. I found that Mr. Patton had fully adopted the opinions of Dr. Hopkins. Against these, as he informed me, he was much prejudiced at first, but had been brought over by degrees, since which time his mind had been completely at ease. Coffin had been somewhat reserved in bringing out the whole system, and we had disputed so much on the way as to several points, that he did not consider me open to conviction. But Mr. Patton considered all my questions in the most candid manner, and admitted all the legitimate consequences of the principles which he entertained. In particular, he admitted, which was unusual, that it would be nowise incompatible with God's holiness and goodness to create beings in a state of total depravity. I received from him a more satisfactory account than I had obtained, of the entire system of Dr. Hopkins, who was still alive. I spent a day with him, but he was now about eighty years of age, and unable to enter much into abstruse reasoning. He seemed perfectly placid, and fully resigned to the will of God. He had just received a volume of Scott's Works, in which the extreme opinions of New England are spoken of as tending to Deism. Dr. Hopkins, in the calmest manner, undertook to show that Scott had mistaken his meaning.

"Dr. Hopkins had nothing assuming or dogmatical in his manner, but showed a childlike simplicity and entire submission to the will of God. His labours as a pastor were by no means successful. The church of which he was now, and had long been pastor, was at this time in a very feeble condition.

"Having preached for Mr. Patton in the morning, I supplied Dr. Hopkins's pulpit in the afternoon. There was a mere handful of hearers, and when the psalm was given out, it appeared that there was no one to lead the music, and the Doctor directed me to proceed without singing."

From Newport the travellers made their way to Bristol, where they were hospitably received by the clergyman. They visited Mount Hope, famous for its prospect and for its connection with the history of King Philip. At Providence they enjoyed the kind attentions of Dr. Hitchcock, a Congregational clergyman of what were called liberal views. They received much kindness from Professor Messer, afterward President of Brown University.

The name of Dr. Emmons was perhaps as extensively known as that of any divine in New England. The perspicuity, vigour and terseness of his style, the ingenious concatenation of his arguments, his adventurous boldness, the startling nature of his conclusions, and the increasing number of his adherents, made him a master not to be despised or overlooked. "Franklin," says our narrative, "the town in which Dr. Emmons lived, joined the State of Rhode Island. Mr. Coffin was desirous that I should see this champion of the new divinity. I have no doubt that he had a design in taking me to this venerable theologian, believing that by his conversation I should be brought over, for I was already quite a follower of Edwards. Nor had I the least objection to receive light from any quarter. We, therefore, turned aside from the main road, and came to the Doctor's house early in the evening. The country around was better cultivated than any I had yet seen in New England, and Dr. Emmons occupied a large and commodious farm-house very near to his church. I found him to be rather taciturn than talkative. He did indeed make many and earnest inquiries of Mr. Coffin respecting the progress of the new opinions in Tennessee, whither Dr. Balch had carried the seed from Massachusetts.

"Mr. Coffin proposed to me, as did Dr. Emmons, to remain there and preach, as he had promised to supply a vacancy at some distance. I consented without hesitation; expecting, however, to undergo a thorough sifting, and perhaps to be under a moral necessity of changing my creed. I found that my remaining for so many days was likely to be an inconvenience to Mrs. Emmons, who appeared to be a discreet, sensible and pious woman. But on the first day of my sojourn, the Doctor took me to a monthly meeting of ministers at old Mr. Sandford's, within a few miles, which, however, he was not in the habit of attending, as he did not belong to the club. A dinner was always provided, after which there was a sermon in the church. The two old gentlemen had long been neighbours, but did not agree in their views either of doctrine or church discipline; but they were friendly when they met. And as the Doctor had brought a Virginia preacher, a nondescript, they made him doubly welcome. They differed even more in politics than in religion; for Mr. Sandford was a democrat of a school hitherto unknown to me, holding that when the church was fully established, there would be no need of civil government. On that day the sermon came in turn to be preached by the Rev. Mr. Alexander, of Mendon, a man of some learning. But he was understood to have gone to Boston, and it was doubtful whether he would be there. It was therefore put upon me to preach, and Mr. Sandford took me up stairs into his study, and left me to make such preparation as I needed. In the mean time Mr. Alexander arrived, having ridden twenty or thirty miles in a very hot day. To his inquiries as to what arrangement had been made for preaching, Mr. Sandford replied, 'We certainly expect Mr. Alexander to preach.' Mr. A. declared it to be out of the question, but Mr. S. continued to repeat, 'We expect a sermon from Mr. Alexander, and no other.' Thus he continued the hoax, until the bell rang for public service, upon which I descended and was formally presented as the Rev. Mr. Alexander from Virginia. I never saw a man more surprised or relieved. We went to the church, and found a respectable number for a week day and a busy season. At that time I used no notes in the pulpit, but being in a country where all sermons were read, I felt it to be incumbent on me to make my discourses as methodical and accurate as I could. And though I never could commit words so as to depend on my memory, I had long accustomed myself to follow trains of thought, and the regular array of an argument. I took as a text, 'He that hath my commandments and keepeth them, he it is that loveth me.' I undertook to show

I. The foundation of love to Christ, as it relates both to the object and subject of the affection.

II. The properties of love to Christ; which I made to be
1. Sincerity.
2. Supremacy.
3. Constancy.

III. The evidences of love to Christ;
1. A desire of pleasing, and fear of offending.
2. A desire of conformity to his character.
3. A desire of communion, and sorrow on account of absence.
4. A desire to promote his glory, and sorrow when he is dishonoured, or when his cause declines.

"As I insisted strongly on the position that love must terminate on the true character of the object beloved, I gave them all great pleasure, as this showed that I did not hold to the selfish scheme of virtue. When I got into the chaise with the old Doctor, he made me quite ashamed with his laudation, and assured me there was nothing in the sermon which he did not approve.

"The next day Dr. Emmons took me to a much greater distance to a weekly lecture. The audience was small.

My text was Luke xiv. 18, 'But with one consent they all began to make excuse.' The next day, being the Fourth of July, he took me to a neighbouring town, where an oration was to be delivered by a certain Dr. Manning, who had once resided in Virginia. The Doctor was greatly out of his element at this meeting, for the oration was rabidly democratic, and the people assembled were generally of this party.

"The next day was Saturday, and Dr. E. left home for the place of his appointment. During the visit he never attempted to enter into any controversy, but seemed rather to avoid all doctrinal discussion. He had a young man studying with him, who was principally occupied in writing two discourses for the Sabbath, and these, according to the custom, he read to his preceptor. I was present on one of these occasions. The main object of the sermon was to prove man's dependence on God for every thing, including every thought and emotion. After this exercise, the young man, whom I took to be very stupid, propounded to the Doctor this question: If man is dependent for all thoughts and feelings, and if the law of God requires him to be holy, while his thoughts are sinful, then does not God require the creature to be independent? I wondered how he would answer it, when, after a few moments' pause, he turned to me and asked me how I should reply to the question. I begged to be excused from any such attempt, and so the matter went off without an explanation.

"In person, Dr. Emmons was a little inclined to be corpulent. His hair was thin, and his countenance rather florid than pale. His knowledge of the Southern States was imperfect. He had just published a sermon on the character of Jeroboam, which was considered excessively severe against Jefferson, who had just ascended the presidential chair; yet, as far as I could judge, he cherished no malignity against any one, on religious or political grounds."

We insert here, for the sake of connection, a statement found in another manuscript. "Old Dr. Emmons once said to me, in defending the bands and cocked hats which were then used in New England; 'Clergymen, when they travel or go abroad, should have some badge of their profession. It preserves them from many unpleasant rencounters, and causes them to remember their sacred office. For,' added he, 'when a clergyman thinks that he is not recognised as such, he is very apt to yield to unsuitable compliances; and often, when he seeks to be incognito, he is known to all the company.' This is a sage remark."*

In the frequent mention which Dr. Alexander was accustomed to make of this visit, he always spoke of him in high terms of respect; while he entertained, as is well known, very different theological opinions. But it was characteristic of him to treat with great liberality, and in some respects with esteem and affection, those whom he at the same time regarded as seriously erroneous. In the next chapter we shall take up his narrative, in regard to Boston, the grand object of his curiosity.

* MS. Life of the Rev. William Graham.

CHAPTER TENTH.

1801.

NEW ENGLAND JOURNEY CONTINUED—BOSTON—DR. ECKLEY—DR. MORSE—HARVARD COLLEGE—IPSWICH—DR. DANA—NEWBURYPORT—EXETER—DARTMOUTH COLLEGE—DANIEL WEBSTER—SHELBURNE—DR. PACKARD—COMMENCEMENT AT PRINCETON—PHILADELPHIA—RETURN TO THE COLLEGE.

"I OBSERVED on approaching Boston," says he, "that few persons rode on horseback, and that I attracted no little attention, having my valise, overcoat and saddlebags, and a horse very different in form from those of New England; for he was of English blood, and had been a racer in his time. I began to feel, as I commonly did when entering a city, a certain shyness, which led me to avoid the most frequented houses. When, therefore, I came to the City Hotel, and observed many men in uniform, and some with epaulettes, I thought I would ride on further, and find a quiet house. But after proceeding some distance, I found that I had gone entirely through the town, and was on the way over the bridge to Cambridge. Here, however, I observed a sign, and as I meant only to leave my horse, I determined to stop. And indeed I found a quiet house, for the innkeeper put my horse into the stable himself, and I saw no one about the premises. I felt that I was out of my latitude, and thought it was too late to present my letters. For Dr. Burnet, at Norwalk, had kindly given me an introduction to the Rev. Dr. Eckley, minister of the Old South. The next day I went in search of this gentleman, and coming to a bookstore, the common refuge of strangers and loiterers, I received the necessary directions and proceeded to deliver my letter.

"Dr. Eckley insisted that I should take up my abode with him, saying that the Rev. Henry Kollock of New Jersey had been his guest, but was now gone to Charlestown to spend a few days with Dr. Morse. After a little time, I returned to my hotel, paid my bill, and mounted my Rosinante, which I proceeded to have put up at the City Hotel. The Doctor informed me that it was the evening for the Boston Lecture, a series of discourses preached in turn by the clergy of Boston and vicinity.

"Dr. Eckley was one of a class I had never known. He was refined, possessing great sensibility, punctiliously courteous, and talkative on all subjects. I accompanied him to the Thursday lecture, where about fifty persons were met, and where old Dr. Howard delivered a downright Arian sermon; not, however, in a controversial way, but just as if all agreed with him. Indeed at that time all controversy was proscribed by the liberal party. After sermon I was presented to Dr. Morse, who greeted me cordially, and invited me to Charlestown. A dozen venerable looking clergymen were present, some with fullbottomed white wigs.

Henry Kollock, to whom I was next introduced, was one of the most affectionate men I have ever known ; his heart seemed to be for ever overflowing with kind feelings.

"Dr. Morse insisted that I should go the next evening and preach at his lecture, which I agreed to do, but soon repented, for my spirits had sunk below par. I however went, and preached, but was much disturbed by the glare of the lights ; for chandeliers were then all the fashion. I did as well as I could, using no notes ; the fact was I had none with me. On the Sabbath I had engaged to preach for Dr. Eckley in the morning, and for Dr. Morse in the afternoon. Poor Kollock was almost torn to pieces, in the anxiety to secure his pulpit services, which were something new in Boston ; for in composition and delivery he followed the French school, and having an impassioned manner produced an extraordinary impression upon his audience. He divided his labours among all sorts. Indeed there was as yet no public line of demarcation among the clergy. One might learn with ease what each man believed, or rather did not believe, for few positive opinions were expressed by the liberal party. Dr. Kirkland was said to be a Socinian, as was Mr. Popham ; and Dr. Howard an Arian. Dr. Eckley had professed to be an Edwardean, but he came out, after my visit, a high Arian. Mr. Eliot was an Arian, Mr. Emerson a Unitarian of some sort, and Dr. Lathrop a Universalist. Dr. Freeman, one of the first who departed from orthodoxy, was the lowest of all, a mere humanitarian. He still used the book of Common Prayer, altered so as to suit his opinions. Dr. Morse was considered a rigid Trinitarian.

Dr. Harris, of Dorchester, was reckoned a low Arminian, and became a thorough Unitarian.

"Harvard College was not yet fully under Unitarian influence, but was leaning in that direction. President Willard was thought to hold the old Puritan doctrine, but had no zeal for orthodoxy. Dr. Tappan, professor of theology, was in his writings a Calvinist of the school of Watts and Doddridge; a very amiable man, of prepossessing manners. Dr. Pierson was professor of Hebrew; he was much opposed to Unitarianism, but did not possess great influence. All were for making little of doctrinal differences. As soon as the liberal men had caused this to be settled as a principle, they devised a way to introduce the ablest Unitarians into the College, as fast as vacancies occurred. When Dr. Willard died, Kirkland, a man of genius and eloquence, was put into his place. Even at the time of my visit, all the young men of talents in Harvard were Unitarians.

"Dr. Morse took charge of me for the most part. He conducted me to the Commencement, and introduced me as the President of a college in Virginia. At my first arrival, there was a laughable mistake about this presidency. I had never intended to mention my connection with a college, and I knew that Hampden Sidney was perfectly unknown. But Coffin had told Dr. Burnet that I had been President of Hampden Sidney, and Burnet in introducing me to Dr. Eckley, had written it Camden Sidney. This letter, Dr. E. showed to Dr. Morse, and the American geographer was nonplussed; he had never heard of the College. There was no way to clear up the difficulty but by applying to me.

But by this, the matter was little mended, for Dr. Morse in his Geography had represented Hampden Sidney as nearly extinct; my honour as a President was not therefore very flattering. All titles of this sort, however, go for much in New England, and I was often placed before my seniors and betters. I was invited to dine with the professors and students, but Dr. Holmes, the author of the Annals, took me to his house.

"I preached a number of times for Dr. Eckley in the Old South, and two or three times for Dr. Morse, in Charlestown, but for no others. The principal surprise at hearing me preach was, that I, a Virginian, should avow such doctrine. A certain Judge Peabody, after one of my discourses, expressed this opinion, adding that he had supposed almost all the educated Virginians to be Deists.

"In the Old South Church I found a lingering relic of Whitefield's times, in a convert of his day, a lady between eighty and ninety years of age, who belonged to a prayer-meeting, founded then, which had been kept up weekly, until within a few years. Of this she was now the only surviving member. The celebrated Samuel Adams, signer of the Declaration of Independence, was a member of the Old South, but too infirm to come out. Having spent a week or ten days in Boston, I mounted my horse and went on my way towards Newburyport."

At Ipswich he found Dr. Dana, father of the present venerable Dr. Dana. He had been engaged in a controversy respecting the use of the means of grace; in which he and Dr. Tappan, of Cambridge, were the leading writers on one side, against Dr. Spring and Dr. Emmons on the other. We here resume the fragment of autobiography :

"I preached at Rowley, the day after I left Ipswich, and saw Mrs. Bradford and family. It is pleasant to meet with evidence of having been the instrument of good to any one, after having remained in ignorance of it for almost half a century. The sister of Dr. Coggswell informs me that she was present at that sermon, and then received her first religious impressions. Mr. Bradford had been in his lifetime a zealous advocate for the new opinions in theology, and his people had caught the itch of disputation. Two of them, of whom one was a deacon, came to the house where I was entertained, that I might settle a metaphysical difference which they had been discussing for some time. It was whether there is any thing in the mind besides exercises ? I found it very difficult to comprehend what they meant ; for at that time, I had never heard of what is called the 'Exercise Scheme.' It occurred to me however, that my best course was to get them into the dispute before me, which I did by asking questions of one and the other. I was greatly amused with the matter and manner of the controversy, and began to understand the subject in debate.

"The next day I went into Newburyport. My letter directed me first to Dr. Spring's ; but when I came to the house, I found them under a great and sudden affliction. The next clergyman on my list was the Rev. Daniel Dana, a son of the pastor at Ipswich. He was about my own age, and received me kindly. There was a considerable excitement in the town, where the Free Will Baptists had just commenced operations, and made a number of converts. I was informed by Mr. Dana, that although there were eight Congregational churches, no two ministers agreed in their theological system. One, an Englishman, was an old-fashioned Calvinist; another, a disciple of Gill, was called an Antinomian; a third was a moderate Calvinist; a fourth an ultra Hopkinsian; a fifth an Arminian, and a sixth a high Arian. These are all that I remember, and I preached for them all. Indeed, they kept me so constantly at work that I broke down towards the last, and was obliged to cease on account of a pain in my breast. In consequence of the affliction in Dr. Spring's family, I saw but little of him; otherwise I should have had a time of severe sifting, as the Doctor was accustomed by a train of logical reasoning, to push his opponent to the conclusion to which he wished to bring him."

One day Mr. A. dined at the house of Dr. Coffin, the father of his late travelling companion. A clergyman present (for the manuscript leaves it obscure whether it was Dr. Coffin or another), entered into discussion with him upon the reigning topics of the day, and supposed him to concede that that which renders an action morally good, is its tendency to produce the greatest amount of happiness. "I told him that I did not believe it. I maintained that holiness has an intrinsic excellence, distinct from its tendency to promote happiness, an excellence greater than that of happiness itself. I added that the animal creation has a constitution which renders them susceptible of happiness, and yet that constitution is not moral; that many inanimate things have a tendency to produce happiness, which nevertheless does not stamp them with the character of virtue. He looked me full in the face and said, 'Where were you educated?' I replied that what little education I possessed was obtained among the wild mountains of Virginia."

Leaving Newburyport, he journeyed towards Exeter. A trait of the times is not without entertainment. "On the way," says he, "I was overtaken by a man on horseback, whom I immediately knew to be a clergyman, by the three cornered hat which all country ministers still wore, when they appeared in public. Dr. Eckley told me that even in Boston, when he visited the older people, he was obliged to put on the cocked hat, as they considered the round hat too 'buckish' for a clergyman. The stranger informed me that he had been out 'candidating,' that is, preaching as a candidate in a vacant church. Before we reached Exeter, he turned aside to visit a rich old farmer, and to fill his saddle-bags with cucumbers from the garden. In those days, a pastor in New England who had been dismissed from his people was in a situation little better than if deposed. Poor Mr. M. N. lived in a dilapidated house, where I visited him, and where there seemed to be no supplies but the cucumbers and some rusty bacon. I greatly commiserated his condition; for he was a man of learning, and his wife was a well-educated and refined woman, of great simplicity.

"The Phillips Academy, at Exeter, was the most celebrated institution of the kind in New England. After spending a week in Exeter, Mr. Rowland, the pastor, accompanied me to Portsmouth. I preached here several times (for Dr. Buckminster) in the week-evenings, and to full houses. I found the Doctor an exceedingly agreeable man; well-informed if not learned, orthodox, without any ultraisms, but not abounding in zeal. He introduced me to his son, who had been graduated at the late Commencement, and was the pride of Harvard. He was full of anecdotes, such as were current at Cambridge, and which were mostly intended to ridicule evangelical opinions."

From Exeter he directed his course toward the mountains of New Hampshire, and was soon in the midst of romantic scenery, which revived the associations of his youth. This is a proper place to insert some paragraphs from a publication made by Dr. Alexander in the year 1850, which derives additional interest from the recent death of our great statesman, since these pages were commenced.

"At Harvard, I had the pleasure of being introduced to President Willard, Professors Tappan, Pearson, and others. I was also able to attend the commencement at Dartmouth College. In passing from Massachusetts over the mountains of New Hampshire, I lodged within a few rods of the house of a farmer, the father of the Honourable Daniel Webster. The old gentleman came over to the tavern in the morning, and chatted for half an hour. Among other things he said that he had a son at Dartmouth, who was about to take his bachelor's degree. The father was large in frame, high-breasted and broad-shouldered, and, like his son, had heavy eyebrows. He was an affable man, of sound sense and considerable information, and expressed a wish that I might be acquainted with his son, of whom it was easy to see that he was proud

"Arriving at Hanover, the seat of the College, a day or two before the commencement, I put up my horse and secured a room at one of the two public houses. On the morning of the commencement I presented my letters to President Wheelock, and was received with a profusion of ceremonious inclinations; for it was pleasantly said that the President suffered no man to have the last bow. This, it was reported, was put to the test by a person of some assurance, who undertook to compete with him in the contest of politeness. He accordingly took his leave, bowed himself out of the mansion, and continued to bow as long as he was upon the premises; but the President followed him to the gate, and remained in possession of the field. Dr. Wheelock was a man of learning, especially in the department of history. It was said that he had a great historical work in preparation, but none such ever appeared.

"When I afterwards returned to the tavern, I was surprised to find the whole house filled with a strange and motley multitude. My own room was occupied by a company of gamblers, and the usual circle of lookers-on. I loudly asserted my claim to the room, threw myself on my reserved rights, and made appeal to the host. He declared himself unable to turn the people out; the Green Mountain Boys appeared to be good-natured, but perfectly impracticable. At this juncture I began to consider my situation quite deplorable, when relief came from an unexpected quarter. A note was delivered to me from a gentleman of the village, inviting me to become his guest; by singular resolution he had kept exclusive possession of his house, the only one in

Hanover exempt from invasion. I found ample room and hospitality. It appeared that a letter from Salem, Massachusetts, had named me to this worthy friend, as a clergyman of Virginia, making a first journey through New England. In this house I made the acquaintance of the only other guest, the Reverend Theophilus Packard, now Doctor Packard; whom I accompanied to his home in Shelburne, and there spent a very happy, and as I think, profitable fortnight.

"At the Dartmouth commencement, General Eaton, of eccentric memory, was marshal of the day, and was unceasing in busying himself about the order of the procession to the church; giving each graduate, of every college, the place due to his seniority. Among the speakers was young Daniel Webster. Little dreaming of his future career in law, elo quence and statesmanship, he pronounced a discourse on the recent discoveries in Chemistry, especially those of Lavoisier, then newly made public."

As the introduction of this extract has carried us a little further forward than we intended, it will be necessary to go back and glance at a few incidents of the road to Hanover.

"The tavern belonged to Capt. Webster, though he lived in a large house a few rods distant. The morning that I was to set out to cross the mountains, two clergymen drove up, both alumni of Dartmouth, and on their way to the Commencement. One of these was Mr. (now the Rev. Dr.) Gillett, of Hallowell, in Maine. They were in a chaise and I was on horseback, but they were very willing to make frequent exchanges. Mr. Gillett was an adept in metaphysical discussion, and we were often in danger of upsetting the chaise among the rocks, from being so intent on our discussion. The other clergyman held the same opinions, but had little of his companion's acuteness.

"On the side of a mountain, for we had many to cross, we came to a house early in the afternoon, which was the only place for a great distance where we could obtain lodgings; here, therefore, we determined to remain over night. On conversing with the woman of the house, I found that she had recently obtained experience of religion, though she had heard no preaching. Her eldest son had gone out into the forest to cut some fire-wood, when the limb of a tree fell on his head and broke his skull. He was brought home dead. For a fortnight the mother wept day and night, and was inconsolable. At length it came strongly into her mind that there was no use in grieving for the child, but that she had great cause to grieve for her sins. From this time she began to experience a change in her feelings. She ceased to mourn for her loss, and sorrowed for her guilt, until God manifested himself as reconciled through Jesus Christ. As the people living on the mountain were entirely destitute of preaching, we proposed to have the neighbours collected in the evening; when Mr. Gillett preached to them on the doctrine of Election.

"Next day we took the road to Enfield, a Shaker village, as we were all desirous to see and converse with this strange people. We arrived about noon, and found all the shops closed, as the men were out clearing new ground; with the exception of the Elders, who never put their hands to any labour."

It is a fact not generally known, that shortly after his return home, and through the influence of Judge Niles, Mr. Alexander received the appointment of Phillips Professor of Theology in Dartmouth College. The book of the Trustees shows that this election took place at the Annual Meeting in August, 1802. From Hanover he went to Shelburne, upon an invitation of the Rev. Mr. Packard, afterwards Dr. Packard. "I was the more willing to do this," he writes, "as Mr. P. had just received a letter from home, informing him that a revival had commenced in one part of his parish. At Westminster, we found, very appropriately, an Assembly of Divines. The Congregational ministers of New Hampshire were met in General Association. During my stay of a fortnight with my friend Packard, he never preached once in his own church. Besides the services of the Sabbath, we had meetings on week days in several parts of the congregation. We also visited from house to house, where there were any under serious impressions. One thing in the exercises and conduct of the awakened surprised me. They sat still and believed it improper to pray or use any means except hearing, until they received the gift of a new heart. I preached as usual, and exhorted inquirers to pray, read, &c. Two cases among the awakened I must mention, because they were brought to my remembrance many years afterward, in a very pleasing way. At the house of a Mr. Fisk, we found his wife and daughter in the deepest distress, yet using no means, but sitting still and waiting for the converting influences of the Spirit. Both were convinced of their lost estate and utter helplessness, taking all the blame to themselves. The next day, as the assembly could not be accommodated within, I preached in an orchard. Before I began I perceived Mrs. Fisk walking briskly towards the table on which I stood, and the first glance I had of her countenance assured me that her feelings had undergone a change. I intimated this to Mr. Packard, who immediately after the service spoke to her and found that she was full of joy and love. Many years after this, the Rev. Pliny Fisk, the missionary to Palestine, called upon me, telling me that he came at the request of his mother, who had enjoined it upon him, if he ever should be within fifty miles of me, to make himself known as a son of the woman who was converted while I was in Shelburne.

"On another day we stopped at the house of an old man, also named Fisk, who had a son with a large family living in the same house with him. One of the children, about nine or ten years of age, was under serious impressions, and was called up for us to converse with him. After a longer period than the one above mentioned, and long after I had known the Rev. Dr. Ezra Fisk, of Goshen, he one day asked me if I remembered talking with a boy in Shelburne, describing the circumstances. And on my replying that I did, he said, 'I am that boy.' Harvey Fisk, once my pupil, and afterwards much engaged in the service of the American Sunday School Union, informed me that another person by the name of Fisk, who became a minister and was eminent for his piety, dated his conversion from the same revival.

"The people of Shelburne seemed reluctant to part with me. The pastor and a number of others accompanied me to Conway, the next town, where I was to preach for old Mr. Emerson, who had been unable to walk for many months. He was a meek and pious man, of the old school of Puritans, and an uncle of the Emerson of Boston, who became a Unitarian. He told me that the father of the latter was a pious and orthodox man ; and that when he had reminded his nephew of this, the reply was, that if his father had lived to this time, he would in like manner have changed his opinions. Here I found many sincere and benevolent persons; but I could observe that I was no longer under the cloud which showered its blessings over Shelburne. Leaving the higher parts of Massachusetts, I descended to the valley of the Connecticut, and soon found myself in Northampton, the town made memorable by President Edwards. At Hatfield I called on Dr. Lyman, whom I had seen before." At Hartford he again visited Dr. Strong, who engaged him to write for the Connecticut Magazine. At his request, Dr. George Baxter contributed to this work an account of the great revival in the South. By easy stages he continued his homeward way, through New Haven and the towns upon the Sound to the city of New-York. Here he preached on a Lord's Day evening in the Brick Church, for Dr. Rodgers. The next day was partly spent at Newark, with the venerable Dr. McWhorter, after which he proceeded to Elizabethtown, and visited the Rev. Henry Kollock, at the house of his father. It was a favourite plan of Mr. Kollock to have his friend settled in the congregation of Orange, but the steps taken by him were unsuccessful.

Princeton was visited in the return, and the following narrative, which has been already printed, is here in place.

"Princeton was taken in my journey homeward. In this town, likewise, it was no easy matter to find a place to lay my head, so great was the concourse of strangers. But my friend Mr. Henry Kollock, afterwards distinguished as a preacher, and who had recently been a tutor in the college, kindly introduced me to the house of old Mrs. Knox, where the students of divinity had their abode.

"The appearance of the Trustees and Professors struck me with awe. I seriously question whether such a body of men, for dignity and importance, as then composed the Board could have been found in any part of the country. I need only name Dr. McWhorter, Elias Boudinot, LL. D., John Bayard, Esq., Dr. John Woodhull, the Hon. William Paterson, Dr. Green, the Rev. James F. Armstrong, the Hon. Richard Stockton, Governor Bloomfield, and Judge Wallace. The class then commencing Bachelors of Arts included the late Mr. Biddle, Mr. Robert Goodloe Harper, the Rev. Andrew Thompson, Mr. Henry E. Watkins, Professor Cook of Kentucky, the Rev. Dr. Johnson of Newburgh, and the Rev. Dr. John McDowell of Philadelphia.

"The President, Dr. Samuel Stanhope Smith, I had met in Philadelphia, six or seven years before; and certainly, viewing him as in his meridian, I have never seen his equal in elegance of person and manners. Dignity and winning grace were remarkably united in his expressive countenance. His large blue eye had a penetration which commanded the respect of all beholders. Notwithstanding the want of health, his cheek had a bright rosy tint, and his smile lighted up the whole face. The tones of his elocution had a thrilling peculiarity, and this was more remarkable in his preaching, where it is well known that he imitated the elaborate polish and oratorical glow of the French school. Little of this impression can be derived from his published discourses, which disappoint those who do not know the charm of his delivery.

"On this occasion Dr. Smith appeared to great advantage, for though he had passed his acme, he was erect and full of spirits. The formality used in the collation of degrees does not appear to be of much importance, but with the sonorous voice and imposing mien of President Smith, it added dignity to the scene, and left an indelible impression.

"The College of New Jersey at that time contained some young men who were far above the ordinary level of attainments; distinguished for a high sense of honour, which preserved them from the despicable courses in which misguided youth sometimes seek distinction. It was gratifying to observe, that these young men were the favourites of the President, and that, in their turn, they were strongly attached to him. Some of them still live, to reflect honour on their Alma Mater; but I will not name those who occur to me, lest I do an unintentional injustice to the rest. Some, alas, are extinct; but some may be found shining as stars, with a mild but brilliant lustre, in the civil as well as the ecclesiastical firmament.

"Doctor John Maclean, a native of Scotland, after pursuing the path of science with indefatigable zeal, so far as it was open to him in Edinburgh and Glasgow, visited France, that he might avail himself of the increased facilities afforded for physical researches in the schools of Paris. After accomplishing this purpose, Dr. Maclean emigrated to America, in 1795, and became one of the most popular professors who ever graced the college. He was at home almost equally in all branches of science; Chemistry, Natural History, Mathematics and Natural Philosophy, successively claimed his attention. It is believed that he was one of the first to reproduce in America the views of the new French school in Chemistry: on this subject he waged a successful war with Dr. Priestley, the great champion for phlogiston. No one could attend a commencement at Princeton, without perceiving that Professor Maclean was, as it were, the soul of the faculty. He enjoyed the attachment of all the students, unless perhaps some of the idle and abandoned; it is these who, in all colleges, display the opposite temper.

"At the time of my visit, Dr. Maclean was in the prime of life, a gentleman of fine appearance, polished manners, and a disposition remarkable for kindness and cordiality. He is now remembered, as the students' friend, with sincere and tender attachment, by many of his surviving pupils. It is no part of these paragraphs, to follow any of the persons named into their subsequent life, but only to note these incidents of a day which was full of interest. After the other honorary degrees had been announced, the Trustees, by a consultation at the moment on the stage, agreed to confer on the writer the degree of Master of Arts; an act, which, it seems, was never entered on their minutes; and in the evening he was initiated into the American Whig Society."* On this occasion he was accompanied to Princeton by Mr. Kollock, and Mr. Beasley, afterwards Provost of the University of Pennsylvania.

In Philadelphia he preached for Dr. Linn, whose health was impaired. In Baltimore he stopped with his old preceptor, Dr. Priestley, already mentioned in these pages. He was further detained to supply the pulpit of Dr. Alison, who had sunk into a melancholy state. The impression made by these services, as will presently appear, was such as made it likely for a while that his lot might be cast in Baltimore; and the remembrance of them was long cherished in that city. After this he hastened to Hopewell, where arrangements were made for his approaching marriage.

In the retrospect of this tour, he was accustomed to speak of it as one of the most agreeable and instructive portions of his life. That part of it which brought him into acquaintance with New England, its clergy, its manners and its revivals, he always recurred to with pleasure. To this may be traced the remarkable absence of all prejudice and rancour which marked his feelings and language towards the churches of that land. Of their hospitality he used to speak in warm terms, and as to the inquisitiveness which he had been taught to expect from the people, he declared it to be less than he had encountered in his native State. And although he spent but a few months in that region, the mode of travelling which he employed, and the intimate relations

* Princeton Magazine, 1850.

he sustained to ministers and private families, afforded far better opportunity for observation than a much longer time, passed in the modern methods of speedy transit, and sojourn at places of public entertainment. In moments of relaxation at the fireside, his fund of anecdote concerning this tour was inexhaustible ; and he loved to recall these scenes on occasions when he was visited by friends from that part of the country.

His return to Prince Edward and to the College was hailed with much cordiality, and the old president's house was put into repair, in expectation of his new relations. During the winter of 1801–2, he spent most of his time in Charlotte, under the hospitable roof of Major Read. His preaching labours were abundant, and were attended with some success.

In the year 1801, on his return from New England, he passed a night, as has been said, at the house of Dr. Priestly, who was at that time a member of the First Church in Baltimore. As Dr. Alison, the pastor, was then in feeble health, Mr. Alexander, somewhat reluctantly, consented to remain and preach, as there was but one intervening day before the Sabbath. Early on Monday morning he proceeded on his journey, but having acquaintances in Alexandria he stopped there, and found the Presbytery of Baltimore in session ; before whom he preached at their request. Before he left the place, letters were received both by himself and Dr. Muir, requesting him to return to Baltimore and preach for several weeks. At the urgent request of Dr. Muir and other clergymen, he complied. The result was, that after his arrival at home he received a call to be the pastor of that church.

CHAPTER ELEVENTH.

1802—1806.

MARRIAGE—COLLEGE LABOURS—PREACHING—CALL TO PHILADELPHIA—SETTLEMENT IN PINE-STREET CHURCH—LABOURS IN PHILADELPHIA—EVANGELICAL SOCIETY—ASSOCIATES—STUDIES—PROGRESS.

ON the fifth day of April, 1802, he was married to Janetta Waddel, daughter of the Rev. Dr. Waddel of the county of Louisa. It may be safely said that no man was ever more blessed in such a connection. If the uncommon beauty and artless grace of this lady were strong attractions in the days of youth, there were higher qualities which made the union inexpressibly felicitous during almost half a century. For domestic wisdom, self-sacrificing affection, humble piety, industry, inexhaustible stores of vivacious conversation, hospitality to his friends, sympathy with his cares, and love to their children, she was such a gift as God bestows only on the most favoured. While during a large part of middle life he was subject to a variety of maladies, she was preserved in unbroken health. When his spirits flagged, she was always prompt and skilful to cheer and comfort. And as his days were filled with spiritual and literary toils, she relieved him from the whole charge of domestic affairs. Without the show of any conjugal blandishments, there was through life a perfect coincidence of views, and a respectful affection which may be recommended as a model. It pleased God to spare to him this faithful ministry of revering love to the very last, and when the earthly tie was broken to make the separation short.

In the month of May, 1802, he removed to Hampden Sidney, and resumed his charge of the college. Mr. Rice was still his principal coadjutor, as Mr. Speece had removed to a pastoral charge in Maryland. Of the ensuing years we have slender records. Their colour was probably not very different from those which have been noticed. Besides the perpetual demand for pulpit labours, in a region where to this day ministers travel far to preach the Word, there was a necessity for unwearied application to the difficult branches of public instruction. His field of knowledge was enlarging its limits, and his opinions on all subjects were taking their settled forms. Having resided in the same region many years since, we can testify that his reputation as a preacher was extraordinary. Making all the abatements which may be needful, it must still be acknowledged that for vigour, animation and charm of delivery, his efforts at this time were surpassed by none during his whole career. His health had been invigorated, he had acquired a confidence which had been wanting in his earlier efforts, his person was attractive, and the vehemence and decoration of discourse were greater than in later years.

The letters of this time which remain are few indeed, which enhances the value of that which follows, short as it is.

MR. ALEXANDER TO MRS. GRAHAM.

"HAMPDEN SIDNEY *July* 19, 1803.

"DEAR SISTER :—

"By John Chavis I received yours, and pass over all the rest to answer that part in which you express some uneasiness at my entertaining doubts respecting the genuineness of the Kentucky revival.

"In answer, I observe, that I have never at any time expressed such doubts, though it is more than probable that I have said what some would suppose to indicate such a state of mind. I have not doubted that much good has been done in that country, and that a considerable number have experienced true religion. All these effects I attribute without hesitation to God. And in proportion as I obtain evidence of the existence of such effects, I am confirmed in the opinion that the Spirit of God has been poured out. But I have supposed, and now think, that those extraordinary bodily appearances furnish no evidence of a saving operation of the Holy Spirit. If I should not be able to account for them upon common and natural principles, I yet have no right to ascribe them to the immediate agency of divine power, unless they are among effects promised to be produced. If no stress be laid on them, I have nothing to say in relation to them. If they furnish no evidence in favour of a work being of God, they can, I presume, afford none that it is not. If they are ranked with tears, crying, &c., the common effects of religious passions, I am neither offended with them, nor am I much delighted with them. I have moreover supposed, and do still suppose, that many measures were adopted by the conductors of this work, which were imprudent and unwarrantable. When people are under strong religious impressions, there is more need of regulation and restraint than of encouragement. To give an instance—six or ten persons exhorting at once—five hundred praying as loud as they can cry; these things occurred in Carolina. My opinion is that the fruit of this revival will by no means answer the appearances, and that the declension will be so apparent, that the unbelieving will be greatly hardened. In all these opinions, however, I have a reserve. I have not been an eye-witness to the work; if I were, I might judge differently of many things.

"I remain your affectionate brother,

"A. A."

"About this time," says he, "the conduct of the students became very irregular, and I grew weary of governing them. I had been invited in the spring of 1806, to visit the Third Presbyterian Church in Philadelphia, made vacant by the removal of Dr. Milledoler to New-York.* I declined the invitation, but in September I was again requested to visit the city, as there was no hope of fixing upon any other candidate. This came just at the time when our students

* The call was approved by the Presbytery, Oct. 22d, 1806.

were in a state of much turbulence and insubordination. Without consulting any of my friends, I set out for Philadelphia, where I preached for two Sabbaths as well as during the week." The result was a unanimous call to the church in Pine Street. Immediately on his return home he procured a meeting of the Presbytery, and the Trustees of the College met on the same day, when he requested to be dismissed from both charges. In all this proceeding he seems to have acted with much decision of purpose ; so that his friends did not venture to lay any obstacle in his way, while they were by no means convinced that he was wise in the removal. The step was an important one, as it severed him from his native State, and led the way to those more important engagements as a theological instructor, for which Providence had all along been preparing him.

In subsequent years, and even to the close of his life, he recurred to these years of ministry in Virginia with fond emotion. They were connected with his most animating labours and most visible success. He never could cease to lament the loss of that peculiar warmth and cordiality which belonged to Southern Christians ; and he was often heard to say, that although he believed he had attained greater usefulness by his removal, he had sustained a great loss as to personal and social comfort. In all those things which attract the observation of the public, these were his best days. An exuberant hilarity made his companionship delightful, as will be readily believed by those who remember the clear loud laugh even of his latter years. The circumstances in which he had grown up in his early ministry, among a number of active and inquiring minds, rendered controversy inevitable; and we can recall the days in which debates on theological topics were carried to all the lengths of excitement, which are not inconsistent with good nature and Christian friendship. We regard the period which we now bring to a close, as that in which, with regard to every important trait and faculty, his mind and character took their form. Wider range of knowledge, richer stores of accumulation, sounder experience, keener sagacity, more prophetic forecast, there may have come with advancing years, but in whatsoever can attract in the man, or impress in the preacher, he was just now at a point of culmination.

Another remark is still more obvious; this was the eventful period of his life. From this time forward, and especially after the single remove to New Jersey, there was no more change of place or occupation, but life flowed on in a placid current. Up to this time on the contrary, events had followed one another in very rapid succession. Indeed, from his very boyhood, he may be said to have been in a continual change. This served in a very remarkable degree to form his character, to enlarge his views, to afford sides of approach to various persons and influences, and to redeem him for all his years of study from every thing like the narrowness, pedantry and stiffness of the schools and the closet. As it regards the most important of all qualifications, it may be affirmed without hesitation, that these were years of spiritual advancement. He was incessantly engaged in efforts to do good as an instructor of youth and as a preacher, in public and private. The savour of his unobtrusive piety remained as a holy fragrance in that part of the church, long after he had removed from it, and a few aged persons still survive, who love to relate how his face seemed to shine from acts of private communion, and how his discourse, even more freely than in later years, broke forth in eloquent and pathetic appeals upon divine subjects. We are induced to believe that the very trains of thought, which went to constitute those practical sermons, which were singularly admirable for the intertexture of doctrine and experience, were constructed during the meditations and labours of this period. By all this process, God was preparing him for the important post, at which his closing years were to be spent.

Having determined to leave Virginia, Mr. Alexander hastened to effect a speedy settlement in his new home. His little family had already been taken to Hopewell, and did not return to Prince Edward.

We have happily recovered a letter to Mrs. Graham, which supplies some facts of this period. "We set out from Dr. Waddel's," so he writes in 1807, "on November 24th, and reached Philadelphia on the 8th of December; the roads were deep and the weather unfavourable. We were detained two days in Fauquier by high water, and two more at Leesburg by bad roads. At the last mentioned place, Mr. Mines is settled, but his situation is by no means comfortable. His expectations have not been realized, either as to support or usefulness. We staid at his house, and were treated with the greatest kindness. There are here some excellent Christians, and upon the whole, the village contains as many respectable families as any one of the same size in Virginia.

"Before I left Prince Edward, I wrote to the people here to meet me with a carriage at Little York, expecting to arrive there by the first day of December; but we were so much retarded by the causes already stated, that we were still in Virginia at the appointed time. After passing Fredericktown a few miles, the axle-tree of our carriage snapped in two, and we were obliged to walk half a mile back to get to a house, and to contrive some means of getting the carriage to Fredericktown to be mended. We felt very little disconcerted, although the prospect was gloomy. I left Janetta and the children in the house, and took a young man back with me to the carriage. We were engaged in fastening it as well as we could, when I lifted up my eyes and saw an empty carriage approaching. As soon as I saw it I said, 'There is the carriage from Philadelphia, which was to meet us!' And so it was. We now understood the reason why our axle-tree broke; for half a mile before us there was an ugly little river which had been much swollen by the rains, and which we should have crossed with danger, our horses being jaded. Besides, on that very night a very heavy snow began to fall, through which we could have made no progress without an excellent driver and good horses; and we were much pleased to have it in our power to send Scipio home from this place instead of taking him further, as something might have happened to him. So this little disaster, as it seemed at first, gave us much pleasure in the end. The remainder of our journey was dreadful, as to roads and weather, but we suffered no injury. Janetta wearied herself in carrying William more than was necessary but she and the children remained perfectly well, and through God's blessing are so still. As for myself, I caught a violent cold in Leesburg which affected my breast very much, as I had much preaching to do upon my arrival here. Living in a large city has in it many things agreeable to me, and some which are not. My principal objection to it is, that I am not sufficiently master of my own time ; but this inconvenience is of course greater just now than it will be hereafter. Our people are, with few exceptions, of the middling class. They do not affect the modes of high life, but glory in being plain and unceremonious. They are remarkable for attachment to their minister, and for affection to one another. There is not a person in the congregation who is not friendly to warm evangelical preaching ; and this they must have fresh from the mint, for they are greater enemies to the reading of sermons than the Virginians themselves. I find that Dr. Smith's and Dr. Milledoler's labours have been uncommonly useful. We have also some hopeful appearances at present. The attention to preaching is great, and a few persons seem to be impressed."

His connection with the institution of slavery was not such as to present any serious hinderance to removal, but one of its incidents is too instructive to be omitted. There was in the family a young woman named Daphne, who had been the attendant of Mrs. Alexander from her childhood, and was treated more as a friend than a servant. When it was left to her choice, she determined to accompany her master and mistress to the North ; and as she had been married to a young man in Prince Edward, she went with hopes that he might in some way obtain his freedom. We shall anticipate so far as to complete her remarkable story. Soon after arrival in Philadelphia, she found many, some being of the Society of Friends, who deeply sympathized with her in the separation from her husband; and there were some who proposed that she should go round among the benevolent with a subscription towards his redemption from slavery. John Boatman was regarded as a valuable servant, and was accordingly held at a high price; but the money was raised, and the master struck off something from the sum which he might have obtained. John, who was a brawny and ill-favoured black, was sent on to accompany the family in travelling northward. Mr. Alexander kept them both as hired servants upon wages. But John discovered that he could procure larger amounts elsewhere, and was immediately released to become the coachman of Governor McKean. Daphne, who was of light complexion and persuasive manners, began to associate with the ladies of colour in Philadelphia, and learned to entertain more lofty thoughts. She soon left her kind protectors and set up for herself. The husband went rapidly astray, forsook his wife, and was cast into prison. Daphne fell into ill health, became unable to work, and at length found a place in the almshouse. Here she was during the earlier part of Dr. Alexander's residence in Princeton. During her retreat in this public institution she was led to reflect on the quiet and ease which she had enjoyed under a nominal bondage, so that when she was visited by two daughters of Dr. Waddel, she embraced with joy the proposal that she should return and find a shelter amidst the scenes of her youth, where her mother and several brothers and sisters still lived. "We agreed," says Dr. Alexander, "to make up among us the sum which was necessary. But I told her that she could not go back as a free woman, as the laws prohibited the return of free negroes to the State ; but that she knew what freedom was, and what slavery was, and might again exercise her choice whether to remain free or to go back as a slave. There had been no formal act of manumission when she was brought away. She did not hesitate a moment. She knew that she had never been a slave except in name, and she felt a strong desire to be with her kindred and the children of her young master." Daphne accordingly returned, and has found a happy home ever since in the family of Dr. Addison Waddel of Staunton, working for herself and going wherever she pleases. She still survives at the time of the present writing, and has always borne the character of an affectionate and humble Christian.

Resuming our narrative, we have to state that Mr. Alexander has recorded his belief that the suddenness of his removal was not without some human impatience and precipitancy. "But," he adds, "what I did rashly, Providence ordered for good." Upon arriving in Philadelphia he found himself embarrassed by the novelty of his domestic circumstances, and the common difficulty of obtaining proper servants. He moreover began his labours with a violent cold, which, however, did not prevent his opening his new career of labour. He was received as a member of the Presbytery of Philadelphia on the 21st of April, 1807. His installation as pastor took place on the 20th of the next month; on which occasion the Rev. George C. Potts delivered the customary sermon, the Rev. Jacob J. Janeway presided and gave the charge to the minister, and the Rev. James P. Wilson, D. D. gave the charge to the people.

MR. ALEXANDER TO MRS. GRAHAM.

"PHILADELPHIA, *March* 5, 1807.

"DEAR SISTER:—

"My time is very much occupied here, but the business on which my duty obliges me to attend is not disagreeable. Almost every day some sick persons are to be visited. Funerals are frequently to be attended, and sometimes persons under spiritual trouble apply in order that they may be advised and comforted. There is a very wrong opinion frequently entertained of congregations in such a place as this; as if all the members were well informed people. The truth is, there is much less religious knowledge among the bulk of the people here than in the country. Multitudes grow up with very little knowledge of the doctrines of religion, and many after they are grown join themselves to a congregation by taking pews, who were never instructed at all. These require very plain preaching, and when they become serious need to be taught the very first principles of the doctrine of Christ.

"I have just now returned from visiting a woman, who sent for me to converse about her being baptized, as this had been neglected in her infancy. I found her very ignorant of every thing except that she felt herself to be a lost sinner, and trusted in Christ alone for salvation. She was so affected when she attempted to speak, that she could utter only a few words at a time. She handed me a book, which she said contained a description of her exercises. It contained Wright on the New Birth, and Haweis on the Sacrament, bound together. I had never seen either of them, and therefore looked a little into the volume, and found it to be sound and very plain. I told her it was well, and that I would baptize her on the next occasion.

"This morning I was a good deal encouraged by an account which I saw in a letter from a gentleman in East Jersey to his cousin, one of our elders. This man paid a visit to his cousin in this city last month ; and although he was deistically inclined, and never went to a place of worship at home, he was induced by his relative, who is fervent in piety, to attend our meetings. Since he went home, he has written that he has determined to turn his attention to religion and to change his manner of life. He was educated in Glasgow for the ministry, but became skeptical, as his cousin informs me, and devoted himself to trade. We have several instances of awakening and hopeful conversion since I arrived here. Two men, particularly, who were considered the most worldly in their disposition of any in their circle, have become serious. One of these professes to have experienced a thorough change. The other has been almost in despair, but begins now to be a little comforted. I have frequently visited a man and his wife, who appeared to me as ignorant as any I ever saw in a gospel land ; but they have, I trust, obtained eyes to see ; and knowledge may be expected to follow of course. I have attempted to mention the principal encouraging cases which have fallen under my observation. But I do not yet know one [half of my] people. They do not know one another; for [many of them] never meet any where but at church. Among the poor I have found some choice spirits, real heirs of the kingdom; one man in particular, who is too infirm to come out, and who [is supported by the] congregation, edifies me every time I call to see him, and is all alive in religion. I find myself greatly benefited by my visits to the sick and afflicted; and it leads me to preach in a strain which otherwise I should not have thought suitable to a great city. My love to all friends. Grace, mercy and peace be with you and yours.

"A. A."

TO THE SAME.

"PHILADELPHIA, *Jan.* 23, 1811.

"DEAR SISTER:—

"Religion in this place is at present in a languid rather than a thriving state. The additions to the church have been less considerable during the last year than for any year since I came here. Mr. Burch continues here, and is, I think, very useful. His people are still fond of him, and are building a beautiful church. People at a distance are much mistaken about the kind of preaching which suits this place. Some congregations, it is true, require men of the best learning and talents, but many others demand preaching of the plainest kind, and less learning and polish than almost any country congregation however remote. We need at this time another preacher of the same stamp as Mr. Burch, to preach to the people in the suburbs.

"We have been pleasing ourselves with the prospect of a trip to Virginia next summer; but whether our hopes shall be realized remains to be discovered. If we should be able to accomplish our wish, you may expect to see us in August. Time glides rapidly along; year succeeds year in swift succession. We must soon begin to descend towards the grave, according to the general course of nature. Lately, as it seems in the retrospect, we were young; but soon, if our lives are prolonged, we shall be old. Well, if we can but live usefully and die comfortably, we need not be concerned how soon we finish this pilgrimage.

"A. A."

The materials for constructing a full and connected narrative of this new period are unfortunately wanting. Dr. Alexander seldom retained a copy of his own letters. And what is still more painfully felt by us in prosecuting our work, the autobiography breaks off about this point, and we henceforward journey on without the guiding thread of his own record which has thus far conducted us.

Philadelphia, though far less populous than in our day, was nevertheless the chief city of the land, and was distinguished as for many years the permanent seat of the General Assembly. Its churches were among the most distinguished in our communion, and were served by clergymen of note. There were at this time four Presbyterian congregations. The pastor of the First Church was the Rev. James P. Wilson, D. D., in some respects one of the most remarkable ministers whom our connection has produced. After having been a lawyer for fifteen years, he devoted himself to the work of preaching the Gospel, and laboured with great acceptance and the admiration of many cultivated minds, until the decline of health brought his active service to a close, when he was succeeded by the Rev. Albert Barnes. Dr. Wilson was a man of varied and recondite learning. Between him and Mr. Alexander there were many sympathies, and a familiar literary commerce was kept up between them. Both were strongly inclined to the study of language, in which Dr. W. was a great proficient, and both addicted themselves to Scriptural exegesis, which was then beginning to receive the new lights of continental editors and critics. They had moreover a community of interest as to their mode of preaching, for at this time, both exercised their pulpit gifts without the use of any manuscript. The Second Church, then at the corner of Third and Arch streets, had for its pastors the Reverend Drs. Green and Janeway as colleagues. Dr. Green was an able and popular preacher, and always threw his influence decidedly into the scale of vital piety. Dr. Janeway, who was like-minded, still lives in an honourable old age. The pastor of the Fourth Church was the Rev. George C. Potts, a clergyman of great worth and benevolence, for whom Dr. Alexander retained a warm regard as long as he lived.

The Third Presbyterian Church was not distinguished in any worldly sense. It was in the southern part of the city proper, and at that time contained a great number of persons from the neighbourhood of the Navy-yard, with a goodly proportion of shipmasters and pilots. The predominating ingredient in the congregation was the old-fashioned

Scotch and Irish Presbyterianism, with its salient points of good and evil, with which the new pastor was familiar. There was all possible zeal or tenacity respecting covenanted doctrine and ancient usage, with a disposition on the part of some to look with distrust on hortatory preaching, and any measures toward revival, as savouring of newlight and methodism. The communion seasons were like those of Scotland, with long tables and 'tokens.' There were not wanting, however, some bright specimens of a piety which has never flourished more than among Christians of this lineage. But the situation was one fitted to make a young Virginian minister feel the transition from a religious climate of great fervour and freedom.

Among the excellent private Christians who were members of this church, Mr. James Stuart deserves honourable mention. He was a native of Ireland, and long occupied the place of ruling elder. To a natural temperament of great ardency, he added evangelical knowledge and a remarkable disposition to be useful. He was gifted in prayer, assiduous and affectionate among the poor and suffering, and a valuable aid to his pastor. It is but a few years since he died, full of years, and venerated by all who knew him. Mr. John McMullin was another elder ; a man of gentle manners, unfeigned piety, and unusual consistency of character. Capt. Benjamin Wickes belonged to the same church ; he was well known as one of the few truly religious captains who in that day sailed from our ports, and was honoured with the charge of conducting numerous missionaries to the East Indies and China. Joseph Eastburn, the first who devoted attention to the spiritual wants of seamen, was forward in every good work at this day, and was in close intimacy with Mr. Alexander. With some families of his congregation he maintained affectionate relations to the very close of life; and among these a prominent place is due to the name of Mr. Thomas M. Hall, in whose house even after the decease of this worthy man he was a welcome guest for more than forty years.

A brisk epistolary exchange continued to be kept up with his bosom friends Rice and Speece. Of letters written by the former, we have more than fifty, being all that remain of some hundreds. These show that their communications turned on matters of experimental and ministerial religion and on literature; and they evince a zeal in the pursuit of knowledge under difficulties, which is as rare as it is stimulating. These earnest young men employed their friend, as near the learned marts, to be on the watch for books in every department. In 1808, we find Mr. Rice writing for Eusebius and Wetstein; and in 1810, saying, "Yes, Sir! If it please God to give me health and strength, I am resolved to be master of those languages in which the truths of Divine revelation were originally recorded, and I am very anxious to get all the helps in these studies that can possibly be procured. I must beg your assistance in this business. If you will accept of it, I hereby give you *carte blanche*, a full commission to buy for me, at any price that you think proper to give, any book which you can find, that it will in your opinion be important for me to have. I have been very anxious to get Horsley's new Translation of Hosea. Are any copies to be found in your city? Be on the watch, if you please, for a Syriac New Testament, for Trommius's Concordance, for Wetstein's Greek Testament; I do not know whether it is worth while to mention Calasio's Concordance, and Michaelis's Hebrew Bible. I question if they are by any means to be obtained."

A literary project of Mr. Alexander, which he had entertained before leaving Virginia, was matter of much entertainment in his little circle of intimates. He had begun, and perhaps had completed, a work of fiction, answering exactly to what has since been called the religious novel. It was entitled "Eudocia," and purported to be the history of a young lady of wealth and beauty, who is led through various changes and degrees, from giddy ignorance to piety and peace. The plot was engaging; there was a thread of romantic but pure love, running through the whole; it abounded in graphic description and lively dialogue. Some of the scenes were eminently pathetic; and Mr. Speece was known to burst into tears, when it was read aloud. The whole was made subservient to the inculcation of evangelical truth. The author finally determined to suppress it. The manuscript was not destroyed, but the delay—beyond the *nonum prematur in annum*—resulted in the destruction of more than one half. What remains would fill a good duodecimo. The allusions which follow will now be manifest.

MR. SPEECE TO MR. ALEXANDER.

"POWHATAN, *August* 15, 1808.

"DEAR SIR:—

"I received your acceptable and instructive sermon some time ago in Prince Edward, where Dr. Hall left it for me on his way home. But your letter of June 8, I did not get, till two days ago. The single reason of my not having written to you during so long a time, was the want of any matter which I could think sufficiently interesting. I persuaded myself, however, that you as well as I could conceive how an affectionate regard might subsist between distant friends, though there were not a frequent intercourse by letter.

"Your approbation of my presbyterial sermon affords me much pleasure. I will remark to you that one reason of my swelling that sermon with so many long doctrinal paragraphs, was a wish to remove some suspicions, which you perhaps remember, that I was verging too much towards Arminianism. I have given a kind of confession of my faith, and hope the motive I have mentioned was not improper.

"I am delighted with the prospect of seeing your sweet Eudocia presented to the public. Before I received your letter I had resolved to write to you soon, principally to entreat that the door which confined her might be opened, that she might walk forth for the entertainment and edification of the world. I hope the humorous and satirical parts of the work will be retained. They will be useful in themselves, and will render the book alluring to a larger number of readers. And though I should not like to differ in a point of taste from Mrs. Alexander, allow me to put in a word in behalf of the dream, or dreams, which you read to me from the manuscript. Dreaming is indeed a delicate subject, both in philosophy and religion. But we believe that God does sometimes speak to men, 'in dreams and visions of the night,' to fasten important instruction upon their hearts.

"I have been long collecting ideas for a dissertation on Liberty and Necessity; not to increase the mass of metaphysical subtilties on the subject, but if possible to diminish it. But I have another design in hand, more likely to be executed; namely, to write a sermon or dissertation on the doctrine of Election. Presumptuous as it may appear, I cannot but think I could produce something more satisfactory than I have met with on that doctrine; especially in the business of answering objections against it.

"Our Magazine is dead indeed; solely, I think, for want of zeal in the members of our Synod. I have long believed it possible to make a better one, under the auspices of Hanover Presbytery. The plan you suggest deserves attention. I had thought of trying to get a suitable printer, who should be furnished with matter and editorial direction, and print and distribute the work at his own charge, and for his own sole profit. The times are so discouraging to most things which require money, that I fear we can do nothing shortly in such a design. Mr. Hoge's reputation as a preacher is rising rapidly with the public, and I hope he will do well as the president of the college.

"I have seen the collection of books which you purchased for Mr. Rice. The cheapness of such a mass of literature quite astonished me. When I can find an opportunity of sending you some money, I shall probably request you to exercise a similar kindness towards me.

"I do not know any interesting news to send you from

this quarter, either on the state of religion, or any thing else. Where is to be the end of Buonaparte's tremendous career? But our God reigns, and we will rejoice. Mention to Mrs. Alexander my affectionate remembrance of her, and believe me

"Yours sincerely,

"CONRAD SPEECE."

MR. RICE TO MR. ALEXANDER.

"CHARLOTTE, *January* 28, 1810.

"MY DEAR SIR:—

"I sometimes feel backward to write to you, because I have so little to communicate that can be at all interesting. But the pleasure which your letters afford me is so great, that, frequently when I have no other reason, I write that I may receive an answer from you, and hear something from Mrs. Alexander and your boys. If you think this is my motive at present, you will not wander far from the mark.

"Three days ago I finished the perusal of 'Cœlebs.' Miss Lightfoot Carrington, who is now in Richmond, met with it there, and sent it to me. I had often laughed at her for spending so much time in reading novels. When she got Cœlebs, 'Here,' says she, 'is a novel at last which I know that Mr. Rice will be pleased with;' and accordingly despatched it to Charlotte. I read it with more pleasure than any thing of the author's writing. It delighted me; I trust it improved me too. It put me much in mind of a certain Miss Eudocia, whom I have been longing to see for some time past. The rage for novels is so great that I have long wished to see that species of writing converted to a better purpose. Miss Hannah More has very completely answered my wishes, and has, by the way, obtained that credit with the religious world which I think in all reason belonged tc you. If you differ with me on this point, we will discuss it after we shall have talked over this new-fashioned school affair and other matters; which I hope to do in May next. At that time Mr. Speece and I hope to be with you, *and then*— ! I give you notice that Mr. Speece will come with his pockets loaded with money, in the full spirit of trade I know that he intends to make some grand speculation, for he has within the year past sold nearly two hundred dollars' worth of books, with a view of taking the money to Philadelphia.

"I think the state of religion in this country worse by some degrees than when you left it. Presbyterian congregations are decreasing every year, and appear as if they would dwindle to nothing. The Baptists and Methodists are at a stand. A strange apathy has seized the people. The judgments with which our nation has been visited, and the more awful ones which impend, have produced no effect; or if any, a most disastrous one. Instead of being a blessing they are a curse. The people feel about nothing but money. As to religion, the very stillness of death reigns amongst us. I can find no resemblance to this part of the country, but in Ezekiel's valley of dry bones. I am sure you do not forget your old friends. Remember them, then, at the throne of grace, and let *me*, particularly, have an interest in your prayers.

"I am affectionately yours,

"JOHN H. RICE."

The years spent in Philadelphia were doubtless important both as to direct usefulness and the formation of character. Yet a change thus abrupt brought with it not a few privations and annoyances. His children were sickly, the salary was small, the modes of domestic management were novel and embarrassing, and he was often tempted to wish himself back among the wide plantations and open forests of Lower Virginia. "But these," says he, "were small matters. I enjoyed health, and had on the Sabbath large assemblies of attentive people; and the preaching did not seem altogether without saving effect. The congregation appeared one and all to be pleased with my services, and many strangers as well as members of other churches came to hear me." It may be safely said, that these expressions much underrate the degree of acceptance and popularity which attended his public ministrations. The vivacity and freedom of his discourses, always during this period pronounced without the aid of any manuscript, attracted very general admiration; and their solid contents and evangelical unction made them peculiarly welcome to experienced Christians. He was, moreover, silently acquiring reputation as a theologian, of original and clear views, and strict adherence to the Reformed tenets; and was thus preparing for the important career for which he was destined by Providence.

Being now brought nearer to libraries, learned men and the means of acquiring books, he entered with great freshness of zeal into several interesting walks of clerical study. In every thing connected with the criticism and interpretation of the sacred text, he used assiduous application; taking Hebrew lessons of a learned Jew, perusing the Septuagint, collating other versions, and pushing more deeply those researches which he had long before commenced, into the original of the New Testament. His shelves began also to fill themselves with those folios and quartos, bound in vellum, of Latin theology, which always continued to be characteristic of his library. In some departments of learning he was no doubt surpassed by many of his brethren; but it is believed that none of his coevals had read more extensively in the theology of the sixteenth and seventeenth centuries; including Romanist and Lutheran, as well as Reformed divines. The practice of preaching without writing produced in him one of its ordinary effects, namely, an indisposition to commit his thoughts to paper. Consequently his judgment and taste in composition so much outstripped his ability to execute, that it was many years before he could bring himself to give any thing willingly to the public. He always wrote with ease and even with rapidity, but never to his own satisfaction. During his residence in Philadelphia, therefore, it is not known that he committed any thing to the press, except two sermons, one at the opening of the General Assembly of 1808, and the other on the conflagration of the Richmond theatre, and a few papers in the old Assembly's Magazine, which cannot now be pointed out with certainty.

In his pastoral work he found increasing satisfaction, and was surrounded by good auxiliaries. "Of my own people," says he, "William Haslitt and John McMullin were my unwavering friends. James Stuart was warm-hearted and very zealous, and often showed me the way to the houses of the poor, the widow, and the suffering; and in the prayer-meetings he was my right-hand man. Joseph Eastburn, who was a kind of city missionary, was often at our social gatherings; his heart was warm and his feelings were kind. Though this truly good man had read scarcely any thing but his Bible, he preached more acceptably and profitably than many learned men. He was originally a member of Arch Street church, but falling into scruples about his infant baptism, he went into the country and got a Baptist minister to immerse him, but on condition that he should remain a Presbyterian, as he did to the day of his death. When the Methodists occupied the old Academy which once belonged to Whitefield, Eastburn, who was his follower, began to exhort publicly, and spoke with so much warmth and tenderness that the people were much impressed. All seemed to think that he ought to be licensed as an exhorter, which was then a new thing in the church. The Presbytery gave him authority to preach in the jail, almshouse, and other institutions. But he could not confine himself to these, and spoke at prayer-meetings, and sometimes supplied the place of ministers, when they were absent or indisposed. He even attended Quaker meetings, and was moved to speak there, so often as to give some umbrage to the old broad-brims. An old Quaker lawyer said "he was afraid that friend Joseph spake sometimes before he was moved by the Spirit."

A surviving member of the congregation thinks that Mr. Alexander read but three discourses during his ministry in Pine street. Dr. Milledoler's preaching had brought in a a number of young persons ; the success of Mr. A. was chiefly among those of riper years. At one of the early communions, out of twenty-seven who professed their faith, only one was in youth. The same informant recalls the interest taken by Dr. Benjamin Rush in the performances of Mr. Alexander. He augured his future eminence, and when told that the discourses were very simple, quoted the Latin adage, *Ex pede Herculem ;* adding that he was reminded of what John Newton says in his Cardiphonia, that in his own preaching he followed the advice of a minister who fixed his eye on one of the humblest of his audience, and adapted his language to this hearer. From another venerable Philadelphian, Mr. William Bradford, a friend has derived a second anecdote. Dr. Rush and Dr. Abercrombie were in a carriage at a funeral, when Dr. Rush said, pointing to the Pine street Church, "That is the church Mr. Alexander is coming to." "Do you call that a *church ?*" said the clergyman. "Yes, sir," replied Rush ; "wherever two or three old women meet together in the name of Christ, there is the Church of the living God, the pillar and ground of the truth." On another occasion, when some one spoke of the crowds who came to evangelical preaching, Dr. Rush replied, "Yes, in this sense also, unto Shiloh shall the gathering of the people be."

He was naturally awakened to compassion by observing the great religious destitution prevailing in the outskirts of Philadelphia. It was not a time of revival, and missionary zeal had scarcely dawned upon our churches. Some of his efforts for the spread of the Gospel in the city are thus modestly related in a memorandum of his own. "After coming to Philadelphia, I formed acquaintance with a number of pious men of other churches, and heard a general complaint concerning the want of activity and enterprise. It occurred to me that there was much which might be done by pious laymen. Sabbath schools had not then been introduced. I sat down one day and drew up a constitution for an 'Evangelical Society,' not to raise funds, nor to employ others to work, but *an association of which every member was to be a working man.* I communicated the constitution to the Presbyterian ministers, in order to secure their approbation, which was readily granted. I then sent an invitation to about twenty gentlemen of zealous character in the different congregations, most of whom came together. When I read to them my plan, they seemed greatly pleased, and all expressed a willingness to do something. The first step was to divide the members into committees of two each, to go out in the evening of the Sabbath, to gather the children of the poor in some convenient place, to talk with their parents, and read the Scriptures and other good books. We met the first evening of each month to hear reports and to confer about new methods of doing good. This society operated successfully and without any serious interruption for a number of years, and still exists in a feeble state." Its operations have since been merged into the more extensive plans of the Sunday School and City Mission enterprises. Several important measures were carried into effect by its exertions, particularly the erection of an African church. Several eminent laymen were trained in these efforts for subsequent usefulness; among whom may be named James Moore and Francis Markoe. The bearing of this humble endeavour on the great work of city-missions, has induced us to glean a few additional particulars from one of the surviving labourers. Until this society was formed, it had been very unusual among Presbyterians to have any religious meetings in the evening; and these were even opposed by some good people. The Sunday evening services, when once commenced, were exceedingly popular and much crowded. Several licentiates began their ministry in these labours among the destitute, which gave origin to new churches now in existence.

The enterprise was so novel and simple, and so foreshadowed later measures for church-extension and education, that we gladly add the view derived from a memorandum for which we are indebted to the venerable Dr. Janeway. "When your father," says he to the editor, "came to Philadelphia, there was in existence a society embracing members of different denominations of Christians, and styled 'The Humane Society.' As its name imports, it was to relieve the wants of the poor. Your father originated a society, called 'the Evangelical Society.' In a certain stage of its development both Dr. Green and I became members, and regularly attended its meetings. It then met in the session-room of the Second Presbyterian Church, adjoining the church edifice, which then stood at the corner of Arch and Third streets. The object of this society was to carry the knowledge of the Gospel to the destitute in various parts of the city. The members went, two and two, to particular districts, assembled individuals where they found convenient places, read to them out of the Scriptures and evangelical sermons or portions of books, and conversed and prayed with them. These committees regularly reported to the Society the result of their labours.

"To refresh my recollections, and especially to get a knowledge of the origin of the Society, I have twice conversed with Mr. Nassau, senior, who was a member of the Third Presbyterian Church, under the ministry of Dr. Milledoler, and of course when your father succeeded him as pastor of that church. He gives the origin of the Society thus On a certain day, I think from the pulpit, your father invited some of his church members to meet at his house. When convened, he said to them, 'Brethren, I have been looking over the congregation, and think that a number of the pious members may be very usefully employed in promoting the interests of religion in different places among the poor and ignorant.' He detailed the plan, and they proposed that he should act as their president; but this he declined, as a needless formality. Another meeting was held, to which more were invited. It was afterwards proposed to embrace in the Society members of other Presbyterian churches. The Society continued to act, I think, until your father's removal to Princeton in 1812." *

We find by examination of the Religious Remembrancer,

* Letter of the Rev. J. J. Janeway, D. D., July 23, 1853.

that the Society was instituted on the eleventh day of April, 1808. The same journal, under date of September 18, 1813, says that "some of the Committees, finding the work to increase on their hands, have thought it expedient to devote an additional evening to the children," and adds, that "several convenient houses on different sites have been erected," for accommodating them. And it is said, October 16, that "at the first formation of the Society a small sum was subscribed, which was applied to the republishing of several tracts."

Mr. William Bradford remembers that Mr. Alexander was present at the opening of the Society's Sunday evening meetings, for preaching and teaching, at the corner of Buttonwood and Eighth streets. The enterprise was novel, and the meeting was so much threatened that two constables were employed to keep the peace. It was a neighbourhood of butchers, and some one said of it, "The people will attend, and butcher the Evangelicals afterwards." These particulars, however slight in themselves, have a manifest bearing on the rise of certain great charities among us.

Among the manuscripts which belong to this period, is one which evidently connects itself with what has just been recited, and with the great work of City Missions. It is in the handwriting of Dr. Alexander, and is subjoined without comment.

"THE POOR HAVE THE GOSPEL PREACHED UNTO THEM.

"It is a truly lamentable consideration, that there are thousands of unhappy persons in and about this city who rarely or never hear the Gospel. This is especially the case with respect to many poor people who are unable to obtain pews in the churches, or who are so careless about their salvation as never to have sought this privilege. Whilst with a laudable zeal we are sending the Gospel to the heathen, and to the ignorant on our frontiers, is it not also incumbent on us to endeavour, by all practicable means, to bring within its sound the multitudes in this city who are nearly as ignorant as heathens? Will it not be proper to show charity at home, and to use efforts to secure perishing souls from impending ruin?

"It is believed that it would be productive of much good to this class of people, to erect a *free church*, a church, the pews or seats of which should never be appropriated to particular persons, but left open for all who might choose at any time to occupy them. Such a church might easily be supplied with preaching every Sunday evening by the ministers of the city, and frequently in the day by strangers who may happen to spend the Sabbath in the city.

"In order to provide such a house, and to devise and execute other plans for the extension of religious knowledge among the poor and ignorant in the City and Liberties of Philadelphia, we whose names are hereunto subscribed do agree to form ourselves into a Society; and to regulate our proceedings we have adopted the following rules:

"1. The style of the Society shall be, The Society for promoting Religious Knowledge among the Poor.

"2. Any person may become a member of this Society, who shall contribute a sum for the purpose of building a free church not less than ten dollars.

"3. As soon as twenty subscribers shall be obtained, a meeting shall be held, at which it shall be determined, whether there is a sufficient prospect of success to proceed with the undertaking.

"4. If it shall be determined to make the attempt, a Committee of five persons shall be chosen by a majority of the subscribers present, to whom the whole arrangement of the business shall be committed, and who shall continue in office until the next regular meeting of the Society, when a new choice shall be made.

"5. When the church contemplated is erected, and fit to receive a congregation, it shall be the duty of the Committee already mentioned, to endeavour to have it supplied with gratuitous preaching, at least on every Sunday evening.

"6. Any three members of the Committee shall be authorized to invite any preacher of any Christian denomination to preach in the aforesaid church.

"7. The Committee shall also take the most effectual means to give notice of sermons to that class of people whose benefit is contemplated, and to use every proper measure to induce them to attend.

"8. Subscriptions of sums less than ten dollars will be thankfully received, but will not entitle the contributor to a vote in the deliberations of the Society."

Mr. Alexander was a commissioner to the General Assembly in 1807, 1808 and 1811, and at the first of these meetings was elected moderator. The following year, agreeably to custom, he delivered the discourse at the opening of the Assembly. It was published, and is upon the text, 1 Cor.,

xiv. 12, "Seek that ye may excel, to the edifying of the church."

In the year 1810, Mr. Alexander received from the College of New Jersey the honorary degree of Doctor of Divinity; the same distinction being at the same time conferred on his friends the Rev. Moses Hoge, and the Rev Leonard Woods.

Among other projects of his scheming and inventive mind, we find one or two mentioned in his private reminiscences, which connect him with enterprises that have since become very important. Speaking of the Philadelphia Bible Society, of which Dr. Rush was the chief founder, and which is the oldest in the hemisphere, he adds: "I made some exertion to have a small Tract Society established, but the attempt was not successful. William Bradford did indeed print a few tracts, and Alexander Henry aided in paying the expense." Mr. Bradford, who still survives, relates that about 1808 or 1809, Mr. Alexander urged him to print Mrs. More's "Cœlebs," in order to correct the taste of female readers for romances; which he accordingly did. Having printed the tract "Jack Covey," he applied to Mr. Alexander to fill two blank pages with prayers. The reply was that he had never written one, but the next day he brought him a prayer of a pious seaman before, and another after a storm, which were printed. Mr. Alexander strongly encouraged the primitive Tract Society, the "Philadelphia Tract Society," which had its origin in Mr. Bradford's reprinting of that incomparable narrative, "Poor Joseph," which he received from Dr. Green.

"In considering the wants of the people and the difficulty of reaching the multitude with religious instruction, I conceived the plan of a religious [newspaper], a thing at that time unknown in the world. But as the thing was new, I mentioned [it] to none but two or three of my elders; and it met with approbation. It was suggested that we had a printer, who was a well informed young man, John W. Scott. I conversed with him, and he drew up a well-written but rather florid Address, to accompany a Prospectus. Before the plan was carried into effect, I was removed to Princeton; but Mr. Scott went forward with the enterprise, and published for a number of years, before any other work of the kind was thought of, *The Christian Remembrancer.* We talked of getting some tracts for the sailors, and I composed a few prayers for their use, which Mr. Bradford printed. We then saw no way of extending religious instruction to that class of men; but Providence afterwards opened the way for much good, by means of Bethel meetings, and the like."

It is worthy of record, that in the year 1810, Mr. Alexander was elected President of the University of Georgia, and was solicited with importunity to assume that important place. The fact was unknown even to his children, until revealed by his posthumous papers.

During the last year of Dr. Alexander's abode in Philadelphia, an event of signal calamity drew his sympathies towards his native State. It is thus related in a journal of the day. "On the night of December 26, 1811, the theatre in the city of Richmond, Virginia, was unusually crowded;

a new play having drawn together an assembly of not less than six hundred persons. Toward the close of the performance, just before the last act of the concluding pantomime, the scenery caught fire from a lamp inadvertently raised to an improper position, and in a few minutes the whole building was wrapped in flames. The doors being few, and the avenues leading to them extremely narrow, the scene which ensued was truly one of horror. It may be in some degree imagined, but can never be adequately described. About seventy-five persons perished in the flames. Among these were the Governor of the State; the President of the Bank of Virginia; one of the most eminent attorneys belonging to the bar of the commonwealth; a number of other respectable gentlemen; and about fifty females, of whom a large portion were among the ladies of the greatest conspicuity and fashion in the city." When the direful news reached Philadelphia, a meeting was held on New Year's Day, of more than one hundred Virginians, being part of the Medical Class of the University of Pennsylvania, who, after suitable resolutions of condolence, requested Dr. Alexander to deliver a discourse on the mournful occasion. We well remember the solemn procession from the University to the church, and the throng of the agitated assembly. The sermon was published, and though unquestionably the most hurried production of its author, contains some passages which deserve to be remembered. The text was Romans xii. 15, "Weep with them that weep;" and it was introduced by some remarks on the sympathetic benignity of the Gospel.

"One leading difference between the system of morals prescribed by the Stoics, and that inculcated by Christianity, is, that while the former aims at eradicating the passions, the latter endeavours to regulate them and direct them into their proper channels. The great Author of our being has implanted the principle of sympathy deeply in human nature, and has made the susceptibility of feeling the sorrows of another, as extensive as the race of man. It is common to the untutored savage and the man of refinement and education; and traces of it are discovered even in the animal creation. This principle of sympathy, while it indicates the unity of our species, seems to form a mysterious bond of connection between all its members. The spectacle of suffering humanity, however great a stranger the object may be, will always excite our sensibility, unless the feelings be blunted by vicious indulgence, restrained by prejudice, or extinguished by the long prevalence of malignant passions. Genuine pity, and compassion for objects of real distress, have been perverted and almost quenched, in a multitude of persons, by the artificial excitement of spurious feelings, produced by scenes of fictitious distress; which tend to no valuable end, and are sought only for the momentary gratification of the possessor. But however sympathy may be abused, it has its proper and legitimate exercise, to which we are not only prompted by nature, but directed by reason and exhorted by religion. There are occasions, when not to 'weep with them that weep,' would be rebellion against every principle which ought to govern us. If the sufferings of an enemy may be such as to affect us—if we are excited to weep at the woes of a stranger—what must our feelings be, when we recognise in the cry of unutterable anguish the well-known voice of an acquaintance, a friend, a brother or a sister? Such a cry of distress, from the capital of our native State, has pierced our ears, and filled our hearts with grief. The sons of Virginia, resident in this place, are to-day called upon to mourn, and to mingle their sympathetic tears with those of the whole State."

After some allusion to the distinguished names in the catalogue of the dead, the preacher indulges in a few rapid pictures, which however uncommon in his severer printed works, were not unfrequent in his extemporaneous discourses, and which for this reason ought to be preserved. "That," he continues, "which winds up our sympathies to the highest pitch, is, that the greater part were young women in the very bloom and prime of life. About one half the names in the whole catalogue are of this description. O! who can think, without exquisite anguish, of so many gay and blooming virgins, decorated with the charms of beauty, accomplished by the refinements of art, tender and delicate to excess, and accustomed only to endearments and caresses, perishing by a death so cruel, and by torments so excruciating! Who can describe the chasm which has been made in numerous families, and the agony which has been, and is still endured! Tell us, ye bereaved mothers (if words can express it), the pangs which have rent your breaking hearts, since you beheld the scorched, bruised, and disfigured remains of your once beautiful daughters. 'In Rama,' of old, 'a voice of lamentation, and weeping, and great mourning, was heard; Rachel weeping for her children, and would not be comforted, because they are not.' How many inconsolable Rachels are there this day, who weep for their children and refuse to be comforted. The hoary head of the indulgent father too must now come down with sorrow to the grave. Perhaps the last prop and solace of his declining years, as well as the darling of his heart, is for ever gone from his sight. The helpless widow and the orphan children also lift up their deploring hands and their streaming eyes to heaven, expressing thereby feelings of grief and agony, to which all words are inadequate. And why need I attempt to describe the poignant pangs of the disappointed lover (the day of whose nuptials perhaps was fixed), as he beholds the form which he idolized changed into a frightful skeleton.

"But the shock is felt not only in the city of Richmond, but in remote parts of the State. Several who perished in the flames resided at a distance. With some, perhaps, it was the first visit of any length which they ever made from their father's house. Methinks I see the fond mother taking the last leave of her beloved daughter, little suspecting that it is the last. Or shall I fancy that some unaccountable foreboding seizes her mind and oppresses her heart, as the object of her hopes and fears is carried from her sight?

"But who shall imagine what her situation and feelings are, when the day arrives which shall bring a letter from her affectionate child! A letter comes, it is true; but what horror chills the blood, when it is seen not to be inscribed in the well-known hand of the dear girl, and to be addressed to the father instead of the mother. I see his veteran hand tremble while he breaks the ominous seal. And the countenance which had remained unmoved, while death was braved at the cannon's mouth, now turns pale as ashes, when he reads the few incoherent sentences, by which he is made to realize more than ever the gloomiest hour had painted on his imagination. These remarks are suggested by the recollection of a modest and amiable young lady, whom I happened to see last summer, in company with a pious mother, at a solemn religious meeting, where she appeared to be deeply interested, and to enter very devotionally into the exercises of the day ; but alas ! in looking over the melancholy list, I find her name enrolled. She perished in the flames on the fatal twenty-sixth of December.

"I feel it to be incumbent on me .... to give my public testimony against [theatrical exhibitions] as being, notwithstanding the partial good which may result from them, unfriendly to piety—unfriendly to morality—unfriendly to health—unfriendly to domestic happiness—and unfriendly to true delicacy and genuine refinement."

The peroration is as follows. "Finally, permit me to conclude this discourse, by considering the dispensation, which has convened us this day, in the light of a solemn warning. Yes, my hearers, if ever the trumpet of a righteous Providence sounded loudly in our ears, it doth so this day. The voice is alarming. Let no weak notions of accident and second causes keep you from observing the frowns of heaven, which lower over us. Think not that these were sinners above all who dwell in the land, because they suffered such things. 'I tell you nay ; but except ye repent, ye shall all likewise perish.'

"Often, since the ominous and fatal handwriting on the wall caused the proud king of Babylon to shake with terror in the midst of his profane mirth and riot, has the awful transition from the gay scenes of dissipation, to the shades of death, been made in the period of a single night. Often have the votaries of pleasure been hurried from the festive board, the merry dance, the opera and play—and what is still more dreadful, from scenes of excess and debauchery—into eternity, to answer for their deeds before the tremendous bar of God. Receive the warning, then, and 'suffer the word of exhortation.' The views and impressions produced by this deplorable occurrence, however painful at the present, may be precious in their effects, and should not be allowed to pass off without originating such resolutions and purposes, as shall become the foundation of a new course of life. You may never in the whole period of your lives find a season so favourable, to shake off the undue influence of the world, and to break with every darling lust and besetting sin. My last advice, therefore, is, BECOME REAL CHRISTIANS. Make religion a personal concern. Attend to it without delay. 'Remember now thy Creator in the days of thy youth.' And may the God of all grace crown the exercises of this day with his blessing, for Christ's sake! Amen."

It is worthy of note, as belonging to a parallel between two long and blended lives, that the Reverend Dr. Miller in New-York preached and published a discourse, commemorative of the same afflictive event. It was upon Lamentations, ii. 1—13, and contains an able and elaborate argument against theatrical amusements.

CHAPTER TWELFTH.

1811—1812.

THEOLOGICAL SEMINARY PROJECTED—ELECTION OF PROFESSOR—REMOVAL TO PRINCETON—STUDIES AND ATTAINMENTS—INAUGURATION.

IT cannot now be ascertained by whom the scheme of a Theological Seminary for the Presbyterian Church was first suggested. In the measures which resulted in such an institution, many minds co-operated. Among these we may safely say none were more prominent than Doctors Green, Miller and Alexander. The increasing fields open for Gospel labour, caused not a few among our ministers to be devising methods for supplying the destitutions. It was also generally believed that the method of pursuing studies in preparation for the ministry, under the guidance of individual pastors, however valuable as a measure of necessity, could not be relied on, as the means of furnishing adequate training for the work of so great a country. In regard to the education of candidates in general, Dr. Green, as early as 1805, sent into the General Assembly an overture, addressed to the Committee of Overtures, which was received with so much favour as to be published in the printed minutes of the year with his name, and which originated a system of measures which occupied this judicatory for several years. This admirable paper, however, did not contain any proposal of a theological institution. Of this particular method of raising up a suitable ministry, the earliest mention which we have been able to discover is in a discourse preached by Dr. Alexander in 1808, before the General Assembly, of which he had been Moderator the year before. The passage is as follows:

"I will now make a few remarks on the subject of purity, as it respects the discipline of the church. The first thing here which deserves our attention, is the introduction of suitable men into the ministry. If you would have a well-disciplined army, you must begin by appointing good officers. There is no subject which more deserves the attention of our church when met in General Assembly than this. The deficiency of preachers is great. Our vacancies are numerous, and often continue for years unsupplied, by which means they are broken up or destroyed. Our seminaries of learning, although increasing in literature and numbers, furnish us with few preachers. This state of affairs calls loudly for your attention. Some measures have already been adopted by the recommendation of the General Assembly to remedy this evil; but although they promise considerable success, they are inadequate to the object. In my opinion, we shall not have a regular and sufficient supply of well-qualified ministers of the Gospel, until every Presbytery, or at least every Synod, shall have under its direction a seminary established for the single purpose of educating youth for the ministry, in which the course of education from its commencement shall be directed to this object; for it is much to be doubted whether the system of education pursued in our colleges and universities is the best adapted to prepare a young man for the work of the ministry. The great extension of the physical sciences, and the taste and fashion of the age, have given such a shape and direction to the academical course, that I confess, it appears to me to be little adapted to introduce a youth to the study of the sacred Scriptures."

In reference to these remarks, Dr. Green says in his Autobiography: "Encouraged by this, I used all my influence in favour of the measure; and in 1809, the Presbytery of Philadelphia, to which I belonged, sent into the General Assembly of that year an overture distinctly proposing the establishment of a theological school. The committee to which the overture was referred, reported to the Assembly three plans, namely: 1. 'One great school, in some convenient place near the centre of the bounds of our church. 2. To establish two such schools in such places as may best accommodate the northern and southern divisions of the Church. 3. To establish such a school within the bounds of each of the Synods. After stating the advantages and disadvantages of each of these modes, the committee recommended and the Assembly resolved, that the above plans be submitted to all the Presbyteries within the bounds of the General Assembly, for their consideration, and that they be careful to send up to the next Assembly at their sessions in May, 1810, their opinions on the subject.' When the votes of the Presbyteries came to be examined by a committee appointed for the purpose in 1810, it appeared that a majority of the Presbyteries under the care of the Assembly had expressed a decided opinion in favour of the establishment of a theological school; and that although there was an equal number of Presbyteries in favour of the first and third plans above mentioned, yet there were those who had voted in favour of the third plan, who had done so from an entire misconception of the nature and intention of the first, which would be completely obviated when the details of that plan should be made known. The conclusion therefore was 'that there was a greater amount of presbyterial suffrage in favour of a single school than of any other plan.' Several resolutions were passed by the General Assembly (which I shall not transcribe) for the immediate establishment of the contemplated institution; and a committee was appointed, of which I was the chairman, to draught a plan, as the constitution of a theological seminary. The draughting of a plan fell of course upon me, as the chairman of the committee. In hope of getting aid from my fellow members, I requested the committee to meet in New-York, at the house of Dr. Miller. The committee consisted of seven members, and if I remember right, but four of them met. We however spent the afternoon in talking about the plan of the contemplated seminary. But when I sat seriously down to make a draught of the plan, I found that there was but one idea suggested by my brethren, that I could introduce into it. Nor had I any other guide than the nature of the subject; and if I ever taxed my faculties to their best effort, it was on this occasion. Two of the articles of the plan, when it was reported to the Assembly, were laid over to be considered in the following year, and to this day they have not been taken up—these articles related to the library and a theological academy.

"When I had completed a draught of the plan for the construction of the Seminary, I summoned the committee to meet at Princeton, on the day of Commencement, 1810. There was a general, but not a full attendance at that time; and I shall never forget with what diffidence I submitted my draught to my brethren, not only being willing, but wishing that they would suggest alterations and improvements, and I was surprised when they suggested none of any importance. We knew that it was *cum periculo* that our plan should be published before it was reported to the Assembly. But we determined to do it, and to have copies enough printed to lay one on the table of every member of the Assembly of the following year, 1811. We were not blamed for this act by any one; on the contrary, the members of the Assembly appeared to be gratified when they found that each was served with a copy. This plan has received a considerable number of modifications by the General Assemblies which have convened during the three and thirty years which have elapsed since its first adoption; and yet no important feature of the plan has been changed, and more than three fourths of the language remains as it was in the orignal composition."

On a subject so important in itself, and so closely related to our chief subject, we may be allowed to go into some particulars, by inserting the brief history of the project, prepared, as we believe, by the Rev. Dr. Miller.

"After much counsel and prayer, the proposal to establish a theological seminary for the Presbyterian Church was first introduced into the General Assembly, during the sessions of that body in May, A. D. 1809. It was introduced in the form of an overture or proposal from the Presbytery of Philadelphia. This overture was so far countenanced by the Assembly as to be referred to a select committee, who, after due deliberation on the subject, brought in the following report, which, being read, was adopted, and became the act of the Assembly, in the following words, viz.

"'The committee appointed on the subject of a theological school, overtured from the Presbytery of Philadelphia, report,

"'That three modes of compassing this important object have presented themselves to their consideration.

"'The *first* is, to establish *one great school*, in some convenient place near the centre of the bounds of our Church.

"'The *second* is, to establish *two such* schools, in such places as may best accommodate the northern and southern divisions of the Church.

"'The *third* is, to establish such a school within the bounds of *each of the Synods*. In this case, your committee suggest the propriety of leaving it to each Synod to direct the mode of forming the school, and the place where it shall be established.

"'The *advantages* attending the *first* of the proposed modes, are, that it would be furnished with *larger funds*, and therefore with a *more extensive library* and a *greater number of professors*. The system of education pursued in it would therefore be more extensive, and more perfect ; the youth educated in it would also become more united in the same views, and contract an early and lasting friendship for each other ; circumstances which would not fail of promoting harmony and prosperity in the Church. The *disadvantages* attending this mode would be, principally, those derived from the distance of its position from the extremities of the Presbyterian bounds.

" 'The *advantages* attending the *second* of the proposed modes and the *disadvantages*, will readily suggest themselves, from a comparison of this with the other two.

'The *advantages* which would attend the *third*, to wit, the establishment of theological schools by the respective Synods, would be the following. The local situation of the respective schools would be peculiarly convenient for the several parts of a country so extensive, as that for the benefit of which they were designed. The inhabitants having the seminaries brought near to them, would feel a peculiar interest in their prosperity, and may be rationally expected to contribute much more liberally than to any single school, or even to two. The Synods, also, having the immediate care of them, and directing, either in person or by delegation, all their concerns, would feel a similar interest, and would probably be better pleased with a system formed by themselves, and therefore peculiarly suited to the wishes and interests of the several parts of the Church immediately under their direction. Greater efforts, therefore, may be expected from ministers and people, to promote the prosperity of these schools, than of any other. The *disadvantages* of this mode would be, the *inferiority of the funds ;* a *smaller number of professors ;* a *smaller library,* and a more *limited system of education* in each. The students, also, as now, would be *strangers to each other.*

"'Should the last of these modes be adopted, your committee are of the opinion, that every thing pertaining to the erection and conduct of each school, should be left to the direction of the respective Synods. If either of the first, the whole should be subject to the control of the General Assembly.

"'Your committee also suggest, that, in the former of these cases, the funds for each school should be raised within the bounds of the Synod within which it was stationed. In the latter, they should be collected from the whole body of the Church.

"'Your committee, therefore, submit the following resolution, to wit:

"'*Resolved,* That the above plans be submitted to all the Presbyteries within the bounds of the General Assembly, for their consideration; and that they be careful to send up to the next Assembly, at their sessions in May, 1810, their opinions on the subject.'

"Agreeably to this resolution, the three alternate plans which it contemplates, were sent down to all the Presbyteries, to be considered and decided upon by them.

"At the meeting of the next General Assembly, in May, 1810, the Presbyteries were called upon to state what they had respectively done with respect to the recommendation of the last Assembly, relative to the establishment of a theological school. The reports from the several Presbyteries on this subject, having been read, were referred to a select committee to consider and report on the same. This committee made a report, which, being read and amended, was adopted, as follows, viz.:

"'The committee, after maturely deliberating on the subject committed to them, submit to the Assembly the following results.

"'I. It is evident, that not only a majority of the Presbyteries which have reported on this subject, but also a majority of all the Presbyteries under the care of this Assembly, have expressed a decided opinion in favour of the establishment of a theological school or schools in our Church.

"'II. It appears to the committee, that although according to the statement already reported to the Assembly, there is an *equal number* of Presbyteries in favour of the *first* plan, which contemplates a single school for the whole Church; and in favour of the *third* plan, which contemplates the erection of a school in each Synod; yet, as several of the objections made to the first plan, are founded entirely on misconception,* and will be completely obviated by de-

* "Some of the Presbyteries objected to a single theological seminary, for the whole Church, because they apprehended that, if this plan were adopted, every Presbytery would become thereby *bound* to send *all* their candidates to study in it, however inconvenient or expensive it might be. Others were fearful, that the Professors, in such a seminary, if they were not formally empowered to *license* candidates to preach the Gospel, might be clothed with powers out of which such an abuse would naturally grow, thereby endangering both the purity and peace of the Church, and giving to a few men

veloping the details of that plan; it seems fairly to follow that there is a greater amount of Presbyterial suffrage in favour of a single school, than of any other plan.

"'III. Under these circumstances, the committee are of opinion, that, as much light has been obtained from the reports of Presbyteries on this subject, as would be likely to result from a renewal of the reference: that no advantage will probably arise from further delay in this important concern; but, on the contrary, much serious inconvenience and evil; that the present General Assembly is bound to attempt to carry into execution some one of the plans proposed; and that the first plan appearing to have, on the whole, the greatest share of public sentiment in its favour, ought of course to be adopted.

"'IV. Your committee, therefore, recommend that the present General Assembly declare its approbation and adoption of this plan, and immediately commence a course of measures for carrying it into execution, as promptly and extensively as possible; and for this purpose they recommend to the Assembly the adoption of the following resolutions, viz.:—

"'*Resolved*, 1. That the state of our churches, the loud and affecting call of destitute frontier settlements, and the laudable exertions of various Christian denominations around us, all demand that the collected wisdom, piety, and zeal of

very dangerous influence. It was for the purpose of obviating these, and other objections to a single seminary, that the *sixth, seventh* and *eighth* resolutions, in a subsequent page, were adopted by the General Assembly."

the Presbyterian Church be, without delay, called into action for furnishing the Church with a larger supply of able and faithful ministers.

"'2. That the General Assembly will, in the name of the Great Head of the Church, immediately attempt to establish a seminary for securing to candidates for the ministry a more extensive and efficient theological instruction than they have heretofore enjoyed. The local situation of this seminary is hereafter to be determined.

"'3. That in this seminary, when completely organized, there shall be at least three professors, who shall be elected by and hold their office during the pleasure of the General Assembly, and who shall give a regular course of instruction in divinity, in oriental and biblical literature, and in ecclesiastical history and church government, and on such other subjects as may be deemed necessary. It being, however, understood, that until sufficient funds can be obtained for the complete organization and support of the proposed seminary, a smaller number of professors than three may be appointed to commence the business of instruction.

"'4. That exertions be made to provide such an amount of funds for this seminary as will enable its conductors to afford gratuitous instruction, and where it is necessary, gratuitous support to all such students as may not themselves possess adequate pecuniary means.

"'5. That the Rev. Doctors Green, Woodhull, Romeyn, and Miller, the Rev. Messrs. Archibald Alexander, James Richards, and Amzi Armstrong, be a committee to digest and prepare a plan of a theological seminary, embracing in detail the fundamental principles of the institution, together with regulations for guiding the conduct of the instructors and the students, and prescribing the best mode of visiting, controlling, and supporting the whole system. This plan to be reported to the next General Assembly.

"'6. That, as filling the Church with a learned and able ministry without a corresponding portion of real piety, would be a curse to the world and an offence to God and his people, so the General Assembly think it their duty to state, that in establishing a seminary for training up ministers, it is their earnest desire to guard as far as possible against so great an evil. And they do hereby solemnly pledge themselves to the churches under their care, that in forming and carrying into execution the plan of the proposed seminary, it will be their endeavour to make it, under the blessing of God, a nursery of vital piety as well as of sound theological learning, and to train up persons for the ministry who shall be lovers as well as defenders of the truth as it is in Jesus, friends of revivals of religion, and a blessing to the Church of God.

"'7. That as the Constitution of our Church guarantees to every Presbytery the right of judging of its own candidates for licensure and ordination, so the Assembly think it proper to state most explicitly, that every Presbytery and Synod will of course be at liberty to countenance the proposed plan or not, at pleasure; and to send their students to the projected seminary, or keep them, as heretofore, within their own bounds, as they may think most conducive to the prosperity of the Church.

"'8. That the Professors in the seminary shall not, in any case, be considered as having a right to license candidates to preach the Gospel; but that all such candidates shall be remitted to their respective Presbyteries to be licensed, as heretofore.'

"The committee appointed to prepare a constitution in detail for the contemplated seminary, made report to the General Assembly which convened in 1811." *

The first meeting of the Directors was held June 30, 1812, and was opened with a sermon by the Rev. Dr. Green, who was immediately elected President of the Board, an office which he held as long as he lived. When, three years later, the beginnings of an edifice were made, the corner-stone was laid by the same venerable man. "I consider," said he, "the agency I have had in providing ministers of the Gospel for the Church, and in securing the means for their adequate instruction, and for an attention to their personal piety, as the most important service that I have ever rendered to the Church of Christ."

Few things which we have to relate could be more interesting, if it were possible to recover it, than an account of the state of mind with which Dr. Alexander regarded the universal disposition of the Church to make him its first theological professor. But not a letter, not a memorandum, not a line remains to tell the story. His characteristic modesty must have made this a severe trial. In his best days, and after his longest experience and completest successes, he

* Brief History of the Theological Seminary. Princeton 1838

was accustomed to bow very low under a sense of his own insufficiency. But then, with powers all untried, to be called from his retirement to assume the teacher's office, was an event as embarrassing as it was unexpected. From the analogy of his whole life and feelings, we are persuaded that his final consent to undertake the task was produced by high religious feelings, and a profound recognition of his responsibility to the Head of the Church.

From a source unknown to us, we insert an affecting account, from one who was present at the election.

"In the year 1812, the General Assembly, then in session in the city of Philadelphia, resolved to go into the election of Professor. The Rev. Mr. Flinn, of Charleston, South Carolina, was Moderator. It was unanimously resolved to spend some time in prayer previously to the election, and that not a single remark should be made by any member with reference to any candidate, before or after the balloting. Silently and prayerfully these guardians of the Church began to prepare their votes. They felt the solemnity of the occasion, the importance of their trust. Not a word was spoken, not a whisper heard, as the teller passed around to collect the result. The votes were counted, the result declared, and the Rev. Dr. Alexander was pronounced elected. A venerable elder of the church in Philadelphia, of which Dr. Alexander was pastor, arose to speak. But his feelings choked utterance. How could he part with his beloved pastor? His tears flowed until he sat down in silence. The Rev. Dr. Miller arose and said that he hoped the brother elected would not decline, however reluctant he might feel to accept; that if *he* had been selected by the voice of the Church, however great the sacrifice, he would not dare refuse. Little did he dream that on the following year he should be called by the same voice to give up the attractions of the city, to devote his life to the labours of an instructor. The Rev. Mr. Flinn called on the Rev. Dr. Woodhull, of Monmouth, to follow in prayer. He declined. Two others were called on, and they declined, remarking that it was the Moderator's duty. He then addressed the throne of grace in such a manner, with such a strain of elevated devotion, that the members of the Assembly all remarked that he seemed almost inspired; weeping and sobbing were heard throughout the house.

"Amid the tears and prayers of the Church, Dr. Alexander was elected to the office. Amid the prayers and tears of the Church, he was laid in the tomb. But three of the members of that Assembly, it is believed, are now living. *Instead of thy fathers shall be thy children.*"*

When it became necessary to announce his determination to the people of his charge, it was in the following terms.

"As it is known to this congregation that I have been appointed by the General Assembly to be a Professor in the Theological School which they are about to establish at Princeton, New Jersey, and as the time draws near when it will be expected that I should declare my mind in relation o this appointment, I have judged it proper and expedient,

* The Presbyterian.

in the first place, to make a communication to you, the dear people of my charge.

"After viewing this important subject in every light in which I could place it, and after having earnestly sought the direction of Heaven, it does appear to me to be the call of Providence, which I cannot and ought not to resist.

"This resolution has not been formed under the influence of any dissatisfaction with my present condition, nor from any want of affection to this people; for since I have been your pastor, no event has occurred to disturb that peace and harmony which should ever exist between minister and people; and I have had no reason to doubt the sincerity and cordiality of the attachment of this congregation to me from the first day I came amongst them until this time. For all their respect and attention, and especially for that readiness with which they have received the word at my mouth, 'I give thanks to God.' I moreover wish to say, that I do not know a single congregation within the bounds of our Church, of which I would choose to be pastor in preference to this. No invitation, therefore, from any other would ever have separated us.

"I did expect to live and die with you, unless ill health (with which I have been threatened of late) should have made a removal expedient. But we know nothing of the designs of Providence with regard to us. God's dispensations are unsearchable. In the whole of this business, thus far, I have been entirely passive. I never expected or sought this appointment. When it was mentioned to me by some members of the Assembly, the day it took place, my answer was, that I sincerely wished they would think of some other person; that it was an office which I did not covet, and for which I felt myself altogether unqualified. But when asked whether I would give the subject a serious and deliberate consideration if I should be appointed, I answered that this I durst not oppose.

"Since the appointment has been made, I have thought much, but said little. I have seriously and deliberately considered the subject. I never viewed any decision to be made by me in so important a light. I think I have desired to do the will of God, and have, as earnestly as I could, asked his counsel and guidance, and the result is, that I am convinced that I ought not refuse such a call.

"To train up young men for the ministry, has always been considered of higher importance to the Church of Christ than to preach the Gospel to a particular flock already gathered into the fold; and it has always been considered as a sufficient reason for dissolving the pastoral relation between minister and people, that he was wanted for this employment; and sister churches, which do not allow of removals from our pastoral charge [?] do nevertheless admit this to be a sufficient reason for the translation of a minister.

"In addition to this, it ought to be considered that this call comes to me in a very peculiar way. It is not the call of a College, or University, or any such institution, but it is the call of the whole Church by their representatives. And I confess that it has weighed much with my mind, that this appointment was made by the General Assembly in circumstances of peculiar seriousness and solemnity, and after special prayer for Divine direction and superintendence, and by an almost unanimous vote. Perhaps it would be difficult to find a disinterested person who would not say, under such circumstances, 'It is your duty to go—it appears to be the call of God;' and I do believe that the majority of this congregation are convinced in their judgment, whatever their feelings may dictate, that I should be out of my duty to refuse. Indeed, I cannot but admire the deportment of the people in relation to this matter. Although tenderly affected, and many of you grieved at heart, you have not ventured to say 'stay.' You saw that there was something remarkable in the dispensation, and you knew not but that the finger of God was in the affair, and therefore, with a submissive spirit, you were disposed to say, 'The will of the Lord be done.'

"It does appear hard, indeed, that this bereavement should fall upon you who have already been bereaved so often; but consider that He who causeth the wound, hath power to heal it, and can turn this event to your greater advantage; and I entertain a confident persuasion, that if you willingly make this sacrifice for the good of the Church, the great Head of the Church will furnish you with a pastor after his own heart, who will feed you with knowledge. Commit your case to him with fervent prayer and humble confidence, and he will not forget nor forsake you.

"My dear brethren, as we have lived in peace and love, I hope that we shall part in the same spirit. I hope that we shall remember one another unceasingly at the throne of grace. Let us recollect the times and seasons when we have taken sweet converse together in this house, and other places where prayer is wont to be made. If any shall choose to be displeased, and follow me with hard speeches instead of prayers, I shall not return unto them as they measure unto me. I will not resent their conduct. I desire ever to be disposed to bear you as a people on my heart with tender love; and now to His grace and kind protection do I commit you. Farewell!"

The inauguration, which we anticipate for the sake of connection, took place on the twelfth day of August, 1812. It was an occasion of great solemnity and feeling. The older ministers, especially those to whom the direction was entrusted, looked with parental yearnings on the infant seminary, and none were more ready to hail with thankfulness and hope the approach of new means for training the ministry, than those excellent men who lamented the scantiness of their own early opportunities. But to none did the service of the day bring greater solicitude than to him who was about to put on armour for which he unaffectedly felt too weak. The first discourse was a sermon by Dr. Miller, of New-York, on the Duty of the Church to take measures for providing an Able and Faithful Ministry; from the words, "And the things which thou hast heard of me, among many witnesses, the same commit thou to faithful men, who shall be able to teach others also:" 2 Timothy, ii. 2. It was an able investigation of the question, what is to be understood by an able and faithful ministry, which was made to include piety, talents, learning and diligence; and of the means which the Church is bound to employ for providing such a ministry.

The Inaugural Discourse of the Professor was founded on the words, "Search the Scriptures," John v. 39; and was a learned argument in behalf of biblical study. In one respect the whole performance was true to the habit and character of the speaker; for it did not contain, from beginning to end, the faintest allusion to his own personality. All deprecation of censure, and all promise of fidelity, were equally absent. It was followed by a charge to the Professor and Students of Divinity, by the Rev. Philip Milledoler, D. D. All concerned have since gone to their reward; and of the Directors, before whom these addresses were delivered, the only survivors are the Rev. President Nott, the Rev. William Neill, D. D., the Rev. John McDowell, D. D., and the Rev. Francis Herron, D. D. It is for the public to determine how far the work in which these good men then engaged, with such earnestness and many prayers, has conduced to the progress of religion and learning in the United States.

It was with an unfeigned reluctance that Dr. Alexander accepted the appointment. No man could entertain a higher estimate of the functions which awaited him; no man of eminence could think more humbly of himself. All his life long he was free to acknowledge, that his training, however laborious, had lacked much of the rigour and method of the schools; and while he had pursued knowledge with enthusiasm, and in many fields, he knew that it had been with the neglect of certain forms which are supposed to give fitness for the academical chair. Theology had indeed been the study of his life. Its difficult questions had been the constant occupation of his profoundest meditations; and he had during his residence in Philadelphia gathered about him the great masters of Latin theology, whose works appeared in Holland, Switzerland, Germany, and France, in the sixteenth and seventeenth centuries. A rare occasion for adding to his stock of Dutch theology was afforded by the sale of a library belonging to a learned minister from Holland, the Rev. Mr. Van Harlingen, of Somerset. In relation to this, his friend, Mr. Rice, thus wrote: "I could not help exclaiming, when I heard of the fine library you have purchased, '*O fortunati!*' but I could hardly add, '*Haud equidem invideo!*' But why should I repine? I have more books than I can read."* These Reformed divines he regarded as having pushed theological investigation to its greatest length, and compacted its conclusions into the most symmetrical method. He was accustomed to say that in his judgment Reformed theology reached its culminating point about the epoch of the Synod of Dordrecht. To these great authors he turned with unabated zest during the whole of a long and studious life. He once said to the writer, that on a perplexed subject he preferred Latin to English reading; not only because of the complete and ingenious nomenclature which had grown up in the dialectic schools of the church, but because the little effort required for getting the sense kept his attention concentrated. It was

* Mr. Rice to Dr. Alexander, November 4, 1813.

indeed almost amusing to observe how he would hang over the massive quarto or folio, with all the awakened interest of a novel-reader. In consequence of the fiery controversy which characterized those times, and the scholastic acumen and philosophic adventure and logical exactness which belonged to the age, he considered these scholars as having anticipated most of the minor questions which have vexed the church in later times. His penchant for metaphysical investigation urged him, from an early date, to make himself acquainted with the philosophies of the periods, from which each system took its tincture, and without which it is impossible to survey the several schemes from a just point of view. Thus he perused, and generally in their sources, not only the peripatetic and scholastic writers, but the treatises of Des Cartes, Leibnitz, Wolff, and Voetius. And there was no subject on which he discoursed with more pleasure or success than on the exposition and comparison of these ingenious though now exploded systems. He made himself familiar with the Christian Fathers, both Greek and Latin, and perused them at intervals during forty years; some of his very last labours having been in this field. At a certain period he examined all that they had written on the Divinity of our Lord; and this formed a subject of lively intercourse between him and Dr. Miller. It is particularly remembered with what surprise and admiration he spoke of the felicitous subtilty of Cyril. It was his delight to seek out the portions of truth in the books of ancient authors. Nor did he confine himself to writers on one side. Through long years he was wont to seek with patience the best works in defence of popery ; the argumentative dissertations of the extreme Lutherans and Dutch Remonstrants, as well as the Fratres Poloni and other champions of Socinianism. It need scarcely be added that he was familiar with English theology, as treated both by authors of the Established Church, and by the great Nonconformist divines. His recent travels in New England, and the prevailing excitement caused by the speculations of Hopkins and Emmons, served to keep him observant in regard to the phases of opinion in the American churches. As it respects his own conclusions, he has left on record the statement, that on his return from New England, and during his residence in Philadelphia, his views, which had been somewhat modified by eastern suggestions, began to fix themselves more definitely in the direction of the common Westminster theology. In many respects, therefore, he was well fitted for the difficult post to which the Church was summoning him.

But there were other branches of learning, tributary to the teacher's place, which had occupied his attention. His extraordinary tenacity of memory, which seemed never to let go a fact entrusted to it, gave him both taste and facility for historical study ; and we have never met with any one who was more at home in all the annals of ecclesiastical record. For reasons already indicated the events were made to revolve in his mind around the momentous points of theological determination ; so that the history of doctrine, including the rise and progress of errors, the decisions of councils, controversial authorship and the establishment of symbols and of sects, became favourite objects of inquiry. On these subjects he amassed an extraordinary amount of original manuscript, and from these sources he was accustomed to enliven and diversify his dogmatical instructions.

In the classical languages he was well read, though without scrupulous care for those niceties of metre and accent, in which English scholars take a pride. The Greek of the New Testament was familiar to him from incessant perusal. No day passed without deliberate study of this sacred original. And in his later years a beautiful Glasgow edition of Griesbach was commonly in his hands during all the private hours of the Lord's day. Indeed, he frequently complained that this practice had, to a certain extent, unfitted him for textual citation of the English version in extemporaneous discourse. He accustomed his children to read the Greek Testament, long before they arrived at it as a school-study; and this exercise, between morning prayers and breakfast, was kept up for some years. We have already recorded his first acquaintance with the Hebrew Bible. From that hour he never relaxed in his efforts to master the venerable language. His first successful attempts were made in Philadelphia, where he was stimulated by the example and the counsels of Dr. Wilson, and aided by the lessons of Hurwitz, a learned Jew. The splendid large paper, Michaelis edition of Halle, which he acquired about this time, now lies before us. It was one of his peculiarities that he treated books with a religious tenderness, never making in any one of them so much as a marginal note. This volume was in his hands for nearly half a century, and to the last of his reading he perused at least one chapter of Hebrew every day.

In natural connection with this was the study of Criticism and Hermeneutics. Although in regard to the latter he was indebted chiefly to the older school, his curiosity was wakeful and his knowledge extensive. The history of great manuscripts, versions and editions was deeply fixed in his mind, and he always spoke of them with the familiarity which the mineralogist has with the specimens of his cabinet. The qualifications on which we have slightly touched were the more important, as the new professor was expected to begin his labours with an attempt in every department of theological study.

In the month of July, 1812, Dr. Alexander arrived in Princeton, with his wife then in the bloom and freshness of a health which endured to old age, and with four children, of whom the oldest was not nine years old. The change to a green and airy village, from a heated and populous city, was exceedingly grateful to one who had been reared in the mountains, and to whom the restrictions and conventionalities of civic life were always a penance. Disposed at all times to give frank and prompt expression to what rose within him, he felt the stricture of a great town and its ways, and often longed for the shade and scope of the country. It was perhaps this which led him to regard his sojourn in Philadelphia as the least agreeable portion of his life. But now he was to resume what might be called a country life, and we remember the almost boyish glee with which he saluted and indicated to his children the salient points of rural prospects. He came with his own horses, and for some years was accustomed with his family to spend much time in easy drives among the pleasing scenes of that delightful neighbourhood, and to places where his appointments lay. In early life he was a bold and dexterous horseman. He came to be the tiller of a garden, in which art, however, he did not lay out special endeavours. The dwelling to which he came was small and inconvenient, in the least inviting part of the borough; later years afforded him a much more suitable abode.

On arriving at so important a point in our simple and uneventful history, and at the place from which it is no more to remove, we may be allowed to pause a little over the locality. Princeton is a village which holds out attractions from its high site and its historical associations. At that time it stood upon the county line between Middlesex and Somerset, and just where the hilly or upland country begins to subside into the tamer slopes which extend towards the ocean, but which swell eastward into a graceful line of blue Monmouth hills. The village was for many years little else than a gathering of houses around the College, which had been here for half a century. It had been further signalized by the battle of Princeton, and by the temporary presence of the old Congress. Every thing, however, had reference to the great and venerable literary institution, whose officers were the most prominent persons in the place. The ancient edifice, the ample lawns, and spreading trees, made its grounds, then as now, the principal charm of the village. Its cemetery contained the ashes of Burr, Davies, Edwards and Witherspoon; and in the neighbourhood, as you rise towards a hard rocky ridge, was the farm of the last named, which he had called Tusculum.

At this time Princeton was not without many persons of note, some of whom may be mentioned as more or less connected with the subject of this memoir. Doctor Samuel Stanhope Smith was living, and was approaching the term of his presidentship ; and he was beyond question the person to whom most eyes were directed with favour and admiration. He is distinctly remembered by us, as he then appeared, in a beautiful old age surpassing any that we have known. He was tall, slender and feeble, but erect. The clear soft skin, and delicate complexion, and mild blue eye, were remarkably exempt from the traces of age. Many a pupil will recall his stately venerable form, as he walked with velvet cap and academic gown, in those processions which took place at least every Sunday, from Nassau-Hall to the church. The days of Dr. Smith's activity were nearly ended, and he soon afterwards resigned. He was celebrated for his acquaintance with elegant letters, for the eloquence of his pulpit discourses, and for the matchless courtliness of his manners. He had formed himself upon the best masters of the French school ; in which endeavour his most celebrated pupil was the Rev. Dr. Henry Kollock, one of the most ornate yet vehement orators whom our country has produced ; and who had until recently been the pastor of the village church.

Dr. John Maclean, a native of Scotland, father of President Maclean, was at this time vice-president of the College, and was eminent as a mathematician and a chemist. The Stockton family, always among the most prominent of the place, was represented by Richard Stockton of Morven, the second of the name, well remembered as one of the most able members of the New Jersey bar, and also as a Senator of the United States. Samuel Bayard, a descendant of the Huguenot refugees, a ruling elder in the church, an author of several works, and a man of mild and affectionate piety, was a friend, who, as long as he lived, was cherished by Dr. Alexander with true regard. To whom may be added, Dr. John Vancleve, Colonel Beatty, and others, long since departed, equally respected, but whose names would scarcely interest the general reader. But time has wrought sad changes. Of some of the families here mentioned not a vestige remains; and the writer feels the flight of years, when he observes that only one house in the long and thickly peopled principal street of Princeton is occupied by the same family as in 1812.

Thus at the age of forty years Dr. Alexander was girding on the harness of his most important exertion; at a stage when, if ever, the human powers are in fulness of vigour, and, as the event proved, at the precise middle point of his life. His health, though never robust, was not threatened by any serious indications, and had not yet succumbed to inordinate study. In Philadelphia he had suffered from short but violent attacks of rheumatism, and he was beginning by slow degrees to recognise a train of nervous symptoms, from which he afterwards endured great discomfort. His habits were settled, and his mental and moral character had taken their leading configuration.

Pausing for a moment to recall the picture as then presented, we do not find many striking lines to be added to those already given. In person he was thin, but his countenance was full of life, his complexion was clear, his teeth as yet spared, his locks, though slightly silvered, unusually full, and his eye mobile and piercing to an extraordinary degree, as none can forget who ever saw him. As compared with his later self, we should say that he was characterized by the great spring and vivacity of his manner and discourse; more disposed to converse, bold and ready in argument, sometimes keen in answer or reproof, always open to the point of what was gay or humorous, free with his children and their comrades, enthusiastic in his love of scenery and of music, with a frankness and naturalness in the expression of opinions and sentiments, which was the more delightful the more it receded from the canons of artificial society. His opinions were formed, his lines of study marked out, and in regard to his manner in preaching the Gospel, he was unquestionably at a point beyond which he never rose.

CHAPTER THIRTEENTH.

1812.

OPENING OF SEMINARY—PLAN—ANTECEDENT QUALIFICATIONS—EARLY METHODS—INTERCOURSE WITH STUDENTS—EVENING SERMONS—ACCESSION OF DR. MILLER—RELATIONS OF THE PROFESSORS.

A MODEST man could scarcely be placed in more trying circumstances than was Dr. Alexander in his new post. It is much easier to carry on the routine of an established institution, than to draught the original plan. In this case many things remained to be done. The scheme was not so much to be carried out as to be created. There was not only no foregoing incumbent, in whose steps to tread, but there could scarcely be said to be any precedent. In our day we are familiar with theological seminaries, among Baptists, Episcopalians, and Methodists; but at that time, such institutions, as distinct from colleges and universities, were new in America, and scarcely known in Europe. In Great Britain, France and Holland, clerical training is pursued at the universities; and even the *Prediger-Seminar* of some German States is of late origin, besides being very different from our theological schools.

From the existence for so many years at Princeton of both College and Seminary, the misapprehension has somewhat naturally prevailed that the two schools are connected; whereas they have always been totally distinct; one being an independent chartered institution under a close corporation, owning no necessary alliance with any sect, and the other a strictly ecclesiastical foundation, managed by trustees, and superintended by directors appointed from time to time by the General Assembly of the Presbyterian Church. There had indeed been theological lectures in the College of New-Jersey, and eminent men had proceeded from the instructions of Witherspoon and Smith, but the experiment was now to be tried of a separate and additional curriculum; and from this time, all strictly professional lessons in divinity ceased to be delivered in the College.

The Committee of the General Assembly had indeed prepared a general scheme or programme of a theological course to be observed in the new seminary, and in the construction of this, which was framed by Dr. Green, Dr. Alexander's views were largely contributed. But now, as sole professor for a time, he was to strengthen this outline, to fill up its details, and to carry the work into laborious execution. It can scarcely be doubted that these were among the most anxious moments of his life. With the highest views of what was demanded, he unfeignedly shrank from the responsibility of realizing his large idea, and would doubtless have laid down the attempt, but from the deep persuasion that the call was of God, and from the hope that his hands would soon be strengthened by the accession of a suitable colleague. His first solicitude was concerned in drafting a plan of study for the three years which had been allotted for the course. He was next to address himself to the work of actual instruction. However well furnished in several departments with the general knowledge implied in ministerial accomplishment, he was necessarily destitute of all special preparations. Not only were lectures to be written, on branches lying far asunder, but such lacunæ were to be filled up, as exist here and there in the acquisitions of the most diligent student ; while the whole modus of communicating knowledge and conducting discipline was as yet an affair of tentative and doubtful effort.

Although called primarily to be a teacher of theology, in its stricter acceptation, he was led both by strong native tastes and by convictions of reason, to give first attention to the criticism and interpretation of the original Scriptures. With the Greek, as has been intimated, he was sufficiently familiar to be a competent instructor ; but Hebrew literature was in its infancy in America. The works of Gesenius were as yet unknown, and the learned labours of Gibbs and Stuart had not been given to the world. Even in New England the vowel-points were for a time held in suspicion, and those who desired to penetrate into their mysteries were fain to seek after the difficult and very rare volumes of Buxtorf, Leusden and Opitius. Conscious of his own imperfect knowledge, he modestly but indefatigably set about the work of inculcation, and the few survivors of those small classes will readily testify how zealously and even enthusiastically he toiled with them among the knotted roots of Hebrew rudiments. For a number of years, and with increasing ability, he worked in this field, until relieved by the services of a beloved pupil, the Reverend Charles Hodge, now senior professor in the Seminary. As it regards Criticism and Hermeneutics, it was a department which had great charms for him, and by extensive reading, compiling and original investigation, he prepared to furnish a system of instruction, which for some years he delivered as lectures, a number of which still remain among his papers. We can call to mind no subject in which he was more uniformly interested, than the fortunes of the Hebrew and Greek text, the annals of translation and recension, and the principles of hermeneutical study. To this he added copious instructions in Biblical Archæology, on which he prepared numerous discourses, and which remained under his control for many years. The manuscripts on this subject in our possession are more than would fill a single large volume. It was a topic which awakened his profound attention and lively feeling; for no man looked more reverently on the typical Christology of the levitical law; and none of his pupils can forget the awe with which he approached the recesses of the expiatory system, or the felicitous use which he made of the altar and the propitiatory, in his more purely theological exposition of the Atonement. Though far from the extreme of Cocceius, and though falling short of Witsius in his interpretation of Mosaic symbols, he nevertheless differed still more from that rationalizing school of American divines, then becoming loud and influential, who were disposed to reduce the contents of levitical typology to a minimum. We have lived to see a healthful reaction against this extreme tendency.

As might have been expected, however, his primary attention was bestowed upon the large round of topics included within the title of his peculiar professorship, that is, the statement, establishment, and defence of the doctrines which constitute the Christian system. Deeply persuaded that many theological errors have their origin in a bias derived from false metaphysics, he set about the methodizing of his thoughts upon mental philosophy, always keeping in hand the clew which he had received from his venerated preceptor, William Graham. The German philosophy was as yet unknown among us, and he was never led to travel the transcendental or "high priori road," but treated mental phenomena on the inductive method, as the objects of a cautious generalization. While he uniformly recommended the perusal of Locke, it was as he often declared, not so much for the value of his particular conclusions, as for the spirit of his investigation, the calmness, patience, and transparent honesty of that truly great man. He likewise expressed great favour for Reid, Beattie, Buffier, Campbell and Stewart, with whose general methods, as well as their views of intuitive truths and constitutional principles of reason, he was in agreement, while he dissented from many of their definitions, distinctions, and tenets. These were subjects which fell in with his tastes, habits of thought and course of reading; and as preliminary to the development of the revealed system, he regarded them as forming a necessary part of every complete theological course. And if the acuteness of his inquiry and the force of his reasoning were ever fully exhibited, it is in his lectures on the Will, and his elaborate refutation of Dr. Thomas Brown's work on Causation. From year to year his scheme of mental philosophy took on a form of stricter method ; yet he may be said to have begun with it at his entrance upon public teaching. No portion of his course more awakened the interest of his auditors ; and such was the ingenuity with which he made these lessons bear on theological questions still in reserve, that in the days of church-controversy it used to be a common remark, that students who had been imbued with Dr. Alexander's metaphysics were sure to swallow his entire system. Perhaps the same is true of every theological instructor who deduces a concatenated system from any clearly defined principles.

From these topics he turned to the closely allied domain of Natural Religion. In regard to this, the only safe way of defining his theological position would be to publish his treatises, and any thing short of this might be misapprehended. While he was far from being a rationalist, he was never satisfied with the tactics of those reasoners who under the pretext of exalting revelation, dismiss with contempt all arguments derived from the light of nature. Here he freely declared his judgment that many sound, able and pious men had greatly erred. He rendered due homage, therefore, to the labours of such writers as Nieuwentyt, the younger Turrettine, and Paley, and spent much time in considering and unfolding with nice discrimination the various schemes of argument for the Being and Perfections of God, and the necessity and antecedent probability of a revelation. Connected closely with this was the discussion of Ethical Philosophy, in which he taught from the outset the same doctrines which have been given to the world in a posthumous work, and which have awakened severe opposition from those who find them fatally inconsistent with modern systems of theology.

The anxieties belonging to an attempt to lay down the great lines of a method for teaching the whole system of revealed truth, to those who were to be the ministers of the Church, were just and burdensome. There are a few living who can recollect the particulars of these instructions. As compared with those later methods which grew out of continued experience with successive classes, they were probably more extemporaneous and colloquial; there was more use of existing manuals, and less adventure of original expedients. Dr. Alexander, herein concurring with Chalmers, conceived that theology was best taught by a wise union of the text-book with the free lecture. Finding no work in English which entirely met his demands, he placed in the hands of his pupils the Institutions of Francis Turrettine. It was ponderous, scholastic and in a dead language, but he believed in the process of grappling with difficulties; he had felt the influence of this athletic sinewy reasoner on his own mind, and had observed that those who mastered his arguments were apt to be strong and logical divines. At this time there had been no modern edition, and copies were rare; but the classes were small, and the book was not laid aside until it became impossible to supply the demand. It would be very unjust to suppose that the young men were charged with the tenets of Turrettine, to the injury of their mental independence. It is indeed difficult to apprehend the force of a vulgar argument which sneers at text-books—the convenient wisdom of the mighty dead—but admits any amount of unwritten dogmatism from the chair of the living professor. Dr. Alexander often dissented from the learned Genevan, and always endeavoured to cultivate in his students the spirit and habit of original investigation. It is likely that his labours at this period derived a peculiar vivacity from his time of life, from the freshness of the employment, and from the necessity of adapting himself to a limited circle. He very laboriously engaged in making such brief aids in the way of syllabus and compendium as might furnish to the student a manageable key to the whole classification. He prepared extensive and minute questions, going into all the ramifications of theology; lists of which still remain in the hands of some alumni. He assigned subjects for original dissertations, which were publicly read, and commented on by both professors and students; a near approach to the acts held in the old university schools, under the scholastic moderator. To this were added, at a date which we find ourselves unable to fix with precision, the debates of a theological society, meeting weekly, always on some important topic, and always closed by the full and highly animated remarks of the professor.

So far as we have been able to discover, the general plan of the studies in the Seminary received its form at this time; there were subsequent additions and emendations, but the main trunks and branches remained the same. This is particularly true of the theological course, properly so called.

The natural and simple light, in which it was a characteristic of the professor to view all subjects, and the predominance of logical nexus as the element of association in his mind, concurred to cause a preference for the ancient and more obvious scheme of classifying Scripture truth. Hence he did not adopt the Federal method of arrangement, as it has been called, of Witsius; great as was his sympathy with the evangelical warmth and unction of that school. For the same reasons his judgment disapproved the order suggested by Chalmers, in the preface to what remains of his original and striking but fragmentary theological course. For, while he agreed with this great author in considering the plan of redemption as the ultimate scope and crowning glory of all theology, he nevertheless preferred as a medium of scientific communication, that disposition of topics which takes its departure from the Being, Attributes, and Works of God; that is, from Theology in its strictest acceptation. On each head or title he was accustomed to assign a considerable portion of the text-book, to be carefully perused by the class, and to be made the subject of a sifting examination; also naming the chief authors who had treated of the points respectively, and sometimes, when these works were numerous, allotting them to different students, with a requisition that they should give some account of each, either orally, or what was more common, in writing. This examination and these essays gave rise to brief but animated remarks from the chair, and he was never more felicitous or more convincing than in such impromptus; in which his eye would kindle and flash, and his expressive face become radiant, as he poured forth the gatherings of an extraordinary erudition, or pursued the thread of nice and delicate analysis, with a clearness and closeness of argument which his partial hearers thought unrivalled. To this was added, however, and with greater fulness as years advanced, the delivery of formal and elaborate lectures on the grand articles of the faith.

The division of this department into Didactic and Polemic Theology, which the Plan of the institution made imperative, gave the professor an opportunity to go over all the leading doctrines in the way of defence against the objections of errorists, heretics and infidels. In doing this he brought to bear his remarkable stores of recondite reading. He gave the biography of eminent opponents, clear analyses of their systems, and refutation of their reasons. Of necessity he was thus carried into the field of *Dogmengeschichte*, the progress of controversies, the debates and conclusions of councils, the construction of creeds, and the whole round of symbolical theology. What might be considered by some an inordinate length of time was devoted to the cardinal differences, such as the controversy with Deists, Arians, Socinians, Pelagians, Arminians, Papists and Universalists ; all being made to revolve around the Calvinistic system, which, upon sincere conviction, he had adopted.

To prevent a return to this subject, we shall here add a few words concerning methods which, as the growth of experience, were not matured until some years later. He was so earnestly in favour of having the young clergyman armed at all points against adversaries, that he greatly extended his lectures, so as to embrace the varieties of Heathenism and Mohammedanism with which missionaries must be brought into conflict ; and also the forms of error which prevail in our Western country. Accordingly he has left copious reviews of Campbellism, Shakerism, and even Mormonism, with details which show how largely and attentively he must have examined all the available authorities of these heretics. In conducting these studies, he alighted on a method which gave him great pleasure, and was always interesting to his pupils. Early in the session each member of the class had allotted to him some erroneous system or controversy, to be made the subject of a dissertation. The whole term was sometimes allowed for preparing these, and some of the essays became almost volumes. Among them were productions which he prized very highly. All this was over and above his extensive course of lectures. He was far from having a stereotyped plan; but besides undertaking new subjects of instruction in the close of his life, as we shall have occasion to say, he made frequent changes in his *modus operandi* to the last.

It is worthy of note, that while he gave diligent attention to this part of his duties, he was in no sense an active controvertist. In private, his error, if he erred, was altogether in the opposite direction. When falsehood was read or heard by him, it was the tendency of his mind, from its strong logical interest, rather to yield himself to the consideration of adverse arguments, and to weigh them with a judgelike calmness, than to seek on the spot for weapons of refutation. His practical maxim was the *audi alteram partem ;* and those who were privy to his daily studies were astonished at the time which he bestowed on the most dangerous writers. And yet his own opinions were held with a firmness which in his mature years seemed to suffer not even a momentary shaking. The habits to which allusion has been made, tended beyond doubt to produce in him a peculiar reserve and impartiality in stating the opinions of adversaries, and in refuting them.

There is one charm connected with the opening of a theological school, which belongs peculiarly to its infant state, and can never be fully regained in years of greater prosperity. This is the intimate association between teachers and scholars. As yet, there were no buildings ; the professor's house was at once library, chapel, and auditorium. The handful of pious young men gathered around their preceptor almost as members of his family ; going freely in and out, sitting at his board, joining in the domestic worship, and, in a sense, not merely learning of him but living with him. This continued to be the case for a number of years, for the Seminary began with three, and did not attain the number of thirty until the fifth year of its existence. In such a state of things, there is more freedom and frequency of intercourse, than when more than a hundred are collected, when it would absorb all the time and strength of the professor to bestow the same personal attentions. In later years, it is but just, however, to observe, Dr. Alexander gave as free access to his study as pupils ever enjoyed of a teacher. Few moments of the day passed without a knock at his door ; and as his apartment was but a few steps from the principal edifice, it was resorted to by the young men with the greatest familiarity, and on every sort of errand both temporal and spiritual. We may here add, that at no time of his life was he accustomed to deny himself to visitors; acting, as it should seem, on the maxim which Payson adopted,—"the man that wants to see me, is the man I want to see." But in these early years, the relation of professor and student was peculiarly intimate, as will be remembered by many now alive, who sought his advice in the greatest emergencies of their spiritual life.

Some extracts from a family letter of the period, will add interest to this time of transition.

"*October* 10, 1812.

"I was dismissed from my charge in Philadelphia, on the 22d of July. You may guess that I felt some regret at leaving a congregation in which I have reason to believe there are many of God's dear children, particularly among the poor. As in every congregation, however, there are some who are not of the right spirit, so also in this there were some men rather turbulent. Though we never had any contention in the Society, I could perceive there was fuel to cherish the flame if it should ever be kindled. The labours of a city minister are necessarily very great, where his charge are numerous; and it is extremely difficult, with any exertion which can be made, to afford universal satisfaction. And upon the whole, a city is not so favourable for religion, except among the poor and distressed. I have every reason to believe that my people were sufficiently attached to me, and parted with me reluctantly; but most of them were convinced that I was following the path of duty. It seems, however, that God had a controversy with that city, for since my removal Dr. Green has been elected President of this College, and has determined to come. Or He may intend to substitute men whose labours He will more abundantly bless.

"On the 29th of July I removed my family to this place, where a house was provided for us, not very large or commodious, but the best which could be obtained. The people here we found very kind and attentive, and the situation of the place remarkably pleasant, especially in summer. Every place however has its inconveniences and difficulties. Heaven is not to be expected in this world. External circumstances go but a little way towards making us happy. The relief which we receive in our afflictions and distresses has often more real pleasure in it than we experience in our greatest prosperity. Little things often disturb our peace as much as great, and we bear small adversities with less patience than greater, because we do not seek 'grace to help.' During the whole summer our family has through God's mercy enjoyed uninterrupted health. I am greatly pleased to learn that some of your children begin to fear the Lord, in the days of their youth. I hope you will not be disappointed in the fruit which these early blossoms promise. There can be no greater pleasure to serious parents than to see their offspring choosing wisdom's ways and 'walking in the truth.'"—"You may suppose that I have abandoned preaching. Very true, it is no part of my office, so long as the school is in a place supplied with the Word; but as I have been so long accustomed to preach, it does not seem pleasant to be altogether silent, and therefore I preach every Sunday evening in my own house; and as often as opportunity offers I ride over to some one of the neighbouring congregations, and assist my brethren."

Adverting to the same topic, he writes January 27, 1813: "It is a part of my duty to preach to my students, who are nine in number, but as I did not wish to interfere with the regular worship of the place, I instituted a meeting on Sunday evening at my own house. No persons attended but such as were invited, and when the winter commenced, very few could attend with comfort; but in proportion to the difficulty of attending was the desire increased, both among the students and citizens. At length a large room was fitted up in one of the College buildings, and I was invited by the Faculty to preach in it. The place was very soon crowded, and all the principal families in the place and vicinity took the lead in attending. We were soon obliged to seek a larger place, which was also found insufficient to contain the people who came. Sometimes more than a hundred have been unable to get in. We have now removed to the Refectory or Dining Room [the present Museum], a room which will hold several hundred people seated, and even this seems as if it would be scarcely sufficient. The attention of the people is uncommonly solemn and many appear to be affected, but what the result will be, God only knows. Two particular facts have encouraged me to hope for some good issue. A young man who came here to study divinity, appeared soon after his arrival to fall under deep convictions. He came to me and told me with many tears, that he was an unconverted man, and that he wished to withdraw. But I insisted on his remaining, and he has ever since been much exercised in mind. The other case was very unexpected to me. A daughter of . . . called on me the day before she left the place, to converse with me respecting the concerns of her soul. She appeared to be deeply affected, and so far as I could judge manifested the temper of a true penitent. She regrets very much that she has not the opportunity of making a profession of her faith before leaving the country. This family has been uncommonly gay and thoughtless, and I suppose she never mentioned her case to any of them."

These evening services are well remembered by many, as connected with their great spiritual delight and progress, if not with their conversion to God. Young men of different religious persuasions prized these evangelical instructions; and it is not many weeks since we heard a bishop of the Protestant Episcopal church declare that this was the best preaching he ever heard. Dr. Alexander's discourses on these occasions were uniformly of the practical and experimental kind. They were extemporaneous and animated, and embodied all those qualities which made him eminently popular, especially among the common people, who preferred his free and often irresistible invitations, and the clear ringing of his lively and penetrative voice, to more staid and scholastic addresses which smell of the lamp and sacrifice religious to literary merit. He was sought after in private by great numbers who were in distress concerning their salvation, and was invited in various instances to labour in fields which the Lord was blessing by the effusion of his grace.

"Two weeks ago," he writes in the same letter, "I visited Elizabethtown, to see the work of the Lord which is going on in that place. Here are about a hundred persons under deep impressions, and the number is increasing every day. A place five miles beyond has also received another shower of divine influence. Some remarkable cases of awakening have occurred in both places. O that the blessed influence may spread far and wide!"

It is greatly to be regretted that no letters can be recovered, entering into any detail of his views and feelings as to the great work of education which he had begun, or the studies which he was pursuing. Such correspondence, it is well known, he maintained somewhat largely with congenial minds, especially with Doctors Rice, Speece, and Campbell of Kentucky; but from the necessity of the case we must allow these years to be very much a blank. And even in regard to those which follow, one year succeeds another with a felicitous sameness which leaves little for the narrator. The same cares, the same labours, the same contentment. A beloved wife and four children, with an increasing circle of pupils, and a great number of visitors, made happy days in the humble, cheerful home. Death came in and bore away the youngest child, an only daughter. Disease gave frequent cause of solicitude respecting the others, whose lives were nevertheless preserved. The employments of the study and the lecture-room were incessant and wearing, but they were enthusiastic. The compilation, collection, translation, revision and refutation, incident to the life of a young and ardent professor, went on with a diligence of which the fruits were extant for many years in piles of manuscripts, some of which became lectures, others parts of published works, while all have long since, and perhaps intentionally, been committed to the flames.

During the first few years there was a peculiar glow of delight in the mind of the professors, when small companies of alumni began to try their gifts as probationers, and leave the nest as the first fledged of the new institution. But greatly interesting as this was to both parties, it affords little for record, and most of the persons concerned have long since gone to their rest. In the years which remain, therefore, we cannot undertake to set down the quiet events in the way of annals. Their true history is in the General Catalogue which registers the names of successive classes.

Externally, the period of which we write was troublous, for the war with Great Britain was in progress. Except, however, that general sympathy which every good man must have with the interests of his country, Dr. Alexander was as little disturbed as any man in the land. From the site of Princeton, the village was again and again traversed by bodies of troops, both going to the field of hostilities and returning. The whole population was much agitated by the controversies leading to the war, and by the progress of the conflict. Privately, he lamented the policy which involved us in these troubles; but he never took any active part in politics, never preached a political sermon in his life, and indeed seldom voted at an election. In common with

Christians throughout the Union, he deplored the spiritual evils consequent on the war; and it was too evident that for many years there had not been a time of so general decay in religious zeal and activity. The even tenor of his studious life was nevertheless pursued, and the gentle stimulus of new employments added to his happiness.

But the event most worthy of being noted in this connection was the accession of a colleague. Hitherto, as we have seen, he had conducted his little band of pupils through all the parts of their preparation. The Reverend Samuel Miller, D. D., of New-York, was elected to the chair of Ecclesiastical History and Church Government, by the General Assembly of 1813; but in consequence of a violent illness he did not assume his duties until the month of December, in that year. Dr. Miller brought with him a high reputation as a preacher, an author, and a Christian gentleman. He was about three years older than his colleague, being accordingly in his prime of mental and bodily vigour. His name was widely known from his "Retrospect of the Eighteenth Century," and more recently from his defence of presbytery against the attacks of Doctors Hobart and Bowden. For many years he had maintained his post with honour and esteem, in the First Presbyterian Church of New-York, where he succeeded the venerable Dr. Rodgers, after having been his colleague.

This seems to be the first place offered in which to speak of the mutual relations of the two professors; a subject to which we shall revert. For six and thirty years they laboured side by side and were in almost daily communication. These were circumstances in which, if any where, one might expect sinister and unkindly attributes to be drawn forth. In many particulars they were dissimilar; indeed two men of genuine piety could scarcely be found more unlike. Dr. Miller came from the training of city life, and from an eminently polished and literary circle. Of fine person and courtly manners, he set a high value on all that makes society dignified and attractive. He was pre-eminently a man of system and method, governing himself, even in the minutest particulars, by exact rule. His daily exercise was measured to the moment; and for half a century he wrote standing. He was a gentleman of the old school, though as easy as he was noble in his bearing; full of conversation, brilliant in company, rich in anecdote, and universally admired. As a preacher, he was clear without brilliancy, accustomed to laborious and critical preparation, relying little on the excitement of the occasion, but rapid with his pen, and gifted with a tenacious memory and a strong sonorous voice; always instructive, always calm, always accurate.

His colleague had received a lasting impress, in manners and labours, from a very different class of influences. The inward principle of delicacy and refinement, the soul of true politeness, we think we may assert, was within him in high measure. Perhaps no man ever more respected the feelings of others. But he was not a man of rules. Eminent natural simplicity was his characteristic. If this led him to be careless or abrupt, at any time, he cared not for the inelegance, even when he grieved over any occasional offence. His studies and his way of life were singularly free from all constraint and plan. Though a perpetual reader, he seemed always to read for entertainment, rather than by constraint A friend once found him deeply engaged in Jack's old work on Conic Sections; and in the earlier part of his life he perused many volumes on physical philosophy. His rest was in continual change of mental pursuit. Never did he seem more at a loss than when called upon to lay down regulations for the hours, the employments or the behaviour of others. Perfect liberty, as to time, pursuits, and even bodily movements, was almost his passion. Scrupulously clean in his person, he never seemed to advert to the fashion of his dress. Animated even to vehemence in conversation on topics which aroused him, he often had his fits of silence. While his door was open to every visitant, and his kind counsel was freely given, he certainly omitted many a received form, and would occasionally, during an inordinate visitation, abstract his eye and his attention, and hum a tune to himself. In the pulpit, he was most himself when he was most truly extemporaneous; which perhaps was in the mind of the learned Chief Justice Kirkpatrick, when he said, with a jocose eulogy, "Dr. Alexander is the prince of Methodist preachers."

With such marked differences, it is certainly no slight matter to record, that during a lifetime of common service, these two men never had an alienation, or the difference of an hour. In opinion they frequently diverged; yet mutual respect and affection were never violated, but rather increased with every year of their lives. Placed in circumstances which might have engendered rivalry, they appeared to rejoice in each other's gifts and success. From the beginning of their acquaintanceship, Dr. Miller always resorted to his younger colleague as his wisest adviser He admired his learning, testified the profoundest reverence for his judgment and piety, coveted his company, and unfeignedly delighted in his ministrations. On the other hand, Dr. Alexander regarded his friend and brother with the heartiest affection. Again and again has he been heard to say, that for the charitable use of his means, for adherence to his rules of self control, and especially for exemption from all traces of vanity and of envy, Dr. Miller surpassed all men he had ever known. He was fond of saying, that after more than thirty years proximity, he had never detected in his colleague the slightest appearance of jealousy. This was the more remarkable, as it is well known that with all his varied excellencies, Dr. Miller as a preacher was less followed by popular admiration than his friend.

Though we say it by anticipation, it is seasonable to add, that as years rolled on, and old age arrived, the concord and affection of these servants of Christ presented a beautiful and edifying spectacle. They conversed together and prayed together; and as their hoary heads appeared, with a punctuality belonging to both, in the devotional and other more public services of the Seminary, the moral influence of the sight upon their numerous and respectful pupils was happy and indelible.

After the arrival of Dr Miller, both professors were actively engaged in preaching the Gospel, not only in Princeton, but in the neighbouring congregations, and even in the two great cities, where their labours were constantly in request. It is impossible to determine which of them most delighted in the actual labours of the pulpit. They never spoke of these as a burden, but eagerly welcomed them as a satisfaction. Before the erection of buildings for the Seminary, there was no separate worship on the Lord's Day, for the students. The professors however preached frequently, and in some years in stated rotation with others, in the village church, and the chapel of the college ; the control of the latter service being in the hands of their friend President Green.

At an early period in the history of the institution, a meeting was established on the afternoon of the Sabbath, for the spiritual edification of the young men, and was maintained during the whole life of these professors ; it will be remembered by hundreds as the *Conference*, and shall be more fully noticed. The colloquial addresses which they delivered here would form a system of experimental theology, if they could be recovered.

CHAPTER FOURTEENTH.

1813—1817.

FIRST YEARS OF PROFESSORSHIP—HEALTH—THEOLOGICAL STUDIES—NUMBERS—FISCAL CARES—REVIVAL IN COLLEGE—PREACHING—SPIRITUAL COUNSELS—VIRGINIA—DR. HOGE—DOMESTIC HABITS.

IN the early years of his life as a professor, Dr. Alexander began to endure trials in regard to health, which were destined to overhang him during the whole middle period of his activity. Princeton, a place proverbially healthful, so as to deserve Witherspoon's appellation, as the Montpellier of America, is nevertheless like that salubrious town of France exposed to the sweep of angry winds, especially about the breaking up of winter. To this influence, his delicately sensitive temperament was peculiarly open. The east winds of March and April harrowed his constitution, and produced a train of most distressing symptoms, chilliness, nervous perturbation and dyspepsy. At this time began that morbid wakefulness, which kept him often whole nights without refreshment. He became thin and haggard, and except in some short intervals this was his condition for many years. It was however more a general malaise than a serious disability, by which he was harassed, and he seldom made these ailments a reason for abstaining from duty, either at home or abroad. Indeed he rather sought a solace in more intense occupation of mind, which in turn increased and perpetuated the evil. His southern friends began to ponder on these appearances. "I have ever believed," wrote the Rev. John H. Rice, "that your present situation is better adapted to your habits of feeling and of previous study, than any other in the Presbyterian Church; and have regarded you as more usefully employed than any other man in our society. Nothing could make me wish a removal, selfish as I am, but a regard for your health—may I not add your life. I do not believe that the climate suits you. If, however, you could be as usefully placed any where to the South, I should think it your duty to remove; or if it were certain that you cannot for want of health discharge or sustain the duties of your office, I should think that another habitation ought to be sought. What may be the result of certain schemes which I now have in view, I cannot tell, and therefore I will not communicate them."*

This was the time of his arduous labour and rapid accumulation. With a restless activity he pushed his inquiries far beyond the field of his prescribed course, which was sufficiently extensive. From this time forward he lost no opportunity of procuring every accessible volume of Latin theology, belonging to the German, French, Dutch and Helvetic schools; of these an unusual store may be seen on

* Rev. John H. Rice to Dr. Alexander, May 4, 1817.

the shelves of the Seminary collection.* Nor did he confine himself to dogmatic or polemic works, but read largely in the departments of Criticism and Hermeneutics. During all his life he manifested a strong turn for languages, which was now indulged in connection with his exegetical studies and instructions. His careful application to the Hebrew and Greek texts was continued as long as he lived. He assaulted the Arabic, but as he said with little proficiency. In Syriac he made further advances; and we remember the lessons in this language which he gave to a student of 1815, afterwards widely known as the Reverend Thomas Charlton Henry, D. D., of Charleston. His children were enlisted in the work of copying, and we have a manuscript on Hebrew Archæology, in the yet unformed hand of one of his sons. The reigning controversies of the day awakened his lively attention, and he repeatedly dipped into the Greek and Roman classics, and even into works on mathematical and physical science. It was characteristic of his habits to seek mental relaxation in a change of grave studies, rather than in what is denominated light reading, and for many years nothing

* It is with a pensive interest that the writer remembers having noted at Leyden, for the entertainment of his father, the series of portraits, executed in the best Dutch style, of those worthies, in learning and science as well as religion, whose names he had so often heard at home; for instance, of Joseph Scaliger, Salmasius, Heinsius, Boerhaave, Wesselius, Cocceius, Wittichius, Hoornbeeck, Van Til, three of the family of Schultens, Ruhnkenius, Havercamp, Wyttenbach, Wynpersse, Van Voorst, Perizonius, Witsius, Hemsterhuis, De Moor, and Schultingius; also of Vorstius, and Arminius and Episcopius, side by side; information which, alas! never came to the ear for which it was intended.

was more common than to find his evening hours spent over some ponderous tome of the seventeenth century. His pen was constantly in activity, and we have been astonished at the extent to which he made compilations and digests from standard works in other languages. By slow degrees his body of lectures on divinity was growing into shape; while, as has been said, he preferred on many accounts to express his thoughts in the lecture-room in the unfettered diction of the moment. Neither now nor at any later period was he much addicted to modern fiction or modern poetry. Without being a politician he was always a reader on politics, thoroughly acquainted with all questions of American statesmanship, and all his life long a serious and diligent student of the best journals; for, like Dr. Arnold, he considered "a newspaper one of the most painful and solemn studies in the world, if it be read thoughtfully." In a word, every thing showed the vigour and spring of a manly spirit, making trial of its best and as yet unwasted energies.

The number of students during these years was constantly on the increase. The matriculations were in 1812, nine; in 1813, sixteen; in 1814, fifteen; in 1815, twenty-two; in 1816, twenty-six; and in 1817, twenty-three. Among these were some who are living as ornaments of our own and other churches, including two bishops of the Protestant Episcopal Church, in Virginia and Ohio. "The true heraldry of the college," says Chalmers, "is her sons." The Princeton Seminary has no reason to be ashamed of her escutcheon. Among those who still survive, it is a pleasing duty to name, as falling within this period, the Rev. Henry R.

Weed, D. D., of Wheeling, and the Rev. William Blain, of Hudson Presbytery, two of the first three alumni ; Professor Hooper, of the Baptist Church ; the Rev. John Barnard, of New-York ; the Rev. Dr. Howe, of the Reformed Dutch Church ; the Rev. Dr. Swift, of Pittsburgh ; the Rev. Dr. Biggs, of Cincinnati ; the Rev. Doctors Henry, Snodgrass, Chester, Hodge, Sprague and Magie, and Bishops Johns and McIlvaine. But nearly thirty from these six classes are no more on earth. President Chamberlain, of Oakland College, belongs to this number, a man of talents and energy, who came to a tragical end. Professor Graham, of the Union Theological Seminary in Virginia, died almost at the same time with his venerated preceptor. Larned, a prodigy of early eloquence, whose name is often mentioned with those of Whitefield and Summerfield, shone brightly for a few years, and then closed his career, in New Orleans. Nevins, of Baltimore, will never be forgotten by any who esteem childlike piety, united to genius, wit, and oratorical impression. Newbold, of 1816, was the first of a long catalogue, who devoted themselves to foreign missions ; he was cut down while meditating a life of hard service on the frontiers of Russia and Tartary.

With these, and with all his students, especially while their number was small, Dr. Alexander maintained the most intimate relations. They had constant access to his fireside and his study ; and were aided by him in their pursuits, and encouraged to propound difficulties and scruples for his resolution. While as yet there was no church-scheme for the education of young ministers, a certain number of the students were sustained by the voluntary contributions of churches and individuals; and the sums for this purpose to a large extent passed through his hands. Having assumed this labour when he was the only professor, he continued it to the close of his life. As the numbers increased, and as the sums came in irregularly as to time and unequally as to amount, the administration of these funds became embarrassing, and but for habits of the most rigorous exactness in accounts would have been onerous in the extreme. At a later period the founding of scholarships, and the digested plans of the Assembly's Board of Education, placed this department of labour on a surer basis. But the whole affair brought the professor into a close and often tender relation to deserving youth, who confided their necessities to him, and never failed to find in him a gentle and sympathizing friend.

In this connection may be noticed his endeavours to gather a library for the institution. At first, the few cart-loads of old, second-hand, often odd volumes, raked together from studies and garrets, scarcely deserved the name of a library. We well remember when the whole collection was contained in the professor's study. The gift of Walton's Polyglott, by the Rev. Dr. Green, was the first token of any thing like a literary apparatus. In later days the munificence of Mr. Lenox, Dr. Sprague, Mr. Agnew and the Messrs. Stuarts, has caused a happy change; but it is still to be lamented that the churches at large are supine upon this important subject. Public libraries will generally be the exponent of the degree of scientific and literary advancement in a Seminary. The liberality of donors should be invited to this object. But the number is small of those who estimate the necessity; and zeal for great libraries always infers a high measure of literary cultivation. In regard to this, we have become accustomed to hear the most narrow and grovelling opinions, from the lips even of clergymen and so-called scholars; as if the only intent of a library was to furnish pabulum for the undergraduates. For almost forty years Dr. Alexander was himself the librarian, and he never relaxed his exertions to make the collection more worthy of the place it occupied.

At this time, it must be remembered, no buildings had been erected for the use of the Seminary. When the number of students became too great to be accommodated in the houses of the professors, they resorted to the public rooms of the College, which, as well as the library of that institution, were hospitably thrown open for their use. During a part of the time, also, the students of the two seminaries, and the village congregation worshipped together in the old college chapel, which is now a gallery of paintings; this was when the Princeton church had been consumed by fire. In this place Dr. Alexander delivered many impressive discourses, which are remembered by persons now living. At one time he received a message from Dr. Chalmers, enjoining it upon him to regard his professorial work as a business sufficient for the powers of any one man, and not to wear out his strength with preaching; but such was the demand for his pulpit labours, that he was as little able to abide by this rule, as was Chalmers himself, when afterwards he assumed the chair of instruction.

About the beginning of the year 1815, there was a general religious awakening in the College of New Jersey. "The divine influence"—we use the language of President Green—"seemed to descend like the silent dew of heaven; and in about four weeks, there were few individuals in the college edifice who were not deeply impressed with a sense of the importance of spiritual and eternal things. There was scarcely a room—perhaps not one—which was not a place of earnest secret devotion!" More than forty students gave favourable evidence of conversion. Among these were a number who afterwards became members of the theological institution, and some who rose to eminence in the ministry. Such an event could not but extend its marked influence to the Seminary. The students of divinity were much engaged in labours and prayer among the youth of the college, and a corresponding solemnity and tenderness were spread over both bodies. Dr. Alexander and his colleague were largely engaged in rendering aid to Dr. Green, by repeated sermons and exhortations, and still more by private counsels, to such as were affected with their earliest spiritual distresses and joys. It was a period never to be forgotten by those who witnessed its remarkable impressions and transformations. Though a still greater revival had occurred in the preceding century, there has been none so extensively affecting the college in any later year. After this, as from time to time the churches of New Jersey and the bordering states were visited with similar refreshings, the seminary professors were accustomed with gladness to give permission to their students, to visit these scenes of grace, for the increase of their experimental knowledge, as well as for the exercise of their gifts. They also made preaching excursions themselves, as far as their home labours allowed; and at such times, and more frequently at sacramental gatherings, Dr. Alexander was wont to break forth in warm and melting harangues, not inferior to the bursting effusions of his youth. For notwithstanding the increasing delicacy of his health, he could endure an extraordinary amount of labour and excitement; and he certainly never seemed so happy or so much raised above himself, as when amidst listening crowds he was proclaiming the boundless riches of salvation.

It was during this lapse of years that he began to be widely known as a spiritual adviser, and to be consulted by distressed minds, on cases of conscience and other spiritual griefs. Without ever seeking this—for he always seemed to assume the place of an adviser with reluctance—he continued all his life to exercise great influence, perhaps his chief influence, in this quiet department of Christian service. For such work he was eminently fitted by his singular caution and wisdom, his personal trials of heart, his deep acquaintance with the inward workings of grace, his sensibility and tenderness in regard to the afflicted, and his characteristic secresy and silence about all that was confided to him. Cases of this sort were constantly arising among his own pupils, and those who had lately been such. As he advanced in life, these confidential applications, both in person and by letter, were surprisingly increased, until the labour became almost burdensome. But it was undoubtedly by this very means, noiseless and unobtrusive as it was, rather than by formal teaching, by sermons, or by authorship, that he built up that character and attained that influence, which were so universally recognised in the church. He lives now, in the memory of great numbers, especially of the clergy, as eminently a wise counsellor and a spiritual guide. In regard to such communications, his reticency was almost extreme, and of his large correspondence on such topics, he committed every vestige to the flames.

While we are alluding to his influence in the Presbyterian Church, some other particulars merit a passing notice. It was not yet by written works, for his career of publication had not yet commenced. The moulding power which he was already beginning to wield, and which has never been denied even by those who viewed it with dissatisfaction, operated in more silent ways; by the truth communicated to his successive classes, and the impressions left on their character; by a large and valuable correspondence, the very delicacy of which has prevented its appearance more largely in these pages; by ministerial visits, and in his more active years by journeys; by the weight of opinion and argument in church-courts, and by the perpetual force of his evangelical preaching, in which he never relaxed till the very end.

The year 1817 brought to him a singular gratification, in a visit from his venerated friend, the Rev. Moses Hoge, D. D. The life of Dr. Hoge belongs so much to the history of the Southern Church, that we feel justified in adding to what has already been said some particulars from another manuscript. "Moses Hoge was the son of a very intelligent, orthodox and pious farmer, who spent the early part of his life in Pennsylvania, within the bounds of the Philadelphia Presbytery. With this aged man the writer, when very young, was providentially led into an acquaintance. Travelling in 1791, he had the misfortune to have his horse badly foundered, and was left by his company at the house of Mr. Solomon Hoge, in Frederick County, Virginia, with whom the old gentleman then lived at the advanced age of eighty-four years. Nearly the whole of several days was spent in listening to Mr. Hoge's explanation of his views on a number of points in theology; and the writer can declare that he never in any equal time, as he now thinks, derived so much light as from this aged farmer. He told me, that when grown to manhood he deliberately and seriously sat down and went through the Westminster Confession of Faith, to see whether the doctrines were founded in Scripture; and after a careful examination of this formulary, he was able to adopt the whole, as indeed the truths taught in the Word of God. He was often present at the meetings of the Philadelphia Presbytery. His judgment in regard to most of the members was not very favourable; the individual whom he valued most was a Mr. Wilson, whom he said the others were continually persecuting on some account or other. The Presbyterian Church was that in which Mr. Hoge had been born, baptized and educated, and with which he first joined in communion; and in this he continued, until the Synod passed the act called the 'Adopting Act,' which indulged such persons as were scrupulous in regard to certain articles to express their exceptions to the Presbytery, who were permitted to license and ordain, if they judged the matter not to be of essential importance. When this act was passed, it gave great dissatisfaction, and some, the number of whom cannot be determined, left the Presbyterian Church, and joined the Seceders, who were then beginning to raise their standard. Among these was Mr. Hoge. This fact, so far as my recollection serves me, was not communicated to me by the old gentleman, but by his son the Rev. Dr. Hoge. And I am certain that when the communication was made, I had never heard of such an Act, nor could ever obtain sight of it until the last minutes of the Old Synod were published a few years since.

"Moses Hoge was considerably advanced in manhood when he commenced the study of the Latin language; but by diligence and assiduous application he made up for the loss of early instruction. Nor had his mind previously been left uncultivated. Being of a sedate and studious turn he read many books, by which his understanding was strengthened and enriched with various knowledge. It has often happened, as we have seen in the case of Mr. Graham himself, that a late commencement of classical studies does not result in an imperfect or superficial scholarship. He became an accurate and profound scholar, and acquired a perfection of mental discipline to which very few attain. Having laid a good foundation in Latin and Greek, he resorted to the academy of Mr. Graham, where he pursued his studies with indefatigable industry, and exhibited that purity, meekness and devotedness of Christian character, which conciliated the esteem of all who knew him. Here, also, under Mr.

Graham's direction, he studied divinity, and was in due time licensed to preach the Gospel by the Presbytery of Hanover, then the only one in Virginia.

"Although Mr. Hoge's talents were of the first order, and his knowledge was accurate and extensive, he had a poor delivery. His voice was husky and irregular in its intonations, and the muscles of his face were subject to a peculiar and visible excitement while he was speaking. When, therefore, he obtained licensure, he did not seek any conspicuous situation. He went and spent some time under the roof of the Rev. Dr. Waddel, then the most celebrated pulpit orator in Virginia. What benefit he derived from intercourse with this great and good man is not known, but it is certain that he ever afterwards entertained for him the highest veneration and the greatest admiration of his talents. Indeed, Dr. Waddel excelled in private conversation as much as in the pulpit, and was always ready to disclose his own views and sentiments to young students and ministers with the utmost freedom.

"Wishing to be useful in conveying the precious message of the Gospel to the destitute, Mr. Hoge had his attention directed to a part of the country on the South Branch of the Potomac, where was a tract of very fertile land, and where a number of Presbyterian families had settled, but where no minister of the Gospel had ever resided. Here he laboured assiduously for several years, in the study and in the pulpit. It was his habit to write every sermon and commit it to memory. At first he cultivated an elegant and rather flowery style; but finding that he thus shot over the heads of his people, some of whom were of German descent, and imperfectly acquainted with the English language, he changed his manner of preaching so as to accommodate himself to the capacity of his hearers. In this sequestered situation, Mr. Hoge was deprived of all literary and refined society, and was very far removed from his brethren in the ministry, and from the meetings of the Presbytery, which he nevertheless felt it to be his duty to attend. An opening [for removal] occurred at Shepherdstown, in Berkeley County, by the dismission of the Rev. John McKnight to Pennsylvania. The congregation at Shepherdstown was small, but intelligent and highly respectable. He had, however, to come after a man much admired for pulpit eloquence. Mr. McKnight composed his sermons with great care, and after committing them to memory, delivered them in a very pleasing and animated manner. As to mere elocution, Mr. Hoge fell immeasurably behind his predecessor; but he possessed qualities which in the esteem of judicious men more than compensated for his want of eloquence. He had a pure and ardent spirit of piety, and always fed his flock with sound evangelical truth, thoroughly digested and prepared before it was exhibited. He had also an invaluable habit of watching for opportunities to be useful. Into whatsoever company he came, he always aimed to say something which he hoped would be useful. Shepherdstown was at that time under the care of the Carlisle Presbytery, but Mr. Hoge was a member of the Lexington Presbytery. He received, therefore, from the former body, a letter inquiring by what authority he occupied a vacant congregation under their care, without their permission. Mr. Hoge wrote back a letter replete with Christian feeling and good sense, and with some sprinkling of wit. He continued, however, in connection with the Lexington Presbytery, to which were annexed, some time after, all the churches in the Valley south of the Potomac.

"Mr. Hoge remained in this place until the year 1807, when he received an invitation to become president of Hampden Sidney College, where he spent the remainder of his days. Soon after his removal to that place the germ of the theological school was formed, and he was appointed professor of theology by the Hanover Presbytery; and a number of young men had the privilege of receiving his instructions in theology. This was the origin of the Union Theological Seminary, which has since risen to importance, chiefly by the unwearied exertions of the Rev. John H. Rice, D. D.

"In the year 1810, Mr. Hoge was honoured with the degree of Doctor of Divinity by the College of New Jersey. On account of his extreme modesty in regard to his own attainments, this was quite unexpected, but it has seldom fallen on one who more truly deserved it. His success in conducting the college was equal to any reasonable expectations. The institution being almost entirely without funds, and having fallen into much irregularity as to the usual order of classes, gave some difficulties to one who had himself never enjoyed the privilege of going regularly through a college course.

"As a preacher, Dr. Hoge was much admired by spiritual and judicious persons. Men who had never been accustomed to Presbyterian preaching, attended with delight on his ministry. Among these was the late eloquent out eccentric John Randolph; who about this time had come under serious impressions of religion. Mr. Randolph courted the acquaintance of Dr. Hoge, and entered freely into conversation with him. During this period of his life, Dr. Hoge preached without writing his sermons, and commonly without much previous study; but he pursued trains of thought which had become familiar to him. The charm of his preaching was the strong genuine feeling by which he appeared to be actuated in all that he said; giving himself up to such sentiments as at the moment rose in his mind; and his pious emotions during utterance were often exceedingly strong. But he was never hurried by his feelings into any thing like rant or extravagance. He never lost the balance of his mind, but preserved that sobriety and solemnity which are always wanting where extraordinary excitement takes place. He was fond of casuistical preaching, aiming by nice discriminating marks to remove the perplexities and doubts which he found to be common among the good people of the region where he now laboured. Perhaps he carried these searching disquisitions too far, and multiplied the evidences of sincerity too much. All who were acquainted with Dr. Hoge admitted that they had never known a man whose whole character both as a Christian and a minister was more unexceptionable and consistent. He seemed habitually to retain on his mind a sense of the Divine presence, and was ever ready to engage in the most spiritual conversation. He was condescending and patient in dealing with the most ignorant who wished for instruction, and seldom lost an opportunity of addressing a word of instruction or exhortation to any servant who might be waiting on him. He seldom met with ill treatment from any, and never indulged in angry or resentful feelings. In regard to the things of this world, I never knew a man more indifferent. Indeed he did not suffer his mind to be harassed with cares of this kind. During a large part of his life his salary was very small, but he was contented in every condition, and trusted in Providence amidst all circumstances. He might indeed have turned his attention to farming, as was the practice of most of his brethren in Virginia. But he had set out with the determination to devote his whole time to the work of the ministry, trusting Providence for a support ; and he advised all young clergymen who consulted him, to pursue the same course. He however never censured such as did otherwise. While president, he suffered no young man who was seeking the ministry to go away for want of support. To all pious youth his purse and his house were open, and he treated them with all the kindness of a father and all the familiarity of a friend or a brother. His influence on young men was exceedingly salutary. When he found them self-confident and dogmatical, he would not attempt to repress this disposition in any other way than by free discussion, and by showing them difficulties in their own theories, which probably had never occurred to them.

" Though his health had been declining for some time, Dr Hoge was induced, in the year 1820, to undertake a journey to the north. He had a particular desire to meet once in his life with the American Bible Society, for which institution he had a high regard. As he could also attend the General Assembly as a commissioner, and visit friends that were dear to him at Princeton, he determined to venture, weak as he was ; and at first it seemed as if his health would be benefited by the journey. He attended the anniversaries at New-York in the beginning of May, and then on his return stopped at Princeton, where he spent several days in cheerful and useful conversation with an old friend. He seemed to take a deep interest in the place and its important institutions, and especially felt himself to be on hallowed ground, when he reflected that the ashes of Burr, Edwards, Davies, Witherspoon and Smith were deposited in the cemetery. It was an object of special desire with him to visit the tombs of these eminent men, to whom the Presbyterian Church is so much indebted. But soon after his arrival in Princeton, there came on a cold eastern rain which continued for several days. He went out in this inclement time, and stood long enough to read all the Latin epitaphs, some of which are long. This imprudence, if it may be so called, was the occasion of his death.

"The writer accompanied him to Philadelphia, and the first night was spent in Trenton, where, at the earnest request of several persons, Dr. Hoge preached in the church by candle-light. Very little opportunity was offered for giving notice, except by the ringing of the church-bell. The sermon was on Romans x. 9 ; and I see that a discourse on that text has been published from his manuscripts ; no doubt the same in substance which he then preached. Soon after arriving in Philadelphia he was seized with a typhus fever, from an attack of which he had recovered but a short time before leaving home. His illness continued several weeks, so that there was opportunity to send for his wife and his son Thomas, a physician, both of whom arrived before his decease. There was nothing remarkable in the exercises of his mind, but a calm submission to the will of his heavenly Father, and a kind and grateful feeling to all around him. His disease was attended with much languor and debility, which could not but affect his spirits, and prevented that cheerful animation which was common in health."*

It has often been observed with justice, that though Dr. Alexander had removed from his native state, he never lost influence there. Until his last breath, he was intensely a Virginian ; and nothing more kindled his restless eye, or animated his nervously mobile frame, or called out his colloquial fires, than any occasion for vindicating the honour of the "old colony and dominion," as the ancient writs have it. In return, his opinions continued to have much weight in the Virginia churches. More than once they sought to win him back to their bosom. In numerous instances, of which the precise dates are unfortunately lost to us, he made visits to this beloved region, preaching everywhere, renewing the friendships of his youth, mingling with the immense gatherings, who, according to the custom of the land, met or followed him at sacraments, presbyteries and synods, and thus keeping up the connection to which he owed so much of his active usefulness. It needs scarcely be said to those who

* MS. Life of the Rev. William Graham.

knew him, that as it regards his judgments, feelings, and policy, he was uniformly reckoned, in every good sense, a Southern rather than a Northern man. More especially in his abhorrence of extreme and fanatical abolitionism, he never bated a jot; having constantly and firmly predicted its degradation into infidelity, which has now become patent to the world.

For evidence of the strong hold which he continued to have upon his friends in Virginia, we need only advert to some transactions which are brought to light by his correspondence, though never made the subject of his conversation. In 1820, he was again elected President of Hampden Sidney College. The congregation of Cumberland simultaneously tendered to him a call to become their pastor, with the understanding that he was also to preach at the College church and at Briery. Immediately after this, the Synod of Virginia chose him their professor of Theology. These offers he declined.*

A glance at his domestic habits during this period will not be here out of place; and what is to be said may be taken as applicable, with certain obvious modifications, to a number of preceding and following years. He was now between forty and fifty, slender in person, clear in complexion, with a slight silvering of his abundant brown hair. His body was open to sudden impulses, seldom long at rest, and prone to motions and gestures which were highly animated and expressive, rather than graceful. Like most new-comers from a city, he for a time devoted himself to horticulture,

* Letter of Col. Samuel Venable, October 28, 1820.

but it never gained his heart, and he pursued it less than even his respected colleague, who likewise fell off in his zeal. . He was always an early riser, and the older inhabitants of Princeton bear in mind his frequent long walks with his three elder sons, who were then little boys. He long retained his youthful fondness for a horse, and indulged moderately in riding and driving. Sometimes visiting the sea-side, he used to vaunt that he could swim as boldly as when he was a child. His delight was in his family. After being deeply absorbed in study or teaching, he would come in, full of animation and ready to relax at the fireside. It was always his custom—a most delightful one for all about him—to pour out the fulness of his thoughts upon all that interested him, at the table and in the domestic group. Coming from his newspaper, his book, his class, from visits, church or journey, he gave forth a perpetual and vivacious flow of information. Nothing had escaped his eye, and nothing even of details seemed to be withheld in his narrative, yet without tedium or repetition. These daily conversations were the chief entertainment of his life, as they are the most delightful recollections of his household. Through his whole life his house was much frequented by guests, but at this period, though his quarters were never so strait, he was most visited from abroad. Giving a hearty welcome, and most elated when his table was fullest, he gave himself little care as to display or fashion. Many who may read these notices will recur with a melancholy pleasure to the days and weeks which they have passed under his simple but hospitable roof. He was addicted to sacred music, and as both he and Mrs. Alexander were gifted with clear and pleasing voices, the hours of family intercourse were enlivened by many a psalm and sacred song. When such men as Dr. John H. Rice, or Dr. Finley, or Dr. Janeway, were added to the circle, the conversation took a higher flight, and we remember in his fireside discourses of that day a vehemence and impressiveness, which were wanting, except at some favoured moments, in his later years. In all that regards the indulgence of the table, he was frugal and plain in his tastes, and happily temperate without any thing like dietetic rigour.

Nothing more characterized him than his fondness for communicating instruction, on every subject, even the most elementary, within his reach. It might be the alphabet, or Hebrew and Syriac grammar, or geometry and surveying, in which he was fully versed, or metaphysics ; he was unwearied and delighted, if only he had willing learners ; and he had the art of making every learner willing. Though he sent his boys to school, always giving his suffrage for the day-school method, he was constantly teaching his children. Every one of them received from him, and commonly on his knee, the rudiments of spelling, arithmetic, geography, algebra, geometry, and the classic languages. He would pass hours in a day giving lessons in the alphabet ; breaking off a hundred times, as he observed the first symptom of weariness. For in regard both to himself and others, he acted on Shakspeare's adage, "No profit grows, where is no pleasure taken." Every corner of the house was occupied by bits of paper, flying like sibylline leaves, and covered with spelling-lessons, executed by himself in printing characters, and decorated with bold but most unartistic drawings of beasts, birds and houses. As the little ones got on to the dead languages, which, on his plan, was very early, similar papers contained lists of Latin words; these were to be committed to memory; and in the case of one son, the number of such words amounted to thousands. He quoted with approval the testimony of Dr. Witherspoon, who in presbyterial trials used to examine the candidates on 'vocables' rather than on translation of books. These avocations were confined to no hours. It might seem strange how he could endure the interruption; but it was his peculiarity that he seemed incapable of being interrupted. Except in hours of devotion, his study was always free to his children, even the youngest; noise made no difference; their books and toys were on his floor; and two or three would be clambering upon him, while he was handling a folio or had the pen in his hand. In times of health and spirits, his manner of playing with his children was amusingly romping and even boisterous, and he threw them about with a sprightliness which often extorted a momentary cry of fear or pain. To this may be ascribed the unusual freedom which they always had in his presence, but which was checked in a moment when he grew suddenly sad or grave, as was often the case. Before dismissing the matter of family training, we ought to mention his constant and animated conversations with his children. It was his solace, at home and by the way. Without the slightest appearance of plan, but with an easy and spontaneous flow, he was, during some hours of every day, pouring forth a stream of useful information, on all subjects, but chiefly on religion. The whole wealth of his extended reading and observation seemed at one time or another to be distilled in these familiar interviews. All the romantic and stirring events of his early mountain life, the tales of Indian massacres, to which his grandmother had fallen a victim, his journeys in new countries, and his schoolboy days, came in for their share. He excelled in graphic narration, and attracted the attention of guests and strangers, even when directly addressing himself to babes. As soon as a child could comprehend the subject, he began with the beautiful stories of the Bible, and repeated them again and again, until the little ones were perfectly acquainted with them long before they could make use of books. It was a common thing for his hearers to be melted to tears. This natural and extraordinary gift led him to indulge in biblical narrative in the pulpit, to a degree which we believe to be uncommon, and gave a singular attraction to certain discourses, especially on the parables and miracles of our Lord. For the same reason his addresses and sermons to children were incomparably winning, and his labours in this kind were sought for, far and near, much beyond his ability of supply. Without trying to speak in monosyllables, as if these were more intelligible than longer words, he always made himself perfectly intelligible to the humblest capacity.

Here it gives us great pleasure to insert the testimony of a venerable servant of God, the Rev. Dr. Samuel B. Wilson, since Professor of Theology in the Union Theological Seminary. The incidents which he relates come within the period of which we have been treating. "In October, 1816, the Synod of Virginia sat in Fredericksburg:—Dr. Alexander came on from Princeton, to meet his brethren in the ministry there. To these brethren, the companions and fellow-labourers of his early days, he was strongly attached. According to the custom of Synod, there was preaching every day and every night during the meeting. The congregations were large, attentive, and deeply interested in the services. The Superior Court was in session there at the same time, and drew together a large collection of men distinguished for their intelligence.

"The fame of Dr. Alexander had gone before him, as a superior preacher, and a man occupying the highest station in the Presbyterian Church. Great anxiety was consequently manifested to hear him. On Sabbath day the sacrament of the Lord's Supper was to be administered, and it was announced that Dr. Alexander would preach the Action sermon. At an early hour the church was filled to its utmost extent. Among the audience was found the Judge of the Court, Judge Brockenborough, of Richmond, many lawyers and physicians, and not a few who seldom entered the house of God. Dr. Alexander began his sermon with that humility and simplicity for which he was ever so remarkable. Such an introduction, to men accustomed to judge of greatness by pompous manners and splendid diction, produced a feeling of disappointment, and one eminent lawyer, who afterwards became a Judge of the Court of Appeals, rose from his seat and left the church.

"The text which he had selected was 1 Cor. v. 7. 'For even Christ our Passover is sacrificed for us.' As he advanced in explaining the origin, design, and typical signification of the Jewish Passover, he became warm and animated, and soon commanded the attention of his whole audience, and awakened a universal and intense interest. During the discourse of that morning, which many will recollect as long as memory lasts, several incidents occurred which showed the power of true Christian eloquence.

"As he passed from the description of the Jewish passover, to the sacrifice of Christ, he said, bending forward and looking intently on the communion table spread before him, where the bread and wine lay covered, '*But where is our lamb?*' At these words, so impressively uttered, and accompanied by a gesture so significant, an old French dancing master, who scarcely ever entered the church, rose from his seat near the pulpit, and gazed intently, to see if there was not something on the communion table, which he had not yet seen. An intelligent little girl, too, who sat before him, after she returned home, said: 'Aunt H. did you ever hear such a man? When he said, "Where is our lamb," he seemed as if he was looking for a lamb on the communion table.'

"As he proceeded in describing the successive scenes of our Saviour's sufferings, his hearers became deeply and almost universally affected. Feelings which could scarcely be suppressed were manifest in every part of the house; and tears were seen rolling down the cheeks of many but little accustomed to weep. When he depicted the last scene of our

Saviour's sufferings on the cross, that power of descriptive painting, for which he was remarkable in his pulpit efforts, was displayed in a manner rarely surpassed by the most accomplished orators. Amidst the unutterable agonies which Jesus suffered while hanging on the cross, he introduced Mary his mother among the spectators, beholding the cruel sufferings of her beloved son, and quoted the prediction of Simeon as there fulfilled : 'Yea, a sword shall pierce through thy own soul.' Such was his gesture, his voice, his whole manner, that had Mary actually stood before the audience, with flowing tears and every token of deepest sorrow, the impression could hardly have been increased.

"Dr. Alexander never aimed to excite mere animal feelings. The effects produced were the result of Bible facts and truths, clearly presented by one who believed them, and felt their power. During the delivery of that discourse, it would have been easy, repeatedly, to have produced an amount of feeling that could not be controlled. Such, however, was his command over himself and his audience, that besides the speaker's voice, nothing was heard but, here and there, a half suppressed sob, and nothing seen to disturb the solemnity of divine worship.

"Many heard Dr. Alexander on that occasion, for the first and last time ; but it is believed that the revelations of the final judgment will prove that his labours then were blessed to the good of many souls." *

To this may be added a short narrative from the pen of

* Virginia Historical Register, Jan. 1852, p. 43.

the late venerable President Brown. "I particularly remember," says he, "some time after he went to Princeton, a sacramental service in the Northern Liberties, where Mr. James Patterson was pastor. There had been an extensive and powerful revival of religion at that time, as there had often been under the ministrations of that excellent though somewhat eccentric man. The church was crowded ; I presume a majority of the ministers [of the Assembly] attended. I suppose near a hundred new communicants stood up in the aisles and were addressed by the pastor. After this Dr. Alexander, who had been previously engaged for this service, arose to administer the ordinance. After some preparatory remarks, before distributing the bread and the wine, he began with a supposition that the Saviour himself was present, and proceeded to inquire what in such case he would probably say. In a manner at once plain, solemn, searching, and adapted to the various conditions of Christians, he presented the most touching appeals I had ever heard on such an occasion. It almost seemed to me that these were the very words as to matter and manner which Christ himself would have uttered. After dispensing the elements, he concluded in the same admirable strain, using language which a child might understand. He addressed different classes ; first communicants in general ; then those newly admitted, in very melting strains ; then the unconverted, and such as had refused to own Christ. He addressed the ministers of the gospel, 'fathers and brethren' then present. He addressed young men and young women, and closed by speaking to little children, in the very manner of Him who took special notice of such, and said, 'Forbid them not.' The effect was extraordinary; all were melted into tears. I had never heard any thing to be compared to it."*

We have thus, in the absence of documents, and in regard to a period prosperously monotonous and void of great external events, endeavoured to fill the blank with minor characteristics, which go to make up the portraiture of the man; and this to some extent must be our resource in the chapter which shall follow.

* Letter of the Rev. Matthew Brown, D. D., to Henry M. Alexander.

CHAPTER FIFTEENTH.

1818—1829.

CHURCH - LABOURS — PROGRESS OF SEMINARY — PRIVATE HABITS AND DAILY ROUTINE—THE CONFERENCE—CHARACTER OF HIS PREACHING—THEOLOGICAL TROUBLES—COMMENCEMENT OF AUTHORSHIP—BIBLICAL REPERTORY — COLONIZATION — CORRESPONDENCE.

THE period of ten or twelve years, beginning with 1818, was so much like that which preceded it, and so void of stirring changes, that we feel the difficulty of treating it, so as to escape the charge of wearisome repetition. Yet it was a time of quiet and happy progress, both as it regards the professor and the school. During this term of years he made several visits to Virginia, in some of these being accompanied by his family. These tours, especially in the years 1818, 1821, and 1825, are remembered by many in his native State; for he was called every where to the work of preaching, and indulged freely in that flow of extemporaneous argument and exhortation, which more than all things else seemed to bring out every latent power of his mind and heart. He was also during these years repeatedly a commissioner to the General Assembly. In this court he was frequently entrusted with important parts of business, and some of the public papers bear the marks of his hand. It cannot be said that he was a frequent speaker; but when he addressed the house on great subjects, to which he very much confined himself, he was uniformly heard with attention, and the candour and force of his argument always carried weight with the hearers. Some testimony of his coeval and friend, the Rev. Matthew Brown, D. D., President of Jefferson College, cannot here seem inappropriate. "I find," says he, "in the minutes of 1803, that (Mr. Alexander) was one of a committee 'to report on the state of religion,' as collected from the statements of the several members who were called on in order. Mr. (afterwards Dr.) Miller was chairman; there is, however, I think, internal evidence that it was written by Mr. Alexander, or at least that the information and sentiments were from him. No man in that house was so well qualified to give a faithful account of these remarkable revivals. This report partakes of the same spirit which led him to write the History of the Log College. —There was one memorable occasion which is worthy of special notice; it was probably in 1820 or 1821. He was the chairman of a committee to report some alterations in the old Confession of Faith, and particularly in the Form of Government. There was a full and free discussion of the changes proposed. He spoke very little, and was always brief, as was his manner in church courts. On this important occasion, he was frequently called upon to explain; and, after attending to the objections and debate, he arose with great modesty, and in a few words, in a lucid and conclusive way removed all the difficulties. This usually closed the discussion, and I do not remember an instance in which his views did not prevail. It reminded me of what is stated of Dr. Witherspoon, that he did not speak until other members had discussed the subject, when in a concise, clear, and forcible manner, he gave his views, and generally with a unanimous result."

On practical questions we are secure in saying that no man was regarded as a safer or wiser counsellor. At the same time, it is fair to add, that when parties ran high, his characteristic mildness and caution led many to designate him, sometimes not without a sneer, as a moderate man. This term was used, however, solely in regard to measures ; for in respect to doctrine, there was no period of his life in which he did not clearly stand forth, beyond suspicion, as a believer and maintainer of the old Westminster tenets, in their strict interpretation.

In the Theological Seminary, every thing was settling itself into an established form of prosperity, which gave general satisfaction to the Church. The numbers had been greatly increased, and the stream of accessions was steady. The matriculates were in no year fewer than twenty ; in 1822 they rose to fifty, and in 1823 to sixty-nine. The number of students, which had been forty-seven in 1817, became considerably more than a hundred. Several Synods began to entertain the project of a full endowment for three professorships. But there was nothing which made a greater impression, on students and on the public, than the erection of an edifice for the accommodation of the young men. Into this solid and excellent building, though but partially finished within, they entered in the year 1818. About the same time Dr. Alexander removed his family into the commodious dwelling in which he was destined to end his days. At this stage of progress, the public rooms of the Seminary were within the large edifice, as yet the only one. These were the Oratory or Prayer Hall, also used for lectures and religious meetings, and theological debates; the Refectory, and two library chambers. All concerned felt the cheering influence of this change to premises which they could call their own, and which had an air of comfort and permanency. The students were brought more near to one another and to their teachers. The result was seen in greater diligence and punctuality, increased fellowship in religion and zeal in the pursuit of knowledge; so that we suppose there has never been a period in the history of the Seminary, during which there was more animation or delight in all parties. Of the alumni of this period, we number among the departed such men as Dr. Wisner, of Boston; Dr. John Breckinridge, and Dr. Potts, of St. Louis; the Rev. Horace S. Pratt, of Georgia; the Rev. James W. Douglass, of Virginia; the Rev. John H. Kennedy, of Pennsylvania; the Rev Joseph Sandford, the Rev. Joseph S. Christmas, of New-York; the Rev. Alexander Aikman, the Rev. Professor Dod, of the College of New Jersey; the Rev. Samuel G. Winchester, of Natchez, and the Rev. Theodore Wright, a man of colour.

In the new circumstances, Dr. Alexander felt himself invigorated and advancing. With his colleague, Dr. Miller, he maintained the most pleasing and harmonious intimacy;

and when an additional helper came, it was in the person of the Rev. Charles Hodge, whose talents he had early discerned, and whom he regarded more as a beloved son than even as a cherished pupil. He had by this time accumulated and digested much of what was to be the matter of his teachings; at least he had surveyed the entire field, and distinctly marked out its boundaries and divisions. His study door was over against the Seminary entrance, and very near to it. These few steps he might be seen to take day by day, at the appointed hours, always in full time. And during many years of his life, this may be said to have been the only bodily exercise he took; as he was now sliding into that habit which afterwards became inveterate. It is not believed that he seriously undervalued the importance of this means of health in others, but it is certain that in the last thirty years of his life, he used as little bodily motion as any man of his times; confining himself not only to one apartment, but to one chair. This was in striking contrast with the customs of Dr. Miller; and there was an amicable but incessant controversy between them on this point, often waged with as much ability as jocoseness. This proximity of the Seminary, and Dr. Alexander's habit of never denying himself to visitors, contributed very much to that frequency of interview with his pupils, which so many of them remember with pleasure. At all hours, and often in an unbroken succession for hours, he would receive visitors, and listen to them commonly with patience. He was certainly to be forgiven, if sometimes, in the presence of the more wearisome ones, he took up his pen, or gazed abstractedly upon that distant horizon marked by blue hills, which he loved to contemplate from his eastern window. Besides the perpetual work of preparation, in which he was now employed literally every day, his regular public services may be stated as follows. He had one lecture, daily, which, with the accompanying examination of his classes, occupied at least an hour. On Tuesday evening, he attended an exercise of speaking, at which every student, at stated periods, pronounced a discourse of his own composition, on some religious subject. To this was added, during some years, the delivery of complete sermons, by the senior students. All these were subject to the professors' criticism, and in these exercises the labour was shared by Dr. Miller. On Friday evening, there was a debate, on some point in theology or allied subjects, in a theological society, comprising almost the whole Seminary. The utmost freedom was allowed, and the debate was concluded by the summing-up of the professors, who were both always present. As this was a period of very active controversy in our Church, on those points of theology which have since divided us, there was, as might have been expected, a peculiar animation in these discussions; and in our opinion he never shone more, or more displayed his stores of knowledge, his grasp of great subjects, or his acumen and dialectical force, than in some of these disputations, when, after being warmed by hearing the defence of specious error, he closed with the establishment of sound doctrine. The professors by turns attended evening prayers with the young men; the morning service being conducted by the senior students. At these exercises, Dr. Alexander sometimes expounded a passage of Scripture, and sometimes made a brief but pointed exhortation. He was accustomed also to join his colleague in the meeting for prayer, known as the Monthly Concert. One day in each month was left vacant, for the class prayer-meetings of the young men, and for their more solemn private devotions, to which many of them added fasting; and it was common for the professors to meet the whole body at a certain hour of the day. From this time forward, even before the erection of a separate chapel, there was a discourse to the students, on the morning of the Lord's Day; it was delivered alternately by Dr. Alexander and Dr. Miller.

But there was no exercise which more impressed its character on the students of that day, than the Conference of Sunday afternoon, which has been already mentioned. This meeting it is believed owed its origin entirely to the suggestion of Dr. Alexander, and was kept up as long as he lived. Indeed, there were some peculiarities in the manner of conducting it, which may be said to have grown out of his remarkable aptitude for free colloquial descant on religious topics. As the other exercises of the Seminary were intended to give fitness for the external work, this was directed solely to the cultivation of the heart, and there are not a few who bless God that they were ever brought under its sacred influence. Nothing could be more simple than the mode of managing this colloquy. After singing and prayer, a subject in experimental or practical religion, which had been named the week before, was discussed. The conversation was opened by one of the students, whose turn it was ; any others were allowed to express their views, as they were called on in order ; until a sufficient time had been spent. The professors then closed, with a familiar discourse, of from twenty to thirty minutes. As we have intimated, this was an occasion which more than any other Dr. Alexander used, for the outpouring of his profound personal experience of divine things. There was scarcely a topic in regard to vital piety, which did not come into discussion during the Seminary course. As he sat in his chair, he would begin with a low voice and in the most ordinary tones of conversation, evidently relying upon the feeling of the moment, as raised by foregoing remark, for all his animation. As he went on and drew more largely on his recollections and his consciousness, he seldom failed to kindle, and sometimes at the conclusion left all present in a state of high emotion. These remarkable effusions sometimes almost took the form of soliloquy, as losing sight of all around him, he uttered the serene or enraptured feelings of a soul in communion with God. Singing and prayer closed the service, which commonly occupied about an hour and half. It is but just to add, that Dr. Miller also delighted in this meeting, and contributed to it some of his most valuable thoughts. His little discourses here were always digested and methodical ; enriched with many golden sayings from old writers, and enlivened with anecdotes from his singularly copious fund. And, as his colleague was often heard to say, Dr. Miller evinced more and more spirituality of view and feeling, until the very last.

This Conference was so nearly connected with the religious development of Dr. Alexander, that we shall subjoin, altogether from memory, a few of the subjects which used to be treated from year to year. They were such as these: The Work of the Spirit on the Heart.—The Nature of true Conviction.—True and false Sorrow for Sin.—Saving Faith. —What are the Evidences of a Change of Heart?—Spiritual Joy.—The Believer's 'first love.'—Indwelling Sin.—Temptation.—The Mortification of Sin.—Symptoms and Cure of Backsliding.—Apostasy.—Spiritual Pride.—The best Method of reading the Scriptures.—How to conduct private Devotion.—Revivals of Religion.—The best Means for the Conversion of Sinners.—Growth in Grace.—Spiritual-mindedness.—Dangers of a Seminary Life.—Religious Conversation.—Fasting.—Nature and Evidences of a Call to the Ministry.—Christian Consolation.—Views proper for those who are about to enter on the Work of the Ministry.—Foreign Missions and the Missionary Spirit.—The Imitation of Christ.—Religious Melancholy.—The Regulation of Appetite.—The Unpardonable Sin.—The Assurance of Hope.—Preparation for Death.—Walking with God.—Divine Meditation.—Brotherly Love.—The Sanctification of the Sabbath. —The Day of Judgment.—The everlasting Rest of the Righteous. Of the opinions which were expressed on these and similar points, some notion may be gained, from the volume of Practical Sermons, and especially from the work on Religious Experience.

During all this time he was preaching as much as many pastors. Both to his own students and to those of the College, he was always welcome in the pulpit. For a time, he and Dr. Miller, assisted afterwards by Mr. now Dr. Hodge, preached on Sunday evenings in the village church. We have said before, that during his whole life as a pastor, Dr. Alexander used the free method, and carried no manuscript into the pulpit. After his arrival at Princeton, he began to change his method in a certain degree, making more experiment of written composition, in sermons on important topics. And what he wrote he also read; for he frequently declared his inability to commit a discourse to memory. We are bound to say that so far as manner and impression are concerned, these efforts fell far below his ordinary discourses. The matter was always equally valuable, and the train of thought was often close and felicitous; but he was sometimes indescribably trammelled by his paper, and was not a rhetorical reader; so that whole congregations used to brighten up as with a ray of sudden sunshine, when towards the close he would throw up his spectacles, cast about his penetrating glances, and, as if indignant at his duresse, break forth in the liberty of his natural eloquence. No two preachers were more unlike, than was he, in the two portions of one and the same discourse. For this reason, those who never listened to him at home, or were acquainted only with his discourses on great occasions, which were carefully written and read, have but the faintest idea of what he was as a preacher. And the period of which we are writing, was that in which he condensed into his pulpit exercises the greatest amount of theological instruction, with the still unwasted vivacity of his earlier years. In two classes of sermons he especially excelled; first, in those which clearly and connectedly set forth the different parts of doctrine, in the way of definition and proof, so as to bring them within the scope of the humblest minds ; and secondly, those in which he gave the history of a religious experience, in its origin, progress and consummation, with minute dissection, graphic detail, and moving appeal to the heart. In the latter of these, there were many who considered him unsurpassed.

There has seldom been a time since the opening of the Seminary, when it did not contain some students of the Baptist persuasion, as many as five such having been there at once. It is to the honour of both parties, that, as Dr. Alexander loved to declare, no one of these young brethren ever gave occasion to censure for indecorous propagandism, or ever took offence at the frank expositions of doctrine which were made. There was, about this time, an increasing anxiety in the Presbyterian Church, upon a number of questions, both doctrinal and practical. These unquiet feelings were naturally reflected in the students of the Seminary, who at that period came from almost every State of the Union, not excepting New England, which was indeed largely represented. It began to be seriously questioned by many, whether the diversity of theological opinion existing among our ministers were not too great to be comprehended within common symbols. The German philosophy was as yet unknown, and even the works of Coleridge, which afterwards opened the door for it, had not been read, if we except his Biographia Literaria. The later forms of new divinity, commonly attributed to certain New England theologians, were only beginning to assume a regular shape. The conflict was therefore still very much upon the old fields of the preceding century, and disputation ran high upon the points mooted by Hopkins and Emmons. It was warmly questioned, whether the mind is a series of exercises ; whether God is the efficient cause of sinful acts ; and whether the unconditional submission of the new creature involves a willingness to be damned for the glory of God. Still more earnest was the debate concerning the effects of the fall ; the imputation of Adam's sin to his posterity ; the imputation of Christ's active righteousness to believers ; the nature of moral and natural inability ; and the extent of the atonement. These questions lie so near the foundations of religion, that they were brought into view, whenever instruction and advice were to be given to new converts. They were therefore much agitated in the great revivals which at this time were spreading through the land. By many, the supposed improvements on some of these heads of theology were held forth as necessary to the work of general conviction and renewal ; they were warmly published amidst the enthusiasms of great awakenings ; and it was not uncommon to stigmatize those who adhered to old theology, as behind the age, if not as the enemies of revivals. Out of the same extensive excitement of religious feeling, arose new questions as to the mode of producing and managing revivals ; and hence the controversy, long since dead, concerning New Measures. There are few of our older readers who need to be reminded of the alarm caused by the methods of Mr. Finney ; the 'anxious-seat ;' and the Lebanon Conference. These once momentous topics belong to our narrative only so far as they had a bearing on the mind and labours of its principal subject. As a theological professor he was awake to the important bearing of all these innovations. The questions of doctrine were continually coming up in church-courts, upon the examination of candidates, which sometimes afforded opportunity for angry and indecorous wrangling between ministers, over the heads, perhaps, of students from Princeton. The young men of the Seminary came in great numbers from the very midst of revival scenes, where these matters of controversy had been agitated, in connection with their most sacred exercises. There often appeared within the walls of the institution, hot and valorous youth, who were wiser than their teachers, and eager to beard a professor, and make converts among their fellows. The whole of this period, therefore, was one of agitation and consequent solicitude ; the rather as the number of students was so great.

These were circumstances which demanded firmness and discretion ; and probably there are few who on looking back will not acknowledge that Dr. Alexander displayed both. As was before said, his theological opinions were settled, and were becoming well known ; he was universally ranked among the leaders of the old, or as many deemed it, the obsolete Calvinism of the seventeenth century. It was always his lot to suffer most in reputation from those who would have had him quicken his pace, so as to keep abreast of the moving column. At no time was he so much aspersed as at this ; and not a few represented him as opposed to the glorious work of grace which was in progress. It was even said that he was utterly unacquainted with the phenomena of religious revival ; but this was of course the language of such as had no knowledge of that early history, with which the readers of this volume have been made acquainted. It may be safely asserted that there was no man in the Church who had studied more closely this whole subject ; and it may now be added, that the sober opinions which he calmly maintained, in the midst of great opposition, are those which have since become the settled judgment of our Church. Under such a pressure he was led to examine more deeply the foundations of his system, and to push his inquiries into the recesses of theology, as concerned in the prevailing controversy. It became also his sacred duty, to inculcate what he held to be truth, with augmented diligence, and by every means to guard his pupils against the errors of the age. This he never attempted in the way of direct debate, or violent assault, but rather by the safe establishment of such principles in the earlier parts of the course, as from a logical necessity should lead to the reception of orthodox opinion. In this endeavour we believe the charge against him never was, either that he did not understand the points at issue, or that he failed of success in implanting his own doctrines in the youthful mind, but rather that he proceeded by the way of circumvallation and gradual approaches, so that the conviction was carried before they were aware. Thus, likewise, in regard to revival measures, he freely expressed the results of his long observation, when opportunity was given, in public or private ; but in such a way as to show how tenderly he distinguished between the genuine work of Divine grace, and the excesses of rash and fanatical instruments He seized every fair occasion to preach the Word, in seasons of awakening, and with a fervour and success that often disarmed the prejudice which was ready to arise from mistaken views of his position. The juncture was nevertheless one which called for circumspect walking, and no doubt led him to anxious study and many prayers.

In this connection it becomes necessary to notice the commencement of his authorship. Few men whose works fill many volumes ever began to publish so late in life; for his first book was issued when he was about fifty-two years of age. The method of preparing for the pulpit by laborious but unwritten meditation, was certainly unfavourable to facility in composition. He had given a few occasional discourses to the press, had contributed some articles to the Virginia Religious Magazine, of which we can discover no copy, to the Assembly's Magazine and other periodical works, and had amassed piles of manuscript upon theological subjects; but he was yet to embark upon the sea of publication. In regard to style he was a rigorous critic, and was always dissatisfied with himself. He never manifested the slightest complacency in any thing which he composed. He would read his manuscript aloud, amend, erase, transpose, and frequently cancel. Never feeling perfect freedom in the flow of composition, he did not venture upon those imaginative flights, nor break into that opulence of expression, which were common in his oral discourses. Hence he satisfied himself with simplicity and clearness; qualities which his written works possess in the highest degree. In regard to his style, it may be observed that he went always for the thought rather than the words, and was never led along by the bait of fine language or the development of a figure. The election between these two kinds of writing, must, we suppose, be made early in life. The occasion of his first published volume is worthy of mention. It was about the year 1823, that a little knot of young skeptics began to make themselves busy in the College of New Jersey, and it was feared that the evil would become diffusive. At the request of one of the tutors, Dr. Alexander prepared a sermon, much longer than his wont, and delivered it in the College Chapel. The text was Luke xii. 57, "Yea, and why even of yourselves judge ye not what is right ?" The subject was the Evidences of Christianity. The discourse had a happy effect, and awakened so much attention that it was requested for the press. On preparing it for this purpose, he saw room for much addition, and at length brought it out as a small volume in eighteens, from the Princeton press, under the title, "Outlines of the Evidences of Christianity." A second enlarged impression was soon called for. It has since passed through numerous editions in England and America, has been translated into several languages, is used as a text book in many colleges and schools, and continues to find sale without any diminution from year to year. Of this little manual, President Talmage observes, "I consider it one of the most perfect models of classic English which is extant ; a book to be closely studied by the scholar not only for its masterly moral demonstrations, but for its lucidness and purity of language.' Yet we remember that the author sent it abroad, with little short of trembling. His analogous treatise on the Canon of the Old and New Testament appeared in the year 1826. At that time, there was no accessible treatise on this important subject. It contains more erudition than any of his productions, and was immediately taken up by the British press. Although the substance of this work was incorporated with the last improved edition of the Evidences, he prepared it afresh for the press in the later years of his life. On the whole, it is one of the best specimens of his learned and eminently cautious mode of investigation. The publication, in 1823, of Professor Murdock's Discourse on the Nature of the Atonement, was a critical event in the theological history of the times. In opposition to the views there avowed, Dr. Alexander contributed a series of articles, occupying about twenty-five pages in Dr. Green's Christian Advocate.*

In the year 1825, a quarterly publication was issued at Princeton, under the title of the BIBLICAL REPERTORY. It was projected and undertaken by Professor Hodge, under whose auspices it has continued to flourish till this day, having now completed its twenty-ninth annual volume. As it is the oldest of existing American theological reviews, so we believe it to have as wide a circulation as any. Its character is too widely known to require our commendation. At its inception, the plan did not look much beyond the reprint of rare and useful treatises on Criticism and Hermeneutics, but it soon became the channel for original articles on theological subjects. Through good and evil report it has pursued its way, and has contributed more than any other agency, to make known those opinions which belong to what

* Christian Advocate, 1824, pp. 76, 119, 168.

some have chosen to call the Princeton School. In times of controversy it has not refrained from a free expression of judgment on great questions; and its pages contain ample discussion of all matters relating to the defence of Calvinism and Presbytery, the policy of the Church, the charities of the age, new divinity, new philosophy, and new measures, and especially the difficulties which preceded, accompanied and followed the division of our ecclesiastical body. Some of the ablest writers in our communion have chosen it as the vehicle of their best thoughts; among these, to say nothing of those who survive, we may mention Dr. Miller, Dr. Green, Dr. Rice, Dr. Fisk, Dr. Breckinridge, Dr. Winchester, and Dr. Dod. From the beginning, Dr. Alexander was active as a counsellor, and from the year 1829 he was a constant and often a large contributor. Its volumes contain some of his most elaborate and memorable treatises on theology, besides many essays and reviews of a minor sort.

So far as can be discovered, his first contribution to the Review was an Essay on the Bible as furnishing a key to the phenomena of the natural world; appearing in two numbers of 1829. But this was followed by one of his most able and striking productions, namely, his review of Dr. Thomas Brown's celebrated work on Cause and Effect. As a teacher of mental philosophy, and one well versed in all the varieties of Scottish opinion, he looked with lively interest upon the speculations of this fascinating writer; and believing them to be fraught with danger to the cause of truth, he attempted a refutation, which has been judged fair and successful. So far as we have learnt, this was the earliest extended reply to

Brown; for Sir William Hamilton's noted review in the Edinburgh did not make its appearance until the following year. To this dissertation we would confidently refer those who would judge of his qualifications for metaphysical inquiry, or would learn the methods of subtile and patient analysis, for which his lectures were remarkable. In this answer, he shows that on Brown's hypothesis all reasoning from the nature of an effect to the nature of its cause, or the reverse, must be futile; that this defeats the teleiological argument for the being of God; that it destroys human accountability; and hence that it is untenable and dangerous. The closing sentence is characteristic: "That his theories have in some instances operated unfavourably on young men of ardent minds, we know to be a fact; but, in our opinion, the right way to prevent the bad consequences of such books, is not to prohibit, but to answer them, and to lead young men to peruse them with caution, and at the right time."

The name of Dr. Alexander has been long associated with the American Colonization Society. Indeed, if those who were of the councils which projected it, and early committed themselves in its favour, are to be ranked as its founders, he assuredly deserves a name among them. The Rev. Dr. Robert Finley, the real father of the enterprise in its modern form, was a native of Princeton, and an alumnus of the College. He was an intimate friend of Dr. Alexander, and we remember the long and anxious interviews which they held upon this subject. Dr. Finley once said to his friend, "When I consider what many others have effected for the benefit of their suffering fellow-creatures at an earlier age than mine, I am humbled and mortified to think how little I have done." This he uttered with ardent emotion, adding his determination to engage in some enterprise for the good of mankind. Not many months afterwards he disclosed to the same friend his plan of a colony of free blacks on the western coast of Africa. The scheme struck most as chimerical; but Finley was immovable, and from the very outset Dr. Alexander was as sanguine as he. The first public meeting which ever took place in the country to consider this matter was held in the borough of Princeton; where Dr. Finley gave an exposition of his plan. The meeting was small, but among those present were the professors and most of the students of the Theological Seminary.* It certainly added to the interest which he felt in this undertaking, that it was his young townsman, Captain Robert F. Stockton, of the United States Navy, who, in 1822, accompanied by Dr. Ayres, effected the purchase of Mesurado from the natives, by a series of prudent and heroic acts, which almost savour of romance. He never faltered in his zeal for colonization. When others fell back, he was always hopeful, and his testimony was often repeated, "I am as fully persuaded that the plan of colonizing the free people of colour in Africa is wise and benevolent, as I ever was of the wisdom and benevolence of any human enterprise." "It behooves those," said he, "who industriously sow prejudices against Colonization in the minds of the free people of

* History of Colonization on the Western Coast of Africa; p. 80.

colour, to consider what injury they may be inflicting on them and their posterity. Let them either propose some method by which these degraded and down-trodden people may be rendered more comfortable and respectable here, or let them cease to throw obstacles in the way of their emigration to a country where they may have the opportunity of enjoying the real blessings of freedom. It is in vain to declaim about the prejudice of colour; however unreasonable, it will long continue to exist, and will prove an effectual bar to the possession and enjoyment of the same privileges and advantages which the white population enjoy. If I were a coloured man, I would not hesitate a moment to relinquish a country where a black skin and the lowest degree of degradation are so identified, that scarcely any manifestation of talent, scarcely any course of good conduct, can entirely overcome the contempt which exists, and which is perhaps stronger in the free than in the slaveholding States; and I would use every exertion to reach a land where it is no crime and no dishonour to appear in a coloured skin, a country where no white superiors look down upon the black race, but where they are lords of the soil and rulers of the nation. I admire the honest ambition and noble daring of the first emigrants. Then no Liberia existed. The Society owned not one foot of ground on that continent, and it was extremely doubtful whether they would be able to obtain any territory for a colony. Yet these lion-hearted men, resolved to run every risk, took their lives in their hands. Like Abram, they went out, not knowing whither they went; and the event has proved that they were called by the providence of God, to engage in this hazardous enterprise. And I cannot but feel pity for the grovelling views of many coloured men, now residing in a state of degradation in this country, who in Liberia might rise to wealth and independence, and perhaps to high and honourable office."

The visit which he made to Virginia in 1825, gave great pleasure to his friends, and to none more than to Dr. John H. Rice, who wrote often concerning it. "If," says he, "you could but have witnessed the universal burst of joy when it was understood that you were coming, and the deep disappointment expressed by every one, on hearing that probably you would not come, you would know what influence under the divine blessing you could exert here." "It is not possible to *hire* a carriage for *you*, in this neighbourhood. Nobody will hear of that. I do trust that we shall have the pleasure of seeing you and hearing you talk once more. Your head quarters must be with us; in the old house occupied by you so many years. This is the central point, to which people are most in the habit of coming; and near which people who come from Cumberland and Charlotte will find it easiest to get accommodations." Thus wrote this warm friend while the journey was in prospect; he afterwards says: "I do believe that it would prolong your life and extend your usefulness, if you could make such a visit every year. It might be the means of bringing your children acquainted with the children of those, who will never cease to love you with a fervour and perpetuity of affection, which is rarely to be found except among old Virginia Presbyterians. Come then often among us, and let us enjoy the pleasure of showing, or rather trying to show how much we love you." And again: "Your visit last summer constitutes an epoch in 'the annals of our Parish.' Things are commonly spoken of, as happening just before, or just after, or while Dr. Alexander was here. And if I could have my wish, you would render your last services to the Church here, and lay your bones to rest in the land of your nativity."*

Amidst public duties, Dr. Alexander found time to indulge the sympathies of Christian friendship. If the correspondence of that day could be recovered, especially with Dr. Rice and Dr. Speece, it would probably give a picture of his inward life which no later pen can supply. A few letters have been preserved, written to his eldest sister, the wife of Professor Graham of Washington College; with this excellent woman he maintained a correspondence for about sixty years. She departed this life in 1853, while this memoir was in preparation. In the year 1822 he wrote thus to her: "I am afraid from what I have heard and from the strain of your letter, that your grief on account of the death of your beloved daughter has been excessive; that you have yielded more than was good to despondency; and that you are in danger of sinking into a settled dejection. I know that your natural disposition exposes you to an extreme on this side, and that unless you vigorously and resolutely oppose it, you will be likely to do yourself a serious and perhaps a lasting injury. Grief, like all other natural passions,

* Letters of Dr. Rice, March 18, May 2, August 6 and October 16, 1825.

becomes sinful when indulged too far. It then involves always some want of confidence in God, some improper feeling in regard to his government and will. It partakes of the nature of that sorrow which worketh death. It wastes the spirits, debilitates the body, predisposes to various diseases, unfits for the discharge of common duties, destroys one's own peace, and adds to the unhappiness of friends. Somehow or other, we are not so much afraid of sin, when it approaches us through this channel. If we grow light and indulge a love of pleasure, conscience is soon wounded ; but we are ready to justify our sorrow, and refuse to make the effort which is necessary to check it. There is often a strong perverseness in the human mind in hugging its sorrows, as if they were valuable or sacred. But while the religion of Christ permits us to indulge our natural feelings, it strictly requires temperance here, as well as in other indulgences. It requires us to rejoice, to rejoice always, and to rejoice even in tribulation." And more particularly in the same strain, at another time : "I feel for you under the sore bereavement which you have suffered ; but the stroke, though severe, comes from the hand of a Father, who afflicts not willingly. Our children are more the property of God than of ourselves. He gave and he taketh away, and it is our duty to submit to his will in all things ; for whatever he does is right, and best for his own children. Hereafter they shall see that there was a propriety in all his dealings. To give up a child or other dear relative whom we believe to be prepared, is comparatively easy ; but to part with one concerning whom we have no sure ground of confidence—this indeed is hard !

But we are poor judges of what preparation is. We know not what God may work in behalf of our children in their last moments. We know not but that the principle of grace may be implanted in such as are piously educated, earlier than we are aware. In some cases, what is called conversion may be no more than the development of a principle implanted before. We know not how far the promise of God to believing parents, in behalf of their offspring, extends, when they are taken away in tender youth. If we believe that all the dying infants of such are undoubtedly saved, why may we not hope that those who have advanced a little beyond infancy may be comprehended in God's gracious covenant? Many who never profess religion exhibit more of the Christian temper than some who are professors. They are diffident of themselves, and do not make known all that they have experienced. I cannot but entertain pleasing hopes of the salvation of such amiable young persons as have been devoted to God, and early imbued with Christian instruction, when they are cut off by premature death. It can do no harm to hope as much as we can respecting the dead. Let us be as rigid as we please in regard to the living; but it is no dishonour to God, nor disparagement of his truth, to entertain enlarged views of his mercy. After all, humble submission to the will of God, from a trust in his wisdom, faithfulness and mercy, is the best refuge. When Eli heard the message of God respecting his sons, his language was, 'It is the Lord, let him do what seemeth him good!' 'Be still, and know that I am God.' These sore visitations are intended to answer wise and gracious purposes. Let us endeavour to profit by seasons of adversity. For most, it is good to be afflicted. Beware of a gloomy, disconsolate mind. Let not grief prey upon your spirits, and unfit you for the duties of a Christian. We must all very soon die, and it is much better that our children should go early, than live to be old in sin, and then die without an interest in Christ. Cast all your care upon the Lord. Commit all into his hands. Blessed are they that trust in him!"

A place is due also, to the only letter to his aged and declining mother, which is known to be in existence.

DR. ALEXANDER TO HIS MOTHER.

"PRINCETON, *May* 25, 1823.

"MY DEAR MOTHER:—

"When I last saw you, it was very doubtful whether you would ever rise again from the bed to which you were confined. Indeed, considering your great age, it was not to be expected that you should entirely recover your usual health. I was much gratified to find that in the near prospect of eternity, your faith did not fail, but that you could look death in the face without dismay, and felt willing, if it were the will of God, to depart from this world of sorrow and disappointment. But it has pleased your Heavenly Father to continue you a little longer in the world. I regret to learn that you have endured much pain from a disease of your eyes, and that you have been less comfortable than formerly. Bodily affliction you must expect to endure as long as you continue in the world. 'The days of our years are three-score years and ten, and if by reason of strength they be four-score years, yet is their strength labour and sorrow; for it is soon cut off, and we fly away.' But while your Heavenly Father continues you in this troublesome world, he will, I trust, enable you to be resigned and contented and patient under the manifold afflictions which are incident to old age.

"The great secret of true comfort lies in a single word, TRUST. Cast your burdens on the Lord, and he will sustain them. If your evidences of being in the favour of God are obscured, if you are doubtful of your acceptance with him, still go directly to him by faith; that is, trust in his mercy and in Christ's merits. Rely simply on his word of promise. Be not afraid to exercise confidence. There can be no deception in depending entirely on the Word of God. It is not presumption to trust in him when he has commanded us to do so. We dishonour him by our fearfulness and want of confidence. We thus call in question his faithfulness and his goodness. Whether your mind is comfortable or distressed, flee for refuge to the outstretched wings of his protection and mercy. There is all fulness in him; there is all willingness to bestow what we need. He says, 'My grace is sufficient for thee. My strength is made perfect in weakness. As thy day is so shall thy strength be. I will never leave thee nor forsake thee. Though I walk through the valley of the shadow of death, I will fear no evil; for thou art with me; thy rod and thy staff they comfort me.' Be not afraid of the pangs of death. Be not afraid that your Redeemer will then be afar off. Grace to die comfortably is not commonly given until the trial comes. Listen not to the tempter, when he endeavours to shake your faith, and destroy your comfort. Resist him, and he will flee from you. If you feel that you can trust your soul willingly and wholly to the hands of Christ, relying entirely on his merits; if you feel that you hate sin, and earnestly long to be delivered from its defilement; if you are willing to submit to the will of God, however much he may afflict you; then be not discouraged. These are not the marks of an enemy, but of a friend. My sincere prayer is, that your sun may set in serenity; that your latter end may be like that of the righteous; and that your remaining days, by the blessing of God's providence and grace, may be rendered tolerable and even comfortable.

"It is not probable that we shall ever meet again in this world; and yet, as you have already seen one of your children go before you, you may possibly live to witness the departure of more of us. I feel that old age is creeping upon me. Whoever goes first, the rest must soon follow. May we all be ready! And may we all meet around the throne of God, where there is no separation for ever and ever! Amen!

"I remain, your affectionate son,

"A. A."

CHAPTER SIXTEENTH.

1830—1839.

DIVISION OF THE PRESBYTERIAN CHURCH—PROSPERITY OF SEMINARY—INVITATION TO VIRGINIA—LITERARY TOILS—WRITINGS OF THIS PERIOD—DOMESTIC LIFE—CORRESPONDENCE—REVIVALS—SLAVES AND SLAVERY—PROSPECT OF DEATH.

FROM the year 1830, there was a period which was as anxious as any equal portion of time, to the Church and the Seminary. We are not called upon to recite those painful controversies, which in 1838 resulted in the secession of a large body of ministers and Presbyteries from the Presbyterian Church. That history has been amply recorded, by persons friendly to both sides of the great question. But it would be impossible to write the life of Dr. Alexander with truth and candour, without representing his views, and stating his position, in regard to matters which connected themselves with all that he held most dear. As has been already suggested, the agitations of the Church communicated their impulses to the Seminary, and during the years of which we are writing, naturally occupied to a great extent the minds of both professors and students. But one reason which conclusively precludes the subject from these pages, as to any discussion of its merits, is that Dr. Alexander never chose to make himself prominent, even as a champion for the opinions which he firmly maintained. To this course he was led, partly by a temper eminently moderate and pacific, which some denominated timidity ; partly by views which he entertained concerning the functions of a theological professor, as to a certain degree withholding him from the field of strife ; but more than all, by his inability to coincide with many respected brethren, as to the particular means by which acknowledged evils were to be remedied. His position in regard to these controversies may be thus simply stated. In doctrine he was a Calvinist of the Westminster type, and was recognised as such, by friends and opponents. No single man can be found, even during this period of excitement, who employed his pen more laboriously or frequently, in defence of the doctrines which distinguish what had begun to be called Old School Theology. This is sufficiently evinced by his articles on Original Sin, on Natural and Moral Ability, on the Atonement, and on Imputation. And the doctrines which he believed, he also diligently, fully, and successfully inculcated upon his students, who were already becoming numerous in the ministry. In regard therefore to theological tenets, and his view of their importance, he did not yield to the most impetuous of his brethren.

A second remark is equally just ; he believed that a considerable number of ministers in our Church had departed from these doctrines, and in so doing had deviated from the standards of the church. Here arose a question, as to the more or less of this deviation; how great it must be, to render one unfit for the ministry; and how much must be left to the individual conscience of him who subscribed articles of faith. On this point, as we shall presently show, his comprehension of slight differences was wider than that of some. It must be added, that he lamented the disunion, embarrassment, and annual contentions, which were making our Church a proverb. He saw clearly that elements thus irreconcilable, ought to be apart, and expected that division must some day ensue; while, as his published opinions indicate, he was unwilling that orthodox men should take the initiative in such division. Of the complicated acts and measures, by which the friends of truth sought to rid themselves of the evils, there were some which he could not approve; and hence he lost the favour of many from whom he was little inclined to be separated. When at length, the division was effected, not by process for error in doctrine, but by the spontaneous secession of large numbers, including all the adherents of new doctrine, he cordially and determinately stood by the constitutional body, and never ceased to rejoice in the quiet and purity of the Church which was the result.

The turbulent spirits of the time were causing dissension in respect not only to theological opinion, but the means of promoting the conviction and conversion of sinners; hence as much was said of New Measures, as of New Divinity. To justify what has just been summarily stated as to Dr. Alexander's position, we shall make a few citations from what is extant in his own words. In the year 1832, he contributed to the Biblical Repertory an article on "The present condition and prospects of the Presbyterian Church." It was the first essay in that work which explicitly recognised the party-troubles in our communion. It sustains what we have affirmed respecting his estimate of the theological errors then rife. "That there exists a difference of opinion in the Church," says he, "in reference to certain doctrinal points, and as to the precise import of the act of adopting the Confession of Faith, by candidates at their licensure and ordination, cannot be denied or concealed. It is also apparent, that the numbers who choose to range themselves under one or the other of these parties, are pretty nearly balanced. Hitherto, in all questions which put the strength of the Old and New Schools, as they have been called, to the test, the majority has been found on the side of the former, until the meeting of the last General Assembly, when a decided majority appeared on the other side. It is true, indeed, that the points on which a division took place between them, on that occasion, were not doctrinal points, but certain ecclesiastical transactions, relative to missionary operations and the training of candidates for the ministry; yet it is understood that generally the respective parties were agreed in their views of theology. This difference may be considered therefore, as having its foundation in a diversity of theological opinion." How grave this diversity was, may be gathered from another article, of which indeed he was not the author, but to which he is known to have given his assent. "We wished it to be understood, that we were the determined opponents of all those in our communion who manifested a leaning towards Arminian or Pelagian opinions in theology, or who discovered a disposition to invade the principles of Presbyterian church government, or to exchange them for those of the Congregational system. Against these, and against all who manifested a desire to favour them, we have lifted our voice from time to time—feebly, we acknowledge, but, according to our ideas of propriety, as distinctly and decisively as we were able." He believed that there were such errors maintained by ministers and authors as should disqualify them for exercising office in our church; but he also believed that there were some differences which did not amount to heresy, and which ought not to be made matter of discipline. And while he always defended the strict interpretation of subscription to articles, he was certainly more lenient in his judgments than some who acted with him. On this point, his views are best expressed by what he uttered in a conference of clergymen, in 1835. "Dr. Alexander expressed his belief that our church could not long be governed by a General Assembly, as constituted at present; but that the evil ought not to be precipitated. He declared his belief that the most important difference between the friends of the truth was as to the degree of theological difference which might be tolerated."* In the same spirit he wrote to Dr. Weed; "We go on here upon our old moderate plan, teaching the old doctrines of Calvinism, but not disposed to consider every man a heretic who differs in some few points from us."†

For a long time he had augured evil from the diffusion

* MS. Notes of a Conference, held April 15, 1835.

† Letter to the Rev Henry R. Weed, March 8, 1834.

of new opinions. As early as 1831, he writes to a friend "My mind is full of gloomy apprehensions respecting the affairs of our church, since the meeting of the last General Assembly. I cannot foresee whither we shall be driven. I had never suspected that the new men and new measures would so soon prevail in the supreme judicatory of our church. But I need not dwell on this subject, as I have nothing remedial to communicate. If the Lord intends good for the church, our exertions will prosper. But if we are to be handed over to the men of the new religion, bound hand and foot, then we must yield, and mourn in secret places over the departed glory. We old men shall soon leave the stage. The burden and heat of the day will soon come upon you young men, who will have great need to be strong, to preserve the ark of the Lord from falling into the hands of the Philistines. Quit yourselves like men. Stand up bravely for the religion of your fathers, which is also ours, by deliberate choice, as well as inheritance."*

Deeply as he felt the evil of increasing error, he had from the beginning a dread of originating any measure of division. That this was his sentiment, at least in 1834, is manifest from his language in an article to which reference has already been made. "If it is now found," says he, "that our differences are so wide, that we cannot live in peace, let us peaceably agree to separate into two distinct denominations. This should, however, be the last resort. The Church of Christ is ONE, and all who agree in essential matters should hold communion together, notwithstanding

* Letter to the Rev. W. S. Plumer, July 6, 1831.

minor differences. And if division on account of some diversity in sentiment commences, there is no telling where it will end; for we presume there are no two men who in all their opinions on every subject entirely agree. And as not only our presbyteries, but our congregations are in a multitude of cases composed of persons who agree partly with one and partly with the other side, a division of the Church by a line of difference on theological points, would split many churches into two parts, neither of which would be able, without the other, to support the Gospel among them. Endless controversies also respecting the church property would necessarily arise, and society would be agitated and convulsed to its very foundations. And as brethren, differing as we now do, have hitherto continued to live in peace, and in most places in great harmony, have loved each other as brethren, and have cordially co-operated in promoting the Redeemer's kingdom, why may not this still be the case, after the present exacerbation of feeling has subsided? Upon mature deliberation, therefore, we declare our sentiments to be opposed to all schemes which tend to the division of the Presbyterian Church. We do not know, indeed, that there are any persons who seriously wish or meditate any such thing; but sometimes hints and rumours come to our ears, which seem to have this bearing."* Such were his avowed opinions at this time; but these were during the first acts of the drama. He very soon came to perceive the causes of separation were almost unavoidable. Thus he writes to a former pupil, in 1837: "I tremble for the ark. I see

* Bibl. Repertory, 1834, p. 39

dark lowering clouds collecting. The new Revival Measures, connected with the New Theology, are gaining strength and popularity every day. The stream is deepening and widening, and will shortly pour forth such a torrent as will reach over the whole surface of this land. Our Church cannot proceed much further under her present organization. The General Assembly ought not to be long continued in its present form. But what can be done? Divide? How? If shades of opinion must mark out our parties, we may have a dozen as well as two. I say, No division. Let us hold together as long as the foundation can be felt under our feet. When that sinks, then 'what shall the righteous do?'" He then proceeds to indicate a new organization of the body, retaining the General Assembly as a bond of union and council of brethren.* Again, about the same time, to a valued pupil of his earliest class: "I hope that your Presbytery has honoured you with a seat in the next General Assembly. Men of nerve should have hold of the vessel in the time of a tempest, for doubtless the New School brethren will rage and clamour loudly. But we mean them no injury. It is necessary for our very existence, that we should be separate."† As early as 1833, he had expressed similar fears to the same friend: "Pittsburg Synod," so he writes, "is the purest and soundest limb of the Presbyterian body. When we fall to pieces in this quarter, and in the far West, that synod will be like a marble column which remains undisturbed in the ruins of a mighty temple. I do not know

* Letter to the Rev. W. S. Plumer, Sept. 13, 1837.

† Letter to the Rev. Henry R. Weed, April 14, 1833.

but that more of us will be obliged to seek an ultimate refuge in that region from the overflowing of new divinity and new measures. As you suggest, through the ultraism of the Old and the New School, the sound and moderate part of the Church is placed in jeopardy."*

From these scattered expressions of opinion, it is sufficiently manifest, that with all his desire for peace, he had slowly and reluctantly arrived at the conclusion, that the two parties could not much longer remain in union. Yet he took no leading part in the immediate causes of the division, which eventually took place in 1838. It is well known that he never gave his assent to the Act and Testimony. As a member of the Assembly of 1837, he advocated the abrogation of the Plan of Union ; he voted for the act disowning the Western Reserve Synod ; but did not vote for the act dissolving the connection of the Synods of Utica, Geneva and Genesee. He was, moreover, with Doctors Baxter and Leland, in preparing the pastoral letter addressed to the churches by the General Assembly. There can be no doubt that all his sympathies were with the majority ; that he approved of the end which they had in view ; and that he was prepared to sanction and defend to a certain extent the means which they adopted to accomplish that end. After the separating acts were passed, and when the churches, presbyteries and synods which they affected, refused to submit to them, or even to regard the abrogation of the Plan of Union as a valid act ; but on the contrary resolved to proceed as if the said plan was still in force, and to claim

* To the same, Feb. 21, 1833.

for all judicatories formed under it a right to sit in the General Assembly; he certainly never manifested the slightest hesitation as to which party was right. After the accomplishment of the division, and especially after the ground assumed by the minority in the Assembly of 1838, when they withdrew and claimed to constitute the Presbyterian Church, there was no man who entertained more strongly than he disapprobation of the whole course pursued by that minority, or who took a livelier interest in the success of the Old School Assembly in all its conflicts. It is believed that the articles on the division of the Church which appeared during this period, though not from his pen, may be taken as expressing his views on the general subject.

There is no friendly and competent reader of this memoir, who will not admit that the writer has had a difficult and delicate task, in making the brief record above given. He durst not suppress it, from any fear or favour; and he has in no case consciously coloured it with any opinions of his own, but has simply endeavoured to record in truth the judgments of an honoured parent.

To not a few it was matter of surprise that the dissensions in the Church produced so little injury to the Theological Seminary. The truth is, it never was in a more healthful condition. Immediately after the disruption of the body, it is true, there was a sudden falling off in numbers, so that in 1839 the whole amount was only ninety-eight. But this loss was almost immediately repaired, and the average of matriculations for the decennium, 1830–1839, was fifty-three annually; rising in 1831 to seventy-eight. The whole number of students was, in 1836, one hundred and thirty-six; in 1837, one hundred and forty-two; and in 1838, one hundred and thirty-five. The disputes of the time gave renewed animation to all concerned; and in particular the widely extended interest in questions arising out of revivals, infused a zeal into the young men, which sometimes demanded the cautious hand of repression and guidance. The three instructors were perfectly united in their views concerning all the points in controversy. It will probably be acknowledged by all who were in the Seminary, during these years, that the course of learning was pursued with uncommon ardour and satisfaction.

We have already noticed the strong desires which had been felt in regard to the return of Dr. Alexander to his native State. These attempts were more earnestly renewed in the year 1831. The nature of the proposal will best appear from an authentic representation of the proceedings of the Synod of Virginia. This was unquestionably the most serious inducement which was ever presented to draw him away from Princeton. The invitation of the Synod was reinforced by numerous private letters. In one of these, a brother clergyman still living thus puts the case: "In reference to the great question submitted to your consideration, I have thought much; and though I may not be able to present the subject in one single point of light in which you have not viewed it, yet the more I reflect on it, the more it seems to me that you may possibly think it your duty to accept the invitation, which I know will be given with great unanimity and warm affection, if there be any hope of its meeting a favourable reception.

"Two reasons influenced the members of the Synod, in making the effort to ascertain beforehand what would probably be the result of the appointment, should it be made. One was that they did not wish to agitate the Church, and raise hopes which might issue in disappointment. The other was that the interests of the [Union] Seminary required, nay imperatively demanded, that as little delay as possible should attend the filling of the vacancy. At the called meeting the nomination could not be made, because it was not contemplated in the call; but it will be made at the regular meeting. But while there are such pressing reasons for coming to a decision as soon as practicable, there seem to me, as before intimated, strong inducements to a favourable determination.

"The Seminary, raised at great expense, with much toil and solicitude, and with the sacrifice of one of the best lives among us, is now on an elevated poise; and I know not who is so likely to sustain it as yourself.—[Dr. Rice] in the last hour of his mortal struggle expressed a strong desire that the institution might continue to be conducted on the same principles as by himself. In you, the Synods would cordially and with great confidence unite. The institution would not be under the control of the jarring elements of the General Assembly." It is scarcely needful to add, that none of the considerations thus proposed had sufficient force to withdraw Dr. Alexander from the post to which he had been assigned by the Church. But this adverse decision cost him a serious struggle of feeling.

This was beyond all doubt the period of his greatest literary activity. Both in pressing his researches into the works of others, and in committing his own thoughts to writing, he was indefatigable, so that he scarcely knew an idle hour. He was constantly adding to his written lectures, filling up gaps in the series, and by compilation and original research preparing himself for treatises and volumes which he afterwards made public. His voluminous manuscripts largely belong to this period. Having discovered a faculty of composition, of which he had long supposed himself destitute, he began to make amends for past inaction. At no time did he contribute so much to the Biblical Repertory, and his choice was generally directed to the most important subjects ; which, however, he saw fit to treat rather in their principles and history, and upon their intrinsic merits, than with express allusion to the controversies then agitating the American Churches. Some of these essays deserve a passing notice in any tribute to his memory.

In 1830 he communicated to the above named quarterly work an essay on the "Early History of Pelagianism." In preparation for this and some kindred articles he read largely in the works of Augustine, as well as the Massiliensian Semipelagians and their opponents. He also made himself thoroughly acquainted with the works of Jansenius, an author in whom he took a lively interest. He communicated to those around him a lively interest in Augustine and his times, and would sometimes go largely into the story of those angry controversies, as he sat among his family, with great animation and effect. We were informed by the Rev. Dr. Symington of Glasgow, that this essay, and several analogous ones yet to be mentioned, are not only commended to students of the Reformed Presbyterian Church, but are even made subjects of examination by the professor.* The writer's own conclusions are indicated by the last sentence of this essay: "It is our opinion, therefore, after looking on all sides, and contemplating the bearing and consequences of all theories on this subject, that no one is on the whole so consistent with facts, with the Scriptures, and with itself, as the old doctrine of the ancient church, which traces all the sins and evils in the world to the imputation of the first sin of Adam; and that no other theory of original sin is capable of sustaining the test of an impartial scrutiny." The same volume contained a contribution on "the Doctrine of Original Sin as held by the Church, both before and after the Reformation."† In the course of the next year he published "An Inquiry into that Inability under which the Sinner labours, and whether it furnishes any Excuse for his Neglect of Duty;" a dissertation which vindicated the Calvinistic views, and was justly regarded as one of the ablest productions of his pen.‡ We have already spoken of his article on a proposed re-organization of the Presbyterian Church. This was followed, in 1832, by a treatise on the Synod of Dort, in which the history of doctrine in that day is treated.§ A fai

* Biblical Repertory, 1830, pp. 77–113.

† Biblical Repertory, 1830, pp. 481–503.

‡ Biblical Repertory, 1831, pp. 360–383.

§ Biblical Repertory, 1832, pp. 239–252.

more able article was the review of the "Essays on the Formation of Opinion and the Pursuit of Truth;" works in which there was an insidious attack upon some fundamentals of ethical science. The questions which are here discussed at great length and with the utmost vigour of his mind, are two: first, the responsibility of man for his opinions, and, secondly, whether any testimony is sufficient to establish a fact which is a departure from the laws of nature.* The next year produced an essay on the Racovian Catechism, in which he details the history and tenets of the early Socinians; and a translation of Melancthon's treatise on Sin.† Besides an article on Transubstantiation, he wrote an extensive historical sketch of the Scotch Secession; and reviews of Wayland's Moral Science, and Woods on Depravity. We omit a number of minor reviews, which appeared during the same period.

But his labours with the pen were by no means confined to sermons, lectures, and periodical essays. In the year 1831, he prepared a new edition of his work on the Evidences of Christianity, with additional matter which tended much to its completeness. His book on the Canon of Scripture was sent to him in a London reprint, in 1832. In 1833, he published a "History of the Patriarchs." He also contributed to a religious journal, in 1839, those essays on Religious Experience, which have since appeared in a volume. It is sufficiently shown, therefore, that neither pro-

* Biblical Repertory, 1832, pp. 394–428.

† Biblical Repertory, 1833, pp. 180–204, and pp. 521–531

fessional toils nor the agitations of church controversy had impaired his relish or capacity for the severe labours of the study.

If now we take a glance at matters more personal and domestic, we must remember that he was no longer in his physical prime, as during this ten years' period he passed his grand climacteric. It was certainly something remarkable, for a man turned of sixty to apply himself with such enterprise and earnestness to new and different pursuits; the rather, when as we afterwards learn this was only the beginning of labours which were to endure for nearly twenty years. During the time of which we write his health was interrupted, not only by his never absent nervous disorders, but by acute sciatica, and in 1833 by a slight hæmoptysis. Sometimes he looked upon the probabilities of extended life as very faint. Thus he writes to his eldest sister, in 1831:

"Although I wrote to you by mail not long since, I will not permit so favourable an opportunity as that which now offers to pass without dropping you a line. The time of our earthly correspondence is drawing to a close. I am now in my sixtieth year, and you are a little older. This is an age to which I never expected to come; but Providence has preserved me, and brought me along; and upon a review of my life I have reason to be thankful for the manifold blessings which I have received. But I have nothing to say respecting my own fidelity and diligence, except what is of the most humbling kind. I must cast myself entirely on the free mercy of God and the rich merits of Jesus Christ. This is all my hope and all my salvation. I find, as I suppose you do, that the arrival of old age does not bring death any nearer to the feelings. I have indeed a rational conviction that I am nearer to my end, but as to realizing apprehensions of death, I am not conscious that this acknowledged nearness has any effect on my views of the importance of that awful event. In regard to the state of the soul immediately after death, I find my mind filled with darkness when I attempt to form particular conceptions of it. My only relief is in relying on the general promises of the Gospel, and dismissing all solicitude about the mode of existence or the special nature of the feelings in that untried state. I have always wished and hoped to arrive at a degree of faith in the things of the invisible world, to which I have not yet attained. In my ideas of divine things there is too much of imagination—of mere notion—too little of the feeling of reality. When, for a moment, I can conceive of eternity, as *a real, approaching state*, I am startled—and feel astonished at my habitual apathy. Sometimes, when I awake suddenly in the night, the thought of eternity and of the judgment is overwhelming. But these impressions soon pass away, I am occupied with visible scenes and earthly cares, and for a great part of the time futurity is out of view.

"I am much concerned about the state of our Church. Every thing in the signs of the times is ominous; for while revivals are multiplied, errors appear to be coming in like a flood. Divisions threaten to rend the body, and thus peace —one of the richest blessings of the Gospel—will be lost. But the Lord reigneth, let the earth rejoice! I do not look forward to any time when I shall have it in my power to visit Virginia again. It is, however, a matter of little consequence. Let us all be engaged in preparing to meet in a happier world." *

This was the very time at which efforts were making in Virginia, as related above, to bring him again to his native State. In writing to his son, he speaks of a letter, "the object of which," says he, "was to learn whether there existed any insuperable objection in the way of my consenting to take Dr. Rice's place in the Union Seminary. They seem to think that the existence of the institution will depend upon the success of this project. I have not had time to give it much consideration. If I were younger and more capable of answering their expectations, I would think seriously of it; for in the distractions of the church in this region I fear that our Seminary will become a bone of contention. And as Mr. Hodge is well prepared to take my place, and nothing would be requisite but to put some young man in his place, I do not see that this institution would suffer much loss by my departure." † These negotiations we have already said resulted in nothing. He made a visit to Virginia in the Autumn of 1835, but no case occurred during the whole remainder of his life, in which he seems to have thought of leaving New Jersey.

To give a recital of his pulpit labours, would be to repeat what has been said in the previous chapters. Scarcely a Lord's Day passed in which he was not preaching, at home or abroad, and he was frequently called to such exercises

* Letter to Mrs. Graham, July 27, 1831.

† Letter to J. W. A., Sept. 15, 1831.

during the week. These labours were made much more abundant by the great prevalence of religious awakenings in the land ; and it is remarkable, that while he was reputed by some an enemy of revivals, or at least one ignorant of their nature, there was no preacher whose services were sought with greater avidity, during such seasons of religious warmth. The controversy ran high about New Measures, or the system of means employed in revivals On this subject, as we need scarcely say, his judgment was with that of the sober party, a judgment which has since become that of the Church at large.

As the number of students was now very large, he had abundant opportunity to exercise that influence which has already been mentioned, by means of private counsel. It is in connection with this that hundreds remember him, with even more warmth than in his character of public instructor. And as many of his former pupils were now established in their posts of usefulness, he kept up a paternal regard for them, and often gave them letters of counsel. An eminent clergyman, whose name would add force to the statement, if we were sure of his permission to publish it, after referring to his own early authorship, speaks thus of Dr. Alexander. "I have said these things because I feel indebted to him for the kindness with which he treated me and my maiden production. I am under many other obligations to him ; yes, more than I can express. His sweet simplicity, his perfect naturalness, his saintly purity ; how deeply have they inscribed themselves on my memory !" The portraiture would be incomplete without some specimens of these. "If you cannot live at * * *," so he writes to a young minister, "on the salary which they give you, you will be under a necessity of removing ; and you ought to consider whether this is not an opening in Providence for your relief. In my opinion, no situation is so desirable for a preacher as a pastoral charge ; and no man called to the ministry ought to relinquish it for any other business, unless there be an evident prospect of greater usefulness ; or some physical disqualification for the work. When a man alleges that he cannot visit, or perform other parochial duties for which he has bodily strength, it is just as if a servant should pretend that he cannot do the work for which he is employed. A minister of Jesus Christ must divest himself of fastidiousness, and exercise self-denial in the performance of his duties. In regard however to what is duty (in the matter of pastoral visits) every man must judge independently for himself, and not be governed by the whims of well-disposed but weak women. In a large city, preparation for the pulpit is the main thing, and except in case of illness, comparatively little good is accomplished by running from house to house. The preacher who ably fills the pulpit will, on the whole, get along very well. The course in such a place as Baltimore would be for the minister first to prepare for his pulpit exercises on the Sabbath ; next he should be attentive to Bible Classes, Sunday Schools, and catechizing ; and should visit the sick. And as to visiting, he should appropriate certain portions of time, and conscientiously perform what appertains to that time. His calls ought to be very short, except in special cases. It is poor economy for a man to exhaust his strength in talking to one at a time, when he has an opportunity of saying the same thing to hundreds or thousands."

The next letter is upon a subject which always lay near his heart, and in regard to which he had some special facilities for forming a judgment.

DR. ALEXANDER TO THE REV. WILLIAM S. PLUMER.

"PRINCETON, *June* 10, 1830.

"REV. AND DEAR SIR :—

"Your letter came to hand just as our examination had commenced, which prevented an immediate answer, and ever since I have been in Philadelphia, or away from home in some other place. The subject on which you ask advice is both delicate and difficult ; and for one so far off, it is impossible to judge correctly on the course most proper to be pursued by a person situated as you are. It seems to me, however, that when Providence has cast the lot of one of his servants in the country of slavery, he ought not to abandon it on account of prospective evils, the existence of which is only conjectural ; or, if certain, which would not be greater than evils of another kind, which must be encountered, let a man go where he will. It is now becoming more and more a subject of consideration with our zealous young men here whether duty does not call some of them to make every sacrifice of personal comfort, and to devote themselves to the instruction of the slaves. Surely they ought not to be abandoned to ignorance and vice, without an effort to rescue them from ruin ; but if ministers will flee from their work in the southern States, simply because of the existence of slavery, how can it be hoped that others, knowing such facts, will venture into such regions ? My opinion, therefore, is, that as you have formed a permanent connection in that country, and have become a slaveholder, you ought to remain, and endeavour by all lawful means to extend the blessing of salvation to that degraded people. And if you wish for my opinion as to how you may best promote the welfare of those whom Providence has committed to your care, and for whom you must give account, I would say, that you can best promote their happiness by keeping them in your possession, and instructing them in the Christian religion. No one can prevent your instructing them in the great truths of religion ; and even if the laws should become so rigid as to forbid their being taught to read, this will render the use of oral instruction far more important. And all experience teaches me, that the *living voice* is the proper medium of instructing the ignorant. Those persons who learn to read imperfectly derive very little benefit from the art ; a few sentences, pronounced *viva voce*, sink more deeply into their hearts than many pages spelled over with great difficulty.

"As to bringing the unhappy creatures to the northern States, it has been demonstrated by experience that it is, in general, ruinous.—My advice then is, that you remain at B., if the people wish it, and lay yourself out to do all the good you can to black and white ; and if you cannot operate in one way, you will be able to do good in another. Remember, however, that 'the husbandman hath long patience,' after he has sowed the seed. Do not expect to effect much by storm, but understand that moral improvement is always gradual, and very commonly imperceptible from day to day. Labour assiduously, and trust in God for the fruit, although every body around should be lamenting that nothing is done. It is too much the error of the day, and especially of the South, to aim at unnecessary excitement; to push things to an extreme from which they must speedily return; and then, like an elastic cord, will spring nearly as far beyond the mark on the opposite side. Observe, I do not say it is unlawful to leave the South, in any circumstances. I only mean to say that the reasons which you mention are not the ones which should induce you to take that step. If Providence needs you more elsewhere the door will be set wide open, and your call clear. As to place, when duty calls you will find the right one. Beware of discouragement. It cuts the nerves of effort—of steady persevering effort—completely. The news from the General Assembly you will receive from others; and I have nothing interesting to communicate from this place. It is now vacation, and we are for a while in solitude.

"Yours affectionately,

"A. A."

DR. ALEXANDER TO THE SAME.

"PRINCETON, *July* 1, 1834.

"DEAR SIR:—

"I have received your two letters, which came to hand the same day, one dated May 27, the other June 10. In regard to historical facts I will keep the subject in mind, and set down such fragments of knowledge as I have. Dates will be defective; but facts may be of use without precise dates.

"As to the instruction of the coloured people, as the blacks are called in this country, I know nothing of importance. The Rev. John Mines, some years since, prepared a catechism for their instruction, which I revised in manuscript. It was printed, but never came into use. It was intended to be used by the catechist in the instruction of such as were unable to read. Dr. Palmer, of Charleston, published one somewhat similar, accompanied with prayers, a copy of which I have. Some years ago, I delivered a hastily written discourse to the Society for promoting religion among the Coloured Population. That discourse is somewhere among my papers; what it contains I know not; but if you wish to have it, I will look it up and send it to you.

"The early Presbyterian ministers in Old Virginia were far more attentive to the instruction of the blacks than their immediate successors. I have had under my pastoral care a number of Mr. Davies's converts, particularly Will and Ned, brothers, who belonged to Col. Thomas Read of Charlotte, and were eminent for piety. Both were natives of Africa. They were brought over when boys, and were taught to read by Mr. Davies, or some one under his direction. Will adhered to the Presbyterian Church while I remained in Virginia, but Ned went over to the Baptists and became a preacher. They were both very aged when I last saw them. Old Harry, who belonged to Ben Allen, in Cumberland, was one of the most fervently devout men I ever met with. He also could read, and had a Bible which had been given him by Mr. Davies; but having come to the country after he was grown to be a man, he spoke our language in so broken a manner that I could not understand much of what he said; but his soul appeared to be all on fire with love to Jesus Christ. One of the most fervent spirits I ever knew was old Molly, who once belonged to Dr. John Blair Smith. At public worship she could not restrain the expression of her feelings. As her noise disturbed the congregation, he expostulated much with her, but all in vain. When I lived at Hampden Sidney, she belonged, I think, to Martin Sadler.

"The Presbyterian preacher who laboured more than any other among the blacks, and with more success, was the Rev. Robert Henry, of Charlotte. He was the pastor of Cub Creek and Briery, and was a very singular man. Though a graduate of Nassau Hall, he was a rough, uncultivated Scotchman, who so blundered in preaching that he often placed himself in a very awkward attitude. Old Father Patillo, upon being asked in my presence about Robert Henry, said, 'He had as much grace as would serve two men, but not half enough for himself.' He delighted in preaching to the negroes, and as the fruit of his labours, had nearly a hundred communicants at Cub Creek alone. When I commenced my ministry there, the number was above seventy. Twenty-five communicants, and several of them distinguished for piety, belonged to Mrs. Coles, on Staunton River; and this lady, the mother of Mrs. [Paul] Carrington, of Sylvan Hill, though not a member of the Presbyterian Church, testified to the good effects of religion upon her servants. Almost all her house-servants were members of the Church, and one man was constituted by the session an overseer of the coloured communicants. It was a lovely sight to see these seventy blacks surrounding the table of the Lord. I see the pious and humble labours of this servant of God are now likely to be overlooked and forgotten. The trumpets for sounding the praises of men were not used in his day. The existence of this body of black communicants, and the great number of other blacks who attended at Cub Creek, induced Dr. [John H.] Rice, when a pastor of this church, to apply for a commission to labour for a part of his time among them.

"Old Mr. Mitchell, if his memory is not gone, can furnish you with facts which no living man beside can. He can tell you of the labours of his father-in-law, the Rev. David Rice, and of his colleague the Rev. James Turner, both of whom, I think, preached often to the blacks.—[In later times] I know it to be a fact that multitudes would walk ten miles to hear a black man who could not read a word, [in preference] to going to hear the best sermons within a few miles. And when we made appointments to preach to them alone, which was often done, their habit of indulging their feelings, by shouting, and their desire to have such feelings roused, presented an effectual bar to regular instruction. This they thought was religion, and the way to glorify God. Still much more might have been done [by later ministers.] When I left the State, upon a retrospect of my ministry, I deeply regretted that I had not laboured more for the instruction of these people; and I wrote to my friend, the Rev. Matthew Lyle, an earnest exhortation to attempt more in this way.—We had no difficulty from the government, when I resided in Virginia; but events occurred soon after, which induced the legislature to enact stricter laws, and which caused the people to be more jealous. In the Valley, when I was a boy, the number of blacks was very small. A few wealthy families only possessed slaves. Ministers there had therefore little to do with this subject.

"I remain, respectfully and affectionately, yours, &c.,

"A. A."

The scheme of Foreign Missions under the care of the Presbyterian Church originated in the West, and became a fruitful cause of contention in the General Assembly. The work which is now performed by our Board of Foreign Missions was begun by the Western Missionary Society. While many continued to harbour doubts, Dr. Alexander fully believed that such enlarged operations as we have since seen realized, were justly to be expected. He therefore wrote to a confidential friend, concerning the Church enterprise: "The reason for encouraging its institution, in most concerned, was to bring out resources from parts of the Church which were perfectly dormant. Thus far, it has succeeded beyond expectation. The Philadelphia Synod will be the principal dependence on this side of the mountains.—New-York city furnishes the richest field for all pecuniary operations."*

He was always a zealous advocate for the work of Foreign Missions, and was accustomed to indulge liberal and sanguine expectations at times when many good men were ready to be appalled. His interest in the work was augmented and enlightened by "that minute and unapproachable topographical knowledge" (we use the words of the Rev.

* Letter to the Rev. Henry R. Weed, March 9, 1835.

Dr. Davidson), "which no other man possessed, and of which nothing in print, or to be put in print, can give an adequate idea." He followed with anxious inquiry those students who became foreign missionaries, and maintained a lively intercourse with some of them. His correspondence with Mr. Whiting of the Syrian Mission, and Dr. Armstrong of the Sandwich Islands, would add to the value of our work, if it could be recovered. At the monthly prayer-meetings held in the Seminary for the spread of the Gospel, he often poured out his stores of information on these subjects; and for a time he delivered a series of weekly lectures, in the evening, in the chapel of the Institution.

We shall next make copious extracts from a communication on a subject of great delicacy and importance; it is that of supposed early conversions:

"I was not aware," he writes to a friend, "until your letter put me on the inquiry, how barren my memory is of facts concerning early piety; I mean such as have fallen under my own observation. In books, you can find many cases, but—strange as it may seem, and it is as discouraging as strange—I cannot remember one solitary instance of decided piety in childhood, where the child lived to adult age to prove the genuineness of the change. And I do not here confine myself to the earliest stages of childhood, but include the whole period under twelve years of age. I will correct what I have said, by mentioning a case which just now occurs to my memory. The Rev. Mr. Robinson, pastor of the Cove, Albemarle, Va., had a little son, who at the age of six or seven years gave evidence of experimental religion. I never conversed with the child, but heard of him from many, and was well acquainted with his father, who on one occasion took the child over the mountain to the Synod, with the view of conversing with the ministers, that he might receive advice about admitting him to the Lord's table. On some account, I was not at that meeting, but heard of the fact from those who were there. Whether he was then admitted, I cannot be sure; but if not, it was soon afterwards. This young man you must have known when you lived in Lexington. I think he was graduated at Washington College. He died of a fever, at the Union Seminary, soon after he was licensed, and I have understood always gave good evidence of piety, living and dying.

"I have, however, seen many beautiful and hopeful blossoms, which were never followed by mature fruit. A. B. was the daughter of an excellent man in Berkeley (now Jefferson) County, and the granddaughter of one still more eminent for piety—one of the fruits of the ministry of 'One-eyed Robinson,' the first apostle of Virginia, though now remembered there no longer. This little girl, in 1791, was about eight years of age. She was intelligent, grave, modest, very conscientious, loved to hear sermons, was ready to converse on religion, and seemed to have a warm affection towards Christian people. I was much at the house, as I made it one of my homes, the first winter after being licensed. I never saw any thing in this child but what was indicative of pure and elevated piety. She was almost entirely exempt even from childish levity, and, as her mother told me, was consistent in private devotion. I did not entertain a doubt of her being a regenerated person. But, as I have been informed, for I saw her no more, as she grew up all her religious feelings wore off, and she became as gay and careless as other young ladies of her own age. Whether she is now living, or what was the course of her after life, I know not.

"C. D., a boy of thirteen or fourteen, attracted universal notice by the apparent fervency of his pious feelings. His prayers in public have melted large congregations into tears, and none doubted the genuineness of his piety. But when exposed to the company of irreligious companions at college, he became entirely careless; and if not skeptical, has lived afar from God until this day, though a man of talents and character, and high standing in the world. He was of my own age, and when I was careless, he faithfully and tenderly addressed me on the subject of religion, and not without some present effect. He said to me then, however, 'The pious are deceived about me; I have never experienced a saving change, and I have withdrawn from the Lord's table.' Some years afterwards, I met him, in company with some of the profanest young men I ever saw; though out of his mouth I never heard a profane expression. I felt that I owed him a debt, and having then more zeal than now, I waited for an opportunity to speak with him. He candidly confessed, that all his religious impressions were gone; that his views of religion were greatly changed, and that when he was the subject of these, he was misled by a set of enthusiastic preachers, in whose opinions he now had no confidence.

"E. F. was another, who about the same age gave pleasing evidence of having received a new heart. Old Christians would smile and weep when they heard him converse or pray. It was a revival season, and he was much noticed and caressed, and after a while evidently became vain. He fell in love also with a lady much older than himself, and appeared like one almost distracted. He turned from religion somewhat suddenly, and became one of the most profane men in the land. His after history is unknown to me.

"G. H. was an obscure apprentice to a tanner. He was seen attending prayer-meetings, and one wet evening, when the good simple old man who conducted the meeting found none to aid him in the prayers, he asked this boy if he would not pray. The youth consented, and the people who were present reported that no minister could make a better prayer. He was thenceforward called out, upon all occasions. Even in church, the minister after sermon would call on G. H. to pray, and all wondered how this boy, who had nothing but the most common education in the world, could excel the most learned and eloquent ministers in prayer ; and some good people would rather hear G. H. pray, than listen to the best sermon. After some time, however, there was a manifest change. The style of his prayers became more artificial and elaborate, and there was an observable straining after striking expressions. But it was resolved that he should be a preacher.—God had determined otherwise ; for though he was sent to school and afterwards to college, the Presbytery would not receive him when he offered himself as a candidate ; his vanity and arrogance had become so manifest and insupportable. He was mortified and grievously offended, and immediately engaged in the study of the law. His course was downward, and his end hopeless. Man looketh on the outward appearance, but God judgeth the heart. Gifts are no sign of grace.

"My old teacher, the Rev. William Graham, had no confidence in any appearances of early piety. He said they were seldom permanent. But read the account of Mrs. Edwards, wife of President Edwards. Did any one ever give better evidence of religion pure and undefiled? Look at a great many other cases, in Janeway's Token for Children, &c. I have taken up an opinion, that all religious impressions made by truth are salutary, even if conversion does not immediately follow. The fruits in a revival are commonly from seed sown long before. This in the spiritual world is precisely analogous to the harvest in the natural world. But to the query, what ought to be done. God has promised to ordain strength out of the mouths of babes and sucklings. It is unbelief to deny that the grace of God can reach children. Why so few are converted in that age, we do not know. Old Dr. Hopkins believed and taught, that God has conditionally promised the salvation of baptized children, to parents in the baptismal covenant. (See his system of Divinity.) But even if this were true, it does not follow that they shall all be brought in while children. Mr. Richard Baxter, in his Dispute with Tombes, says that the time will probably come, when there will be but few conversions within the pale of the church by the public preaching of the Word, as children will be pious under parental culture, before they can attend with profit on the ministry of the Word. Do you ask what should be done for children? Persuade parents to do their duty; to bring them up in the nurture and admonition of the Lord. But I have a favourite notion, that this is a rich uncultivated missionary field. There should be a class of preachers for children alone. If I were a young man, I would, God willing, choose that field. Twenty-five years ago, a little man by the name of Robert May, came to Philadelphia, from the London Missionary Society, on his way to Hindostan; for the European war rendered it safest to come here and go in an American vessel. He and his wife were I think the most diminutive couple I ever saw matched, and they were childlike in their feelings of vivacity and versatility. Mr. May never entered a house without inquiring for the children; and his manners were so puerile and affectionate, that they would soon cluster around him, and clamber on his knee, or cling to his skirts. In fact he conversed very little with grown people. He was not in his element with such, while with children he was all alive, full of anecdote and pleasantry; but every story had a good end, and the winding up would make them feel serious and often weep after all their mirth. On Saturday afternoon, when the schools were not in session, he would preach or lecture to them, and sometimes a thousand would attend. A small volume of these lectures was printed. This dear little man remained several months in Philadelphia, before he met with a passage. In India, at a place called Chinsurah [in Bengal, eighteen miles north of Calcutta], he commenced his operations among heathen children; and when he was called home, which was about three years after his arrival there, he had twenty-five schools under his care. Look into the Reports of the London Missionary Society, or the Evangelical Magazine, for some account of him.

"Our common preaching does the children no manner of good. I am doubtful whether the custom of taking and confining them during the service is not injurious. But pass this; sermons suited to children can be preached. I have tried it over and over, and I never had an audience more attentive, or who better understood my meaning. I often go now, and deliver addresses to them at Sunday-school anniversaries; and to keep up and enliven attention I commonly stop and ask them questions, which I expect them to answer. They seldom refuse to speak, and their answers give opportunity for further explanation. I delight in such discourses, and if I had health and leisure would have one every week. Perhaps I shall, as it is. But I am constrained to remark, that the talent of preaching to children is of all other preaching talents the most rare. A brother who has better preaching talents than myself, and more piety, when he speaks to the children reads them a discourse from a paper, so composed as to be fit for the press; but while it is in the course of delivery, almost every one is vacant or wandering. I. J. K. has a great love for children, and has devoted himself to the Sunday-School cause, and thinks he has the talent of addressing them. I went to hear him, and of all the affected, vulgar, quaint, ill-adapted discourses this exceeded. The more sensible children laughed in his face. L. M., once a student here, often undertook to address children. His method was to entertain them with figurative and exaggerated stories. Sometimes he terrified the little urchins almost into fits. One of my children was present at his meeting when a thunder storm of some violence arose; to increase the terror he blew out the candles and intimated that perhaps the day of judgment was come. Another dear old brother screams at the top of an astounding voice, and they gaze in stupid wonder. Too much noise drives away thought. No man can have any variety of ideas, nor any connected train, beneath the deafening roar of a cataract. I thought at first that the sea shore would be an excellent place for meditation; but the ocean-war drove away every thing but the one uniform sombre emotion. You perceive by my egotism and digressions that I am growing old." *

The letters just cited illustrate a disposition of Dr. Alexander to draw largely on his own early observation, and this was still more strikingly exemplified in his ordinary discourse. The same will appear in a paragraph which we refer to this period, and which undoubtedly refers to the late Dr. Livingston, of New Brunswick, for whom he entertained an unusual veneration.

"Another divine, who belonged to a different denomination, and left the world a few years ago, seemed to me to be eminent in piety. Religion appeared uppermost in his mind at home and abroad. I believe he was seldom in company with any one without saying something about the worth of the soul, or the excellencies of the Saviour. When he entered any house, he seldom sat many minutes without introducing some discourse respecting divine things, and this no

* Letter to the Rev. William S. Plumer, February 26, 1834

in a stiff formal manner, but affectionately and earnestly He was fond of conversing on experimental religion, and freely communicated many interesting particulars concerning the exercises of his own mind, and the various trials and conflicts which he had experienced in his religious progress. He mentioned, that when a young man he had long laboured under distress of mind, which was not removed until he heard Whitefield preach; when a single text repeated by the speaker seemed directed to him individually, and all his darkness was removed. He had much confidence in the powerful application of particular texts or promises to the mind; believing that the Spirit directed them to the heart, for the relief of distressed souls. He mentioned a particular verse, which had been thus remarkably brought to his mind in answer to prayer for some brighter manifestation of God's favour.

"On a particular occasion I had occasion to observe how he seized every opportunity, at public houses, to say something which might leave a good impression. The keeper of the inn himself attended at dinner, and my venerable friend began a story, addressing himself to me. The man presently went out; he paused in his narrative, and as I was surprised at his breaking off so abruptly, he said to me in a low voice, 'I commenced this story with a view of benefiting our host; wait till he comes in;' and then resumed it. At another place where we stopped, when about to depart, he took the owner of the house to one side and gave him a pointed and powerful exhortation. Wherever he was, he made all know that there was one in company who feared God, and who was neither afraid nor ashamed to acknowledge his dependence on him. On crowded steamboats, he would always publicly ask a blessing at meals. His appearance favoured this, being truly venerable. He was a man of large frame, and wore a flowing white wig. His heart seemed to be always overflowing with kind affections. Most of the middle-aged ministers of the Reformed Dutch Church studied under his direction, and revere his memory."

Among other tokens of advancing life, Dr. Alexander was warned by the removal of several early friends, who were called away during the years to which this chapter refers. His friend and kinsman, the Rev. Matthew Lyle, had been called away in 1827. We have already recorded the death of Dr. John H. Rice, for whom he entertained as warm a regard as for any man living. He was not only a great man, but a man of great affections. A little domestic instance will place his friendship for Dr. Alexander in a strong light. Soon after the removal of the latter to the north, Mr. Rice wrote to him thus: "And here let me make a request of you, which I have often thought of making before. I do it seriously, and in the spirit of a friendship which I am assured will last while life lasts. If it should please the All-wise Disposer of events to remove you from your family before they are educated and settled in the world, and I should be spared, it is my most earnest wish that you would leave to me that one of your children to whom you may judge that it would be most advantageous. He shall in such case be to me a child, and I to him as a father. I hope that you will excuse me for making such a request, and that it may not be forgotten."* And after the lapse of twenty years, he resumes the subject: "I owe you more than I do any other man in existence. It is not in my power to do any thing for you personally; but should the Sovereign of the universe be pleased to order that I should survive you, it may be in my power to act the part of an efficient friend to some of your children."† In 1836, the Rev. Conrad Speece, D. D., another companion of his youth, already named in these pages, was suddenly taken to his rest. These and similar events had an obvious effect upon the temper of his mind; not in the way of gloom, but as producing an elevated solemnity and habitual expectation of the time when his own change should come. Yet he urged forward all his pursuits with unabated vigour, and rejoiced to see others rising up to vindicate the truth which he loved. That some of these persons belonged to other denominations, did not seem to diminish his regard for them. When in 1839, Dr. Nettleton spent some time in Princeton, Dr. Alexander found much satisfaction in observing the coincidence of their views on the great and contested points of evangelical theology. And in the same year, when the accomplished and pious Joseph John Gurney exercised his public gifts among us, he took equal pleasure in the remarkable approaches which this good Quaker made to the doctrines of sound faith. At the age of sixty-seven, no feeling of religious warmth manifested any abatement.

We suppose that no one was ever long conversant with

* July 15, 1810. † July 21, 1830

Dr. Alexander, without being astonished at his turn for the particulars of localities, and his topographical knowledge. In the estimate of those who knew him most closely, this was by far the most remarkable of his endowments. It was doubtless fostered by his living in boyhood in a wild country, and by the continual and often solitary journeys of his early manhood. However much he might seem to be otherwise employed, his eye was always directed to the surface of the country and its natural configuration. To have travelled a road once was to know it, with all its landmarks for the whole of his life. Wherever he had wandered, he knew the direction of all the streams, their rise and flow, the chains of hills or mountains, the nature of soils, timber and crops, and the ridges which mark and divide the water-systems. And he had the faculty of extracting the same sort of information from travellers and others coming from regions which he had not visited. It was a standard topic of merriment with him to banter his children upon their occasional blunders in determining the species of a forest tree. As he began his eager inquiries on these subjects when our States were few in number, he was able to add to his knowledge as new countries were settled; so that we suppose there was no man living whose acquaintance with the geography and topography of America was more extensive or exact. In times when private modes of travel were common, we have known him to draw plans of journeys, extending through several hundred miles, for missionaries leaving home, with a note of distances and a specification of every night's sojourn; without the consultation of book or map. This knowledge reached also, far beyond what is common, to foreign countries, and was perpetually increasing by his study of every thing new in the shape of voyages and travels. For the same reason he took a lively interest in all that belongs to the natural delineation of the earth, and in his later years perused with much zest the works of Mrs. Somerville and Professor Guyot on Physical Geography.

As connected with what has just been mentioned, and in some degree falling under the same faculty, we may note his acquaintance with all the churches and pastors of our Presbyterian connection. If we did not know that hundreds now living can bear witness to what we say, we should be led to modify the strength of the statement which we are about to make. The whole territory of the Church was so mapped out in his head, that it is scarcely too much to affirm that he knew who was the pastor of every Presbyterian Church in the United States. Notices in journals and elsewhere, which made little impression on others, seized his attention, and seemed to fall into the right places and fill up the proper blanks. In most cases he knew also the whole line of incumbents from the beginning. This knowledge extended quite largely to other branches of the Church. As his pupils from year to year spread themselves over the country, he followed them in their wanderings, and particularly kept his eye upon those who went to foreign lands. There was not a missionary, of either our own Church or the American Board, with whose locality he was not perfectly familiar.

CHAPTER SEVENTEENTH.

1840—1851.

DECLINING YEARS—UNABATED STRENGTH OF MIND—CORRESPONDENCE RESPECTING DEATH—STUDIES—EXTRAORDINARY LABOURS IN WRITING—DOCTOR JOHN BRECKINRIDGE—SLAVES AND SLAVERY—VISIT TO VIRGINIA—LOSS OF FRIENDS—PUBLICATIONS—ACTIVITY AND HAPPINESS OF HIS OLD AGE.

FROM part of his public duty he was now to be relieved, in consequence of the resolution of the General Assembly of 1840, that Dr. Hodge should be made Professor of Exegetical and Didactic Theology, and that his own title should hereafter be Professor of Pastoral and Polemic Theology. The closing period of his life occupies somewhat more than ten years, and begins about his sixty-ninth year When we speak of him however as declining, the word must be received as applicable rather to body than to mind. No one could perceive any abatement of his intellectual vigour, and in regard to professional and literary labour he never was more abundant. His was in the highest sense a happy old age; and the remembrance of it fills his surviving friends with satisfaction and thankfulness.

He had lived to see the institution to which his life had been devoted, not merely established, but at its very highest prosperity; and during these years the number of students attained its maximum. In every part of the country, and in the missions of other lands, were men of piety and distinction, who looked back with affectionate veneration to his paternal care.

As the horizon of his view was thus extended, he seemed to glow with a larger benevolence, and at no time manifested more lively interest in every new proposal for the spread of the Redeemer's kingdom, than now when he felt that his days on earth were numbered. It was a common observation concerning him, that while his judgment was cool and his policy conservative, he never rejected any scheme because it was novel; and no man was more sanguine in hope than he, with regard to great enterprises from which even younger persons were disposed to recoil. Yet he was not slow to recognise the tokens of decaying nature, and to draw from them appropriate reflections. In 1840, he thus begins a letter. "This day, forty-nine years ago, I was licensed to preach. You may know from this that I am growing old, and of course approaching the end of my pilgrimage. My health, however, is as firm as it has been for years; only I am still distressed with weakness of nerves. Dr. Miller has had several attacks of low fever this year, but is now restored to his usual health. My family have been blessed with uninterrupted health for more than a year, so that we have not once had to call in a physician. For this we desire to be humbly thankful to Him 'who forgiveth all our iniquities, and healeth all our diseases.'" * And some months after this, to his elder sister: "For some time I entertained a thought of visiting my friends in Virginia this summer; but after reflecting seriously on my age, and on the expense of the journey, on the small benefit that would accrue, and the important duties which require my attention, I came to the conclusion that it was rather my duty to stay than to go. Whether I shall ever see you and my other friends again, is uncertain, but it is a matter of little consequence. If we can only so live and act as to have an entrance administered to us into the kingdom of our Lord and Saviour Jesus Christ, it will not be long before we shall meet where parting is no more. Our contemporaries are fast dropping off, and indeed very few of our early acquaintances are now left. The death of Dr. Baxter was a solemn admonition to me. We were in the same office, and nearly of the same age, and his constitution seemed much more robust than mine; but he is taken and I am left." †

The same year deprived him of a younger friend, the Rev. John Breckinridge, D. D., once his pupil, and for a time his colleague; a man whom he respected for his talents, eloquence and chivalrous bearing, and loved for his affection-

* Letter to the Rev. Henry R. Weed, D. D., October 1, 1840.

† Letter to Mrs. Graham, May 31, 1841.

ate converse and ardent piety. It was often remarked by the household, that no one had the faculty of drawing forth his powers in animated conversation, so fully as this warm and brilliant friend. And though Dr. Breckinridge was eminently remote from any thing like undignified levity, he knew so well how to present that side of any subject which was entertaining, that his presence used to make itself known by the peals of genial laughter which would burst from the study. He was equally skilled to touch the chords of Christian pathos. And we may be allowed to say, that the Church has seldom lost a man who more happily united devout tenderness and philanthropic zeal with manly honour and high courage in his Master's cause.

Though the difference in age was so great, Dr. Alexander looked on his junior colleague with high respect; which is testified by the following sentences from his Introductory Lecture, next following the bereavement; it is likely that much more was uttered by him: "On this occasion also it seems to be highly proper to make solemn mention of the decease of one of the most active, energetic and eloquent ministers of the Presbyterian Church, who had been not only a student but for some time a Professor in this Seminary. You will all understand me to speak of the late Doctor John Breckinridge, whose death, in the midst of his years, and in the midst of the most enlarged and flattering prospects of usefulness, is an event which should not be overlooked by the Church, nor cursorily passed over by this Seminary, to which he was ever an ardent and efficient friend. Few men filled a larger space in the view of the Church and the public, and few men could be taken from the earth who will be more missed. He was indeed 'a burning and a shining light,' but we were permitted to rejoice in his light only for a short season. Our only solace under this affliction is, that it was the stroke of our Heavenly Father, who is infinitely wise and good; and that our brother departed in the full assurance of faith and hope, and now rejoices in the presence of Him whom unseen he loved, and in whom he believed, which is far better than any pleasure to be enjoyed on earth. But let the memory of the devoted servants of the Lord, and of their work of faith and labour of love, be affectionately cherished by the Church."

In the spring of 1842, Dr. Alexander made a flying visit to Richmond, where he delivered a discourse which was published. The subject was, "The People of God led in unknown ways;" from Isa. xiii. 16. On his return he writes to his sister: "My going to Richmond was a sudden thing, and I was obliged to come back immediately to fulfil appointments made in the State of New-York. I therefore could not with any ease or comfort extend my visit to Rockbridge. During this vacation I have been almost constantly in motion, and my health has generally been good; they tell me every where that I have grown much more corpulent than I formerly was. My principal weakness is in the stomach and nerves; and though diseases of this kind are not attended with immediate danger, they make us very miserable at times, and at last become incurable and end in lingering death. I have been appointed by the Board of Missions tc visit, in company with a younger man, the western counties of New-York; to ascertain the state of the churches there. But I am very doubtful whether a person of my age should undertake so long a journey, or whether any good is likely to arise from such a visit.—I am thankful that my life has been spared to see all my children educated. And now if I could see them all pious members of the church, I should be disposed to say, 'Now, Lord, let thy servant depart in peace.'" *

Notwithstanding the adverse prognostics of this letter, he was permitted to revisit Virginia in the summer of 1843. On this occasion he delivered a discourse before the Alumni Association of Washington College, on the Commencement Day, June 29th. From the crowd of persons and the extreme heat, he was during the address seized with a faintness, which was alarming, and which made it necessary for him to be carried into the open air. No expostulations, however, could induce him to desist. He was especially desirous to say something in honour of his old teacher, Mr. Graham. He therefore returned and completed the delivery of the Address. Its last words were these: "Having now finished what I wished to communicate at this time, I must, my beloved friends, take a solemn and last farewell of you all; expecting never again to see the faces of most of you in the flesh.. May Heaven's richest blessings attend you!"

From the columns of a religious journal, published some

* Letter to Mrs. Graham, July 5, 1842.

time after the event, we derive the following statement: "I shall never forget some circumstances connected with his last visit to Virginia. It was the summer of 1843. He came, as he told me when I met with him, reckoning upon it as his last visit to his native region. Dr. Alexander opened the Commencement exercises with a short prayer. A generation long gone by seemed to be represented in him, and while he sat looking down upon the scene, and partaking of the varying emotions that swayed the auditory, I could not but fancy what thoughts and feelings must have been passing through his mind, far out of the range of those that were present to the minds of others there. He had been one of the early students of Liberty Hall Academy, under its first rector, William Graham, a man of eminent talents and piety, who well deserves to be honoured as the father of learning in West Virginia, and who was the preceptor likewise of Baxter, Speece, J. H. Rice, and other men of note, both in church and state.

"In the afternoon the audience again filled the spacious building to hear Dr. Alexander, the most of them for the last time. The heat of the crowded house, and the effort of the occasion, coming after the fatigue and excitement of the morning, were too much for an aged man, like Dr. Alexander. He faltered in the midst of his discourse, grew pale, stopped and sank back into his seat, every heart in the vast assembly beating quick at such an interruption. In a few moments he rose, and renewed the effort; but it would not do. It was not long before he gave way, and had to be carried out of the house in his chair. I had listened in painful anxiety from the time that he had commenced again, and the feelings of the audience were now all absorbed in concern for him. Who could tell but that the cords of an aged and feeble life, too tensely stretched, might suddenly snap, and the scene wind up with a melancholy and thrilling event.

"Friends gathered around him, and begged that he would leave off, suggesting that, with his consent, the address would be printed. He declared his intention of going on. It was then suggested that the rest should be read by some person for him. But no, he persisted strangely, and as it almost seemed, obstinately. What was the secret of his pertinacity? He had an office to perform, he had a tribute to pay on that last occasion. And there, under the shadow of the old church, surrounded by the descendants of his own paternal family, and of his contemporaries, amidst the tombs of his own generation, and within a few yards of the graves of his own parents, he sat and read his tribute to Mr. Graham—the audience clustering around him, and hanging with fixed and tearful attention on his closing words. He sketched the character of Graham, spoke of his services to the cause of learning and religion, and concluded with a few impressive remarks, in which he spoke of himself as the sole survivor of the whole number of officers and students, connected with Liberty Hall at the time of his entrance, and for two or three years afterwards, and exhorted those about him, as one who never expected to see them again, to seek salvation through the infinite merits of a Redeemer.

"The address has been printed. But it needs that one should have been present to feel the full impression of it, as delivered.

"That face and form, that group, the old church, the churchyard with its monuments, all seen amid the lengthening shadows of declining day, formed a scene for a painter's pencil. It was a most striking and appropriate picture for the last page of such a man's pilgrimage to the place of his birth and of his fathers' graves.

"N. L."

Concerning this visit, his eldest brother, Andrew Alexander, Esq., thus wrote: "We have been very much gratified with the visit of your father. There were frequently present the three brothers and two sisters. It is not common for so many aged brothers and sisters to meet; the youngest being sixty-seven years old. It is not at all probable that we shall ever again meet in this world." It is instructive to add, that at this present writing, only one of that venerable circle survives.

On returning from this memorable visit, Dr. Alexander thus addresses his sister: "After an absence of sixty-four days, I returned home; preserved from illness and all fatal accidents. But the day before I reached home I met with a slight disaster, which, if a kind Providence had not interposed, might have been very serious. For in going from Chambersburg to Carlisle, when in sight of Shippensburg, the car in which I was with many others, ran off the track into a ditch. The locomotive which did not leave the track broke loose from the car by snapping the chain ; otherwise we should have been dragged along, overturned, and perhaps killed. Whereas we all escaped with very slight injury. I believe that I was more hurt than any other person, having been driven against the seat before me, by which I got a stroke on the leg, just below the knee. I felt it so little, however, that I walked nearly half a mile to Shippensburg, and then did not think it worth while to examine the place. But at Carlisle I found the leg much swelled, and the skin torn off. I had an appointment to preach in the evening, and though I was unfit for public service I found it necessary to go into the pulpit and make the effort. Next day I came all the way home, and have been ever since almost entirely confined to the house ; for by some means, I know not how, my ankle was sprained. But I am now nearly well of my bruises, and all the time have enjoyed excellent health. I found all well at home.—I have sent on my Alumni Discourse to Dr. Ruffner. I might as well have left it, for I had no opportunity of transcribing it, or doing any thing to it, except adding a few particulars respecting the Rev. William Graham. They must make the best of it. I have now very little literary ambition, and am therefore reckless as to what becomes of the address.—Upon a retrospect of my late journey, I feel glad that I was persuaded to undertake it ; though I now feel that home is the best place for old people. Whether I shall live to take such another journey, I certainly cannot tell ; but the probability is that my next journey will be to that land from whose bourne no traveller returns. The only preparation for death which can be effectual to give solace to the mind is a lively faith in Christ. If we confide implicitly in him we shall fear no evil. All before us is dark and unknown, but our Great Leader can conduct us safely over this Jordan. The valley looks gloomy, but the Shepherd's voice can cheer us while we pass through. Let us dismiss a timid, unbelieving spirit, and be strong in the Lord and in the power of his might. We should not look into our own hearts for comfort, but directly unto Christ. The more we trust in him, the more we honour him. Nothing in us or about us is more displeasing to him, than our fear or distrust of his power and grace. He seems to say, as to his disciples of old, 'Why are ye so fearful ?' 'Wherefore did ye doubt ?' 'Only believe ; all things are possible to him that believeth.' "

It is in harmony with such remarks to add here, that during this and the following year, he was called to mourn over several dear friends. Mrs. Paulina Le Grand departed this life in 1843. No Christian woman in Virginia was more widely known. Having come out of a family circle of great wealth and extreme worldliness, during the great awakenings of which we have already had occasion to speak, she signalized a long life by a sincerity of Christian deportment which made her example noted. She was a lover of good men ; she entertained strangers ; she washed the saints' feet. Her home was open to all disciples of every name ; she not only sometimes entertained many families of her friends at once, but gave a welcome to the humblest wayfarer who needed shelter. For months and even years she gave a home to ministers of the Gospel. While her personal experience was not joyful, she loved evangelical truth, and spared no pains to promote it. Having a masculine skill and generalship in the conduct of affairs, she extricated a large estate from embarrassment, and was able to contribute largely to good objects. Her courage was remarkable, and no instance was ever known in which she shrank from reproving sin, even in distinguished persons. For more than half a century she was the friend and correspondent of Dr. Alexander. Nearly about the same time died his elder brother, Andrew Alexander, Esq., of Lexington ; a man of probity, sagacity, and consistent life. After a brief interval, two beloved sisters were taken away, Mrs. Ann Turner, relict of the Rev. William Turner, and Mrs. Martha Rice, wife of the Rev. Benjamin H. Rice, D. D.

DR. ALEXANDER TO MRS. GRAHAM.

"PRINCETON, *Jan.* 20, 1844.

"DEAR SISTER :—

"The occasions of our writing have of late been of a sorrowful kind. Your last contained an account of the decease of our dear sister Turner, who died in a strange land, but surrounded by kind friends, and supported by Christian hope and comfort. It has now become my painful duty to inform you and other friends of the death of Anne Forman, second daughter of our sister Martha Rice. You know that she was married to a young clergyman in Kentucky, who was settled in or near Versailles. She visited her parents last spring, and brought with her a little son, a year old, named Benjamin Rice. Though Anne had been delicate from childhood, her health appeared not only good, but robust, when she was here. But five or six weeks ago she was seized with some disease which affected her head and stomach, and on the 11th inst., gently departed this life, having given every evidence of being a sincere Christian. Her last words were, 'I wish to be a better Christian!' from which it would seem that she was not aware of the nearness of her end. Her parents, as you may suppose, are much distressed; but while they sorrow, it is not as those who have no hope; and they will no doubt derive spiritual benefit from this heavy affliction."

TO THE SAME.

"PRINCETON, *March* 6, 1844.

"MY DEAR SISTER:—

"Your last letter conveyed to us the mournful intelligence of the death of our oldest brother; and now it falls to my lot to inform you that our youngest sister, Martna Rice, has also been taken away from us. She gave up her spirit into the hands of her Redeemer about two o'clock this morning. About three weeks ago she was seized with a violent chill, followed by a high fever. Three or four days ago her fever subsided, and we hoped that she might recover; but a dreadful oppression of the lungs came on, owing to what cause is not known. This difficulty of breathing continued to increase until she expired. With the fever, which the physicians call congestive, she had also an inflammation of the tonsils, which rendered it difficult for her to speak. Being confined to the house by a severe attack of sore throat with fever, I was unable to see her before yesterday morning. I found her mind in a calm and comfortable state, in the midst of bodily pain and oppression. During her whole illness her understanding was undisturbed, and her faith was strong. The only doubt which she expressed to me was a fear lest her perfect peace of mind, devoid of every doubt and fear, might be the effect of her disease. But the fever had then left her, and the same peace and confidence continued to the last; for even when speechless, she understood every thing; and when her husband asked her whether she could now say that God had given her victory over death, and requested her to signify it by raising her hand, she immediately did this, and soon after expired. Her loss will be greatly felt in the family. She will be greatly missed in the congregation, especially among the poor and afflicted. She was active in works of faith and labours of love. I could not bring myself to believe that this sickness would be unto death. I prayed often and earnestly that she might be restored to health and to her husband and children. But the will of God was otherwise.—I have seen Dr. Rice this morning. He bears his bereavement like a Christian; his feelings are very tender, but he bows with entire submission to this afflictive dispensation.—Thus our family, the members of which have been so long preserved in life, are now taken away in rapid succession. Out of eight, three have departed within less than six months; and it cannot be long before the remaining five shall be summoned. O may we all be ready! And may we be enabled to meet death with as little fear as those who have already died! Farewell. God bless you all!

"Your affectionate brother,

"A. A."

TO THE SAME.

"PRINCETON, *May* 13, 1845.

"We have been preserved to a good old age, and as God has been so favourable to us thus far, we ought not to distrust him for the remaining part of our journey. We need not be troubled about the dissolution of these frail bodies. 'Dust thou art, and unto dust shalt thou return.' It is a way which all must travel once; grace and strength for the day we must trust Him to grant, who hath said, 'I will never leave thee, nor forsake thee.' If Christ be near to us in that hour when heart and flesh fail, we need fear no evil. He hath himself suffered all the bitter pains of death, and is therefore able to sympathize with those who walk through the gloomy valley. His people, who trust in him, are seldom left to darkness and discouragement in that last conflict.—As we shall in all probability never meet again in this world, may we have a joyful meeting in the world to come! And while continued here beyond the time usually allotted to mortals, let us pray for each other daily, that we may be counted worthy, through the grace of the Lord Jesus, to inherit the kingdom prepared for the people of God, from the foundation of the world!"

TO THE SAME

"*June* 21, 1847.

"As to my own health, it is very good in the general; though I have had several sudden and severe attacks of disease, which seems to have its seat in the stomach. The crazy tabernacle must come down, and it matters little by what means this end is attained. The only wonder is that it should last so long. I have been trying of late to realize my nearness to the eternal world; but though my judgment is fully convinced that I shall soon cease to be an inhabitant of this world, and be in an unchangeable state of happiness or misery, my feelings are not in accordance with my judgment. I cannot bring death near so as to apprehend the reality of the solemn circumstances in which I stand, on the breaking brink of eternity. But perhaps it is best that our minds should not be continually occupied with the thoughts of death. When I attempt to think distinctly of what my views and feelings shall be the moment after death, I feel lost in the obscurity of the subject. I seem to dread the awful surprise which will burst on the mind. But my only relief is that the Great Shepherd, who accompanies his sheep through the valley of the shadow of death, will be their guide afterwards, or will furnish them with a convoy of angels. We need not trouble ourselves about the particular circumstances of our future state of existence, if only we are found among the number of Christ's sheep. For all his people he has provided suitable mansions in his Father's house. Some will occupy much higher places than others;

but if we are admitted into the very lowest, it will be enough.

"I have often resolved to begin to make special preparation for an event so certain and so near; but I find I can do nothing towards it by my own exertions. Dying grace is commonly reserved for a dying hour. The best preparation is, to be found watching and actively engaged in our Master's service. In thinking what will make death easy, it has occurred to me, that a lively faith is all that we need. To have an humble, confident trust in Christ, will bear us up, however the waves of Jordan may swell around us. Let us not torment ourselves with unnecessary fears and scruples. We must trust entirely to the mercy of God, and the merit of Christ; and if we do so sincerely, we shall be safe. Every letter which I write to you, of late, I think will be the last; for considering our advanced age, it is to be expected that one of us will soon be called away; and it cannot be long before we shall meet in another, and I hope a better world."

TO THE SAME.

"PRINCETON, *June* 18, 1848.

"DEAR SISTER:—

"I am sorry to find by your letter that your health is not as good as usual; but at our age we must expect to be subject to many and increasing infirmities, until death comes to release us from all the evils of our present condition. Though death is called the king of terrors, and the last enemy, yet to the believer he is a conquered foe, or rather is converted into a friend. Therefore Paul, in giving an inventory of the possessions of the Christian, places death among the number: 'For all things are yours; whether Paul, or Apollos, or Cephas, or life, or death, or things present, or things to come; all are yours, and ye are Christ's, and Christ is God's.' And he says again, 'For me to live is Christ, and to die is gain:' having a desire to depart and be with Christ, 'which is far better.' There is much sin in indulging unbelieving and unreasonable fears of death. We ought to place more confidence in the Captain of our salvation, who has promised never to leave nor forsake his people, and to be with them in the valley and shadow of death. How often do we see those who were subject to bondage all their lives, delivered from all fear when they are laid on their death beds. And thus, I trust, it will be with you. 'Jesus can make a dying bed feel soft as downy pillows are.' Be determined to trust in the Lord and fear no evil. He is a powerful, a loving, and a faithful Shepherd."

TO THE SAME.

"PRINCETON, *August* 7, 1849.

"DEAR SISTER:—

"Yours of the 3d inst. came to hand this morning. I am gratified to learn that your health continues so firm, at so advanced an age. It is certainly a cause of great thankfulness. What you say of your health during the past year is with some exception true in regard to myself. My general health was never so good since I was in the ministry, as for a few years past; and I am more fleshy than in any former period. But in the last month I had a pretty violent attack, which, if it had not been taken in time, might have ended in Cholera. In regard to this desolating pestilence, which is a heavy judgment on our land for the sins of the people, our town like yours has hitherto been exempt."

Again in 1850, he writes: "My time must come soon. If I can only be ready, it matters not whether I pore over the inevitable event or not. Our departure will probably not be very far apart. May we meet in a happier world!" * The last letter to this estimable sister, and indeed the latest date which has come to our hands, is of June 12, 1851, and closes a correspondence of at least fifty years. It is written in a fair and firm hand, and is filled with lively domestic details.

We have varied from chronological exactness, and omitted certain things, in order to give these letters and extracts in unbroken series. They evidently proceed from one who had learnt to look death in the face, and are from first to last a comment on the maxim, *Disce mori.* If we had nothing else to judge by, we might suppose them to have been penned by one who had laid aside the entire business of life, and devoted his mind to the recluse contemplation of eternity. But so far was this from being the case, there was no time in his whole life in which he was more full of employment, or set about it with higher zest. His sympathy with the world about him was uncommon. He had not ceased to take pleasure in the affairs of the Church or the intercourse of friends, and seemed bent on working to the last both publicly and privately. The prosperity of the institution was

* Letter to Mrs. Graham, Jan. 30, 1850.

great. For part of the time the number of students was nearly one hundred and fifty. In 1843, the beautiful library building, reared by the munificence of Mr. Lenox, was completed. Health prevailed in his own family, of whom five children out of seven now surrounded him. It was by far the most serene, if not the happiest portion of his life. It was in his view an addition to his comfort, that two of his sons were his colleagues. The visit of a deputation from the Free Church of Scotland, in 1843–4, greatly awakened his feelings. The visit of the Rev. Dr. Cunningham in particular, offered an occasion for long and interesting conference upon the state of the Church and the methods of theological education. Some of the enterprises to which he had adhered in their darker hour, such as the Foreign Missions of our Church, and the colonization of the Free Blacks, began to show signs of eminent success. In 1849, a benevolent Episcopalian of the South, in founding a seminary in Liberia, requested that it might be called the "Alexander High School;" adding, "to him they are indebted; for but for said article [proposing the plan] this donation would not have have been made, and I trust it will in due time grow into a college bearing the same name." *

It is generally known that the various benevolent schemes of the Presbyterian Church are conducted by large commissions of clergymen and laymen, which are denominated *Boards.* These are elected from time to time by the General Assembly. Dr. Alexander was from their origin an important member of these bodies. Of the Standing Committee of

* Quoted in a letter of Elliott Cresson to Dr. Alexander, April 20, 1849.

Missions he was chosen a member in 1807 ; and continued in this and in the Board of Missions which grew out of it, until his death. As long as he remained in Philadelphia he met constantly with the Committee, and sometimes went from Princeton afterwards for the same purpose. He was a member of the Board of Education, from the beginning. We have elsewhere spoken of his interest in the Board of Foreign Missions. At the first meeting of the Western Missionary Society, which preceded the Board, he was elected a Vice-President. In 1837 he was chosen a member of the Board, and remained such as long as he lived. "He was punctual," says the Hon. Walter Lowrie, "in his attendance at the meetings ; and from his minute knowledge of all its operations was a most useful and influential member. After the death of Dr. Miller, he was on the 6th of May, 1850, elected President of the Board, and was such until the time of his death." He was likewise President of the Board of Publication from its origin, was constantly invited to their counsels, and prepared a number of their works.

In addition to these strictly Presbyterian schemes, he was greatly interested in the American Sunday School Union, the American Bible Society, and the American Tract Society. For the first named he furnished several valuable publications. In regard to the Tract Society his affection and zeal never abated. For a time he was a member of their Publishing Committee ; he wrote some of their smaller publications, and was a frequent contributor to the American Messenger ; in which, it is believed, his very last communication for the press appeared. One of the closing acts of his life was to give a sum to send one of their small libraries to a destitute pastor. He was particularly solicitous to extend their circulation of volumes, and said, late in life: "I reflect on no part of my life with more satisfaction than any little agency I have had in encouraging and promoting the Society's volume circulation. I do consider the success of this enterprise as intimately connected with the prosperity of vital scriptural piety in our land; not in any one church, but in all evangelical churches, and beyond them all, by conveying a sound and practical knowledge of the Gospel to multitudes who enjoy no public means of grace, or have not attended on them. If I could do any thing more to urge on this blessed work which has been so auspiciously commenced, I would cordially lend my aid." Again he says, under a later date: "The success of the volume circulation gladdens my heart every time I think of it; and I sincerely wish that, instead of twenty volumes, you had a hundred in circulation."

It is proper that we should add something of the literary labours of this period. He was accustomed to say that he wrote more than in any previous part of his life. Indeed it was his solace, and the pen was continually in his hand. This is the more surprising, as for some of his closing years, he scarcely made any use of one eye, and was frequently threatened in the other. Yet when he was not hurried, his manuscript character was round, clear and bold; though he never used desk or table, but held the paper before him, on a wide book or port-folio.

His volume entitled "Thoughts on Religious Experience,"

already mentioned, appeared as a separate work in 1840. It contains the results of his matured thinking upon the inward work of grace, and has been extensively useful. No one of his writings more fully reveals his own opinions and feelings upon the rise and progress of godliness in the soul. The work was adopted by the Presbyterian Board of Publication, and in 1853 appeared in a German translation.

In 1841, he reviewed the Works of Dr. Chalmers, for whom he cherished the greatest respect, but from whom he was constrained to differ on some points of metaphysical theology. Especially he objects, as McCosh has since done, to Chalmers's opinion, that morality can be ascribed to no feeling or emotion unless it be the consequence of volition, or somehow connected with volition.* He also wrote, as he had often done before, on the "Religious Instruction of the Negroes." He likewise reviewed Dr. Hetherington's History of the Westminster Assembly.† He contributed a warm and instructive article in behalf of American Colonization, in which he reiterates his opinion thus: "We do believe, that it is the design of a wise and benignant Providence to make Liberia the asylum of the whole African race now dispersed over this continent and the West India islands. It is our sincere persuasion, that no event which has occurred in the world since the commencement of the nineteenth century, is at all equal in real importance to the successful establishment of this little colony." He furnished reviews of

* Princeton Review, 1841, p. 30, ff. The article is only in part from his pen.

† Princeton Review, 1843, pp. 30–41; and pp. 561–587.

Dr. Reid's "History of the Presbyterian Church in Ireland ;' and of the "Debate on Baptism" between Dr. Rice and Alexander Campbell.* He wrote and published at some length on the Life of Dean Milner, whom he greatly admired, on Struther's History of the Relief Church in Scotland, and on the collected works of Andrew Fuller.† The *Horae Apocalypticae* of Elliott drew from him a long and careful dissertation ; and he wrote an extended review of Dr. Davidson's valuable History of Kentucky.‡ The publication of Chalmers's Sketches of Mental and Moral Philosephy urged him to appear again in the way of candid and decided animadversion on some points, mingled with hearty praise and admiration.§ He gave a notice of the "Free Church Pulpit," a Life of Robert Blair, and a discussion of Free Communion, as against the rigid view of the Baptists ; which, if we mistake not, closed his labours in the Princeton Review.‖ Meanwhile he was preparing and at length published his volumes on the "History of the Log College," and the "History of African Colonization ;" the latter being a volume of 603 octavo pages. During this time, there was scarcely a week in which he did not contribute some paper to the religious journals.

No one accustomed to consider the progress of literary performances can run over this list of publications, without some astonishment, that they should have proceeded from

* Princeton Review, 1844, pp. 57, 199, 581

† Princeton Review, 1845, p. 191, and 1846, pp. 26, and 547.

‡ Princeton Review, 1847, pp. 141, and 4f0.

§ 1848, p. 529, ff.

‖ 1849, p. 82, and 1850, pp 185, 557.

one who was nearly approaching fourscore ; especially when on examination they are found to betray no marks of senility, but to furnish instances of his most acute reasoning powers and most ardent emotion. But in truth these were but a small portion of his labours with the pen, during his last ten years. Not to mention new lectures on the branches which he had long taught, he was making incursions into new fields. Among the manuscripts which remain are many of this period, on important subjects, and some which were produced during the very last year of his life. Certain of these are on the Composition and Delivery of Sermons. He drew out the careful plan of a work on the Duties and Consolations of the Christian, and began to fill up the outline, at moments of leisure ; this seems to have been one of his last employments. He completed his volume on Moral Science, which was published soon after his decease, and which leaves its testimony to the unimpaired vigour of his understanding. He projected, and carried out through some hundreds of pages, a work on Patristical Theology, intended to exhibit the opinions of the Fathers, on all leading points in divinity. It is a contribution to what the Germans call *Dogmengeschichte.* He began a Memoir of the Rev. William Graham, to whom his grateful affection seemed always ready to turn, as long as he lived. This fills a small quarto, and is nearly complete. He had for years been gathering materials for a History of the Presbyterian Church in Virginia ; and from time to time was engaged in entering in an immense folio, biographical sketches of distinguished American clergymen, and alumni of the College of New Jersey. To these must be added the whole of those autobiographical sketches, filling numerous volumes, to which we are indebted for the earlier portions of our narrative. These do not extend further than the year 1810. They are interspersed with memoirs of almost every distinguished minister of his acquaintance ; to which indeed their extraordinary extent is to be ascribed. But for the express inhibition of their author, they should have been made public in their original shape. But nothing more evinces his untiring diligence, and the spring of his enterprise, than the fact that when, in 1851, the chair of Church Government was left vacant, he not only assumed the duties of this department, but immediately addressed himself to the work of preparing a course of lectures. We have before us his fair and sightly manuscript, of sixty-three large folio pages, on " Church Polity and Discipline." It was evidently broken off by his last illness, and ends with an unfinished sentence, on the independency of churches. This was in September, 1851.

In this same lapse of time he wrote numerous sermons, and preached upon an average once every Lord's Day. He likewise corresponded with friends, answering perpetually recurring queries on important points connected with religion and the Church. The routine of his Seminary appointments was followed with the punctuality and much of the vivacity of former years. What was wanting of earlier grace and sprightliness was more than replaced by the dignity and wisdom of age. At no time did he carry more weight among his attached pupils than in these years of venerable decline. In May, 1849, the resignation of Dr. Miller, which he had sought two years earlier, was finally accepted. It was a touching sight to behold the forms of himself and his aged colleague on those occasions when they appeared together at the head of their students. Many an observer was prompted to exclaim, "The hoary head is a crown of glory, if it be found in the way of righteousness!"

It was during the year in which he died, that Mrs. Mary Lundie Duncan, of Scotland, visited Princeton. "The hours passed in Princeton," says this Christian lady, "amid the courtesies and hospitalities of the venerable Dr. Alexander, are among the hoarded gems of memory. A powerful interest hangs around that aged man, so true of heart, so distinct of mind, so affable of manners. He is full of Christian sympathies, and ready to communicate, so that you require but to put an inquiry and he flows out, whether the subject be of sixty years since or of yesterday, and it is your own fault if you are not the wiser for his communings. Perhaps others may have remarked, what added much to the interest that cleaves to this excellent gentleman—his strong resemblance to Wilberforce. Though much more bulky, yet the figure is like that of a twin brother. His manner of sitting in his easy chair, of speaking, of smiling, and above all his ready way of giving information, and his edifying Christian remarks, showed a resemblance both in the mould and in the jewel within." The resemblance in the points mentioned has been noted by others, and will not fail to be suggested to any who examine the striking statue of Wilberforce, in Westminster Abbey. But we ought not to withhold a marginal note of Mrs. Duncan's, upon the above paragraph. "How touchingly," she adds, "are these remembrances deepened in pathos, by the tidings just arrived, that the Patriarch is with Abraham, and Moses, and all the prophets, in glory. It is true he has reached the consummation of his faith and hope, but then his family have lost him—his students have lost him. Princeton will see his face no more. The Church will never again appeal to his wisdom and experience. America must number him with her patriots, and heroes, and divines, who have departed—and I, a passing stranger, while I prize the more the privilege of having seen him, feel but the more keenly that the anticipated 'passing away' has begun."*

The death of numerous distant friends has been recorded; but we have to mention some nearer home, which cast a heavy shade over the society of Princeton. One of these was the decease of the Rev. Albert B. Dod, D. D., Professor of Mathematics in the College of New Jersey; a man whose brilliant genius, social charms and high promise caused his loss to be keenly and widely felt. In 1848, the Rev. Ashbel Green, D. D., late President of the College, departed this life. His remains were placed among the sepulchres of the great presidents and divines in the Princeton cemetery. Between him and Dr. Alexander, who was his junior by about ten years, there existed a strong and unbroken Christian attachment. But the event which more than all others in life made old age significant, was the departure of the Rev. Dr. Miller, on the 7th of January, 1850.

* "America as I Found it. By the mother of Mary Lundie Duncan." Carters, pp. 107–8.

Although the public has reason to expect a memoir of this venerable servant of Christ, we cannot refrain at this point from adding something to what we have already said concerning his character. His excellencies were admitted widely in the church, for he was known throughout our own country and in foreign lands. His publications were numerous, and were to a large extent vindications of the doctrine and polity of the Church which he loved. No Presbyterian is ignorant of the promptitude, courage and address with which he came forward on more than one occasion, when what he deemed important truth was assailed. As a writer he was remarkable for the purity and perspicuity of his style, and the absence of all meretricious ornament. He was a great reader, and was accustomed to enrich his works with numerous and apt citations from other authors. As an instructor, he was laborious, full and lucid. For six and thirty years he occupied the chair of Ecclesiastical History and Church Government; with a respect from all concerned, which augmented with his age.

It is impossible to remember Dr. Miller, without thinking of him as a Christian gentleman. Without an approach to stiffness, he was urbane and elegant in all the forms of the best society, with which indeed he had always mingled. He was cheerful and cordial in his greetings, lively in conversation, and fond of social intercourse. It was to this that the founding and continuance of a clerical association was due, in which he and his ministerial friends met at one another's houses during many years. He was the charm of mixed companies; being rich in topics of discourse, and happy beyond most men in apposite anecdote and historical reminiscence. Indeed we have never known any one who could give such magical effect to little ebullitions of humour, which repeated by the lips of others seemed to lose all their aroma. But nothing so marked his character as his evangelical piety. It was the opinion of his colleague, that in this Dr. Miller steadily grew, till the very last. He loved the cause of his Master, and was unwearied in his endeavours to promote it. The work of preaching the Gospel was his delight. Unsatisfied with the opportunities afforded by the Seminary Chapel, the College and the village church, he readily complied with every invitation from abroad, and until extreme old age was accustomed to go to the neighbouring congregations on every side, and unsought to bestow those labours which were always welcome and edifying.

We have already spoken of the inviolable sacredness of fraternal regard which for nearly forty years subsisted between him and his colleague. During this long period the thread of their lives had been entwined together, with increasing closeness. They were mutual advisers and confidential friends, and rejoiced in each other's progress, happiness, and acceptance with the church. Their differences of opinion, which were slight and few, were matters for amicable repartee, but never caused them even for an hour to draw in different directions; no one ever dreamed of such a thing as a faction for one or the other. It was most natural, therefore, that Dr. Alexander should look with sadness upon the tokens of decline in his respected brother. For some months Dr. Miller had been subject to attacks of disease, and at length was entirely confined to his house. His decline, however, was denoted more by great debility than by severe pain. Amidst it all, he was calm and believing. Foreseeing his departure with an unerring eye, he was resolute in his assertion of all the truths which he had taught, and humbly confident in his expressions of hope in Jesus Christ. Dr. Alexander thus briefly records his decease. "Dr. Miller's health had been declining for several months. He had scarcely any disease, except the decay of old age. By degrees he sunk, until the seventh of this month, when he gave up his spirit to God who gave it. He was calm and comfortable in mind during his whole confinement. He expressed no very lively feelings, but was troubled with no fears or doubts. A day or two before his death, I asked him whether any dark cloud at any time came over his mind; he replied, 'None whatever.'" *

Among all who surrounded his grave, there was none whose mind was more deeply solemn than his aged colleague, who pronounced a simple but touching funeral discourse. It is much to be regretted that no full report of this was ever made. The notes which exist among his papers are no more than hints for the aid of memory: yet even these fragments we feel it to be duty to subjoin in part. A large portion is manifestly lost. The text was Hebrews xi. 13; "These all died in faith," &c.

"The Reverend Dr. Miller was born in the town of Dover, in the State of Delaware. His father was the pastor of a Presbyterian church in that place, then flourishing, but of late years almost extinct. His early education was ob-

* Letter to Mrs. Graham, Jan. 30, 1850.

tained under the special tuition of his father. In this best of all schools he was prepared to enter college ; and when of suitable age he resorted to the University of Pennsylvania, where in due time he was graduated. He had selected the ministry of the Gospel as his profession ; impelled, we have no doubt, by a sincere desire to glorify God and do good to men ; but the speaker has no particular acquaintance with the early religious exercises of the deceased." Here occurs a chasm.—"Being always careful in his preparations, and possessing a neat and perspicuous style and a graceful elocution, he continually grew in popularity ; and as his preaching was truly evangelical, it was highly acceptable to serious Christians. At an age much earlier than usual, he was honoured with the degree of Doctor of Divinity, by one of the eastern Colleges ; a distinction which he afterwards received from other sources ; as well as recently that of Doctor of Laws. During twenty years he continued as a pastor in the city of New-York. Before the decease of Dr. Rodgers, the Rutgers-street church was separated from the Collegiate church, and called Dr. Milledoler ; and at the decease of Dr. Rodgers the Collegiate church was divided into the Wall-street and the Brick church. Of the former Dr. Miller became the pastor, and laboured acceptably among that people, until in the spring of 1813 he was chosen Professor of Ecclesiastical History and Church Government, in the Theological Seminary at this place ; and in the autumn of the same year, he entered upon the duties of his office.

"It may be remarked, that no man in the Church had been more zealous and active in founding this Institution, than Dr. Miller. He and Dr. Green may more properly be considered its founders than any other persons. Others aided by their counsels and occasional exertions, but these two devoted themselves with untiring zeal to the prosecution of the object, and had the pleasure of seeing their exertions crowned with success. At this time, Dr. Miller, so far as I know, was not thought of as a professor ; and I am persuaded the thought was entirely foreign from his own mind. In connection with this Institution he has continued until the day of his death.

"Besides labouring in his appropriate vocation, he has very frequently preached in this and the neighbouring churches ; and I think I may say, that I never knew a minister, who delighted more in preaching the Gospel. As he advanced in life, it appeared to his friends that his preaching became more spiritual and evangelical. Even to the time when the decay of physical strength confined him to the house, he sought opportunities of delivering the Gospel message to the congregations in the vicinity. As to his writings, which are numerous, and his professional labours, I need not speak. Of his ability, learning and fidelity, there are hundreds of witnesses scattered over the land."

"The character of our deceased friend and brother may be thus summed up. In all the private and domestic relations of life he was exemplary.—As a neighbour he was kind and courteous to all, and exactly just in his dealings. As a minister he was faithful and evangelical, and was accustomed to present the truths of the Gospel in a manner so distinct and methodical, that his discourses could not only be understood with ease, but readily remembered by the attentive hearer.—As a member of church judicatories, he was an able advocate for [truth], a warm friend to experimental and practical piety, and of course a friend of revivals. No member of our Church has done more to explain and defend her doctrines than our deceased brother. With his colleagues he was uniformly cordial ; and *I have never known a man more entirely free from vainglory, envy, and jealousy.* To the students under his care he was paternal and affectionate."

We cannot more appropriately close what relates to the union of these two men, than by giving insertion to an extract from a letter from Dr. Miller, to the Rev. Henry A. Boardman, D. D., of Philadelphia. It has a pathos which will go to many a heart.

"PRINCETON, *Feb.* 28, 1849.

"I thank you, my dear brother, for the kind expressions which you employ on the prospect of my retiring from office. I am, indeed, nearly worn out. Far advanced in my eightieth year, I have outlived all my relatives, and all my own expectations, and am compassed about with so many infirmities, that I am persuaded a longer continuance in office would be in no respect just, either to the Seminary or myself. Yet in looking forward to retirement from official labour, and especially to that day which is near at hand, when I must 'put off this tabernacle,' I desire to bless God for the humble hope which I am permitted to entertain, that I have so good a home to go to, where there will be no more infirmity, and especially no more sin ; but perfect union and conformity to Him who, though he was rich, for our sakes became poor, that we through his poverty might be rich.

"I desire to unite with you, my dear brother, in thanksgiving to the Great Head of the Church, that our beloved Seminary has been made so useful to our Zion, by training so large a portion of our ministry under the same teachers; and I hope I have some sincere gratitude that I have been permitted to occupy a place, and take some humble part in this hallowed work. But I can truly say that the sentiment which most strongly and prominently occupies my mind, is that of thankfulness that the Lord has been pleased to unite me with colleagues so wise, so faithful, so much superior to myself, and so eminently adapted to be a blessing to the Church. I consider it as one of the greatest blessings of my life to be united with such men, and pre-eminently with my senior colleague, whose wisdom, prudence, learning, and peculiar piety have served as an aid and guide to myself, as well as to others. I desire to leave it on record for the eye of intimate friendship, that in my own estimation my union with these beloved men has been the means of adding to my own respectability and my own usefulness far more than I could ever, humanly speaking, have attained, either alone or in association with almost any other men. I desire especially to feel thankful that I ever saw the face of my venerated senior colleague. He has been for thirty-six years, to me a counsellor, a guide, a prop, and a stay, under God, to a degree which it would not be easy for me to estimate or acknowledge.

"The union in our Faculty has been complete. And the solid basis of the whole has been a perfect agreement on the part of all of us in an honest subscription to our doctrinal formularies. There has been no discrepance—no pulling in different directions here.

"Hoping to see you in a few days, I am, my dear sir, your friend and brother in Christian bonds.

"SAMUEL MILLER."

There were two of his last public appearances away from home, which seem to deserve a record from us. The first of these concerns the meeting of the Synod of New Jersey at Elizabethtown in 1850.

DR. MAGIE TO JAMES W. ALEXANDER.

"*Jan.* 20, 1854.

"MY DEAR SIR :—

"You ask me for some account of your father's last visit to Elizabethtown ; and with sincere pleasure I comply with your request. It was to attend the meeting of the Synod of New Jersey, just one year before that held in Princeton, during the sessions of which the Lord permitted him to enter upon his final rest. Many of us never expected another opportunity of looking upon his beloved face, or listening to his cheering and animating voice.

"A few months before, he had spent a Sabbath with my people, and preached a sermon to youth, which is still remembered and spoken of with the deepest interest. We then considered it doubtful whether he should be able to attend the meeting of Synod. Still on the appointed day he was here, and appeared to be in quite good health and spirits On both these occasions he was an inmate of my family, and had I leisure, I should love to speak of his pleasant intercourse with us, and especially of the calm, earnest, and comprehensive prayers he offered for me and mine. His presence seemed to make our house like 'a field which the Lord has blessed.' As the meetings of Synod were progressing, I invited a number of his former students to meet him at my table. We enjoyed these interviews, and he evidently enjoyed them too. Now and then he indulged a little in the quiet humour which always distinguished him, and which added zest and life to his conversation. But every thing was seasoned with grace.

"It was, however, of his appearance in the Synod that I intended chiefly to speak. There he was the same wise, kind, unobtrusive man he ever was in such bodies, neither putting himself forward to mingle in every little debate, nor declining to give his opinion when the nature of the business required it. I have often admired his conduct in this respect, and could wish it had more imitators. Dr. Alexander was not one of those who conclude that nothing is well done which they have not had the shaping of.

"You know it is the custom of our Synod to devote one evening to public prayer and exhortation; and I was very desirous that your father should make one of the addresses. Accordingly as Chairman of the Committee of Arrangements, I mentioned the matter to him. At first he said, 'I am too old, you must select some other person.' I replied—'You see, sir, that a large proportion of the ministers of the Synod have been your pupils, and this may be the last time that they will ever have the privilege of listening to your voice. He seemed struck with the suggestion, but said nothing farther. In the evening he made his address, and though he seemed feeble at first, his words had the same life and power with those which we had often heard in his earlier days. It was such a strain of affectionate counsel as only a man like him could give. He commenced with a reference to the fact, that he found himself standing in the presence of many who had once been his beloved pupils; and as he went on to urge us to quit ourselves like men, for God, and the great interests of his kingdom, he appeared to be talking to us as from the very gates of the celestial city. It is scarcely too much to say, that we beheld his face as if it had been the face of an angel. His heart was melted, and our hearts were melted likewise.

" Even making some abatement for the mingled feelings of veneration and love with which we regarded him, I must say, it was one of his very best efforts. He felt evidently that it was the last time. Every thing in his manner, his looks, and the tones of his voice, as well as in the words he uttered, indicated that he stood on the very verge of heaven, and was fully ready to say, I have fought a good fight, I have finished my course, I have kept the faith; henceforth there is laid up for me a crown of righteousness, which the Lord the righteous Judge shall give me at that day. And it was the last time. Most of us saw his face no more.

" Great and good man! May his mantle, as well as that of the beloved Miller, fall on all our rising ministry! Then would Zion arise and shine, her light being come, and the glory of the Lord risen upon her.

"Very truly and affectionately yours,

"DAVID MAGIE."

The other visit was to the church in South Trenton, which he had regarded with much interest, as the pastor had been one of his pupils. From this friend we have derived the statement which follows. It was a beautiful summer day, July 27, 1851, and a communion Sabbath. As the church-edifice was incomplete, the services took place in the Mercer Court House. Dr. Alexander preached on that occasion to the edification and delight of all who heard him, and also rendered most valuable assistance at the table. He was apprehensive lest he might be seized with a faintness, to which he had been subject at times, but nothing of the kind occurred. The sermon was rich in Bible truth and Christian experience, and in manner he was more than usually animated, solemn and impressive, to the very close. In the afternoon he made an address to the Sabbath School. The room was crowded almost to suffocation. His venerable appearance, penetrating eye, silvery locks and tremulous voice, all had a tendency to increase the interest which all present, from the oldest to the youngest, felt in the distinguished speaker, as in a serious but familiar manner he commenced by saying: "In a hundred years, every one who hears me now will be in heaven or in hell! . . . . . This is the last time I expect to address you. You will probably never see me again. But you will remember what I tell you long after

I am dead and gone. You will remember that an old man addressed you on this occasion. When a little boy, only five or six years old, I remember hearing an old man preach the Gospel, just as you hear me now. I remember how gray his hair was, and how old he looked, and how he was dressed. And I never can forget the text that he preached from. It was these words: 'If any man love not the Lord Jesus Christ, let him be *anathema maranatha.*' I did not then know the meaning of these hard words, but the minister went on to explain them, and said that if we did not love the Lord Jesus Christ, we should all be accursed of God and devoted to destruction. And this I repeat in your hearing this day, my young friends. If you do not love the Saviour you will be destroyed. You can never enjoy his favour and blessing unless you love him with all your hearts, and do whatsoever he has commanded you. Remember it is an old man that tells you so—on the authority of the Word of God. When you go home, write it down that on this, July 27, A. D. 1851, Dr. Alexander, an old man, addressed the Sunday School, and said, 'If any man love not the Lord Jesus Christ, let him be anathema maranatha.' Remember it is an old man that tells you so.' These are a few of the words, and a very imperfect sketch at best of what fell from his lips on that occasion, which can never be forgotten by the hundreds of children and youth, together with their teachers, who heard him. Even the youngest child had its eyes fastened on him to the last, drinking in the words which he spake, while all listened with breathless attention to this farewell address.

"This I believe was the last time this venerable man ever preached the Gospel out of Princeton, and it was a good day's work. How faithfully that work was performed, how full of holy zeal for his Master and of love to the souls of his fellow-men, there are multitudes of living witnesses in our midst who can testify, some of whom we humbly hope shall rise up in the judgment and call him blessed."

Our labours concerning the events of Dr. Alexander's active life are now brought to a close. But before we approach the scenes of the termination, it may be allowed us to recur for a little to the general aspect of his declining years. In person he was certainly much changed, but not in the way which gives painful indication of infirmity. As we have found him repeatedly saying in his letters, he was enjoying the sense of health, more than in his years of prime. His body was fuller, and his eye had not waxed dim. When he chose it, which was rarely, he was competent to extraordinary exertion. His hearing was acute to the last, and with the aid of glasses he used his sight without complaint. His love of children, of family chat, of visits from friends, of psalmody, and of the daily journals, was undiminished. As he walked home from an evening service, he said to one of his family, whom he almost outstripped in the rapidity of his step, "I begin to think there is a literality in that saying of the prophet Isaiah, xl. 30, 'But they that wait on the Lord shall renew their strength.'" On the day of his entering his seventy-eighth year, he visited the house of his eldest son, played gaily with the children, and seemed as alert and keen as in his best days. His attention to his grandchildren was remarkable. They clambered upon his knee as freely as their parents had done before them, were instructed by his drawings and his tales, and seemed to give him unmingled delight. He often prayed over them, laying on them his hands in benediction.

It was almost a daily remark in the house, that these were his best days, even in natural things, and that he never had so vivid an enjoyment of life. Such was his own delightful admission. "Old age," said he, "is not an unpleasant part of life, where health and piety are possessed."* A host of physical evils which had beset him in earlier days, had now been mercifully removed. His simple nourishment was enjoyed without rule or scruple, and the morbid vigils which once distressed him gave place to balmy sleep. It was apparent to every one that he was in higher spirits, even if sometimes his alternations of depressed feeling would return. Occasionally he would break out in conversation with all the exuberance and glee of his youth; but the characteristic of his temper was a benignant serenity. From our earliest recollections, he had been accustomed to sit and muse in the evening twilight, often prolonging these hours far beyond the time when lights are usually demanded. These moments, though solemn, appeared to be pleasurable. In these he pursued his most fruitful trains of thought. As he grew older, this solitary exercise was more frequent and protracted; and in no instance did it seem to merge into any thing like slumber. It was a period to be gratefully remembered, as one of singular peace.

* Letter to Mrs. Graham, August 15, 1850.

From what has been extracted from his correspondence, it may be gathered that he was continually meditating on his approaching departure ; but this gave no sombre colouring to his manner or his words. Though he never spoke, except by incidental allusion, of his personal experience, it was too evident to admit of doubt, that his countenance was often radiant with uncommon spiritual joys. It broke out in his family prayers, in his singing of psalms and hymns, which he continued in the domestic service till the very last, and especially in his sermons and addresses at the Lord's Table.

Old age never seemed to occur to him as affording a motive to relax in labour. His principle was, that the faculties were to be kept in vigour by perpetual use. The same had once been expressed to him by his friend Dr. Rice : "As far as my observation goes, there are two errors to which aged men are exposed. One is, of holding on, and refusing to admit that they are old. We have seen some instances of this. The other is precisely opposite. It is allowing themselves to grow prematurely old. Failing to exercise their faculties, they become rusty and move like an old door whose hinges are never oiled. I have no doubt about the fact, that when the organs through which the mind acts, fail, mental imbecility ensues. But I am equally certain, that ceasing to exert our faculties greatly impairs their strength. And I am convinced that when a man, whose life has been very active, *retires*, he very soon sinks into second childhood."* The opinion here advanced was one which Dr. Alexander cherished, often uttered, and persistently acted on ; with an

* Letter of Dr. John H. Rice, January 8, 1830.

entire success which seems to us instructive. His own words express somewhat characteristically the temper of his mind in regard to public duty; it was only a few months before his death, that he thus wrote.

DR. ALEXANDER TO THE REV. DR. PLUMER.

"PRINCETON, *April* 16, 1851.

"REVEREND AND DEAR SIR:—

"To relieve your mind from all uneasiness respecting the expression in my letter, about not 'continuing much longer to be a professor,' I would inform you, that on this day week I expect to enter on my eightieth year; and of course I cannot expect to 'continue here much longer.' I have no intention of resigning, while my health is good, and my mind sound. If I should be seized with paralysis, or some other disease which would entirely disqualify me for performing the duties of my office, I might deem it expedient to resign; but it is my general purpose and hope, *to die in the harness.* My health and spirits were never better than at present; although the excitability of my nervous system occasions seasons of depression and uneasy feeling, from the physical state. All I want is a stronger faith. This I hope I shall receive in the hour of need, in answer to many prayers. And you could not gratify me more than by your declared purpose to remember me in your prayers.

"With kind regards to Mrs. Plumer and your daughters, I remain very truly yours, &c.

"A. A."

During this time he very much ceased to go abroad, and confined himself most of the day to his study. Here, however, he was to be found neither idle nor resting, but generally engaged in study, and to an extraordinary extent in writing. There was scarcely a new work of interest in any of his chosen departments, which he did not peruse. There was no person of our acquaintance who kept himself more abreast of the literature which regards the Millennarian and the Geological controversies. On all such topics his conversation was as flowing and as judicious as in former days. What is most worthy of mention is, that no one discovered or suspected the slightest decay of the mental powers. On every subject to which he applied his mind, he manifested not only soundness but quickness. Though he sometimes complained of some difficulty in remembering names, his friends remarked that he was annoyed by the same many years before. It was observed with wonder by all his family, that Providence seemed to have given him full exemption from the common weaknesses of old age.

At the stroke of the bell, he might be seen without fail, issuing from his study door, and going across the small space which divided the Seminary from his grounds; much bent, and with eyes turned to the ground, as he paced slowly on, wrapped in his cloak and with his profuse silver locks waving in the wind; but often, as if at some sudden dash of thought, he would quicken his steps almost to running, and ascend the threshold with alacrity. This was a peculiarity of his motion all his life. His children always knew his whereabout, by the vivacity of his changes, and used to say jocosely that he never closed or opened a door softly, and always ran up stairs. With his manuscript rolled up in his hand, he took the chair, and after a short and pertinent prayer, began his instructions. They were always such as kept his pupils in wakeful attention, and so far as we know were not less acceptable than those of his younger life.

It has been said that he continued to preach. That he should have done this with so much pleasure to himself and so little abatement of interest in his audiences, is not a little surprising; especially when we consider the bodily changes which he had sustained. His voice remained clear, and though tending to play too much among the upper notes of the register, had no weakness; and notwithstanding the total loss of teeth his articulation was perfect. He read from his manuscript more than in his middle life; but often threw in new matter, and almost always closed with an extemporaneous application. The signal for this was the sudden throwing up of the spectacles upon his forehead; and he would then enchain the attention and control the feelings of the assembly in a manner which sometimes reminded them of his best efforts. At the Sunday afternoon Conference, he still loved to indulge his talent for original and animated remark; we suppose there was no one of his intellectual efforts which abode more in its pristine vigour.

No observation was more common than that Dr. Alexander was unlike most old men, in his tolerance for the changes of the day. If a new scheme of any promise was on foot, he was really more inclined to listen and to favour, than most younger men. The passing events of the neighbourhood and the country awakened his inquisitive interest. In this he has strikingly reminded us of Chancellor Kent. One reason for this was his persevering habit of learning all that public journals could convey. Another reason may be found in his almost total exemption from what may be called the pride of years. He was in no such sense a *laudator temporis acti*, as that he undervalued or disparaged contemporary men and things. We have no recollection of ever hearing him hold up former generations of ministers as models, or lauding the works and methods of his youth, or complaining of deterioration in preaching. He was sanguine in his hopes for both Church and country, and favourable even to a fault in regard to the performances of junior brethren. Every one was welcome to his door; and many are the instances in which he has spent an hour in lively conversation with some itinerant chapman or agent, whom most would regard as a nuisance; but from whom he always contrived to learn something.

On a former page we have employed a word which was often on his lips, and which more than all others denotes the blessedness of his Christian evening; it was Peace. Sometimes it seemed to be 'perfect peace.' No cloud is known to have darkened his prospect for years, in regard to his personal acceptance with God. And though his prayers and discourses more than his common talk were the vehicle of his joyful thoughts, it was a pleasure to all who were near him to observe how he had outlived and thrown off one care and anxiety after another, until he stood almost *in procinctu*, stript and ready, for the last conflict. This was not the less edifying or delightful, for being accompanied with a serene and healthful interest in all the concerns of his family and his calling ; and it seems incredible that any one could pass through a long period of decline with less burden to others or less exaction from them on the score of infirmity or years. After all, we feel how impossible it is by any report of ours to convey an adequate impression of this truly happy and beautiful old age.

CHAPTER EIGHTEENTH.

1851.

ILLNESS—LAST HOURS—DEATH.

IT has been already said that the months immediately preceding his last illness were marked with unusual bodily comfort. He was alert and cheerful, and said that he never felt better. The last sermon that he ever preached was delivered to the students in the Seminary Chapel, on the 7th of September, from the words, Isaiah 54 : 13, "All thy children shall be taught of God." The Lord's Supper was administered in the First Church of Princeton on the 14th of September ; on which occasion he made an address to the communicants. This was his last public service. In the afternoon he was present at the Conference in the Seminary. The subject treated was the Sacraments, considered as Means of Grace. Feeling slightly indisposed he at first declined to offer any remarks ; but after Dr. Hodge had spoken, he added a few words. The summer heat of that year was remarkably extended into the month of September, and, in his own apprehension, predisposed him to disease.

About the 18th of September he began to be more indisposed, but for a number of days only in a slight degree ; and he continued to attend his classes. On Sunday, the 21st, he would have gone to the regular service in the Chapel, but was dissuaded from it by his family. He seemed exceedingly reluctant to omit his lectures, and even after becoming too unwell to leave the house, dictated the syllabus of a lecture on Mental Philosophy.

About a week after his seizure he had an interview with Professor Hodge, from whose notes we are permitted to make an extract, preferring his simple statement to any prepared report. "On going over," says Dr. Hodge, "I found him reclining, in his ordinary dress, upon a sofa in the study. As I entered the room, he reached out his hand to me, and for the first time in my life called me his dear son ; and said he had a few things to communicate, to which he did not wish me to make any reply. He said that his impression as to his situation was different from that of his family. They thought he was getting well ; he was sure he was going to die. His increasing weakness, and the entire loss of appetite convinced him that he could not recover. After much reflection, he had come to the conclusion that there never was a time in which it would be or could be better for him to leave the world. He never had felt that his work was done before now. He had accomplished every thing he could for his family, and thought he could no longer be of service to the Seminary, and he therefore considered that it was desirable he should not recover. He said, he spoke thus not from any bright views of the future, which he had not, but from the convictions of his understanding. He had never known any man after eighty years of age to be useful, and he did not wish to drag on a few more years a burden to himself or others. His views of divine truth, he said, remained the same ; and as to comfort and support in dying, he had as much reason to expect them now as ever. He added, 'Now, my dear son, farewell—you will never see me again.' He told me to make a short prayer—which I did, he adding Amen—with peculiar emphasis.

"As I was about to withdraw, he said—'Yes ! I must see you again, as I have some things to say about the Seminary.'

"October 15th.—Dr. Alexander sent for me again. He was still in his study. He gave me his account-book of the scholarships and explained to me what he wished done in reference to that matter. He was more cheerful than when I last saw him. Spoke of his dissolution as certainly near at hand, and gave general directions about his funeral."

The disease, which took the form of a diarrhœa, now increased, so that he had no rest day or night. In the morning, instead of being refreshed he was quite exhausted. But until a week before his death, he came down regularly to his study, as early as six o'clock in the morning, and lay upon the sofa until bedtime. During the latter part of this time, however, he required the assistance of an arm to lean upon. For the last week of his thus coming down he seemed better ; the disease was somewhat checked, he was driven out occasionally, and continued to walk into another room, where he listened to the newspapers and other reading, and seemed much interested in all that was going on. The only distressing symptom was a total loss of appetite, which all around him tried in vain to tempt.

While his family were all hoping with much cheerfulness, his own judgment of his case never wavered. He declared that his stomach had lost all tone, and that he should gradually sink. In remembering the perfect calmness with which he contemplated every symptom, his friends now wonder that they were not more alarmed; for in his previous slight ailments he had usually been much discouraged. But his composure in speaking of his approaching dissolution tended to dispel all serious apprehensions of the result. When any new article was prepared for him by his loving family or sent in by kind friends, he would say with the utmost cheerfulness, "My stomach has lost its power, and cannot react." From the very first, it is obvious that he had a clear understanding of his case, such as precluded all expectation of recovery.

On the 17th of October, for the first time, his family were compelled to give up all hope of his amendment. The change on that day was marked and sudden. He had walked down as usual to the study, with the assistance of his beloved daughter, but was evidently weakened by the effort. During the day his debility increased so much that when night came he was utterly unable to walk. He was very desirous of being taken to his chamber, from which he said he should never descend alive. Accordingly, by the kind aid of Mr. Cleghorn of the Seminary and a few other persons, he was carried up stairs and laid upon his bed. It is proper to say that the day before, his eldest son, who had been absent in Europe, was permitted to meet him. He was lying on the sofa, much emaciated, but with a countenance strikingly like that of thirty years before. Taking his son by the hand, he gave thanks to God for having preserved him, and for allowing this interview, which he had greatly desired. He then proceeded to give a number of directions and orders, with perfect composure and the deliberation of one who utters a series of charges from a memorandum. There was an air of unearthly authority which we remember with awe. He said that his end was approaching, and that all arrangements had been completed for the comfort and sustenance of his family. To this son he then gave the Hebrew Bible which had been his daily companion for forty years. He designated for his eldest grandson the fine Clarendon Cicero, in ten quarto volumes, and caused us for the second boy to choose between Hesychius and Burmann's quarto Quintilian. He had previously pointed out for little William Alexander, one of his grandchildren, the walking-stick which he had long used. These things were done with all the calmness and cheerfulness of his most untroubled days. He proceeded to name two of his sons, who should have the entire control of his manuscripts, and of any notice that might be published of his life. He said that his treatise on Moral Science was in his judgment the most worthy of being edited. After having thus settled his last worldly affairs, he proceeded to talk freely about the work of God in the Reformed Churches abroad, and when his strength was exhausted, dismissed his son. In all that he uttered he was clear, succinct, and decided, speaking with a mien which carried something of command. The writer of these pages may be allowed to record his heartfelt thanks to God, for the privilege of thus beholding once more the face of an honoured father.

During his illness he dictated a paper to be taken round for subscriptions towards the relief of a young man whose studies had been interrupted by disease. Only two or three days before his death he spoke of a clergyman whom he had met on the railroad some time before, and to whom he was very anxious to send some books. The name of this stranger had escaped his memory, though he remembered the county and presbytery somewhere near Buffalo.

On the 16th, already mentioned as his last day below stairs, he gave his last directions to his beloved wife and to his children. On the same day he had a last interview with his cherished colleague and friend Dr. Hodge, whose memorandum we will not mar by abridgment or change.

"Oct. 17. Saw Dr. Alexander for the last time. He was upstairs in bed. He said he had sent for me to speak about his funeral. He said as Dr. John McDowell had from the beginning been a Director of the Seminary, and was one of its best friends, he thought him the proper person to preach on the occasion. He commissioned me to make the request as from him, with the injunction not to utter one word of eulogy. 'We cannot,' he added, 'prevent people from talking about us, but I do not wish any delineation of character attempted, nor any praise.' He then, with a smile, handed me a white bone walking-stick, carved and presented to him by one of the chiefs of the Sandwich

Islands, and said, 'You must leave this to your successor in office, that it may be handed down as a kind of symbol of orthodoxy.'

"The students of the Seminary had set apart this day as a season of fasting and prayer. When he was informed of this he said, 'Give them my blessing; but tell them not to pray for my recovery, which is now out of the question.' I never saw him more himself—more cheerful—almost playful. There seemed in his case to be no difference between faith and sight. He spoke of this world and of the next in the same tone of cheerful assurance, passing from one topic to the other without the least change of manner. There was no excitement nor tension of feeling, but the most perfect simplicity. I never saw and never imagined a death-bed where there was so little of death. It seemed to him as an ordinary matter, and he spoke of dying with the same natural cheerfulness, with which he would have spoken of going from one room to another. Indeed his chamber was the most cheerful room in the house."

Either on this day or the preceding, he had an interview with the Rev. William E. Schenck, pastor of the First Church, a gentleman for whom he had always cherished much affection. From minutes of Mr. Schenck, intended solely for his own eye, we make the following extracts.

"It was on the morning of the Thursday preceding Dr. Alexander's death, that I called to inquire after his health. My inquiries having been answered at the door I was about to leave, when I was called back by one of his sons, who said that his father had heard I was at the door and desired to see me. As I entered the study he was lying on the sofa in his usual dress, but supported by pillows. He extended his hand in a very cordial manner; on taking it I found it icy cold. He at once said to me in a very warm and tender tone, 'My dear young friend, I have much desired to see you once more, and am glad to have this opportunity. I wish to bid you farewell. You will see me no more in this life.'

"I was so greatly overcome by this address that I hardly knew what to reply. I merely said, 'I trust and most earnestly hope, dear sir, that you may yet be mistaken. Should it be so, we are confident it would be your inexpressible gain; but it would be a sorrowful day indeed for all of us that should survive.'

"'I feel confident,' said he, 'that I am not mistaken. I shall not live long. Nor have I any wish to stay longer. I have lived eighty years, which is more than the usual term of human life, and if I remain, I have little to look forward to, but infirmity and suffering. If such be the Lord's will, I feel thoroughly satisfied, and even would prefer to go now. My work on earth, I feel, is done. And it does seem to me (he added with great earnestness), as if my Heavenly Father had in great mercy surrounded me with almost every circumstance which could remove anxieties and make me feel that I can go without regret. My affairs have all been attended to, my arrangements are all completed, and I can think of nothing more to be done. I have greatly desired to see my son James before my departure, and sometimes feared I should not have that privilege, but the Lord has graciously brought him back in time to see me, having led him safely through much peril on the ocean. My children are all with me.................................. The church of which you are pastor is prosperous and flourishing. The Seminary Faculty is again full, and the Institution in an excellent condition. The more I reflect upon the matter, the more all things seem to combine to make me perfectly willing to enter into my rest. The Lord has very graciously and tenderly led me (he added, closing his eyes and clasping his hands in a devotional manner) all the days of my life—yes, all the days of my life. And he is now with me still. *In Him I enjoy perfect peace.*' The last sentence he uttered in a quick, earnest and happy tone of voice, such as was peculiar to him in certain moods. Pausing a moment or two, as if to recover breath, he then said:

" 'I have much desired to see you, that I might bid you farewell, and once more invoke God's blessing upon you and your ministry. You have had a strong hold on my affections, and I have felt much satisfaction in your preaching. Continue as you have begun, and have done thus far, to preach Christ and Him crucified, scripturally, plainly, earnestly, and God will continue richly to bless your ministry, even as he has here so lately done. He lifted his hands, as if to pronounce a benediction. I fell on my knees, beside the sofa, with my head bowed, and weeping bitterly; nevertheless I tried hard to restrain my feelings, while with his hands extended over me, he offered a short and fervent prayer, closing with these words: 'God greatly bless his servant, in his person, in his family, and in his ministry. May it please God to give him great usefulness and success.

May many souls be saved through his efforts ; and when his work is done, may we be permitted to meet again in a happier world, Amen.'

"As I arose from my knees, he reached out his hand as if to bid me farewell.

"'I cannot go (said I) until I attempt to thank you, which I do with my whole heart, for your long and unvarying kindness to me. You have been to me the best and most valued of earthly friends.'

"'You must thank God for that, (said he quickly.) All kindness and all friends are His gifts. Give my love to your wife and children.'

"The last sentence he repeated when I had reached the door, and very slowly, as if he were loath to have me leave him—

"'Give my love and a very affectionate farewell to your wife and to your dear little children.'

"As I walked away from the house I could not repress my tears, and a sense of utter desolation came over me for a little while as I thought that I had probably taken a last view, and received the last words of affectionate counsel from that beloved and venerated friend, to whom I have been accustomed to resort, and on whose counsels I have been accustomed to rely as on those of no other man on earth. But soon my feelings grew calmer. I felt that I had been breathing an atmosphere redolent with the very fragrance of heaven. The room that I had left seemed to have been perfumed with holy composure and immovable confidence in a glorified but present Redeemer. As I reflected upon the scene, I gained new views of life, of death, and of Heaven. I felt, as I had never felt before, how 'sure and steadfast' is that anchor of Gospel hope which 'entereth into that within the veil.' I could not help asking myself, 'Is it possible to die so? Does the Lord Jesus give his people such complete and quiet victories over the grim King of Terrors?' There was nothing excited, nothing exultant; and yet it seemed to be thoroughly triumphant; a calm, believing, cheerful looking through the gloomy grave into the glories of the eternal world. It was the steady, unfaltering step of a genuine Christian philosopher as well as an eminent saint, evincing his own thorough, heartfelt, and practical belief in the doctrines he had so long and so ably preached, as he descended hour by hour into the dark valley and shadow of death. And I could not help praying as I had never prayed before, 'Let me die the death of the righteous, and let my last end be like his.'"

In his illness his early days seemed to pass before him in review. The anniversary of his licensure, sixty years before, had recently occurred. To this he alluded on the last day that he sat up, recurring to his unwillingness to be licensed, and his dislike to the text assigned to him, as before related. During one of these nights, while his devoted wife was watching by his side, he broke out into something like a soliloquy, rehearsing God's gracious dealings with his soul. There was so great an elevation in his language, that Mrs. Alexander was unwilling to be the sole witness, and called in their daughter. He recounted the particular exercises of his youth, and especially dwelt on that scene in the Bushy Hills, of which notice has been taken in one of our early chapters. On this occasion, more than any other in his illness, his views and emotions appeared to acquire the form of holy rapture.

Disease was now rapidly doing its work. His appetite was gone. Through the night he would occasionally take a little ice or a spoonful of ice-cream. There was something touching in the value which he set on the most ordinary attentions. He was especially thankful that our dear mother was permitted to wait on him to the last. She was much attenuated and exhausted by solicitude and loss of sleep, and could scarcely have held out many days longer; yet the support of her faith and patience was little less remarkable than his own. When approaching his end, he said to her with great tenderness, "My dear, one of my last prayers will be that you may have as serene and painless a departure as mine." How wonderfully was this prayer soon to be answered! He said, "Now I understand, as I never did before, what is meant by that promise, Psalm xli. 3, *Thou wilt make all his bed in his sickness.*" Before this time he had suffered little acute pain, but his disease was of such a nature as to allow him no rest. Yet no word of complaint or dissatisfaction fell from his lips. He often said, "Why should a living man complain, a man for the punishment of his sins?" To his daughter, who was leaving him in the morning, he said, "You have been a watcher indeed—ever on the alert."

On the day after he finally went to his bed, he gave his last directions about the Seminary, and many little things which were on his mind. He seemed to forget nothing, but made suggestions even to the last of matters pertaining to the health of the family. On Saturday, October 18th, his weakness was extreme, and from this time he positively refused to take any anodyne. He said he knew that death could not be far off, and he wished his mind to be entirely free from the effects of stupefying drugs. During the night he suffered more pain than at any time previous, but in the intervals was perfectly calm and peaceful—more than peaceful—he seemed as happy as if he was already in heaven, and talked without intermission in the most delightful way. His discourse was much about dying, and he expressed a wish that he might pass away on the morrow, which was the Lord's Day; but added, "Just as God sees best." When relieved from pain, he said that such relief was often to be attributed to the ministration of angels; and afterwards, "They are always around the dying beds of God's people." He repeated part of Watts's hymn, "O for an overcoming faith, To cheer my dying hours." He spoke of the preciousness of the word on which God had caused him to hope; "just the same word," said he, "that caused me to hope so many years ago, when I was in such distress because I thought I had not conviction enough; and could get no comfort till a good minister (the Rev. James Mitchell) told me that there was no certain degree of conviction prescribed as necessary to salvation; and it was by hearing this again and again that I found comfort." All this with a serene and heavenly glow, which can never be described.

About the same time he said to one of his sons, who inquired whether he was at peace; "O yes!" with a tone which implied, "How could you doubt it?" Then he added, "No ecstacy—but clear faith. I have been reviewing the plan of salvation this morning, and assuring myself that I do accept it.—The transition to a state so unknown is certainly awful; but Christ can prevent the shock. I have never been afraid to die, and I have never before seen a time so suitable for my departure. I am in the fortieth year of my professorship. I have seen all my wishes accomplished. God has answered my prayers, even in averting particular diseases which I feared. The Seminary has never been in so prosperous a state. If I were to recover, it would be for no use; I have seen no man fit for much after eighty. But I shall not recover." To others he had said, "My views of theological truth are what they have always been."

On Sunday he was still weaker, and said that he could not last long; but his mind was just as clear as ever. He designated a passage of Scripture, which he wished to hear read by one of his children, and when some difficulty occurred in turning to it, he mentioned the beginning of the verse, *Who shall lay any thing to the charge of God's elect?* When the family returned from church, and spoke of Dr. Hodge's sermon, he was much interested, and said with much animation, "He is a noble man." About noon a very perceptible sinking took place, so that we looked every moment for his last breath. He lay quiet, breathing quick but feebly, and with his eyes closed. During Monday the 20th, he slumbered, but now and then uttered broken expressions which were truly characteristic of him; such as "We must devise something for them," "Penitence and faith." Towards night he was seized with a hiccough, which con tinued through the next day ; yet he seemed little annoyed by it. His voice was hardly audible, and his eyes were very dim. On the morning of Tuesday the 21st, he seemed somewhat revived, and talked a little. Though he had some return of appetite, he was averse to taking food ; and when the physician urged it, asked if it was to strengthen him, and spoke of that as useless and absurd. But when told that it was only for his temporary comfort, he assented. His taste seemed as acute as in health, and he never had greater quickness of hearing. After this he lay in the same tranquil state, though perfectly collected in reason, growing weaker and weaker, until about six o'clock in the morning of Wednesday, October 22d, he ceased to breathe. It was observed by his older children that as he drew near to death, his countenance assumed more and more the look which he had when they could first remember him. To the last he was exempt from the marked changes of appearance which are common in illness ; his face looked comelier, and as if chiseled out of marble.

The event was the more impressive, because the Synod of New Jersey was at the very time assembled in Princeton. To this he made frequent allusion, a very short time before his death. There were many devotional acts held by this body, in reference to the illness of their venerable member. An end so blessed, so edifying, so fitted to suggest high thoughts of God's covenant faithfulness, could not fail to make its deep impression on these servants of Christ. In looking back upon the scene, we find nothing absent which he could have desired. It was a comment on the words which were often upon his lips, *How excellent is thy loving kindness!* It was, to the letter, a fulfilment of wishes expressed by him some years before, in the following devotional exercise, which he doubtless penned with reference to his own case.

"PRAYER FOR ONE WHO FEELS THAT HE IS APPROACHING THE BORDERS OF ANOTHER WORLD.

"O most merciful God! I rejoice that thou dost reign over the universe with a sovereign sway, so that thou dost according to thy will, in the armies of heaven and among the inhabitants of the earth. Thou art the Maker of my body, and Father of my spirit, and thou hast a perfect right to dispose of me, in that manner which will most effectually promote thy glory: and I know whatever thou dost is right, and wise, and just, and good. And whatever may be my eternal destiny, I rejoice in the assurance that thy great name will be glorified in me. But as thou hast been pleased to reveal thy mercy and thy grace to our fallen miserable world; and as the word of this salvation has been preached unto me, inviting me to accept of eternal life, upon the gracious terms of the Gospel, I do cordially receive the Lord Jesus Christ as my Saviour and only Redeemer, believing sincerely the whole testimony which thou hast given respecting his divine character, his real incarnation, his unspotted and holy life, his numerous and beneficent miracles, his expiatory and meritorious death, and his glorious resurrection and ascension. I believe, also, in his supreme exaltation, in his prevalent intercession for his chosen people, in his affectionate care and aid afforded to his suffering members here below, and in his second coming to receive his humble followers to dwell with himself in heaven ; and to take vengeance on his obstinate enemies. My only hope and confidence of being saved, rests simply on the mediatorial work and prevailing intercession of the Lord Jesus Christ ; in consequence of which the Holy Spirit is graciously sent to make application of Christ's redemption, by working faith in us, and repentance unto life : and rendering us meet for the heavenly inheritance, by sanctifying us in the whole man, soul, body, and spirit. Grant, gracious God ! that the rich blessings of the new covenant may be freely bestowed on thy unworthy servant. I acknowledge that I have no claim to thy favour, on account of any goodness in me by nature ; for alas ! there dwelleth in me, that is in my flesh, no good thing ; nor on account of any works of righteousness done by me ; for all our righteousnesses are as filthy rags. Neither am I able to make atonement for any one of my innumerable transgressions ; which, I confess before thee, are not only many in number, but heinous in their nature, justly deserving thy displeasure and wrath ; so that if I were immediately sent to hell, thou wouldst be altogether just in my condemnation. Although I trust that I have endeavoured to serve thee with some degree of sincerity ; yet whatever good thing I have ever done, or even thought, I ascribe entirely to thy grace, without which I can do nothing acceptable in thy sight. And I am deeply convinced, that my best duties have fallen far short of the perfection of thy law, and have been so mingled with sin in the performance, that I might justly be condemned for the most fervent prayer I ever made. And I would confess with shame and contrition, that I am not only chargeable with sin in the act, but that there is a law in my members, warring against the law of my mind, aiming to bring me into captivity to the law of sin and death. This corrupt nature is the source of innumerable evil thoughts and desires, damps the exercise of faith and love, and stands in the way of well-doing, so that when I would do good, evil is present with me. And so deep and powerful is this remaining depravity, that all efforts to eradicate or subdue it, are vain without the aid of divine grace. And when at any time I obtain a glimpse of the depth and turpitude of the sin of my nature, I am overwhelmed, and constrained to exclaim with Job, 'I abhor myself and repent in dust and ashes.' And now, righteous Lord God Almighty, I would not attempt to conceal any of my actual transgressions, however vile and shameful they are ; but would penitently confess them before thee ; and would plead in my defence nothing but the perfect righteousness of the Lord Jesus Christ, who died the just for the unjust, to bring us near to God. For his sake alone do I ask or expect the rich blessings necessary to my salvation. For although I am unworthy, he is most worthy ; though I have no righteousness, he has provided by his expiatory death, and by his holy life, a complete justifying righteousness, in which spotless robe I pray that I may be clothed ; so that thou my righteous Judge wilt see no sin in me, but wilt acquit me from every accusation, and justify me freely by thy grace, through the righteousness of my Lord and Saviour, with whom thou art ever well pleased. And my earnest prayer is, that Jesus may save me from my sins, as well as from their punishment; that I may be redeemed from all iniquity, as well as from the condemnation of the law; that the work of sanctification may be carried on in my soul by thy Word and Spirit, until it be perfected at thine appointed time. And grant, O Lord! that as long as I am in the body, I may make it my constant study and chief aim to glorify thy name, both with soul and body, which are no longer mine but thine; for I am 'bought with a price'—not with silver and gold, but with the precious blood of Christ, as of a lamb without blemish and without spot. Enable me to let my light so shine that others seeing my good works shall glorify thy name. O! make use of me as an humble instrument of advancing thy kingdom on earth, and promoting the salvation of immortal souls. If thou hast appointed sufferings for me here below, I beseech thee to consider my weakness, and let thy chastisements be those of a loving father, that I may be made partaker of thy holiness. And let me not be tempted above what I am able to bear, but with the temptation make a way of escape.

"O most merciful God! cast me not off in the time of old age; forsake me not when my strength declineth. Now, when I am old and gray-headed forsake me not; but let thy grace be sufficient for me, and enable me to bring forth fruit even in old age. May my hoary head be found in the ways of righteousness! Preserve my mind from dotage and imbecility, and my body from protracted disease and excruciating pain. Deliver me from despondency and discouragement in my declining years, and enable me to bear affliction with patience, fortitude, and perfect submission to thy holy will. Lift upon me perpetually the light of thy reconciled countenance, and cause me to rejoice in thy salvation, and in the hope of thy glory. May the peace that passeth all understanding be constantly diffused through my soul, so that my mind may remain calm through all the storms and vicissitudes of life.

"As, in the course of nature, I must be drawing near to my end, and as I know I must soon put off this tabernacle, I do humbly and earnestly beseech thee, O Father of mercies, to prepare me for this inevitable and solemn event Fortify my mind against the terrors of death. Give me, if it please thee, an easy passage through the gate of death Dissipate the dark clouds and mists which naturally hang over the grave, and lead me gently down into the gloomy valley. O my kind Shepherd, who hast tasted the bitterness of death for me, and who knowest how to sympathize with and succour the sheep of thy pasture, be thou present to guide, to support, and to comfort me. Illumine with beams of heavenly light the valley and shadow of death, so that I may fear no evil. When heart and flesh fail, be thou the strength of my heart, and my portion for ever. Let not my courage fail in the trying hour. Permit not the great adversary to harass my soul in the last struggle, but make me a conqueror and more than a conqueror in this fearful conflict. I humbly ask that my reason may be continued to the last, and if it be thy will, that I may be so comforted and supported, that I may leave a testimony in favour of the reality of religion, and thy faithfulness in fulfilling thy gracious promises; and that others of thy servants who may follow after, may be encouraged by my example, to commit themselves boldly to the guidance and keeping of the Shepherd of Israel.

"And when my spirit leaves this clay tenement, Lord Jesus receive it! Send some of the blessed angels to convoy my inexperienced soul to the mansion which thy love has prepared. And O! let me be so situated, though in the lowest rank, that I may behold thy glory. May I have an abundant entrance administered unto me into the kingdom of our Lord and Saviour Jesus Christ; for whose sake and in whose name, I ask all these things. Amen."*

The unvarnished narrative of such a scene might perhaps claim to be left to make its own impression; but there are a few reflections which force themselves upon our thankful minds, and which shall be simply and briefly expressed.

The first is, that death approached in a great degree disarmed of its ordinary terrors. Here was nothing ghastly. Though not painless, his dying bed was exempt from agony. He was surrounded by his family, was waited on by the wife of his bosom, and was in full possession of his intellectual powers.

Another remark is, that in his last hours there was no vacillation, as to the truth of the system which he had spent his life in maintaining. He may be said to have reasserted it with his last breath.

* Thoughts on Religious Experience, p. 307

But more striking than all, is it, that in dying he was pre-eminently true to the natural simplicity of his character. Not one syllable was there for effect. All was as in his days of health. He looked collectedly on the awful change, and met the enemy as one whom he had long surveyed and was now to overcome.

CHAPTER NINETEENTH.

1851.

FUNERAL SERVICES, AND OTHER TESTIMONIALS OF RESPECT.

GREAT solemnity was added to the scenes which have just been reported, by the fact that the Synod of New Jersey was meeting in Princeton at the time. This venerable body adjourned to attend the funeral services, which took place on Friday, the 24th of October. The concourse of awed and mourning friends was extraordinary. Many members of the New-York and Philadelphia Synods were present, as well as numerous fellow Christians of other persuasions. The Synod of New Jersey, after meeting in the Chapel, assumed the principal part in the solemnities. The Presbytery of New Brunswick accompanied the remains as pall-bearers. Then followed the family, and Professors, the Directors, the students, the clergy and a multitude of mourning friends. The assembly gathered in the First Presbyterian Church, where the galleries were filled with the students of the two institutions, and the body of the house with the

Synod, while the aisles and even the pulpit stairs were occupied by the attendant throng.

A prayer by the Rev. Dr. Murray opened the service. The students of the Seminary then sang a hymn Part of the fifteenth chapter of the first epistle to the Corinthians was read. The hymn, 'Why should we mourn departed friends,' was sung. After which, in pursuance of a wish expressed by the departed, a funeral discourse was delivered by the Rev. John McDowell, D. D., the oldest Director. His most appropriate text was Revelation xiv. 13. "And I heard a voice from heaven saying unto me, Write, Blessed are the dead that die in the Lord from henceforth; yea, saith the Spirit, that they may rest from their labours: and their works do follow them." The preacher pointed out the prominent marks which indicate the character referred to —he that is *in the Lord;* and then remarked, that blessedness was predicted of him who sustained this relation in life and in death. The nature of this blessedness was a second topic—a blessedness in union with Christ; a blessedness in dying while thus united with the living head; a blessed rest after all the toils of life, and in the full enjoyment of heaven, whither every good work followed the believer, and received its gracious reward. The beautiful and appropriate theme was treated in the most practical manner, with much earnestness and feeling; and there appeared to be but one impression among the auditors of the entire fitness both of the subject and its treatment to the solemn occasion. It was just such a sermon as should be preached on a funeral occasion, and we doubt not, that the deceased, could he have heard it, would have expressed his approbation. After the sermon proper, the preacher read an extract of a letter which he had received from one of the Professors in the Seminary a few days previous to the death of Dr. Alexander, in which it was stated, as the twice repeated injunction of the deceased, that the funeral sermon should contain no delineation of his character and no eulogy. This inhibition, so much in keeping with his general character, was in fact his eulogy. It was so felt to be by the audience, although the preacher must have felt embarrassed by a restriction which precluded him from expatiating in so fruitful a field. He confined himself accordingly to a few historical details.

"After the religious services in the church," says a contemporary account, "the body was borne by ministers of the Gospel to its burial. The arrangements for the procession had been made with great skill, and the whole was conducted without the slightest confusion. It was one of the most impressive spectacles we have ever seen. In the middle of the broad street fronting the College and Church, the students of the College, with their Professors, amounting to more than two hundred and fifty, walked four abreast; then followed the Synod of New Jersey and clergy from the neighbouring cities and towns, numbering more than one hundred clergymen; then the corpse, borne by members of the Presbytery of New Brunswick, and accompanied by the sons of the deceased; these were followed by the students in the Theological Seminary, with the Directors, amounting to about one hundred and forty, together with citizens. There were no females in the procession, although many were in attendance at the church.

"The numerous cortége formed an extended circle around the grave, and after the body was deposited, the audience were briefly addressed by Rev. Dr. Magie of Elizabethtown. His remarks were most happily conceived, and uttered in silvery and tremulous tones. In speaking of depositing all that was mortal of this good and great man in the silent tomb, of the many evidences of usefulness he had left behind him, and of the halo of light which the doctrine of the resurrection shed upon the grave, he with difficulty commanded his feelings. Had it not been for this self-imposed restraint, he could have dissolved the large audience in tears. One of the most striking features of the solemn ceremonial was the six sons of the deceased, three of them in the ministry, standing side by side on the margin of that grave which held the mortal part of their venerated parent, to whose instructions and example they were so deeply indebted. It was a funeral never to be forgotten. It was a funeral without gloom, which bore the thoughts quite to the verge of heaven. The light of the resurrection and of immortality seemed to dispel the shades of death and the grave, and the spectators of the scene could say, and no doubt did say, 'Let me die the death of the righteous, and let my last end be like his.'" The closing prayer was offered by the Rev. Dr. Plumer.

We must be permitted to add, that the brief address of Dr. Magie, at the grave, was eminently simple, graceful and pathetic. The throng had become great, but they now formed a hollow square, the students of the Seminary on the west, the College students on the east, the Synod on the north, and the citizens on the south. The sun of a matchless autumnal day was just going down, as the beloved deposit was lowered into the earth which contains the relics of Burr, Edwards, Davies, Witherspoon, Smith, Green and Miller. Dr. Magie broke the silence by words something like these :

"There is the end of eighty years—of sixty years of faithful service in the Christian ministry—of forty years of eminence in our highest institution of sacred learning. That place looks cold, and dark and gloomy to lay such a man in ; but it is just as good a place as that in which his Master rested. The dust we lay here is precious. It has been the dwelling-place of an immortal soul—it has been the temple of the Holy Ghost." A few other touching words were spoken.

It would be difficult, and might even seem invidious, to single out any from the numerous discourses which were delivered from the pulpits of his pupils and other friends, in every part of the country. To some of these we may be indebted for a few corroborative testimonials, in another place. The same remark applies with less force to the acts of public bodies. Several of these, on account of statements which they contain, deserve to be perpetuated.

The Synod of New Jersey, being on the very spot, naturally took the lead in expressions of filial respect.

EXTRACT FROM THE MINUTES OF THE SYNOD OF NEW JERSEY, IN SESSION AT PRINCETON, N. J., OCT. 22D, 1851.

"The Committee appointed to bring in a paper expressive of the views of the Synod, with reference to the death of the Rev. Archibald Alexander, D. D., made the following report, which was adopted and ordered to be published in the New-York Observer.

"Since the Synod opened its sessions in this place, God in his wise and holy Providence has seen fit to take the Rev. Archibald Alexander, D. D., to himself, in the eightieth year of his age.

"This event has been preceded by an illness of a few weeks, during which the venerable man gradually declined, until about six o'clock this morning, he sweetly fell asleep in Jesus, and was gathered in as a shock of corn fully ripe. His departure was so gentle, and attended by so entire an absence of distress of any sort, that the family were scarcely able to fix upon the precise moment when the spirit was released, and went up to hear the plaudit,—'Well done good and faithful servant, thou has been faithful over a few things, I will make thee ruler over many things: enter thouin to the joy of thy Lord.'

"This is not the time for a sketch, however brief, of the life and character of one who occupied so elevated a position, and had been so eminently useful in our beloved Church. Nothing more can be done than simply to say that the circumstances connected with the death of Dr. Alexander—a death, in all respects so befitting his previous life—ought to be regarded by the members of this Synod, as highly instructive and impressive. It has occurred during the regular sittings of our body, and while a large number of his brethren and former pupils were assembled to hear the first tidings of its announcement, and make arrangements to attend the honoured dust to its resting-place in the grave. It was a meeting of which the deceased himself spoke with tender interest, and which it is hoped may become memorable for the happy influence produced upon many hearts.

"Dr. Alexander was the first Professor in the Theological Seminary in this town, and in the bosom of our Synod. This office he was permitted by the favour of the Great Head of the church to fill with distinguished credit to himself, and with equal benefit to others, for upwards of thirty-nine years. Placed over the Institution in its infancy, he had the satisfaction of seeing it increase in numbers and usefulness, until it has become a blessing to the land and to the world. A large proportion of all the clerical members of this Synod had the privilege of sitting at his feet and drinking in instruction from those lips which are now sealed in death. Whatever of influence many of us have gained, or power of doing good we have exerted, are due very much, under God, to the labours and prayers of this distinguished Professor.

"A year ago Dr. Alexander was with us in the meetings of our Synod, to cheer us by his presence, and aid us with his counsels. Never shall we forget the address which he delivered on the evening of our Devotional Exercises, and which, as many at the time remarked, was characterized by almost all the vigour and unction of his earlier days. We listened to him with mingled emotions of delight and sorrow —delight that we could once more listen to the well-known voice—and sorrow that we should probably see his face no more. This was evidently his own anticipation, and so the event has proved.

"The death of Dr. Alexander will reach the secret place of tears, in multitudes of different and distant parts of our land. Missionaries in China, India, Africa, and the Islands of the Sea, will receive the intelligence and cry, My father, my father, the chariot of Israel and the horsemen thereof! Good men here and there will call to mind his venerable appearance, and bless God for giving to the Church such a minister.

"When such a Prince and Great One falls in Israel, it is proper for devout men to carry him to his grave, and make great lamentation over him. Grieve for him we cannot—we dare not, but surely we may grieve for ourselves and for the rising ministry. When we reflect upon his long and useful life as an ambassador for Christ, begun when he was but nineteen years of age, and extending through a period of more than sixty years, all spent in successful efforts to build up the kingdom of the Redeemer among men, and retaining its mild and genial lustre to the last, and add to this the sweet serenity of the closing scene, we feel constrained to unite in devout thanksgiving to the King of Zion. We bless God for such a life, and with equal warmth would we bless God for such a death.

"In this our departed father was pre-eminent. He followed his pupils when they went forth to their work, and kept himself acquainted with all their trials and successes. He could tell where they were, and how they were.

"Our beloved Seminary is bereaved, and though sadness fills our own hearts, we cannot do otherwise than tender our affectionate sympathies to the Professors that remain.

Within two short years, Dr. Miller and Dr. Alexander have gone down to the grave. United pleasantly together in a long and honourable life, in death they are not much divided. May the spirit of Elijah rest on Elisha! But all is not lost. We have still brethren beloved to conduct the studies of our Samuels and Timothys; above all we have the mercy and the faithfulness of a covenant keeping God to confide in. It is still permitted us to say, The Lord liveth, and blessed be our Rock, and let the God of our salvation be exalted.

"Attest, R. K. RODGERS,
"Stated Clerk of the Synod of New Jersey."

It is a truly pleasing reflection to those who are most nearly concerned, that the party divisions of our Presbyterian body seemed to have lost all such influence as could prevent a hearty condolence in those who fell into the other branch of the Church. No public testimonial was therefore more grateful than that of the New School Synod of New-York and New Jersey; concerning which we borrow from a journal of the time as follows:

"BLOOMFIELD, *Thursday, Oct.* 23*d.*

"At the close of the public services in the Synod last evening, an announcement was made from the pulpit of the death of the venerable Dr. Alexander, and the concluding prayer was offered with special reference to the fact that so great and good a man had fallen in Israel. This morning at the prayer meeting the subject was again renewed. The moderator led in prayer in reference to it, and various touching and interesting statements were made by Dr. Cox, the

Rev. John N. Lewis, Dr. Campbell, &c., as to Dr. Alexander's literary and theological history. Afterwards a committee consisting of the Rev. J. F. Stearns, D. D., T. H. Skinner, D. D., A. H. Campbell, D. D., were appointed to draft appropriate resolutions. Among other circumstances that showed the high estimate in which the deceased was held, we noticed his likeness which had been hung up in the Synod's place of meeting, where all could refresh their recollections of one so dear in life, and so lamented in death. A meeting was also called of all the members of the Synod, who had been his pupils in the Seminary."

The resolutions were these:

"*Resolved,* That we have heard with profound sorrow, not unmingled with grateful praise, of the peaceful, saint-like death of the venerable Dr. ALEXANDER.

"*Resolved,* That the rare constellation of excellencies which met and blended in the life and character of this eminent servant of God; his child-like simplicity, warm-hearted piety, rich religious experience, fervid Christian eloquence, together with a sound practical judgment, fine natural endowments, accomplished scholarship, and fidelity and perseverance in the discharge of every duty, conspired to make him one of the highest ornaments which have adorned the Church of Christ in our country. The cause of Theological Education, to which his ripest years were devoted, found in him one of its most active and successful promoters; and the Christian Ministry, especially of the Presbyterian Church, is under an inestimable and lasting obligation to his truly apostolic service and example.

"*Resolved*, That in this affecting dispensation of Divine Providence, we recognize a call to new fidelity and watchfulness in the service of Christ, and devoutly pray that the Great Head of the Church would make it a means of spiritual blessings, not only to ourselves but to the school of the Prophets, so highly favoured of God in commencing its existence under the guidance of such a teacher, and to the whole Presbyterian family throughout the land, to whom in common his memory will ever be fragrant.

"*Resolved*, That we tender our affectionate sympathy to the bereaved family of the deceased, and would crave the privilege to mingle our tears as at the grave of a father.

"JOHN N. LEWIS, Stated Clerk."

From his native State the tribute of respect was warm and significant. In communicating it, the Rev. Dr. McFarland, the Stated Clerk, uses the following language: "I feel as though I ought to embrace the occasion to say a few words for myself. I doubt whether any, out of the family connection, feel the death of youı beloved father more deeply than I do. There was no man on earth for whom I felt such love. Ever since I knew him, he has been my counsellor in all the important changes of my life. I felt unbounded confidence in the soundness of his judgment, and he always took a great interest in my affairs.

"I felt under obligations to him in common with others for his invaluable instructions; but when I was associated with him, I enjoyed his personal friendship to a degree which I had no reason to expect, and of which he gave me many substantial proofs, and I regard it as one of the richest blessings of my life. I will thank you to convey to my beloved friend, your mother, the assurance of the sympathies of a heart that feels BEREAVED in some humble measure like her own. God grant her the abundant consolations of his grace. Please also to present my kind sympathies to your sister and to your brothers."

"THE SYNOD OF VIRGINIA IN SESSION AT NORFOLK, VA., *November 1st*, 1851.

"It having pleased the Great Head of the Church to remove by death, on the 22d ult., the venerable and reverend Dr. Archibald Alexander, from his long and useful labours on earth to his reward in heaven: this Synod, in whose bounds he had been born and reared, and of which, during the early part of his ministry, he had been a valued member, feel themselves called upon to testify their affectionate remembrance of his great excellence as a faithful servant of Jesus Christ; and to record on their Minutes the mournful bereavement which the whole Church, and this Synod in particular, feel, in the death of so eminent and useful a minister of Christ. His character as a faithful and successful preacher of the Gospel for more than half a century, and his eminent services as a teacher of Theology in the Princeton Seminary, from its foundation till his death, are known to the entire Church of Christ in our own country, and to most of the Evangelical Churches in Europe.

"'The righteous shall flourish like the palm tree; he shall grow like a cedar in Lebanon. Those that be planted in the house of the Lord, shall flourish in the courts of our

God. They shall still bring forth fruit in old age; they shall be fat and flourishing: to show that the Lord is upright; he is my rock, and there is no unrighteousness in him.'

"Resolved, That the Stated Clerk of Synod transmit to the family of Dr. Alexander a copy of this record, with the assurance of the tender sympathy of Synod in their affliction.

"The foregoing is a true extract from the minutes of Synod.

"FRANCIS McFARLAND, Stated Clerk.

"To the family of the late Dr. A. Alexander."

We need not offer an apology for adding a few paragraphs in this place respecting Mrs. Alexander, who survived her husband less than one year. So united were they in their lives, so helpful, and as it were necessary to one another, and so seldom seen apart, that those who remember either will willingly read of both.

Janetta Waddel was the second daughter and fourth child of the celebrated James Waddel, D. D., already mentioned in this work. She was born in Augusta county, Virginia, but was early removed to the other side of the Blue Ridge, where she spent her happy youth in the county of Louisa. As she grew up she was greatly admired for her beauty, grace, and mental promise. During the long blindness of her father, she was eyes to his infirmity, acting as his amanuensis, and making him acquainted with the contents of many volumes. He taught her to pronounce Latin, at a very early age, that she might read works to him in that language. Under his guidance her education was conducted, partly by the aid of domestic teachers; for she never went abroad to school. In early youth she made a profession of her faith in Christ; but of her private exercises at this time, no particular account has been preserved.

As before related, Dr. Alexander turned aside from a journey, and gained her plighted affection. She was young and blooming, full of vivacity, and the charm of all his house. Matronly virtues in process of time took the place of youthful attraction; but we may be allowed to say, she was always lovely, as a wife, a mother, and a friend. It is impossible to describe what she was to her husband. It was not merely affection that she bestowed, though the tenderness of her attachment was anxious if not overweening; she rendered wise counsel; she assumed every domestic care with untiring industry, frugality, and hospitable warmth; she disguised her own solicitudes, to cheer him when he desponded or was ill; she gave her full soul to all his pleasures and all his pains; she was permitted to be as a ministering angel beside his dying bed. Through God's singular mercy, she enjoyed life-long health and spirits. Her very countenance and greeting shed sunshine over the house and its guests; and the earlier students of the Seminary remember her as a mother or an elder sister.

Without pretension, she was well informed in the usual range of female literature. In conversation she excelled, being free, full of vivacity and humour, and ready to cheer the hearts of all who approached her. It is impossible for her children to think of her, without an affectionate and pensive delight. Into her bosom they familiarly poured all their pleasures and grief, from infancy till some of them attained to gray hairs. Her mind was quick, and her memory remarkable. In later years her reading was chiefly of a religious kind, and her taste was for a class of authors who are savoury and evangelical. It is pleasant to recur to her favourite books: Wilson's *Sacra Privata*, Bennet's Divine Oratory, Traill's Sermons on the Throne of Grace, Flavel's Treatises, Newton's Cardiphonia, Cowper's Poems and Letters, and Boston's Fourfold State. In the school which Providence had given her, she grew up to a modest, gentle and consistent piety. Her coincidence of views with her husband was perfect, and she shared his interest in all that concerned Christ's kingdom. During the first years of the Seminary she was active and successful in gathering support for needy students. The humble poor found her bountiful, assiduous and constant. She delighted in religious services, and gave them much of her time.

The bereavement which made her a widow was a stroke which paralyzed her energies in some degree. Yet her resignation was absolute. She uttered no word of murmuring; she even showed a melancholy smile as she turned to her darkened house and to the service of her family. But a shade had fallen on her, and she never was the buoyant person she had been. Still she pursued her solitary path with uncomplaining diligence and kindly affection. It pleased God to make her departure eminently peaceful, as if in answer to prayers which we have recorded. It took place after a brief illness, accompanied with few violent symptoms, on the 7th day of September, 1852. Though the nature of her malady prevented her from much expression of her views, she has left her lamenting family fully confident of her Christian character and eternal peace.

The surviving children of Dr. Alexander are six sons and a daughter. Of the sons, three are ministers of the Gospel, two are lawyers, and one is a physician. In addition to changes already mentioned, it only remains to be said, that the last of Dr. Alexander's brothers, Major John Alexander, of Lexington, departed this life in 1853, while these labours were near their end. We annex a tribute to his memory, from the pen of his pastor, the Rev. Dr. White :

"Major Alexander was the son of Wm. Alexander, Esq., of Rockbridge, Virginia, and brother of the late Dr. Alexander, of Princeton. He enjoyed the benefit of early religious instruction, and from his early youth was remarkable for integrity, industry, enlightened economy, and true benevolence. These virtues rendered him successful in getting an ample estate, and what was far better, gave him an unusual hold on the confidence and love of the community in which his whole life was passed. His high moral qualities were the result of religious training and religious principle. At an early period of life, he embraced Christ as he is freely offered in the Gospel, and served him as a member of the Presbyterian Church for more than fifty, and as a Ruling Elder for forty-seven years. His devotion to the Church of Christ was enlightened, warm and generous. He had long been the senior Elder in a Session of twelve members. He was no less active and liberal in his efforts to promote the cause of sound learning.

As the generous friend, and senior member of the Board of Trustees of Washington College, his memory is held in grateful remembrance. The same is also true of the relations he sustained and the part he acted toward the Ann Smith Female Academy of this place. He served his country with unswerving fidelity as an officer, in the War of 1812, and for many years as Brigade Inspector for Western Virginia.

"In a word, the various relations he sustained both to the State and to the Church, the true patriotism, the sterling integrity, the eminent good sense, the modest, but enlightened and warm piety with which the high duties, flowing from these relations, were all discharged, render his death a very great public calamity.

"Although he had reached the seventy-eighth year of his age, he had retired from none of the active duties of life—for, 'his eye was not dim, nor his natural force abated.' No one ever thought of the 'good Major,' as he was familiarly called, as an old man. Though old in years, he was young in spirit. He possessed the wisdom of the one beautifully blended with the vivacity of the other. Whether you met him in the social circle or the street, at the prayer-meeting or in the great congregation, you were always cheered by the cloudless sun-light which his peaceful spirit threw over his benignant face. Never did there live and die a man whose hospitality, both to friends and to strangers, was more unpretending and generous. His house was the home of all who ever sought and deserved his confidence. He was literally happy in contributing to the happiness of others.—

Thousands scattered all through the States of this Confederacy, yet live to testify to the truth of this statement.

"His lonely widow, with three sons and two daughters, survive in deepest affliction. They mourn—the Church, the whole community mourn, but not as they who have no hope. Full of years, yet strong in faith, he has gone to join his distinguished brother, his estimable, pious sister, who so recently preceded him, and with them to make a part of that great multitude which no man can number, who are before God's throne, 'having washed their robes and made them white in the blood of the Lamb.'

"He died of apoplexy. Consequently his fall was sudden, but it was safe. He was not called to endure protracted pain and sickness; nor were his loved family called to suffer from prolonged solicitude. Like Enoch he 'walked with God, and he was not; for God took him.' Truly it was much more like a translation than death."

CHAPTER TWENTIETH.

CONCLUDING SUMMARY.

IN conducting the narrative part of our labour which has now been brought to a close, we have chosen to introduce general sketches of mind and manners, wherever they seemed to be naturally suggested; and this has made it less necessary to annex a formal and extended delineation of character. Yet there are some points which require a concluding notice, such as we shall now attempt in the way of general summary; with the full conviction that in no part of our task is there so much danger of being misled by a filial bias. A sense of this has led us in the preceding chapter to borrow from others expressions of eulogy much stronger than we durst use in our own person.

Of those who peruse this narrative some were personally conversant with him of whom it treats; but of these the greater part remember only his years of decline. To most his very figure reappears in memory as bowed down with age. A small number can recall the image of one who was bright and buoyant and whose frame beyond most was informed with a spirit of life. The universal testimony of aged persons is that in his youth he possessed a high degree of manly beauty. His stature, which was precisely five feet and seven inches, was certainly not commanding, but his limbs were shapely and well compacted, and the whole impression was that of symmetrical balance. His walk and motions were too much swayed by the inward pulses of feeling to be either staid or graceful. But the head was unquestionably one to be remembered. A high and spacious forehead, receding into deep angles among an abundance of nutbrown hair, an eye of dark hazel, a delicately chiseled nose, a mouth of singularly variable expression before the ravages of age had caused it to fall in, and a complexion of uncommon delicacy and transparence, combined to produce a physiognomy which no one of numerous portraits has reproduced. But the dead face was nothing. There was a lighting up of the speaking surfaces by the internal glow, which continued long after the grace of contour and colour had departed. This was a large part of that eloquence, which was felt in his conversation and public discourses. The gleam of his piercing eye, sometimes rapidly roving, but often long fixing itself with a peculiar search of expression, added indescribably to the effect of what he uttered. And there were times when an illumination overspread his features, under strong emotion, which we have very seldom seen. As days advanced, he became more wrinkled and haggard ; his teeth were early lost ; and he acquired a stoop in the shoulders. In his latest years, he had better health and even grew fleshy, but except the eye and the expression, there was little to remind of his former self.

The most formidable threatenings of his health were in his early life. The middle portion, as we have already stated, was annoyed by numerous dyspeptic and nervous symptoms, which caused discomfort rather than alarm. He never had a greater sense of health than in the years immediately preceding his last illness. This is wonderful, when we recur to his fixed habit of taking no exercise. He was far from prescribing this method to others, but either some obscure instinct pointed out to him the course which in his case would conduce to longevity and comfort, or the strength of original stamina availed to overmaster a series of influences which in ninety-nine instances out of a hundred would have proved fatal. We certainly never knew any one who quaffed the cup of mere physical life with more zest than he, in the moments when he was exempt from the depressions already often mentioned. And it was delightful cause of thankfulness to their children that their beloved mother retained to so unusual a length of days her youthful freshness and animation. They were early risers and plain livers, but perfectly free from all dietetic hobbies and whimsies.

In recalling the natural traits and character of Dr. Alexander, all persons seem at once to alight on his remarkable simplicity. It is a quality which defies description. We believe that no child could be more free from affectation. It was no fruit of study, principle or purpose ; it was naked nature. In all our lives we never saw any one who so completely did just what he liked ; and yet without cynicism or invasion of others. He was what he appeared to be ; if this gave offence—he could not help it. This naturalness showed itself in his dress, his carriage, his gesture, his tones, his style of writing. In early life he was shy and bashful, and there was always a discernible trace of this. Though his tell-tale face generally revealed his feelings, he had a great talent of silence. There were some things of which he never spoke ; as of his pecuniary affairs, his invitations to important posts, his devotional exercises, his success in preaching. Secrets confided to him were buried in the grave.

We suppose him to have been a man of true modesty. Not only in a sense which we lament to say requires to be recommended—for we believe no one ever heard him relate a story which might not have fallen from a virgin's lips—but in the common acceptation of moralists. He uniformly shrunk into the back ground. He neither sought praise nor tolerated it ; but this he was wont to ascribe more to a sort of pride than to humility. He in no instance ran after the great, or addicted himself to the ministry of the rich and famous, or sat prominent on platforms, or shouldered himself into the van of popular enterprises. It is believed that he lost nothing in favour or even reputation by such a reserve. Men of the world were often struck by a self-retirement which is so uncommon. This was well expressed by that great ornament of the legal profession, George Wood, Esq., of New-York. In speaking of Daniel Webster, this learned jurist and acute observer says : "The people can distinguish between pride or ostentation and that kind of retired habit which results from diffidence or deep reflection. Some of the most retired men I have ever known have been the most free from vanity and pride. Witness the late Dr. Alexander of Princeton, one of the most modest men that ever lived; yet no one ever approached him without the conviction that he was a truly great man."* That he was reserved is certain; that he was sometimes silent and distant has often been said; but it ought to be added that in such silence there was no assumption of dignity, and not a vestige of sullenness. When he shrunk into himself, it was from some great burden on his spirits; for in the presence of the very same persons he would suddenly come out of his temporary gloom with a spring and suddenness as fitful as the moods of infancy. No man had less of what may be called moroseness.

The kindliness of his temper was known to all with whom he ever exchanged hospitalities. He was easily pleased, and even to an extreme ready to be interested in whatever interested a friend. If his host were a farmer, he was untiring in looking at his grounds, crops and stock; if he were a scholar, quite as much delighted with his library or his writings. Every where he was the welcomed friend of children; among them he became a child himself. In his own house these traits of course manifested themselves in a thousand ways which cannot be exposed to the public. The sacredness of relation to a beloved wife does not admit of delineation; its tributes of affection were infinitely above the blandishments of a juvenile attachment. They were all the world to each other; and each had that which was complementary of the other's character. Surely never were there children on happier terms with their parents. They reverenced their father,

* Speech of George Wood, Esq., before a Committee of the friends of Daniel Webster, New-York, May 1852, page 10.

but their approach to him was perfectly free. His door was always open, and he listened to every childish report and narrative, with a burst of unaffected glee such as they never can forget or see again. In earlier years he joined in their sports, and he never grew too old to be as loquacious as themselves about all their innocent pleasures. When one of them entered his study—always without a signal—how gaily, how brightly, would he look around from his pen or his book; and how would the smile caused by any little domestic story irradiate his face, even when he went on with his labour! There was nothing in his character which so much caused his loss to be felt in the circle of his intimates as this unfeigned sympathy with what was interesting to those around him. It was an intense humanity, which enlivened all his words, gestures and acts. This kept him to the very close freely acquainted with passing events, as well of the village and neighbourhood as of the Church and world. It shone out in his regards for his pupils. Every new student was reported at the fireside. He habitually looked on them all with a benignant allowance, and took no pleasure in descanting on their faults; indeed his judgment of them leaned towards the side of undue favour. He followed them in their wanderings, and met them after the lapse of years with hearty and often loud salutations. From all this it may be gathered that in his brighter days, and these were the more numerous, he lived in a perpetual state of genial animation. The reverse was always to be traced to physical causes, and to the morbid susceptibility of a temperament suspended on nerves which trembled at a breeze. Connected with this exuberance of feeling was the childlike sincerity and transparent candour, which did not even know how to adopt a mask. If the playfulness of his evening hours admitted of description, it would add unusual colours of interest to our imperfect sketch. These peculiarities often surprised new acquaintances, who had previously known him only from his works, and who approached him as a man of learning and a grave divine.

The mental elasticity of which we have spoken had its share in all the labours of his research and all his attainments of knowledge. In new fields he evinced for many years the inquisitiveness of boyhood. According to the report of his friends, this was what attracted the attention of his teachers while he was in early youth. It is true they descried also the promise of faculties which were yet to be developed. His powers seem to have attained maturity in the morning of his life. No extravagance or indiscretion has been charged upon his language or preaching at the age of nineteen. To estimate the quality and force of his mind with entire justice, would demand perhaps a biographer of fewer prepossessions. We think we reflect the opinions of other and wise judges, when we ascribe to him natural powers much above the common order. In no other way can we account for his having emerged so early into general esteem, not to say admiration, from amidst an unlettered circle and in the face of great difficulties. Whatever position he attained was without his own seeking; and as truly without the adventitious aids of variegated diction and oratorical display; and this position was more firmly held in the estimate of none than of those who knew him most closely.

From his earliest days his memory was remarkable, as we have had occasion to say before. It was not however the memory of words or any conventional signs. But in regard to faces, localities, historical events, the opinions of authors and classes of men, the sources of knowledge, and above all whatever was held together by a logical thread, his recollection almost surpassed belief. We have heard him say that any interpretation of a biblical passage, if once fixed in his mind, never left it. To this may be added acuteness and perspicacity, in regard to obscure and entangled objects and their intricate relations. The patience of his investigation on such subjects was very great. He loved to ponder long, without book or pen, and often with eyes closed or in darkness, upon the trains of metaphysical and theological argument, which afterwards became the staple of his instructions. This persistency of meditation was the more wonderful in one who was so much moved by impulse and so given to ardent sallies. If we understand the term, he was eminently a close thinker. He weighed his terms, as the instruments of thought, and dwelt long on the sequence of apparently clear propositions. Hence he was slow in coming to his conclusions on important matters. He recommended and practised the survey of a wide field in order to safe inductions. To mental labours so arduous he was prompted by a sincere love of truth. And the consequence was, that if he attained a reputation for any one quality, it was sound judgment. Whatever may have been ascribed to him, he was never accused of rashness in the formation of his opinions. After such processes, it was natural that he was not subject to hasty changes. His system of philosophy and theology took its form early in life, and was avowed by him with firmness on his dying bed. When his thoughts were brought to bear on practical matters and questions of action, the same qualities displayed themselves, in the way of what is justly denominated wisdom. We have already observed that he was largely honoured as a sound adviser.

In the beginning of his ministry his discourses displayed a rich vein of imagination. Nothing would more exhibit the fertility of his invention, than the work of fictitious narrative to which allusion has been made. In his printed works there are few traces of this power. But when he preached in the free method which was most familiar to him, he would sometimes expatiate in descriptive flights which carried away his hearers. The characteristic caution of his mind, however, had early put him on his guard against the seductions of a faculty which however important, often works mischievous disturbance where the discovery of truth is in view; he therefore unquestionably pushed forward the discipline of his thoughts most signally in the direction of intellectual research and ratiocination.

Enough has been said to show that his diligence was unwearied, until the very end of his course, and that he fell in the harness. He was always a busy man. None can remember him as ever idle or ever lounging. It was only when overtaken by the debility of age that he ever was accustomed to assume a reclining posture during the day, still less did he ever nod in his chair. From morning till night, year after year, when not engaged in devotion or some social intercourse, he was reading or writing. Every one marvelled that his organs could hold out. His vacations were not less occupied than the regular terms of study.

There appears to be a discrepance of statement among his friends, as to the nature and amount of his attainments; as these have been looked at from different points of view. Some have declared them to have been deep rather than extensive; others have reversed the statement. Those who knew them best regard both as true, in a certain sense. From his great avidity of knowledge and the rare versatility of his tastes and faculties, he was all his life a reader in various fields. With the exception of the modern languages and natural history, we know of no branches of science or literature which he did not cultivate, at some time or other. But in these widely separate domains he did not pretend to make exact or technical progress; in these therefore his researches could not be said to be profound. In a certain round of sciences, however, he penetrated with a thoroughness and minute accuracy of detail which it would be difficult to exaggerate. We refer to the Scriptures, to theology in all its parts, and to the preparations and auxiliaries of these. The Philosophy of the Mind and Moral Science were his perpetual study. On these he constantly exercised his thoughts; and if there was any department of knowledge in which he excelled, it was the observation of his own mental states and exercises. In regard to this branch of philosophy, he was acquainted with all that could be obtained from ancient and modern authors, and was able with distinctness to rehearse the tenets of masters and of schools.

Of his long continued studies in theology we have already given some account. Scarcely less versed was he in history, both civil and ecclesiastical. To which may be added his attainments in bibliography, physical and political geography, and in politics and general law as connected with morals. On all these matters, the only wonder is, that the mass of his reading had not overwhelmed the original vigour of his understanding. In all these his attainments may be declared to have been profound.

In the communication to others of all that he knew he took great delight, as has been stated in the narrative. So far as we know, there is but one testimony as to his colloquial powers. He was not a perpetual or an exacting talker. There were days when his mouth was sealed ; and in his free moments he had also his times of reserve. He never allowed himself to become the haranguer of a coterie, and in large companies was with difficulty drawn out. When he did speak, it was without the tone or mien of the orator. Yet thousands will remember the instructive entertainment and awakening derived from his colloquial flow. This was chiefly opened in his own family circle, and at the houses of his friends. The peculiar hilarity and rapidity and variety of his household discourse can scarcely be represented ; in his later days he had strong points of resemblance in these respects to Mr. Gallatin and Chancellor Kent. There were the same sudden transitions and the same dashes of humour. At times, when he gave himself scope and yielded to strong emotion, these utterances were scarcely different from his great pulpit efforts. As he evidently talked for the simple purpose of unbosoming his present sentiments, the range of his remark was extensive ; he talked of every thing that interested him, but chiefly of that which had last awakened his mind. The most serious studies of the morning were often given out in distillation to his household and friends. He rehearsed the history of his contemporaries and the stirring news of the day. But he gave himself up to the current of topics, and seldom forced his own subject on others. It was his universal practice to converse with visitors on those things with which they were most familiar. By this means he enabled them to show their best side, while he was gaining stores of varied information, in regard to new countries and remote places and people. When a clergyman or a new student came from some region concerning which he knew little, this examinatory process was sometimes carried on for hours ; and the results were sure to be given out again with minuteness and animation, at the next fireside meeting. Indeed such was his love of communicating with his friends, that in these cases he would often come with immense haste and glowing features into the parlour, and with pen in hand keep the floor for a good half hour in relating the cheering intelligence ; darting back to his books with an amusing precipitation.

His sense of the ludicrous was acute ; hence he was a delightful listener to all entertaining visitors, and a hearty laugher of the best old school. Dr. Rice, himself a very grave man, Dr. Speece, Dr. John Breckinridge and Dr. Young, possessed a great power over his feelings in this respect. The number of visitors in his study was so large as often to become a sort of levee, at which whole forenoons were consumed, in the most cheerful intercourse ; nor did he ever consider this as lost time, always preferring the converse of the living to that of the dead. The humblest callers at his door, not excepting beggars, engaged him in long and animated dialogues. These were frequently wound up with an extended and pungent exhortation to the new comer. There was an old stroller, who came at short periods, and received a frown at many a house, but who always found Dr. Alexander ready to question and advise him. One of his choicest refreshments was to chat with children, and he had the faculty of winning their confidence in a moment. It was very uncommon for the hours of meals to be passed without free and full conversation. It is hardly needful to say that none of these colloquies disclosed any desire of display. He was a great questioner, it must be confessed, but not with a view of either gauging or puzzling others ; it was to increase his own stores, and he was always inquiring and always learning. Of set and formal religious conversation he practised little. Religion transpired through all his words and looks. Occasional remarks of a spiritual kind were ever and anon thrown in. When his heart was full, it ran over the brim ; but he relied little upon studied exhortations in ordinary circles. In private he often, almost daily, discoursed to individuals on the most sacred and confidential parts of experimental religion. To the doubting, desponding and bereaved, he was always a soothing and welcome visitor. By the bedside of those who were ill or dying, he attained an elevation of consolatory power which has made many such occasions memorable for a lifetime. The tenderness of his heart made him a reluctant reprover ; but when he opened his lips for this purpose his words were keen and scorching, often we suppose beyond his intention. It is to be added, that his love of conversation and his social faculties abode in perfect strength, until he was on the very verge of the grave.

From his conversation the transition is easy to his preaching, which was, more than can be said of most, an expansion of his ordinary discourse. It is a topic which we have touched upon more than once ; our purpose now is only to gather together a few additional remarks and reminiscences. The true notion of Dr. Alexander's preaching will not be obtained, unless we consider elevated conversation as the root out of which it grew. Protract the remarks, enlarge the circle of auditors, give correspondent stimulation to mind and feeling, and all the rest follows of course. Though a theologian, and that of the sterner and stricter sort, he did not deliver theological lectures from the pulpit. Formal and elaborate argumentation on doctrinal points was not common in his sermons. It is true, he expounded and defended the great doctrines of the faith, but it was in a method which was homiletical and popular, rather than scholastically didactic. Nothing could be more unlike his doctrinal sermons than the dry and attenuated diatribes of certain metaphysical divines of the last century. It was the Scottish school of sermonizing which he most nearly approached ; varieties of which may be studied in Finley, Davies and Waddel. Even when his object was to establish doctrine, he preferred the textual method. His division and treatment of the subject were generally governed by the text. Any figure which it contained was apt to colour the whole discourse.

There is a testimony here to be added, which from the eminent source from which it flows will not fail to command the respect of every reader. It is from Joseph Henry, LL. D., the Secretary of the Smithsonian Institute.*

PROFESSOR HENRY TO THE AUTHOR.

"SMITHSONIAN INSTITUTION, WASHINGTON,
January 31, 1854.

"MY DEAR SIR :—

"Your letter requesting my recollections of your lamented father was duly received, but a pressure of business connected with the annual meeting of the Board of Regents has prevented me from answering it before this evening.

"It gives me much pleasure to recall to my mind the first discourse I heard him deliver. It was a simple and apparently unpremeditated exposition of truths highly important to the young, and admirably adapted to the students of the college to whom it was addressed. I say apparently unpremeditated, though it must have been the result of much previous reflection in the way of settling definitely in his mind important general principles.

"I think Dr. Alexander had a remarkable faculty of philosophic generalization, and it was this that made him em-

* This admirable letter, though pertinent here, would have found its exact connection better at an earlier place; but it came to our hands while this very page was going through the press.

phatically a full man. He was enabled to discourse by the hour, not from mere memory, but in the way of deduction from the general truths which he had made his own, and which he was in the habit of applying to the conduct and duties of life. For example—in the discourse to which I have alluded ; he discussed the great principle of the permanency of early impressions upon the character, of the philosophy of habit, the importance of a good reputation commencing with the boy, of the negative influence of a single bad act committed in a moment of thoughtlessness which might neutralize almost a life of benevolent action ; of the influence possessed by every individual, and of the responsibility connected with it.

"He had studied in early life the subject of mental philosophy, and had adopted the principles of the inductive method. All ideas he considered as derived from sensation or consciousness, and without attempting to explain the essence of mind or of matter, he contented himself with a knowledge of the laws of their phenomena, and with referring these to the will of the Creator of the universe. All knowledge superior to this was derived from revelation, the truths of which, however mysterious and beyond reason, he adopted with implicit confidence. He was much interested in all questions of physical science, and particularly in the researches in which I was engaged. All his conceptions of truth were simple and clear. His was not a mere speculative faith, or a theoretical system of Christian duty, but one which was eminently reduced to practice. He taught by his example as well as by his precepts, and his influence will long live after him, not only in his published works, but in the memory of his pupils, and in its effect on the character and conduct of all who enjoyed the pleasure and profit of his quaintance.

"I consider it one of the most happy circumstances of my life, that I was permitted so long to enjoy the acquaintance and friendship of so good and so great a man, and to live under his influence.

"I remain, very truly, your friend and servant,

"JOSEPH HENRY."

Experimental, casuistical, practical, consolatory preaching, may be said to have been the field of his strength. In dissecting the heart, unravelling long trains of experience, discovering hidden refuges, holding the mirror up to self-deceiving souls, and flashing rays of gracious hope on the lingering and self-righteous, he was equalled by few. He gloried in preaching a free Gospel. The longer he lived, the more wide, cordial and generous was his offer of Christ to the chief of sinners. Not for an instant was he ever tempted to join with those who, because of the abuses of Antinomianism, would tamper with sovereign boundless gratuitous salvation, or hang legal weights on the wings of ascending faith. So high a value did he set upon the maintenance of an awakened interest among hearers, that he never entered on any avowed series of discourses, or wearied out his auditors by numerous sermons on the same text. Here his practice concurred with the reported remarks of Cecil, in his Remains. The strong historical, we might even say biographical turn of his mind, led him to dwell much on scriptural personages. Surviving hearers will remember his portraitures of Abraham and Joseph, of Ruth, Eli and Hannah, of Josiah and Daniel, of Paul and John. In connection with the same trait, he was uncommonly large in his delineation of individual types of Christian life, or what may be called characteristic preaching. Here he evinced his delicate acquaintance with the anatomy of saint and sinner. The outline was firm and unmistakable, and the hues bright and decided. Such pictures of particular experience dwell in the recollection of his hearers, who often felt the probe entering their consciences to the very quick. To sum up what concerns the matter of his preaching, he set forth the whole system of Divine truth, with a felicitous mixture of doctrine and experience; not separately but intimately blended; the didactic warp being traversed by a woof of variegated emotion; the steel links of reasoning being often red with the ardours of burning love.

Modes of preparation for preaching are always matter of lively interest to preachers; and it is wonderful how much they differ. Dr. Alexander was never accustomed to tell of his own ways, or to enjoin them upon others. Perhaps he was extreme in his disposition to let every man "scuffle through his experiment," as he used to call it, so as to alight on the plan which was best for himself. His written sermons were his later ones. For the most part they were the reproduction of trains of thought which he had arranged in his head many years before. It is not known that his mode of bringing these to paper had any thing peculiar. He was fond of saying, that if he wished to produce a discourse better than common, on a new subject, he should like to write away as fast as he could, and even voluminously. This he called getting the rock out of the quarry. During this process he thought two good results were pretty sure to ensue. One was that the writer would strike on some "rich vein" (another of his phrases) out of which he might draw the chief wealth of his discourse ; the other was, that he would find the rudiments of a method and partition emerge out of this at first chaotic mass. Then, and not till then, he thought the arrangement should be completed ; and then he would sit down and put the sermon into its final form, by an entire new writing. This device no doubt originated in his long-practised method of thinking long and arduously on the topics which he meant to discuss without notes. His written sermons however are but the bony structure of his preaching ; they lack the illustrations, descriptions, flight and pathos of his freer productions.

It has been said, even to repetition, that his chosen method of preparation was independent of the pen. Mr. Gallatin once said to us : "I know nothing of what is called growing warm in writing. In my most elaborate speeches, I have prepared the matter mentally ; and when I have had to write, I have frequently walked up and down the floor, and collected my material and given it shape and diction, just as if I were speaking off-hand." In our belief, this would be a just description of Dr. Alexander's experience. Long and silent meditation preceded his great efforts. In this he declared that he dismissed all consideration of the language to be employed, deliberately thinking that this would suggest itself best during delivery. Neither did he prearrange the exact sequence of sentences or even of propositions ; leaving the mind free to work in new directions while speaking. He used to declare that he preferred not to burden his mind with the recollection of a single expression which had occurred to him in his study. Such was his faculty of abstraction and concentration, that these preparatory lucubrations were conducted in walking, riding, or even sitting among his children. He would say laughingly that he often could think to most purpose, when there was a little clatter of voices around him. Hence it was surprising to observe how little he shut himself up before preaching ; when he did so, it was with a devotional end in view. He was a great advocate of habitual, as distinguished from special preparation. His individual sermons were chapters from a very copious volume in his head. Though he seldom spoke of these things, he once told us, that being about to preach on a text from that part of Scripture, he had rapidly perused the whole epistle to the Hebrews ; and at another time that he had in like manner read the whole Gospel of John over in Greek, on the Sunday morning. On a single point, our recollections vary from those of some authorities to whom we defer with high respect. It strikes us that in general, he not only divided his subject with distinctness, but declared the heads of his argument. The other mode we regard as the exception to his common rule. This is confirmed by a reference to his printed sermons and his manuscripts. He knew very little medium between reading closely, and speaking without any notes. The bit of paper which he usually laid on the Bible scarcely deserves the name. It was seldom of more than ten lines, and was often not looked at ; indeed he said that he used it as a precaution against a total loss of memory as to text, topic and plan, which used to befall him in his younger days. These scraps of writing were not intended as aids in preparation. We have no knowledge of his ever using what is called "a full brief." He frequently ceased to read what he had prepared, and interpolated new trains of argument which occurred to him, and in other cases even did not return to his manuscript at all. This was true in regard to some of his most effective sermons, which were thus drawn out to as much as ninety minutes.

He never seemed to look on preaching from its literary or rhetorical side. To him it was a high spiritual function, and he approached it with much of the awe which had attended his first efforts. It is believed that some trepidation preceded every discourse which he delivered ; as Luther reports concerning himself. Far more than is common, and beyond what he ever explicitly declared, he seems to have believed in special aids, elevations and illuminations, conferred on the preacher during his delivery of the message ; such afflatus from the Spirit he was accustomed to distinguish from the personal graces of the preacher. These impressions doubtless brought his mind into a state highly susceptible of those gusts of sudden feeling, which sometimes swayed not only himself, but whole assemblies. Perhaps this, rather than any rhetorical canon, led him invariably to begin his discourse in the most simple, subdued, and if we may so speak, expectant manner. It was the tone of ordinary conversation on an important subject. Hardly any thing could be augured from his beginning. He allowed himself to rise and glow in a manner almost imperceptible As might be expected, he did not always soar ; but when he did, it was without effort and without abruptness. As he kindled, his language became more vivid, ornate, and powerful ; it even acquired an elegant fitness and accuracy, which is not found in his writings. Towards the close of his greatest sermons, the audience was usually in a state of rapt attention ; nothing was more common than for people to say that they would gladly have listened to him all day.

The style of his more impassioned preaching was indescribably warmer and more coloured than any thing which he has left in writing. Yet it was always simple, and cannot be better described than in words which Dr. Arnold uses of his own : "I am sure an attempt at ornament would make my style so absurd, that you would yourself laugh at it. I could not do it naturally, for I have now so habituated myself to that unambitious and plain way of writing, and absence of Latin words as much as possible, that I could not write otherwise without manifest affectation." In his most elevated passages Dr. Alexander never indulged in the sweep of periodic and climacteric sentences. And as his style, such was his delivery. Gesture was forced from him, and was not undulatory or studiously graceful ; he had no dread of the abrupt or the angular in his motions. Those who speak of his voice as shrill, must be governed by the remembrance of later days, when he could make himself heard furthest in his upper notes. In youth and in his prime, his tones were silvery and his modulation exceedingly varied. The lower and even whispering modes of speech were often very effective. His inflections, especially at the close of sentences, were all his own, and were unlike those laid down in the books ; it was an attempt to reproduce these which made some of his imitators quite ridiculous. The language of his eye was extraordinary, even to a proverb. He was wont to fix his glance on individual hearers, with a penetration which often produced painful shrinking. We have no remembrance of ever seeing him weep in preaching, even when almost a whole assembly was in tears. The impression upon his hearers was at times so extraordinary, that we do not allow ourselves to describe it in detail. One quality was never absent, whether he was gently familiar or suddenly impetuous ; he maintained the unbroken interest of the assembly, however long he spoke. He once said of Summerfield, whom he greatly admired, that this wonderful young orator possessed the art of keeping up fixed attention and awakened expectation ; and that it consisted in passing rapidly from point to point, never dwelling on a thought when once it was fully lodged, never beating his material too thin, and thus never allowing the hearer's mind to get before him. It may be inferred from this that he depended little on rhetorical amplification. The beautiful illustrations which sometimes arose like visions before his audience, seldom held them long ; but he often added scene to scene with a felicity which was above all art, and which was evidently the result of thoughts suggested at the moment. It was manifest from his manner, that in addition to all he had preconceived, his mind was working strongly in new directions, while he was in the act of speaking. At such times his eye would fix itself on vacancy, or on some distant object, revealing by its peculiar expression that he had almost lost sight of his audience, and was expatiating in tracks of original musing. But we despair of conveying any precise notion of his peculiar manner to those who never heard him in the day of his unbroken physical vigour ; especially as we cannot suppose that our ears were not held by the fascination of a filial partiality which cannot be largely shared, and which must be our excuse if we overstate the case.

In the period when he made preaching his great business, his labours were every where owned of God to the awakening and conversion of many souls ; and all through his life such tokens were granted to him from time to time. Yet it is believed, that his work was far more remarkable in edifying the body of Christ, simplifying and enforcing the statements of doctrine, removing scruples, nourishing faith, stimulating to holy life, and consoling the tempted and distressed. In these fields, the effects of his labours, being more remote from public notice, are beyond all calculation, and must be left for the disclosures of the other world.

In closing our survey, we may be expected to say something of his personal piety ; yet nowhere have we so much felt the burden of our task. If the general tenour of this narrative has not set him forth as one who was eminently sanctified, we should fail to reach this end by heaping up assertory declarations. If, as a genial writer has said, "we should be modest for a modest man, as he is for himself,"—reserve on this point is the more demanded; for of all the human beings we ever knew he was the most silent about his own personal experience. At certain times he entered into his closet, and shut the door, but in what manner he conducted his private exercises, no mortal, we believe, is competent to relate. In these hours he is thought to have made more use than is common of the original Scriptures. He had a way of chanting to himself the Hebrew Psalms; for many years using for this purpose a beautiful psalter, which was the gift of Dr. Hodge. From what was observed by his family, and from what he recommended to others, it is supposed that he spent much time in deliberate spiritual contemplation. His piety was to a remarkable degree blended with his system of truth. In his mind doctrine and experience were inseparable. This was consistent with the high place which he always assigned to spiritual understanding and to faith. He observed frequent days of entire seclusion, sometimes adding an abstinence which was almost rigorous.

Prudence was a prominent trait in his character. That this did not sometimes degenerate into excessive solicitude and caution, we will not assert. The courage of adventurous daring, he possessed in his youth. The courage which enabled him to maintain his judgments, not only against all opponents but often against all friends, he might well claim all his days. It was kindred to his great sincerity, candour and love of truth. In his most unguarded moments, he was never known to exaggerate a statement. He was free from censoriousness of judgment, and scrupulous in speaking evil of any human being. Hence he passed a long life, almost absolutely free from strife with any fellow-creature. If he had enemies, they are unknown to us. In all the circle of his acquaintance he was not more truly reverenced than loved.

Of nothing did he seem so much in dread as of pride. From numerous indirect statements, we judge it to be what he regarded as his easily besetting sin. Its outward manifestations were however as rare in him as in any man. It seems to us that his whole life was an arduous study of humility. While he was burdened with a sense of indwelling sin, he was eminently free from doubts as to his own acceptance with God. Though he never said so, we are persuaded that his habitual state of mind was one of confirmed assurance. His conversation, sermons and books show that he set the highest value on personal communion with the Lord Jesus Christ, as the very heart of religion and happiness. On this subject, his sentiments often arose to a blissful rapture ; something of which he was enabled to communicate to others

As practice is the great criterion of piety, we may confidently refer to this. His whole life was spent in an endeavour to do as much good as was within his power. Without unduly lifting the domestic veil, it would be impracticable to represent how gentle, how tender, how sympathizing, how anticipative of every emergency, how laborious, how delicate and yet how faithful, he was to those who were nearest to him. This kindliness extended itself to a wide circle. He was perpetually teeming with plans for the good of mankind. His inventive faculty, in regard to charitable schemes, was a striking trait in his character. A bare survey of the books and papers which he wrote, and the manner in which he applied his learning, suffices to show the benevolence of his soul.

There is reason to believe that during most of his life he suffered from inward struggles and temptations. Yet again and again did he come forth from his study radiant with spiritual refreshment. His religion was characteristically composing and tranquil. As he advanced in years he became more and more happy; until at the very close he was happiest of all. In those last hours his lips were unsealed on many points concerning which he had been as silent as the grave; and he revealed some glimpses of that "secret of the Lord" which had been his portion for years. All was symmetrical and consistent, and hence one of the chief difficulties of description. Of his entire course there was nothing more true to nature and to grace than its close. The intelligent tranquillity which there reigned was beyond any powers of recital. MARK THE PERFECT MAN, AND BEHOLD THE UPRIGHT; FOR THE END OF THAT MAN IS PEACE.

PUBLICATIONS.

The following is as complete a list as our memory enables us to produce, of those books and pamphlets of which Dr. Alexander can justly be considered as the author.

A Sermon at the opening of the General Assembly. Philadelphia, 1808.

A Discourse occasioned by the burning of the Theatre in the City of Richmond, Va., on the 26th of December, 1811. Philadelphia, 1812. pp. 28.

An Inaugural Discourse delivered at Princeton. New-York, 1814.

A Missionary Sermon before the General Assembly. Philadelphia, 1813.

A Brief Outline of the Evidences of the Christian Religion. Princeton, 1825. 12mo.

The Canon of the Old and New Testaments ascertained; or the Bible complete without the Apocrypha and Unwritten Traditions. 12mo.

A Sermon to Young Men, preached in the Chapel of the College of New Jersey. 1826.

Suggestions in Vindication of Sunday Schools. Philadelphia, 1829.

Growth in Grace. Two Sermons in the National Preacher. New-York, 1829.

A Sermon before the American Board of Commissioners for Foreign Missions. 1829.

A Selection of Hymns, adapted to the Devotions of the Closet, the Family and the Social Circle, and containing subjects appropriate to the Monthly Concerts of Prayer for the success of Missions and Sunday Schools. New-York, 1831. (Seven hundred and forty-two hymns.)

The Pastoral Office. A Sermon preached in Philadelphia, before the Association of the Alumni of the Theological Seminary at Princeton, May 21, 1834. Philadelphia, 1834. pp. 30.

The Lives of the Patriarchs. American Sunday School Union. 1835. 18mo. pp. 168.

History of Israel. 12mo.

The House of God Desirable. A Sermon in the Presbyterian Preacher. 1835.

The People of God led in Unknown Ways. A Sermon preached May 29, 1842, in the First Presbyterian Church, Richmond. 1842.

An Address delivered before the Alumni Association of Washington College, Va., on Commencement Day, June 29, 1843. Lexington, 1843.

Biographical Sketches of the Founder and Principal Alumni of the Log College; together with an Account of the Revivals of Religion under their Ministry. Princeton, 1845. 12mo. pp. 369.

A History of Colonization on the Western Coast of Africa. Philadelphia, 1846. 8vo. pp. 603.

A History of the Israelitish Nation, from their origin to their dispersion at the destruction of Jerusalem by the Romans. Philadelphia, 1852. 8vo. pp. 620.

Outlines of Moral Science. New-York, 1852. 12mo. pp. 272.

Introduction to Matthew Henry's Commentary.

Introduction to Works of the Rev. William Jay.

Introduction to Dr. Waterbury's Advice to a Young Christian.

The following books and tracts, as well as some of those mentioned above, are issued by the Presbyterian Board of Publication.

Practical Sermons; to be read in Families and Social Meetings. 8vo.

Letters to the Aged. 18mo.

Counsels of the Aged to the Young. 18mo.

Universalism false and unscriptural. 18mo.

A Brief Compend of Bible Truth. 12mo.

Divine Guidance; or the People of God led in Unknown Ways. 32mo.

Thoughts on Religious Experience. 12mo.

The Life of the Rev. Richard Baxter. (An abridgment.) 18mo.

The Life of Andrew Melville. (An abridgment.) 18mo.

The Life of John Knox, the Scottish Reformer. (An abridgment.) 18mo.

The Way of Salvation, familiarly explained in a Conversation between a Father and his Children. 32mo.

To which must be added the following Tracts:

The Duty of Catechetical Instruction.

A Treatise on Justification by Faith.

Christ's Gracious Invitation to the Weary and Heavy-laden.

Ruth the Moabitess.

Love to an Unseen Saviour.

Letters to the Aged.

A Dialogue between a Presbyterian and a Friend (Quaker).

The Amiable Youth falling short of Heaven.

The Importance of Salvation.

Future Punishment Endless.

Justification by Faith.

Sinners Welcome to Jesus Christ.

The following Tracts have been published by the American Tract Society:

The Day of Judgment.

The Misery of the Lost.

THE END.

www.ingramcontent.com/pod-product-compliance
Lightning Source LLC
LaVergne TN
LVHW021230110826
845150LV00002B/293